International Handbook of ORGANIZATIONAL **CRISIS** MANAGEMENT

To Judith Wegner, Dennis Rondinelli, Bob Adler, and Marty Geer, the noblest crisis management team one could hope for.

—Chris

To Nathalie, Valentin, Melodie, and Alexandre in recognition of what they give me and the way they do it.

—Christophe

To the boys.

—Judy

International Handbook of ORGANIZATIONAL CRISIS MANAGEMENT

CHRISTINE M. **PEARSON**
Thunderbird, The School of Global Management

CHRISTOPHE **ROUX-DUFORT**
E. M. Lyon, France

JUDITH A. **CLAIR**
Boston College

EDITORS

SAGE Publications
Los Angeles • London • New Delhi • Singapore

Copyright © 2007 by Sage Publications, Inc.

All rights reserved. No part of this book may be reproduced or utilized in any form or by any means, electronic or mechanical, including photocopying, recording, or by any information storage and retrieval system, without permission in writing from the publisher.

For information:

Sage Publications, Inc.
2455 Teller Road
Thousand Oaks, California 91320
E-mail: order@sagepub.com

Sage Publications India Pvt. Ltd.
B 1/I 1 Mohan Cooperative Industrial Area
Mathura Road, New Delhi 110 044
India

Sage Publications Ltd.
1 Oliver's Yard
55 City Road
London, EC1Y 1SP
United Kingdom

Sage Publications Asia-Pacific Pte. Ltd.
33 Pekin Street #02-01
Far East Square
Singapore 048763

Library of Congress Cataloging-in-Publication Data

International handbook of organizational crisis management / edited by Christine M. Pearson, Christophe Roux-Dufort, Judith A. Clair.
    p. cm.
Includes bibliographical references and index.
ISBN 978-0-7619-8851-9 (cloth)
  1. Crisis management. I. Pearson, Christine M. II. Roux-Dufort, Christophe. III. Clair, Judith A.

HD49.I59 2007
658.4′056—dc22
                                             2006102717

07 08 09 10 11   10 9 8 7 6 5 4 3 2 1

Acquisitions Editor:	Al Bruckner
Editorial Assistant:	MaryAnn Vail
Project Editor:	Tracy Alpern
Copy Editor:	Kevin Beck
Typesetter:	C&M Digitals (P) Ltd.
Proofreader:	Theresa Kay
Indexer:	Kathy Paparchontis
Cover Designer:	Candice Harman
Marketing Manager:	Nichole Angress

Contents

Introduction   vii

PART I. NEW RISKS, NEW CRISES, NEW DANGERS

1. Organizations in World Risk Society   3
   Ulrich Beck and Boris Holzer

2. Crisis Management and Legitimacy:
   Facing Symbolic Disorders   25
   Romain Laufer

3. Understanding and Managing
   Crises in an "Online World"   85
   Sarah Kovoor-Misra and Manavendra Misra

PART II. NEW CRISES, NEW MEANING

4. Organizational Sensemaking During Crisis   107
   Karlene H. Roberts, Peter Madsen, and Vinit Desai

5. Crisis Sensemaking and the Public Inquiry   123
   Robert P. Gephart, Jr.

6. A Cognitive Approach to Crisis
   Management in Organizations   161
   *Jean-Marie Jacques, Laurent Gatot,
   and Anne Wallemacq*

PART III. NEW CRISES, NEW BARRIERS

7. The Psychological Effects of Crises:
   Deny Denial—Grieve Before a Crisis Occurs   195
   Ian I. Mitroff

8. A Passion for Imperfections:
   Revisiting Crisis Management   221
   Christophe Roux-Dufort

9. The Eight Characteristics of
   Japanese Crisis-Prone Organizations   253
   Toshihiko Hagiwara

10. Voices From the Terraces: From "Mock
    Bureaucracy" to "Learning From Crisis"
    Within the UK's Soccer Industry   271
    Dominic Elliott and Denis Smith

PART IV. NEW CRISES, NEW SOLUTIONS

11. A "Total" Responsibility Management
    Approach to Crisis Management and
    Signal Detection in Organizations   299
    Judith A. Clair and Sandra Waddock

12. Crisis Management Simulations: Flaws and Remedies   315
    Bertrand Robert and Christopher Lajtha

Author Index   327

Subject Index   333

About the Editors   347

About the Contributors   349

Introduction

Organizational crisis management once occurred as little more than a gut reaction in the heat of an incident. The first employee to see smoke in the refinery sounded the fire bell; the first supervisor to see damaged components in the assembly line replaced them; the first employee to reach the company's derailed train guided escaping passengers to safety. From the beginning of the industrial age, companies coped; little crisis-management preparation existed because little was expected. Then, just a few decades ago, as technological advances outpaced their containment, dramatic media coverage vied for the public eye, and litigation depleted corporate coffers, companies began to weigh the costs and benefits of crisis preparation, and the field of crisis management took hold.

Today, many organizations carry out orchestrated forms of crisis management, whether for natural disasters, potential damages to their core technology, or a broader array of possible threats. Crisis-management programs are designed to help organizations both avert crises and mitigate those that occur. Effective crisis-management programs enable organizations operating under the extraordinary conditions of crisis to make timely decisions based on clear thinking about the most important facts. Over time, many organizations have learned that optimally managed crises can bring positive recognition and enhanced stakeholder value, while poorly managed crises can short-circuit organizational viability. Given the nature of today's organizational crises and the broad-reaching environments in which they occur, the stakes can be devastatingly high. No executive is likely to have earned his or her position without recognizing this.

Nonetheless, the intellectual foundation of crisis management is somewhat disappointing. Despite the organizational stakes, the understanding of the depth of crisis management remains underdeveloped. Although there are numerous books on the topic, few capture grounded perspectives. Prescriptions lack rigorous testing. Some authors target quick fixes for managers by encouraging their fear of classic organizational crises, such as media exploitation, product tampering, and environmental disaster; others fuel panic about dramatic crises that are highly unlikely to affect most organizations, such as regional instability and terrorism.

Within the field of organizational science, crisis management is a rather isolated endeavor. Whereas crisis is a powerful and structuring concept in economics, sociology, history, and political science, organizational scientists remain reluctant to consider the usefulness of crisis in accounting for organizational phenomena such as change, learning, leadership, and evolution. Organizational researchers' interest in crises is itself ambiguous: Crises seem to arouse paradoxical attitudes. While organizational crisis-management scholars may be fascinated by the intensity, brutality, and drama of crises, they may also be discouraged by their abnormality, complexity, and destructiveness.

Apart from this ambiguity, research is underdeveloped because of the isolationist nature of crisis researchers themselves. There are at least three reasons for such isolation. First, research in crisis management tends to be dispersed and noncumulative. This leads to rather weak and incomplete conceptual underpinnings for a virtual galaxy of critical concepts and characteristics. Without common and precise theories and definitions, crisis-management scholars lose legitimacy and credibility, and they run the risk of poorly discerning what they aim to investigate. Second, crisis management suffers from a monolithic methodology. The fundamental work in crisis management was based on industrial catastrophes (e.g., Bhopal, *Exxon Valdez*, Three Mile Island); these still constitute a major source of inspiration and serve as unavoidable sources of reference for any researcher. The difficulty in departing from this frame has two consequences: (1) Research in crisis management is far more descriptive than theoretical, and (2) we learn more about accidents than crises. The third reason is that crisis management has become a *science of the exceptional*, focusing on rare and anomalous events rather than on the process through which normality becomes abnormality, reliability becomes vulnerability, and imperfection becomes catastrophe. Largely missed are the processes that start long before an event triggers the acute dynamics of crises.

Although research in organizational crisis management is dispersed and underdeveloped, crises continue to shape the future of organizations and their stakeholders. Novel and poorly understood technologies, changing political climates, globalization, immigration, and a shifting social landscape are just a few of the forces that continue to change the nature of work as well as the nature of organizational crises. Crisis-management research must evolve to meet the unforeseen challenges of these changes. Our goal in this book, then, is to share the latest understanding of organizational crisis management as gathered from prominent crisis-management scholars and practitioners around the globe. Contributing authors have attempted to push the boundaries of their crisis-management thinking and research to envision the field in a broader perspective and to position their reflections across new horizons. We seek here to offer frameworks and findings that will not only capture leading-edge thinking but also provide useful insights and guidance to researchers and thoughtful practitioners.

Introduction

When we began this book, our objective was to include expertise in organizational crisis management from around the globe. After diverse and creative attempts to tap international colleagues knowledgeable about organizational crisis management, we came up short. Like the stream from which it originated, crisis-management scholarship seems to remain largely a product of Western Europe and North America. In fact, we were unable to locate a single organizational or management scholar who is exploring crisis management in Latin America or Africa. Of course, we cannot say definitively that this signals a lack of scholarly interest in crisis management around the globe. Rather, it may reflect the limits of our own scholar networks. We hope, in fact, that the publication of this book will prompt those whom we were unable to locate to inform us about their own crisis-management studies. In the meantime, we are very pleased to have obtained the diversity that we found; we highlight the national origins of the authors in the brief summaries that follow.

We have divided this book into four sections. In the first section, "New Risks, New Crises, New Dangers," contributing authors explore the evolution of crises and crisis management. In the opening chapter, "Organizations in World Risk Society," Ulrich Beck and Boris Holzer (Germany) describe the world's transition into a risk society, including the development of a public audience that is global. Their contribution underscores the importance of including uncertainty as an organizational-crisis-management reality that must be considered when building relationships, making decisions, and taking action. In Chapter 2, "Crisis Management and Legitimacy: Facing Symbolic Disorders," Romain Laufer (France) continues the discussion of links to uncertainty and adds intriguing paradoxes characteristic of this association. This chapter traces the history of risk and legitimacy and provides a complex illustration of the challenges of managing major risk. In Chapter 3, "Understanding and Managing Crises in an 'Online World,'" Sarah Kovoor-Misra and Manavendra Misra (United States) move the crisis management literature into new territory, examining e-challenges as well as broader notions of time, space, and speed as relevant to crisis thinking.

The second section, "New Crises, New Meaning," explores the ways in which key stakeholders make sense of crisis situations. Chapter 4, "Organizational Sensemaking During Crises," examines swift sensemaking in turbulence as key to crisis containment and learning. With the contextual zest of explosions, shockwaves, and evacuation, Karlene H. Roberts, Peter Madsen, and Vinit Desai (United States) bring to life the challenges, opportunities, constraints, and practical implications of sensemaking. In Chapter 5, "Crisis Sensemaking and the Public Inquiry," Robert P. Gephart, Jr. (Canada) expands on the theme of sensemaking through a depth study of the central role it plays during public inquiries and hearings. This chapter introduces additional sources of meaning for understanding crises, including narrative and counternarrative approaches, rhetorical analyses, and ethnomethodology. Chapter 6, "A Cognitive Approach to Crisis

Management in Organizations," by Jean-Marie Jacques, Laurent Gatot, and Anne Wallemacq (Belgium) integrates the definition and characteristics of crises into a cognitive frame. To ground their theory, the authors present the management of a real crisis center as an example that uncovers typical crisis-management shortcomings, e.g., lack of coordination, insufficient standardization, and infrequent communication among diverse operators.

The third section of the book explores "New Crises, New Barriers." In Chapter 7, "The Psychological Effects of Crises: Deny Denial—Grieve Before a Crisis Occurs," Ian I. Mitroff (United States) provokes us to consider the new normalcy of abnormal crises, including how betrayal met by denial may be characteristic of all crises. Supported by a vivid case, this chapter proposes psychodynamics as a window to understanding organizational crises. Chapter 8, "A Passion for Imperfections: Revisiting Crisis Management" by Christophe Roux-Dufort (France), addresses the downward spiral of cognitive narrowing, ego defense, and denial and how these relate to crisis managers' threatened self-esteem. In Chapter 9, Toshihiko Hagiwara (Japan) discusses "The Eight Characteristics of Japanese Crisis-Prone Organizations." As Hagiwara notes, although the characteristics emerge from the context of Japan's business culture, their lessons are applicable to organizations around the globe. From Japan, we move to the United Kingdom with Chapter 10, "Voices From the Terraces: From 'Mock Bureaucracy' to 'Learning From Crisis' Within the UK's Soccer Industry." In an engaging presentation of crises within the British Soccer industry, Dominic Elliott (England) and Denis Smith (Scotland) tackle means of acquiring and disseminating knowledge that seem to foster persistent "pathways of vulnerability," with the result that incidents escalate repeatedly into crises.

The closing section of this book, "New Crises, New Solutions," addresses current thinking about ways out of crises. In Chapter 11, "A 'Total' Responsibility Management Approach to Crisis Management and Signal Detection in Organizations," Judith A. Clair and Sandra Waddock (United States) propose adaptation of the quality, environmental-management, and responsibility-management movements to the crisis-management field. They consider inherent implications and apply their thinking to the crisis-management challenge of early signal detection. Finally, in Chapter 12, "Crisis Management Simulations: Flaws and Remedies," Bertrand Robert and Christopher Lajtha (France) offer a practical introduction and assessment of simulation, a popular crisis-management training tool. Their concise discussion exposes traditional limitations of this method, as well as alternative innovative means for crisis-management training.

As these chapters demonstrate, the field of crisis management is still focused on a very wide reach of topics. The potential for conceptual contributions to our understanding of crisis management seems limited only by contributors' imaginations. For scholars, the unanswered questions far outweigh the answers. To some extent, the inherent contextual challenges of organizational access during crisis continue to stymie some research. For practitioners, although some decisions and actions are clearly ill-advised, no single best way to plan for, manage, or learn from an organizational crisis has yet emerged. In this book, we hope to capture a rich sampling of today's crisis-management research and practice. We hope that your reading will recognize that outcome.

Part I

New Risks,
New Crises,
New Dangers

Organizations in World Risk Society

Ulrich Beck and Boris Holzer

Today's critical debate over—and, sometimes, severe doubts about—risk-management practices ironically follow in the wake of massive endeavors to control and rein in the risks associated with industrialization. Accidents and unforeseen side effects time and again belied the promises of risk management and damage control. The hidden risks of risk models lie under the surface of controllability. Because modern risk management is often designed to maximize predictability, it frequently underestimates the occurrence of unexpected and unlikely—yet nonetheless possible—events, in terms of both the frequency and the severity of hazards. This unfortunate combination is due to the "uncertainty trap" in which many industries are caught: Industries have to be reasonably optimistic so as to base their decisions on rational, probabilistic criteria. Thus they have to look at the most—sometimes maybe the worst—*probable* risk, but not at the worst *possible* risk. The latter perspective, however, characterizes much of the late modern public attitude toward business and science. It is based on a "culture of uncertainty." In order to understand the consequences of this emerging global culture of uncertainty, it is necessary to develop a broader understanding of risk and risk management within the context of social and political theory.

In this chapter, we discuss the emergence of a culture of uncertainty and its consequences for organizations against the backdrop of the theory of risk society. We shall proceed as follows: (1) We will discuss the transformation of late modern society into a risk society—that is, a society increasingly confronted with the undesired side effects of successful modernization. (2) In the process of this transformation, the modern concept of "calculable risk" comes under pressure by the reemergence of uncontrollable uncertainties that are often due to scientific and technological innovations. (3) That has profound implications for organizations which have hitherto played a significant role both as sources of acceptable entrepreneurial risks and as "trustees" in charge of managing collective risks. (4) In contrast to the past, public scrutiny of organizational decisions is not confined to the national domain anymore. Over recent years, the debate about the uncontrollable risks of industrialization has galvanized a global public that casts a critical eye on technological developments and the benefits of innovation and scientific progress. (5) As a consequence, organizations as actors in the transnational realm face an increasing "legitimacy gap." They make decisions whose consequences transcend any particular time or place—and thereby the regulatory apparatus of the state. (6) It is unlikely that the legitimacy gap can be closed by the development of more sophisticated risk management practices. Rather, organizations have to broaden their own understanding of risk so as to include fundamental uncertainties as part of both their decision-making and their relationships with the public.

Modern Society as a Risk Society

Modern society has become a risk society in the sense that it is increasingly occupied with debating, preventing, and managing risks that it has itself produced.[1] The risks of risk society are neither the results of external, natural forces nor of deviant behavior, but of the societal, usually technology-based pursuit of legitimate and valued objectives. Other hazards and dramas of human life—such as plagues, famines, and natural disasters—may sometimes have consequences just as disastrous as modern megatechnologies. Yet they differ essentially from the "risks" of risk society since they are not based on decisions, or, more specifically, decisions that focus on techno-economic advantages and opportunities and accept hazards as the dark side of progress. Risks therefore presume industrial—that is, techno-economic—decisions and considerations of utility. They differ from other hazards and dangers by their "normal," "peaceful," and often systematic origin in the centers of rationality and prosperity. They differ from preindustrial natural disasters by their origin in decision-making, which is of course primarily conducted by organizations and corporate actors and only rarely by individuals.

The association of risk with decision-making has important consequences: Preindustrial hazards, no matter how large and devastating, were "strokes of fate" raining down on humankind from "outside" and attributable to the external world. Blame and accusations were of course formulated, but they were directed against agencies that could hardly be held responsible. They were thus in the broadest sense "religiously motivated" and not—like industrial risks—politically charged. For with the origin of industrial risks in decision-making the problem of social accountability and responsibility irrevocably arises, even in those areas where the prevailing rules of science and law permit accountability only in exceptional cases. People, firms, state agencies, and politicians are responsible for industrial risks. The recognized social roots of risks make it nigh impossible to externalize the problem of accountability.

Therefore, it is not the number of dead and wounded and not the financial damage either, but rather a social feature that makes the hazards of mega-technology a political issue: their ultimate origin in decision-making. The question remains, however: Have we not witnessed a period of continual growth in calculability and precaution in dealing with industrially produced insecurities and destruction in the past two hundred years? To be sure, the institutional history of industrial society also is the history of the various regimes for dealing with industrially produced risks and insecurities (Beck, 1996a; Bernstein, 1996; Bonß, 1995; Ericson et al., 2003; Evers & Nowotny, 1987; Ewald, 1986; Lau, 1989). The idea of reacting to the uncertainties of new markets or new technologies with collective agreements—insurance contracts, for instance, which allow the individual person or organization to trade in a small regular premium against the potential losses in cases of dramatic damage—is not particularly new. Its origins go back to the beginnings of trade and intercontinental navigation. But with the growth of industrial capitalism, insurance was continually perfected and expanded into nearly all problem areas of social action. Consequences that at first affected only the individual have become "risks"—systematically caused, statistically describable and thus predictable types of events—which can therefore also be subjected to collective rules of recognition, compensation, and avoidance.

In order to grasp the dialectics of endangerment and insurance, we must not forget that the term *risk* has two radically different meanings. It applies in the first place to a world governed entirely by the laws of probability, in which everything is measurable and calculable. But the word is also commonly used to refer to nonquantitative uncertainties, to "risks that cannot be known."[2] When we speak about "risk society," it is in this latter sense of manufactured uncertainties. These uncertainties, enforced by rapid technological innovations and accelerated societal responses, are creating a fundamentally new global risk landscape. It is characterized by a "culture of uncertainty" that picks up and amplifies the shortcomings of the industrial paradigm of calculable risk.[3] For society as a whole, and for industrial enterprises in particular, that leads to a precarious erosion of the securities hitherto afforded by the legitimate use of expert knowledge to define risks and their acceptability. For a long time, the calculus of risk has provided a sound and socially appreciated connection between the physical, engineering, and social sciences. It can be applied not only to completely disparate phenomena in health management—from the risks of smoking to those of nuclear power—but also to economic risks as well as risks of old age, unemployment and underemployment, traffic accidents, certain phases of life, and so forth. In addition, it permits a type of "technological moralization" that no longer needs to employ moral and ethical imperatives directly.

The triumph of the calculus of risks would probably not have been possible if fundamental advantages were not tied to it (see Beck, 1999c, p. 51f.). The first of these lies in the fact that calculable risks open the opportunity to "deindividualize" the danger of potential damages. Risks are then revealed as systematic events, which are accordingly in need of individual insurance and general political regulation. In both cases the individual exposition to dangers is mollified by collective provisions. Through the statistical description of risks (e.g., in the form of accident probabilities) the blinkers of individualization drop off. A field for corresponding political action is opened up: Accidents on the job, for instance, are not blamed on those whose health they have already ruined anyway, but are stripped of their individual origin and related instead to the plant organization, the lack of precautions, and so on. A second advantage is that insurance payments paid on a no-fault basis (setting aside the extreme cases of gross negligence or intentional damage) make it unnecessary to identify cause and perpetrator in too much detail. In that way, legal battles over causation become unnecessary and moral outrage is moderated. Instead, an incentive for prevention is created for businesses, in proportion to the magnitude of the insurance costs—or perhaps not.

The important social function of the calculus of risk, then, is to make the industrial system capable of dealing with its own unforeseeable future. The calculus of risk, protection by insurance liability laws, and other devices promise what is basically impossible: Future events become the object of current action—of prevention, compensation, or precautionary after-care. As François Ewald (1986) has shown, the major innovation of the calculus of risk lies in making the incalculable calculable, with the help of accident statistics, through generalized settlement formulae as well as through the generalized exchange principle of "money for damages." In this way, a system of norms for social accountability, compensation, and precautions—though controversial in its details—creates present security in the face of an open uncertain future. Modernity, which brings uncertainty to every niche of existence, finds its counterprinciple in a *social compact against industrially produced hazards and damages*, stitched together out of public and private insurance agreements and thus activating and renewing *trust* in corporations and government.

From Calculable Risk to Uncertainty

The transition from industrial to risk society is deeply intertwined with the waxing and waning of trust in calculable risk. There are two different stages of risk society. In the *first* stage we see a "residual risk culture": the belief that risk-taking is necessary to realize opportunities and that the potential hazards will be cured by further progress. In this stage, there is faith that the consequences of industrialism can be tackled in the same way they have been dealt with in the past: by developing more efficient markets, better technology, and better rules of law. In this context, people who point to systemic risks are usually regarded as scaremongers who just do not get the facts right. But during this stage, global risk factors are constantly piling up. The fact that environmental problems go largely unnoticed simply helps to exacerbate them. Eastern Europe under Communism displays an informative case of how the denial of environmental problems can lead to environmental disaster.

Three factors contribute to the largely unnoticed production of risk factors. First are the metanorms of risk definition, particularly the legal norms of how to attribute liability—that is, causes and consequences, under conditions of high complexity and contingency. If it is necessary to name one and only one actor, in the overwhelming majority of cases *no* actor can be named. This is exacerbated by the fact that, second, a significant number of technologically induced hazards, such as those associated with chemical pollution, atomic radiation, and GM organisms, are characterized by an inaccessibility to the human senses. They operate outside the capacity of (unaided) human perception. Everyday life is "blind" in relation to hazards that threaten life and thus depends on experts and counterexperts. Not only the potential harm but this *"expropriation of the senses"* by global risks makes life insecure. Third, then, there is a significant interrelationship between *ignoring* a risk that cannot be attributed according to the metanorms of risk definition in law and science and *enforcing* risk production as a consequence of industrial action and production.

It is only in the *second* stage in the emergence of risk society that the growth of global risk factors enters public discourse and everyday life. At this stage, risk society becomes reflexive, and thus changes its political dynamics. Everyday life becomes significantly conditioned by risk recognition and response, from the food we eat to the business decisions we make. Once the link between the definition of risk and the breakdown of markets (and sometimes the emergence of new markets) is recognized, a social learning mechanism unfolds. It is an emergent structure of innovation that affects the economy, politics, and culture. Early risk society thus has no significant consequences for the established coalition of industry, science, and state administration that oversaw the development of modern industrial society. In the second stage, however, industrial enterprises cannot count on state administrations in the same way. They cannot count on either the lawmakers or the judiciary to continue to base their judgments on the assumption of continual progress. It is not merely a matter of the democratic process splitting the old coalition into separate interest groups, but a conflict of social paradigms: different principles of society, different principles of knowledge, and different principles of experience.

During the transition, the new risk paradigm of uncertainty is gradually entrenched and professionalized. It is embodied in new industries and new experts. There arises a fundamental split between those who do not believe anything should be changed in our relation to risk, that we should continue on as we always have, and those who now perceive the situation in the context of much wider risk horizons.

In both stages there are different paradoxes involved. In the first, dominated by a residual risk culture, the ignorance of the globalization of risk increases the globalization of risk. In addition, scientists allow themselves to get caught in a safety trap. When they are confronted with skepticism and what they call "irrationality," they promise—as they did in the case of genetic engineering—that everything is "absolutely" safe, controllable, and reversible. The consequence of such absolute claims is that every new risk and new accident shakes the foundations of an inalienable right to safety that seems to have been promised. In the second stage, characterized by a culture of uncertainty, the safety trap takes a different form. Instead of untenable promises of safety, widespread distrust prevails, and consequently, intense debates about and scrutiny of new technologies are the order of the day. The acceptance of every new technology or product is increasingly determined by risk considerations. But since the whole premise of this new attitude is that uncertainty is ineradicable, carrying out this procedure in full would completely stifle innovation. If the world is perceived only in terms of risks, then nobody can act. Yet as Wildavsky aptly put it, "no risk is the highest risk of all" (Wildavsky, 1979). The concept of uncertain risk only says what should *not* be done. It does not address what should or could be done.

There is no safety in calculable risk, but giving priority to uncertainty does not guarantee safety either. These impasses of both a residual-risk logic and the culture of uncertainty show that we cannot expect a straightforward solution to the problems of risk society. Through a host of challenges and uncertainties with which we are concerned today—nuclear power, many types of chemical and biotechnological production, as well as the continuing and threatening ecological destruction—the foundations of the established risk logic are being subverted or suspended.

The emergence of risk society is emblematic of the process of *reflexive modernization*, which entails the self-confrontation of modernity with the side effects of modernization (Beck et al., 2003; Beck et al., 1994; Benton, 2000). The risks of risk society are not external threats that call for new technologies and better knowledge. They are side effects of new technologies and of the growth of scientific knowledge. Accordingly, the problem of modernity has moved from solving externally imposed problems to solving self-produced problems. The fact that modernity and its very institutions are at the core of many of the most pressing problems such as the ecological crisis raises doubts as to whether the *institutions* of modernity are capable of solving the *problems* of modernity. This marks the break with "linear" modernization: In reflexive modernization, the very *method* of problem-solving itself becomes problematic.

From Trustee to Suspect: Organizations in Risk Society

Risk refers not to "objective" probabilities but to the "subjective" expectation of possible damage related to one's decisions. Although knowing the probabilities can serve to legitimize risk-taking as such, it cannot eliminate the necessity of decision-making. The evaluation of a risky choice depends on the realization of uncertain outcomes *in the future* and is thus only possible after the fact. Risk is the possibility of future damage that is attributed to a *decision*—that is, to causes internal to a person, an organization, or society. Danger, in contrast, is the possibility of future damage that is attributed to factors over which we have no control.[4] Thus, an earthquake would usually qualify as a danger, whereas a skiing accident would be regarded as a consequence of a risk that a person undertook. If we distinguish between danger and risk, we can conclude that risk society may well be less "dangerous" but more "risky" than any other kind of society—precisely because *dangers* are increasingly turned into *risks*.

Organizations relying on technology have been important vehicles for the expansion of risk and uncertainty in modern society. Technology in particular plays a crucial role in transforming dangers into risks. Many events formerly regarded as beyond the scope of human influence and intervention are now routinely a matter of human control by virtue of technology. To use a very simple but convenient example (Luhmann, 1986): If one leaves the house, one always runs the "danger" of getting wet. It is a danger since rain is not, in our society, attributed to anyone's decision.[5] Yet the availability of a specific technology—the umbrella—can transform rain from being a danger to being a risk. That is, once one has the option of taking along an umbrella, the question of whether or not to get wet depends on a *decision:* to use the umbrella or not. In many areas, technology has thus greatly extended the scope of human decision-making—and accordingly the possibility of risk and error.

Modern organizations are also an important factor in the production of risk through technology in a more general sense (Perrow, 1984; Short & Clarke, 1992). Much more than individuals, who are not normally required to reconstruct all of their actions as the outcome of conscious decision-making, modern organizations are social systems of decision-making—from the decision to hire someone as an employee to the decision to file for bankruptcy (Baecker, 1999; Luhmann, 2000). Most importantly, organizing involves decisions that create premises for further decisions: decisions about personnel, hierarchies, and rules. Organizations thus have a deep affinity to risk. They construct themselves (and their environment) as the outcome of decisions, because whatever happens in an organization can and must be interpreted as a decision. Modern technology and organizations contribute to a process through which a world of dangers is transformed into a world of risks. The world and its dangers are not "givens" anymore, as technological tools and organizational routines make them increasingly a matter of decision-making.

Yet the emergence of risk society not only results in new risks faced by individuals, states, and organizations, but also fundamentally alters the way in which organizations relate to their social environment. In a way, the organization may be regarded as a convenient vehicle for efficiently achieving clearly defined objectives, as a "system of consciously coordinated activities or forces of two or more persons" (Barnard, 1938, p. 73). In this sense, they are problem-solving institutions. Seen through the lens of reflexive modernization theory, however, they are also problem-producing institutions. They partake in a shift characteristic of risk society: from the distribution of "goods" to the distribution of "bads." This is evident for organizations of the industrial sector. While observers once focused on their achievements, products, and services, they are now equally interested in the side effects of their operations:

> Where once the individual large corporation was free of public pressure unless it specifically misbehaved—stifled competition, endangered its employees, or whatever—today it is being challenged for virtually everything it tries to do and, indeed, for not taking the initiative in the social sphere. Once there were only the owners' goals to attend to, later the systems goals. Today the corporation is being asked to respond to a confusing host of public goals, social as well as economic. (Mintzberg, 1983, p. 464)

The anticipation of side effects also means that corporations are increasingly faced with anticipatory resistance to their decisions: No power plant is built without protest from nearby residents, no oil field explored without critical scrutiny by transnational non-governmental organizations (NGOs), no new pharmaceutical drug hailed without qualifications about its side effects. In other words, as highly visible and ubiquitous institutions of modernity, organizations have to cope with a situation in which the basic principles of modernity are not taken for granted anymore. Consequently, organizations cease to be primarily conceived as instruments of risk *management;* instead, their decisions are often perceived as *sources* of risk.

This signals a significant paradigm shift. Early theorists of modernity regarded the bureaucratic organization not only as an efficient means of instrumental action (e.g., producing goods and services) but also as a tool of planning. The calculus of risk that we have described above could not have become a social institution without being anchored in the modern organization. Organizations are capable of planning their actions. In the process, according to early organization theorists such as March and Simon (1958), they "absorb" uncertainties and replace them by seemingly calculable risks: "When organizations analyze problems, they try to transform *uncertainties* into *risks,* rationalizing problems previously outside the realm of systematic control" (Clarke, 1999, p. 10). Any socially significant imponderability or uncertainty seems to trigger organizational responses: From military security over health care to disaster control, organizations are involved in any serious societal effort to cope with an uncertain and possibly dangerous future. As responses to uncertainty, the aforementioned insurance principle and organizational planning go hand in hand. Insurance serves to defuse individual uncertainties by turning them into collectively faced, calculable risks. Organizational planning creates the impression that anticipatory policies can be devised for any imaginable uncertainty faced by larger groups of people.

However, with the emergence of an increasingly "self-conscious" risk society, it has become more and more obvious that organizations are not simply efficient tools of purposeful action and risk management. Rather, the principles of organizing themselves often seem to contribute to the proliferation of risk. Organizations are not only part of the solution but also very much part of the problem: "We have more to fear from organizations and experts overextending their reach, propelled by forces endemic to modern society, than from conniving conspiracies," argues Clarke (1999, p. 2). As extraordinary, and perhaps even exaggerated, as such a statement may appear at first glance, it ties in with both the increasingly common distrust of organizations and experts and the sociological analysis of reflexive modernization. As indicated above, the latter argues that modernity has become *self*-endangering. The biggest challenges faced by modern society are of its own making—manufactured uncertainties rather than external threats (Beck, 1996b). As an epitome of the modern trust in control, rationality, and objective knowledge, the organization partakes of the process of reflexive modernization. While organizations in First Modernity could by and large rely on a tolerant, even supportive social environment, organizations in Second Modernity have to adapt to a culture of uncertainty that does not uncritically accept received standards of knowledge and calculation.

Again, it is important to understand that the contemporary culture of uncertainty is a consequence of the rather exaggerated claims of certainty made during earlier phases of modernity. Many of them have been shattered by the well-known and much-publicized accidents and disasters of the second half of the 20th century—in particular, by the Chernobyl and *Challenger* accidents that combine to the "Ch-Ch-syndrome" (Funtowicz & Ravetz, 1990, p. 1), that is, the collapse of mega-technologies. But others, such as Bhopal, *Exxon Valdez,* and Three Mile Island, need to be included, too, if we are to understand the changed situation at the beginning the 21st century. Those accidents certainly inform the collective consciousness of risk society. However, on top of the sheer monstrosity of the inflicted damages, the mounting evidence of the systematic connection between risk and organization has made a lasting impression. At least since Perrow's (1984) *Normal Accidents*, the attribution of risks to certain organizational structures has gained currency. The accident has ceased to be a mere mishap; it has become a regular feature. Society has been used as a "laboratory" for new technologies in the past (Krohn & Weyer, 1989), but it is uncertain to what extent it will tolerate such an enterprise in the future.

The Global Public and Its Problems: The Politicization of Risk Conflicts

In the process of reflexive modernization, the foundations of traditional risk management are eroding. Risk in Second Modernity is a cipher for irreducible uncertainty rather than for a calculable future. Neither improved expertise nor better communication can restore the old certainties. The resistance of society toward scientific and technological innovations such as GM foodstuffs is therefore not, in essence, a matter of understanding or misunderstanding calculable risks. What needs to be understood—both by practitioners and theorists—is that the basis of power and legitimacy has changed.

Rather than particular technologies or the decisions made about them, it is the *unforeseeability of the consequences* that has become the source of politics. The risk profile of new, controversial technologies is determined by the uneasy dissent in terms of risk perception rather than by the agreed consent among stakeholders concerning opportunities. The question, therefore, is not whether a given technology is dangerous, but whether it is *perceived* as being dangerous. Genetic engineering is one of the prime examples. Some call its much-debated consequences "phantom risks" or "virtual risks." Such theorists inadvertently highlight an important fact: In the case of manufactured uncertainties, most cause-and-effect relationships are and often remain controversial. What they miss is that this controversial nature is itself a risk—an economic one for corporations and a political one for governments.

The awareness of the unpredictability of ultimate consequences has given rise to a world public that is highly "risk-sensitive." But on the other side of the risk-sensitive public are increasingly unpredictable consumers, among whom a chain reaction can be triggered by the merest hint of plausible evidence. Since uncontested scientific evidence is increasingly rare, public perception becomes the decisive element in such scenarios. And because of its political weight, it is public perception that ultimately defines the likelihood of product bans or the success of liability claims. In risk conflicts, the central question of power therefore is a question of *definitional authority*. It is the question of who, on the basis of which legal and intellectual resources, gets to decide what counts as a "risk," what counts as a "cause," and what counts as a "cost." The question of determining who is responsible and who has to bear the burden of paying for damages has been transmuted into a battle over the rules of evidence and the laws of responsibility. The new global public challenges the existing system of "organized irresponsibility" (Beck, 1988). The dynamic that fans risk failures into risk crises is the attempt to shift the burden of proof and the burdens of cost that have thus far been borne by consumers and the environment back onto corporations and governments. Put another way, they are driven by the attempt to institutionalize the concern for ultimate consequences.

Current and future risk conflicts seem to crystallize around a specific set of risks often referred to as "new" risks (see Lau, 1999). These new risks are characterized by new relationships between the actual decision-making and the spatial and temporal scope of the resulting risks (for the latter see especially Adam, 1998). New risks can no longer be delimited in time and space. They affect everyone but can hardly be attributed to anyone anymore. Properly considered, risk society has always been "world risk society" (Beck, 1999b; Beck & Holzer, 2004), but it is only slowly taking shape as the border-crossing implications of global risks are felt. The risk landscape thus created has the following elements:

(1) *Irreversible consequences, unlimited in time and space, that occur only after a long latency period.* Measuring "risk" probabilistically presupposes a concept of "accidents" as things that happen at a particular time and in a particular place to a particular group. But none of these tacit assumptions hold for the "accident" that occurred at Chernobyl. Even 20 years later, some of the victims have not even been *born* yet. Similarly, an accident caused by GM organisms would be just as unbounded as a nuclear accident. Everything that is celebrated as a triumph of gene technology—e.g., its universal applicability and its power to increase productivity—will have the effect of spreading it much faster throughout the food chain. Theoretically, then, the ultimate risks of this technology would be even more unlimited and incalculable. We can get out of nuclear power, at least in principle, and nuclear waste sites are at least *sites* (i.e., discrete locations). In this regard, biotechnology opens up a completely new arena for the near-invisible production of risk.

(2) *Contradictions of globalization.* Citizenship is usually conceived of in terms of national rights and national duties, and this is the framework that regulates the risks that anyone living within the national territory may face.

But the globalization of risk has created huge difficulties for the nation-state in its effort to manage risks in a world of global flows and networks, especially when nobody takes responsibility for the outcomes. Bovine spongioform encephalopathy (BSE) is an explosive reminder of the inability of nation-states to predict, manage, and control risk in a chaotically interacting world of politically hybrid forms. Politicians say they are not in charge, that they at most regulate the framework for the market. Scientific experts say they merely create technological opportunities; they don't decide how they are implemented. Businesses say they are simply responding to consumer demand. Society has become a laboratory with nobody responsible for the outcome of the experiment (Krohn & Weyer, 1989). This is increased and enforced by the transnational diversity of regulatory standards. And this diversity can cause enormous tensions not only domestically but also in global, regional, and bilateral trading systems. Even existing supranational democratic institutions have difficulties reaching decisions. For instance, in the European Union (EU), which has probably made the greatest progress in establishing transnational decision-making bodies, member states during the BSE crisis followed their own national policies regarding the acceptance of the clearance certificates for British beef. While the exercise of national sovereignty might appear a viable solution in this case, the ramifications of other global risks are not as easily contained and therefore highlight the structural inability to manage manufactured uncertainties either nationally (through independent regulation) or globally (through collective action and supranational institutions).

(3) *Known unawareness and the unreliability of knowledge.* The unknown far outweighs what is known. That is the undeniable consequence of the steady but invisible production of risk. Clearly scientists now know much more about BSE than before. But even now, more than a decade after the disease's discovery, its origins, its host range, its means of transmission, the nature of the infectious agent and its relation to its human counterpart, new variant Creutzfeldt-Jakob disease (nvCJD), remain mostly unknown. Ultimate risk may offer no narrative closure, no ending by which the truth is recovered and the boundaries are stabilized. The lack of past experience means that in the context of manufactured uncertainties, the subjunctive has replaced the indicative. This is in large part because the past has been so thoroughly rewritten. Many things that were once considered universally certain and safe turned out to be deadly. Applying that knowledge to the present and the future devalues the certainties of today. This is the soil that nurtures the fear of conceivable threats. Virtual risks no longer need to exist in order to be perceived as fact. You might criticize them as phantom risks, but this does not matter economically. Perceived as risks, they cause enormous losses and disasters. Thus, the distinction between "real" risks and "hysterical" perception no longer holds. Or more precisely: *Economically,* it makes no difference.

(4) *The dominance of public perception.* Risk acceptability depends on whether those who carry the losses also receive the benefits. Where this is

not the case, the risk will be unacceptable to those affected. If even the benefit is in dispute—as is the case with GM foods—it is not enough to demonstrate that the "residual risk" is, statistically speaking, very small. A risk is always framed by the criteria used in evaluating it, and colored by the cultural assumptions that surround it. One might say: Risks are as big as they appear. From a social-constructionist perspective, this is obvious. Yet it becomes a universally relevant social fact in the case of manufactured uncertainties.

It is against this background that technical experts perceive the lay population as irrational or hysterical, either because people seem to be making bad calculations of personal risk—e.g., when smokers protest against nuclear energy—or because they express themselves with lurid images—e.g., when many people in Great Britain, seemingly invaded by German angst, demonize their genetically modified (GM) wonders as "Frankenstein food." In the public domain, statements of risk are based on cultural standards, technically expressed, about what is *still* and what is *no longer* acceptable. When scientists say that an event has a low probability of occurring, and hence is a negligible risk, they also express a judgment about relative payoffs. Social and cultural judgments do not simply distort the perception of risk. Without social and cultural judgments, there *are* no risks. Those judgments *constitute* risk, although often in hidden ways.

It is almost trivial to state that risk is more than ever a social construction (see Adams, 1995; Krimsky & Golding, 1992; Short & Clarke, 1992). Yet such a statement has important consequences for our analysis. It means that we have to focus our attention on the power relations of risk definition. Once we define risk conflict in these terms, each conflict reveals a microstructure of subsidiary struggles over the same set of questions that repeatedly recur: Who has the burden of proof? What constitutes proof under conditions of uncertainty? What norms of accountability are used? Who is responsible morally? And who is responsible for paying the costs? And this is true both nationally and transnationally, including along the North-South divide. When the politics of risk are explicated along these lines, they cast a rare light on shifts in epistemology and their relation to political strategy. Changing power relations of definition are closely connected to changes in some of society's central self-definitions. And to the extent that power in risk conflicts has changed to favor social movements, it shifts the whole context of risk conflict into a more reflexive constellation.

The key to a positive response to the culture of uncertainty lies in the readiness to make risk a topic of public debate; the willingness to negotiate between different rationalities, rather than to engage in mutual denunciation; and a recognition of the central importance of acting responsibly and accountably with regard to the losses that will always occur despite every precaution. A culture of uncertainty shuns the notion of "residual risks" because risks are only residual if they happen to other people. But the culture of uncertainty is also different from a "safety culture"; that is, a culture in which absolute safety is considered an entitlement that society should strive toward. Such a culture would smother all innovation in its cradle.

In some ways, this argument elaborates a central idea of John Dewey in his 1927 book, *The Public and Its Problems*.[6] Dewey saw local communities being overrun by corporations that operated on a national scale, much as we now see national communities being overrun by corporations operating on a world scale. For him, the only way for communities to regain their function of integrating individuals into society was to somehow match the scope of corporations and of the consequences of their actions. Dewey makes an important contribution to the theory of global risks by observing that a public is something that stands between causes and their consequences, and gives them a symbolic meaning they would not have otherwise. That meaning is what makes politics and society possible. And therefore it is not actions but *consequences* that are at the core of politics. And it is by giving consequences meaning that the public plays its key role in the formation of society:

> The doctrine of economic interpretation as usually stated ignores the transformation which meanings may effect; it passes over the new medium which communication may interpose between industry and its eventual consequences. It is obsessed by the illusion which vitiated the "natural economy": an illusion due to failure to note the difference made in action by perception and publication of its consequences, actual and possible. It thinks in terms of antecedents, not of the eventual; of origins, not fruits. (Dewey, 1954, p. 156)

Although Dewey was certainly not thinking of global warming, GM food, and BSE, his theory is perfectly applicable to the situation of risk society. In his view, public discourse grows not out of consensus over decisions but out of *dissent* over the *consequences* of decisions. Modern risk crises are constituted by just such controversies over consequences. Where some may see an overreaction to risk, Dewey thus sees a reason for hope. He thinks that such conflicts serve an *enlightenment* function. They bridge the gap between experts and citizens. And this is what gives them the political explosiveness that the technical diagnosis of the problem seeks to cover up.

The problem that Dewey started from—that local communities were being overwhelmed by the side effects of modernization—exists today on a global scale. The border-spanning long-term consequences of industrialization have the capacity for igniting transnational "communities of risk" or "risk publics." From the perspective of industry and governments, the fact that social movements can now reach beyond the boundaries of national legal systems in their attempt to hold corporations responsible for the long-term consequences of their actions seems like a recipe for destabilization. From Dewey's perspective, the same events look like a vital step toward the building of new institutions. Risk has the power to rip down the facades of organized irresponsibility. One can see a premonition of this power in the lightning flash of media publicity. It tears the decent drapery for just a moment, and pushes groups into contact from across the world that had hitherto been ignorant of each other's existence. This communication of risks not only happens despite people's original intentions, it goes particularly against the grain of experts and governments.

Social scientists have shown that many risks that are technically quite small loom larger than they "ought to" from the perspective of everyday life. But if we start from the hypothesis that people are acting rationally, where does this difference come from? It comes from what we just discussed, from being exposed to risks against one's will. An omnipresent mass media spreads an omnipresent knowledge of an omnipresent risk, say, contracting the BSE virus through your food. Even though the risk may be very small, its presence completely changes the experience of eating. Even if the chance of dying from a horrible brain-wasting disease is very small, it is not a lottery anyone wants to participate in. So they vote for another product, thereby making possible the collapse of whole markets. The propensity of consumers to act accordingly—to "vote with their shopping trolleys," as it were—has increased and nowadays presents a formidable challenge to many industries (Friedman, 1991; Micheletti, 2003; Micheletti et al., 2003).

The Legitimacy Gap in the Transnational Realm

The mobilization of an increasingly risk-sensitive public has severe consequences for governments and corporations. From the perspective of the public at large and the critical consumer, corporations are making *de facto* political decisions while still attempting to shift responsibility for their long-term risks onto others. In other words, corporations engage in a form of *subpolitics* that shares many attributes with traditional formal politics but bypasses the established institutions (Beck, 1999a; Holzer & Sørensen, 2003). The resulting *incongruity between power and legitimacy* generates a latent tension. It works fine so long as things are run smoothly. But in a crisis situation, the new emperors are often revealed to be naked of legitimacy. The chronic yet regularly unnoticed legitimacy deficit makes it possible for accidents to amplify quickly into crises and collapsed markets.

Conversely, this lack of legitimacy is also the main source of power for social movements. Social movements are neither organized democratically nor legitimated by democratic institutions. However, many people regard them as credible representatives of the public interest. While profit-seeking enterprises are necessarily associated with self-interest, social movement organizations can benefit from the legitimacy that modern culture bestows on actions seemingly motivated by altruistic motives (Boli et al., 2003). When one surveys young people as to which political actors they respect the most, it is these movements that occupy the highest rank. Movements and corporations thus occupy opposite positions in the power-legitimacy matrix: Transnational corporations have many resources of power but little legitimacy, while social movements have few resources of power but a deep well of legitimacy (Beck, 2002, Ch. 6; Holzer, 2006). On that basis, social-movement organizations and advocacy networks are likely to be followed when they seek to mobilize the public against corporations. The incongruity between power and legitimacy is the Achilles heel of the transnational firm, and it is the point at which the public strategies of social movements take aim. In the end, even powerful companies can find themselves backed up against the wall by relatively tiny and poorly outfitted networks of activists.

The Brent Spar affair is a good illustration of how huge the legitimacy gap has grown, and how, once uncovered and harnessed, it makes available a force by means of which David can defeat Goliath (Grolin, 1998; Tsoukas, 1999; Wätzold, 1996). In this case, David was Greenpeace, a voluntary organization without a formal public mandate; it has employees as well as ships, helicopters, hot-air balloons, and quite a considerable budget. But it is definitely a David when ranged against a multinational oil company such as Royal Dutch/Shell. In the Brent Spar case, Shell also had the law on its side as well as the police and the support of the elected British government. And, perhaps most interestingly of all, it had environmental science on its side: Greenpeace's initial claims about toxic waste onboard the Brent Spar later turned out to be wrong. And yet in the end, with every conceivable advantage, Shell lost. There could be perhaps no better demonstration of what an enormous resource is now available to be tapped by a skillfully organized public campaign.[7]

The Brent Spar controversy is a particularly instructive example of the challenges that corporations face when they have to defend themselves against the campaigns of social movement organizations. Both scholars and practitioners regard it as a paradigmatic case study in the field of corporate crisis management (see Paine, 1999; Paine & Moldoveanu, 1999). Although the setting and trajectory of the conflict—as well as its public resonance—was exceptional, it must be seen in the context of a range of similar events—both before and after the Brent Spar case. Those range from the early anticorporate campaigns orchestrated by consumer advocates such as Ralph Nader (see Vogel, 1978) over the long and ultimately successful activism against Nestlé's infant-formula marketing in the Third World (Sethi & Post, 1979; Sikkink, 1986) to the antisweatshop campaigns against Nike and other global companies (Global Exchange, 2003; Micheletti & Stolle, 2005).

Although these and various other campaigns have a lot in common, there are also important differences. For instance, some conflicts revolve around the divergence of standards regarding working conditions or environmental protection. To the extent that the campaigns aim to harmonize those standards across the world, one may expect fewer protest motives in the future. Other cases, however, cannot be as easily resolved by more encompassing regulation: They concern the foundations of regulation as such and are thus directly related to the aforementioned culture of uncertainty. Confrontations about fundamental uncertainties such as the impact of toxic waste on marine life or the introduction of GM organisms into the food chain are not simply about regional variations in regulation and can therefore not be addressed by a convergence of standards alone. They concern the relationship between decision-making power on the one hand and the rules of accountability and responsibility on the other: In world risk society, the consequences and side effects of risky decisions transcend the routines and boundaries of a predominantly territorial mode of regulation.

The resulting legitimation deficit, which grows out of the gap between increasingly global and long-term risks and spatially and chronologically limited responsibility, is now a constant potential, waiting to be transformed at any moment into a radical loss of confidence in established institutions. It has changed the balance of power between the risk-critical public and the transnational corporations. Globalization thus does not simply mean that corporations grow more powerful. Rather, the accelerating pace of international economic integration serves to increase the legitimation deficit of border-spanning economic decision-making. This chronic legitimation deficit renders consumer markets extremely fragile and makes international corporations extremely vulnerable (Willetts, 1998). The more they manage to escape from the power of governments, the more they seem to depend on direct relationships with consumers, markets, and civil society. Globally operating actors such as transnational corporations are confronted with the problem of diverse and often contradictory legal frameworks and societal expectations. They face new uncertainties as societal demands appear increasingly contradictory and elusive. The globalization of communication systems has further exacerbated this problem because activities in one locale are now scrutinized by a transnational public representing various value systems. For the implementation of decisions this may lead to problems, as Phil Watts of Shell International observed:

> Communications technology has created a global goldfish bowl. All multinational companies operate in front of a hugely diverse worldwide audience.... [S]ince the ethical, social, cultural and economic priorities which underlie their demands are... often local and personal, those demands will differ, will often conflict, and may be irreconcilable. (Watts, 1998, p. 24)

The crucial point for corporations is that the legality of their operations may be insufficient to ensure legitimacy. For instance, Shell's planned Brent Spar disposal was entirely legal. The operation complied not only with British but also with international law. Initially, none of the affected *states* objected to it. What Shell did not and probably could not ensure, however, was the acceptance by the (transnational) *public*. The latter becomes problematic when decisions and their consequences are regarded as transcending the boundaries of the nation-state. Accordingly, the legitimacy and acceptance of decisions that comply with legal rules cannot be taken for granted anymore.

It is hardly surprising that organizations, in particular business enterprises, should have sought to address that problem. The recent focus on "stakeholder relations" (Donaldson & Preston, 1995; Freeman, 1984; Weiss, 1998) is instructive in this respect. More and more organizations seek to identify those groups and issues that could throw their operations into turmoil. The only way to regain legitimacy appears to be a systematic effort to engage the public.[8] As the public has grown wary of the side effects of economic activities, the thoroughly private nature of business has been called into question. Echoing Dewey's arguments, the distinction between public and private is redrawn—this time not on the basis of property, but on the basis of the *consequences* of decisions.[9] Thus, one may argue that business decisions are increasingly becoming *public* in nature because of their alleged impact on others. The ensuing scrutiny and distrust of business practice has transformed large corporations into "quasi-public institutions" (Mintzberg, 1983, p. 525; Ulrich, 1977). Taking stakeholders and public demands seriously could become a viable alternative to the expert-based safety culture of the past. Although such an approach cannot pretend to ensure the predictability of future events, it certainly represents a more realistic answer to the challenges of a culture of uncertainty.

Conclusion

In the risk-sensitive social environment of world risk society, organizations have to realize that "crises" do not always have a clearly identifiable origin or cause. A general shift from calculable risk to uncertainty means that it is impossible to control or even accurately predict a firm's external environment. The shift from a safety culture based on the acceptance of residual risks to a culture of uncertainty has made the challenges faced by organizations more incalculable. Furthermore, the globalization of organizational activities and public arenas has multiplied the observers and audiences and has thus only exacerbated this problem. The lesson learned by society—that calculable risk is a useful but not necessarily correct interpretational device—may still have to be learned by some organizations, too. The risks they regularly produce are reflected back by the fact that public outrage can wreak havoc on a company's reputation. The problem of manufactured uncertainties and their consequences thereby becomes relevant to everyday decision-making processes. Organizations cannot stop making decisions, but they can be cognizant of the fact that others will increasingly judge them by their consequences and side effects—and not by their good intentions.

Notes

1. This section draws on arguments developed in more detail in Beck (1992; 1996b; 1999c).
2. Some theorists follow Knight (1921) and distinguish between risk and uncertainty. However, most modern observers would not subscribe to Knight's objectivist interpretation of risk. Even probabilistic risk always entails uncertainties that are simply obfuscated by mathematical precision. The difference Knight had in mind seems to be whether fundamental uncertainties are acknowledged in the decision-making process—or not.
3. By referring to a "culture of uncertainty" we take up a line of investigation pioneered by Mary Douglas and her collaborators (Douglas, 1992; Rayner, 1992; Schwarz & Thompson, 1990; Thompson et al., 1990). However, we perceive the culture of uncertainty as a growing and increasingly encompassing pattern of late modern culture that, as we shall argue below, is also becoming global in scope.
4. See Luhmann (1990, 1991) for a detailed discussion of how this distinction between risk and danger has become increasingly relevant for modern society.
5. To be sure, the decision to go out in the first place may also be construed as acceptance of the risk of getting wet. Yet since it is impossible to stay at home forever, there is no real alternative, and therefore no opportunity for decision-making: no risk, but danger.
6. The following draws on a line of argument developed in Beck (2001).
7. It is important to note that discursive skill and not just professional organization played a major role in Greenpeace's success. Shell's insistence on rational-scientific argument could not match Greenpeace's discourse of possible risks and environmental responsibility (see Holzer, 2001).
8. "Organizations in modern societies are public not only in the sense that their structures, processes and ideologies are open to observation, but also in their ultimate dependence on public acceptance, i.e., of positioning themselves in relation to the perceptions and policies of society at large" (Brunsson, 1989, p. 216).
9. See Dewey's (1954, p. 15) dictum that "the line between private and public is to be drawn on the basis of the extent and scope of the consequences of acts which are so important as to need control, whether by inhibition or by promotion."

Bibliography

Adam, B. (1998). *Timescapes of modernity: The environment and invisible hazards.* London/New York: Routledge.
Adams, J. (1995). *Risk.* London: UCL Press.
Baecker, D. (1999). *Organisation als system.* Frankfurt am Main: Suhrkamp.
Barnard, C. I. (1938). *The functions of the executive.* Cambridge, MA: Harvard University Press.
Beck, U. (1988). *Gegengifte. Die organisierte unverantwortlichkeit.* Frankfurt am Main: Suhrkamp.

Beck, U. (1992). *Risk society: Towards a new modernity* (M. Ritter, Trans.). London: Sage.
Beck, U. (1996a). Risk society and the provident state. In S. Lash, B. Szerszynski, & B. Wynne (Eds.), *Risk, environment and modernity: Towards a new ecology* (pp. 27–43). London: Sage.
Beck, U. (1996b). World risk society as cosmopolitan society? Ecological questions in a framework of manufactured uncertainties. *Theory, Culture & Society, 13*(4), 1–32.
Beck, U. (1999a). Subpolitics: Ecology and the disintegration of institutional power. In *World risk society* (pp. 91–108). Cambridge, UK: Polity.
Beck, U. (1999b). *World risk society.* Cambridge, UK: Polity.
Beck, U. (1999c). From industrial society to risk society: Questions of survival, social structure and ecological enlightenment. In *World risk society* (pp. 48–71). Cambridge, UK: Polity.
Beck, U. (2001). *Risk and power: The loss of confidence and the fragility of markets in global risk society.* Lecture at Harvard University, Cambridge, MA.
Beck, U. (2002). *Macht und gegenmacht im globalen zeitalter. Neue weltpolitische okonomie* [Power in the global age: A new global political economy]. Frankfurt am Main: Suhrkamp.
Beck, U., Bonß, W., & Lau, C. (2003). The theory of reflexive modernization: Problematic, hypotheses and research programme. *Theory, Culture & Society, 20*(2), 1–33.
Beck, U., Giddens, A., & Lash, S. (1994). *Reflexive modernization: Politics, tradition, and aesthetics in the modern social order.* Cambridge, UK: Polity Press.
Beck, U., & Holzer, B. (2004). Wie global ist die weltrisikogesellschaft? In U. Beck & C. Lau (Eds.), *Entgrenzung und Entscheidung* (pp. 421–439). Frankfurt am Main: Suhrkamp.
Benton, T. (2000). Reflexive modernization. In G. Browning, A. Halcli, & F. Webster (Eds.), *Understanding contemporary society: Theories of the present* (pp. 97–111). London: Sage.
Bernstein, P. L. (1996). *Against the gods: The remarkable story of risk.* New York: John Wiley & Sons.
Boli, J., Elliott, M. A., & Bieri, F. (2003). Globalization. In G. Ritzer (Ed.), *Handbook of social problems: A comparative international perspective* (pp. 389–415). London: Sage.
Bonß, W. (1995). *Vom risiko: Unsicherheit und ungewißheit in der moderne.* Hamburg: Bund.
Brunsson, N. (1989). *The organization of hypocrisy: Talk, decisions and actions in organizations.* Chichester: John Wiley & Sons.
Clarke, L. (1999). *Mission improbable: Using fantasy documents to tame disaster.* Chicago: Chicago University Press.
Dewey, J. (1954). *The public and its problems.* Athens, Ohio: Swallow Press/Ohio University Press. (Original work published 1927)
Donaldson, T., & Preston, L. E. (1995). The stakeholder theory of the corporation: Concepts, evidence, and implications. *Academy of Management Review, 20*(1), 65–91.
Douglas, M. (1992). *Risk and blame: Essays in cultural theory.* London: Routledge.
Ericson, R. V., Doyle, A., & Barry, D. (2003). *Insurance as governance.* Toronto: University of Toronto Press.

Evers, A., & Nowotny, H. (1987). *Über den umgang mit unsicherheit.* Frankfurt am Main: Suhrkamp.
Ewald, F. (1986). *L'Etat-providence.* Paris: Édition Grasser & Fasquell.
Freeman, R. E. (1984). *Strategic management: A stakeholder approach.* Marshfield, MA: Pitman.
Friedman, M. (1991). Consumer boycotts: A conceptual framework and research agenda. *Journal of Social Issues, 47,* 149–168.
Funtowicz, S. O., & Ravetz, J. R. (1990). *Uncertainty and quality in science for policy.* Dordrecht: Kluwer.
Global Exchange. (2003). *Nike campaign.* Retrieved December 28, 2006, from http://www.globalexchange.org/campaigns/sweatshops/nike/faq.html
Grolin, J. (1998). Corporate legitimacy in risk society: The case of Brent Spar. *Business Strategy and the Environment, 7*(4), 213–222.
Holzer, B. (2001). *Transnational subpolitics and corporate discourse: A study of environmental protest and the Royal Dutch/Shell Corporation.* Unpublished doctoral dissertation, London School of Economics, University of London.
Holzer, B. (2006). Corporate power and transnational civil society. In I. Richter, S. Berking, & R. Müller-Schmid (Eds.), *Building a transnational civil society: Global issues and global actors.* Basingstoke, UK: Palgrave Macmillan.
Holzer, B., & Sørensen, M. P. (2003). Rethinking subpolitics: Beyond the iron cage of modern politics? *Theory, Culture & Society, 20*(2), 79–102.
Knight, F. H. (1921). *Risk, uncertainty and profit.* Boston: Houghton Mifflin.
Krimsky, S., & Golding, D. (Eds.). (1992). *Social theories of risk.* Westport, CT/London: Praeger.
Krohn, W., & Weyer, J. (1989). Die gesellschaft als labor: Die erzeugung sozialer risiken durch experimentelle forschung. *Soziale Welt, 40*(3), 349–373.
Lau, C. (1989). Risikodiskurse: Gesellschaftliche auseinandersetzungen um die definition von risiken. *Soziale Welt, 40,* 418–436.
Lau, C. (1999). Neue risiken und gesellschaftliche konflikte. In U. Beck, M. Hajer, & S. Kesselring (Eds.), *Der unscharfe Ort der Politik* (pp. 248–266). Opladen: Leske + Budrich.
Luhmann, N. (1986). Die welt als wille ohne vorstellung: Sicherheit und risiko aus sicht der sozialwissenschaften. *Die Politische Meinung, 31*(Nov./Dez.), 18–21.
Luhmann, N. (1990). Technology, environment and social risk: A systems perspective. *Industrial Crisis Quarterly, 4,* 223–231.
Luhmann, N. (1991). *Soziologie des risikos* [Risk: A sociological theory]. Berlin/New York: Walter de Gruyter.
Luhmann, N. (2000). *Organisation und entscheidung.* Opladen: Westdeutscher Verlag.
March, J. G., & Simon, H. A. (1958). *Organizations.* New York/Chichester, UK: John Wiley & Sons.
Micheletti, M. (2003). *Political virtue and shopping: Individuals, consumerism, and collective action.* New York: Palgrave Macmillan.
Micheletti, M., Føllesdal, A., & Stolle, D. (Eds.). (2003). *Politics, products, and markets: Exploring political consumerism past and present.* New Brunswick, NJ: Transaction.
Micheletti, M., & Stolle, D. (2005). A case of discursive political consumerism: The Nike E-mail Exchange. In *Political consumerism: Its motivations, power, and conditions in the Nordic countries and elsewhere (TemaNord 2005:517),*

proceedings from the 2nd International Seminar on Political Consumerism, Oslo, August 26–29, 2004 (pp. 255–290). Retrieved December 28, 2006, from http://www.norden.org/pub/velfaerd/konsument/sk/TN2005517.asp

Mintzberg, H. (1983). *Power in and around organizations.* Englewood Cliffs, NJ: Prentice Hall.

Paine, L. S. (1999). *Royal Dutch/Shell in transition (B).* Boston: Harvard Business School.

Paine, L. S., & Moldoveanu, M. (1999). *Royal Dutch/Shell in transition (A).* Boston: Harvard Business School.

Perrow, C. (1984). *Normal accidents: Living with high-risk technologies.* New York: Basic Books.

Rayner, S. (1992). Cultural theory and risk analysis. In S. Krimsky & D. Golding (Eds.), *Social theories of risk* (pp. 83–115). Westport, CT/London: Praeger.

Schwarz, M., & Thompson, M. (1990). *Divided we stand: Redefining politics, technology and social choice.* New York: Harvester Wheatsheaf.

Sethi, S. P., & Post, J. E. (1979). Public consequences of private action: The marketing of infant formula in less developed countries. *California Management Review, 21*(4), 35–48.

Short, J. F., Jr., & Clarke, L. (Eds.). (1992). *Organizations, uncertainties, and risk.* Boulder, CO: Westview Press.

Sikkink, K. (1986). Codes of conduct for transnational corporations: The case of the WHO/UNICED code. *International Organization, 40*(4), 815–840.

Thompson, M., Ellis, R., & Wildavsky, A. (1990). *Cultural theory.* Boulder, CO: Westview Press.

Tsoukas, H. (1999). David and Goliath in the risk society: Making sense of the conflict between Shell and Greenpeace in the North Sea. *Organization, 6*(3), 499–528.

Ulrich, P. (1977). *Die großunternehmung als quasi-öffentliche institution: Eine politische theorie der unternehmung.* Stuttgart: Poeschel.

Vogel, D. (1978). *Lobbying the corporation: Citizen challenges to business authority.* New York: Basic Books.

Watts, P. (1998). The international petroleum industry: Economic actor or social activist? In J. V. Mitchell (Ed.), *Companies in a world of conflict: NGOs, sanctions and corporate responsibility* (pp. 23–31). London: Royal Institute of International Affairs/Earthscan.

Wätzold, F. (1996). When environmentalists have power: The case of the Brent Spar. In H. Madsen & J. P. Ulhoi (Eds.), *Industry and the environment: Practical applications of environmental management approaches in business* (pp. 327–338). Gylling: Naryana Press.

Weiss, J. W. (1998). *Business ethics: A stakeholder and issues management approach.* Fort Worth, TX: Dryden Press.

Wildavsky, A. (1979). No risk is the highest risk of all. *American Scientist, 67,* 32–37.

Willetts, P. (1998). Political globalization and the impact of NGOs upon transnational companies. In J. V. Mitchell (Ed.), *Companies in a world of conflict: NGOs, sanctions and corporate responsibility* (pp. 195–226). London: Royal Institute of International Affairs/Earthscan.

Crisis Management and Legitimacy

2

Facing Symbolic Disorders

Romain Laufer

> *Certainty is not a mood, it is an institution.*
> —Mary Douglas (2001)

It is tempting for managers and entrepreneurs to consider crisis management as a matter best delegated to specialists. Indeed, it has become standard practice to hire the services of specialized professionals in the area of crisis management or crisis communication. These services have recently become an important and growing source of business for consulting firms and advertising agencies. Deference to the principle of division of labor and respect for the expertise of specialists are not the only reasons, however, why managers and entrepreneurs prefer to outsource crisis management. As a matter of fact, a deeper motivation lies at the heart of the need for managers to limit the time and space devoted to such issues. Crises are usually associated with the idea of an exceptional, negative occurrence of catastrophic dimensions. They are usually associated with the idea of events so abnormal that the mere thought of them has the power to distract from the positive, organized, optimistic, and recurring nature of the world that is supposed to characterize managerial activities. To evoke the possibility of a catastrophe—of its circumstances, of the way in which it may affect our ability to think, act, and forecast—undermines the trust and common sense required to plan and to do business.

This does not mean that firms ignore risk or even uncertainty. On the contrary: Economists tell us that profit is the counterpart of the risks—the "speculative risks"—taken by entrepreneurs. Much like a captain braving the vagaries of an ocean, the entrepreneur's talent lies in his ability to confront the uncertainty of markets. A firm's competitive advantage results from its capacity to innovate, which in turn depends on daring, imagination, and decisiveness.

Entrepreneurs are familiar with the idea of crisis. In Greek, "krisis" means "decision." It is a medical term that defines the specific moment when urgent action becomes both necessary and possible in order to combat an illness successfully. To the extent that a business executive constantly needs to call the shots at key moments, one could say that all management is crisis management. If a specialized field of management has emerged under the name of "crisis management," it is because of a need to distinguish between two types of decisions and two types of uncertainty: those commonly dealt with by managers and those that exceed the realm of their customary sphere of action. What distinguishes them is the positive nature of the first as opposed to the negative nature of the second. If the uncertainties faced by managers presuppose daring and imagination, they are compensated by the hope of reaching an objective. Managers do not ignore dangers, or as it is customary to say when discussing strategy, they know they have to confront threats. These threats, however, are only stumbling blocks to be avoided in order to achieve a set of objectives.

The uncertainties that characterize crisis management are of a different nature: They presuppose contemplating and exploring all of the fears that a man of common sense keeps at bay because they are too unlikely or too threatening to be anything else but the expression of a kind of pathological anxiety inhibiting decisive action. The distinction between the risks and the threats that are traditionally the responsibility of management and those delegated to a specialized profession is exemplified by the role played by the insurance industry. A business cannot be managed if too much time and attention has to be spent thinking about all of the possible accidents that could occur. The desire to isolate this kind of worry is such that, most of the time, it is only once a crisis occurs—in a sense, when it is too late—that "crisis management" appears in the life of firms.

This raises three questions. First, why has it become necessary for management to devote attention to concerns a priori so unsuited to its normal frame of mind? Second, is it possible to delegate these kinds of worries to a group of specialists—i.e., crisis-management specialists—both within the firm and outside of it? Finally, what are the methods and logic specific to crisis management?

We shall address these questions in four successive sections of the present chapter. In the first section, we shall argue that a new type of risk is emerging,

Crisis Management and Legitimacy

which we shall call "major risk." In the second section, we shall argue that the emergence of this new type of risk corresponds to a major historical transformation of the context of business life such that the responsibility of the management of major risk cannot be limited to specialists. This will be shown by defining the social acceptability of risk in terms of systems of legitimacy, the history of the system of legitimacy, and the crisis of the system of legitimacy in and of itself. This will allow us, in the third section, to define the principles guiding the management of "major risks"—of which crisis-management is but one specific dimension—as corresponding to a deep transformation within management itself. In conclusion, it will be argued that today, "to manage is to legitimize."

Given the relative complexity of the theoretical argument developed in the second section of the present chapter, it is preferable to limit our developments to what is required to understand the logic underlying the methods of the management of major risk. However, the complete presentation of the argument will be found in a fourth section of the present chapter. It provides a theoretical justification of the propositions stated in the second section. It is required to gain a better understanding of a world universally considered to be ever more complex and uncertain (Beardon et al., 1993; Laufer, 1993; Laufer & Burlaud, 1980; Laufer & Paradeise, 1990).

Uncertainty Is No Longer What It Used to Be: The Notion of "Major Risk"

A COMMONPLACE

It is commonplace to state that the world is changing ever more rapidly, that it has become increasingly complex and uncertain. This fact is associated with the impression that threats and catastrophes are growing in size, diversity, and importance. It is important to describe some of the factors that have contributed to this impression.

Natural disasters are nothing new. What is new is the extent to which their consequences imply human responsibility. Earthquakes have always existed, but the extension and density of human population has multiplied the number of victims. Moreover, the development of information and telecommunications heightens our awareness of events whose consequences, via the global economy, have an ever-widening impact on people all over the world. The development of the insurance industry has transformed natural disasters into potential financial catastrophes. In addition, our sense of responsibility in relation to these catastrophes has increased with the advances in science and technology: Floods or storms can, to an extent, be forecasted; buildings can be designed to resist earthquakes; tsunamis can be detected and advanced warnings sent out. The example of the 2004 tsunami illustrates all of these points, not to mention the implication of the international community as a whole, which considered itself morally responsible for the consequences of this natural disaster.

An analysis of the impact of natural disasters reveals the extent to which man and nature interact. The greenhouse effect, the ozone layer, deforestation: These are the new long-term ecological threats to the future of humanity and the short-term sources of new and powerful meteorological disturbances.

Then there are industrial catastrophes, which are also nothing new. Mining accidents at the beginning of the 20th century (and still witnessed today in China) killed thousands of workers. However, for reasons that we shall explain, these catastrophes did not lead to either the development of the notion of "major risk" or the emergence of crisis management as a new field of management. This is in part because new products, new processes, and new technologies are often associated with new dangers. Two examples come to mind: dioxin after the catastrophe near the Italian city of Seveso (July 10, 1976) and methyl isocyanate (MIC) gas at the origin of the Bhopal tragedy (December 3, 1984). Much the same can be said regarding the development of new technologies (e.g., nuclear energy, genetic engineering, and information processing) also associated with specific fears. The development of nuclear energy brings to mind Chernobyl (April 26, 1986) and Three Mile Island (March 28, 1979). Genetic engineering is associated with the issue of biological diversity, rousing fears of unintended consequences related to the development of genetically modified organisms or provoking awe at the idea of producing monsters or clones. Information processing is associated on the one hand with worries about protecting privacy and on the other with fears of a major systemic breakdown (sneak-previewed by the Year 2000 "bug").

Product liability is another area where uncertainty and crises have arisen. Two examples illustrate the deep transformations seen in this field. When Ralph Nader published *Unsafe at Any Speed* (1965), denouncing the dangers of riding in a specific car model, the firm tried to deny the facts and refute Nader's credibility. Today, recalling cars singled out as defective for one reason or another has become standard procedure as well as occasion to apply the methods of crisis management.

The changing nature of the risks linked to product liability can also be seen in the rise of legal complaints. The multiplication of class actions in which financial stakes can be extremely high are legion, as in the case of tobacco companies and companies associated with the use of asbestos, and more recently, in cases surrounding the issue of junk food and obesity. Actually, in the United States, the system is such that, according to critics,[1] it fosters a kind of blackmail. Firms prefer to make out-of-court settlements rather than run the risk of incurring massive fines and unwelcome media attention.

Associated with the development of legal risks are the risks linked with recent accounting and financial scandals, such as those leading to the demise of firms as important as Enron in the domain of energy trading and Arthur Andersen in the area of auditing.

Last but not least, alas, a new type of risk has arisen recently: that linked to the development of terrorism. This risk is compounded with the development of science and technology, sources of ever more frightening means of destruction. A few years ago, the fear of the presence of traces of anthrax in the mail completely disrupted work at a branch of the U.S. Post Office as well as at the headquarters of a major publishing company in New York. There is no safeguard against the risks and uncertainties threatening our world today.

PARADOXES

The most obvious characteristic of all of the types of risks we have just considered is their diversity. This leaves us with the question of whether they share something else in common that could help us understand the new uncertainties faced by management. As we shall see, risk and uncertainty are also associated with the presence of logical and practical paradoxes.

1. Complex organizations and complex systems

Today's level of uncertainty is often associated with the world's increasing complexity. Expressions used to describe this situation—such as the development of "complex organizations" or of "complex systems"—are somewhat paradoxical.

Let us first consider the expression "complex organization." In the dictionary, the word "complex" is defined as "consisting of many different and connected parts." An "organization" is made of parts defined as a "systematic arrangement of elements."[2] The term "complex organizations" implies that "an arrangement of elements" can be made of "many connected parts." As all organizations are complex, the term "complex organization" is redundant. Similarly, the expression "complex system" is composed of "complex," which is defined as "consisting of many parts," and "system," which is defined as "a set of things working together as a mechanism." Here again the expression is redundant: A system (i.e., "a set of things") is qualified as being complex (i.e., as "consisting of parts"). To avoid this redundancy, it is necessary to distinguish between two types of complexity: one corresponding to the ordinary complexity of an organization or a system, and another defining a new, higher degree of complexity.

Systems theory distinguishes between closed systems and open systems. In the first case, the "parts" or elements of systems—their borders and hierarchical relations—are perfectly defined. In the second case, this definition can only lead to a satisfactory definition (or "satisficing" to quote Herbert

Simon). It depends on a model whose borders and hierarchies are not unequivocally specified.

For a modern manager, this second model is not an abstract notion. It corresponds to systems made of parts whose number, borders, and hierarchies remain uncertain—as exemplified by the meltdown of Enron. The actual financial situation of the group remained unclear as long as it was possible to disguise the number, nature, status, and control mechanisms of "special entities" where losses were located. This led to the explosion of what was known then as one of the "big five" auditing companies, Arthur Andersen.

2. The emergence of physical paradoxes

A paradox is "a seemingly absurd or self-contradictory statement or proposition that may in fact be true." In principle, a paradox has to do with language and logic and finds its resolution when confronted with reality. One of the most troublesome characteristics of the paradoxes confronting managers today is that, instead of being solved when considered in light of reality, their contradictions only get worse. For example, ecologists are adamant about the dangers linked to the development of nuclear energy. However, reducing the production of nuclear energy implies producing more fossil fuel, which in turn has been shown to be at the origin of the greenhouse effect, another danger for the future of the planet and denounced by ecologists.

The choice here is not unlike that between Scylla and Charybdis. Of course, one can develop renewable energy and diminish energy consumption. But this in turn raises arguments about the time and money required to develop efficient sources of renewable energy and the economic difficulties associated with the reduction of energy consumption. There are no easy answers to the growing energy needs of modern developing economies.

3. Examples taken from the literature on technological risks and crisis management

The intimate link between paradoxes and the nature of the risk is readily expressed in the literature on crisis management, which in itself resorts to paradoxical expressions in order to describe the object of its study.

A noteworthy example of this is *Normal Accident*, the title of a famous and seminal sociological analysis of technological risks by Charles Perrow (1999). It is important to note in passing that he does not use the kind of statistical logic instrumental to the development of insurance policies against events that are, by definition, numerous, limited in scope, and bound to certain laws of probability. He refers to a type of risk involving large systems, whose breakdown has very broad, unbearable consequences and whose probability is, as a result, required to be as small as possible. Perrow's argument is that such large systems always break down sooner or later. The more a system is "tightly coupled" (i.e., strictly defined in all its interactions), the higher the risk that the breakdown will degenerate into a catastrophe. The more the system is "loosely coupled" (i.e., leaves room for adjustment at the level of each subsystem), the more it can escape the negative spiral of consequences generated by a dysfunction. Paradoxically, if the strict control of processes associated with the security requirements of large and dangerous systems helps prevent breakdowns, it has the opposite effect when it comes to limiting the *consequences* of a breakdown.

Along the same lines, the title of one of Karl Weick's latest books, *Managing the Unexpected* (2001), is also paradoxical, especially when considered in the wake of Fayol's principles of administration, which imply the ability to plan and forecast events. Weick argues that the ability to face uncertainty is linked to the development of managerial processes favoring the coexistence of a wide variety of potential responses. Ideally, management can cope with uncertainty when the associated level of complexity (as measured by a variety of potential responses) matches the familiar complexity of the world. Referring to Perrow, Weick links loose coupling to the variety of potential answers given by a system to unexpected stimuli. However, Weick rejects Perrow's fatalism, and states that accidents can be avoided. To sustain this point, Weick relies on another paradox: Organizations confronted with hazardous situations (such as fire stations, airplane security systems, and nuclear plants) are precisely the ones that have the best safety records. He proposes to use these organizations (which he calls high reliability organizations, or HROs) as models for crisis management. The paradoxical nature of this proposition becomes more clear if we consider that these management systems—to whatever extent they may lower the number of accidents—do not guarantee that accidents will not occur. A single occurrence of an accident on this scale would, in and of itself, lead to a catastrophe.

Karl Weick stops short of dealing with unexpected events that are paradoxical in and of themselves. Consider the example of an organization that has to react to a message worded in the following way: "O2 967 complains he is being dealt with like a number." It will be argued that this type of event, which is made possible (and perhaps unavoidable) by the development of information technologies, belongs to the type of puzzling situation increasingly faced by organizations. But this shall be become clearer once we have formally defined the notion of "major risk."

4. Paradoxes in the area of responsibility

Before turning to the new types of risk confronting firms, some attention must be devoted to the notion of responsibility. How does one determine who is supposed to be involved in the process of crisis prevention and crisis management and to what extent?

Traditionally, firms distinguish between the risk they must confront and the risk they choose to delegate. The first, the risk of the entrepreneur or "speculative risk," will be henceforth referred to as "R1." The second, corresponding to risks they can delegate (either against a premium to insurance companies—i.e., what is known in economic theory as "pure risk"—or against taxes to the state in the case of natural disasters) will henceforth be referred to as R2.

The feeling that we are confronted with new forms of risk and uncertainty expresses itself in the growth of R1 and R2. This gives rise to a debate between those who are supposed to be in charge of R1 (the firms, here labeled "A") and those who are supposed to be in charge of R2 (such as the state, ecological associations, etc., here labeled "B"). This debate can be represented by the following schematic dialogue:

A: How am I to take into account R2 when dealing with R1 in the face of stiff international competition? If the cost of R2 becomes too big, I'm out of business. The expenses linked to R2 must remain at a reasonable level so that, combined with the cost of prevention and insurance and eventually with the state's guarantee, my costs are maintained at a level that allows me to remain competitive. Otherwise I am condemned to disappear.

B: Being responsible for R2, it is my duty to ensure that it remains manageable. In any event, if an R2 catastrophe occurs, the activity of your firm grinds to a halt, irrespective of other considerations. The good management of R1 depends on the good management of R2.

It nevertheless remains that:

1. If R1 causes a large firm (or a group of firms) to go bankrupt, the social and economic environment will be so disturbed as to affect the activities of public authorities and social movements.

2. If some catastrophic event of the R2 type occurs and affects the physical environment of economic activities, these activities will in turn be disrupted.

This paradoxical situation may lead organizations engaged in potentially dangerous activities to use what Freud called "the argument of the cauldron." It runs as follows: "First, there is no real danger. Anyway, I have taken all the necessary precautions. Moreover, others aren't doing anything more than I am. And if I do anything more, I'll go bankrupt"[3] (Freud, 1916). It is a type of reasoning in which each separate argument is perfectly legitimate, but any combination of arguments is contradictory.

A FORMAL DEFINITION OF "MAJOR RISK"

The question remains whether all of the examples and considerations discussed above actually correspond to a new form of risk, and if so, whether it is possible to propose a single definition for events that seem so numerous and heterogeneous and whether this definition allows us to account for the paradoxes that, as we have just seen, seem to characterize these new risks.

We will argue that it is possible to answer this question in the affirmative. We will give a precise definition to the emerging notion of "major risk" and describe the new types of risks social and economic actors have to face today.

1. The subjective nature of risk

To define "major risk," one must first define "ordinary risk." By definition, risk is *an anticipation*. Its definition supposes the existence of *a frame of reference* that allows us to define the following:

(a) possible *future events Ei* ($1 < i < n$),

(b) the *probability of occurrences pi* (equal to the total number of cases where the occurrences of Ei is anticipated divided by the total number of future cases anticipated),

(c) *the positive or negative value of the consequences* of each event Ei, Vi.

On this basis, one can define the various moments that characterize the risk considered, and especially the two first moments, called expectation and variance.[4]

This definition allows us to see to what extent the notion of risk can be said to be subjective:

(a) It is an anticipation;

(b) This anticipation depends on the definition of a frame of reference;

(c) The evaluation of the *pi* and of the *Vi* are in and of themselves subjective.

2. Defining "major risks"

There are three ways of defining "major risks" as opposed to ordinary risks. It will be shown that the third includes the first two, which is why we shall choose it as our definition.

Size: It is often said that what distinguishes "major risks" from ordinary risks is their size. For instance, the cost of a platform used to drill petrol in the North Sea is about one billion dollars, which in the case of an accident represents a huge loss for insurance companies. But this does not answer the question of defining precisely the limit between a "big" risk and a risk that is so big that it deserves to be put in a special category with a special name (i.e., that of "major risk"). As long as we have not defined this threshold, we cannot say that we have a precise definition of "major risk."

Causal chain: "Major risk" is often associated with chaos theory, exemplified by the so-called butterfly effect, which states that the development of major (even catastrophic) meteorological phenomena, such as storms or tornadoes, can be deeply modified by the effect of a very minor event. There is something paradoxical in this definition of "major risk," as it can only be defined ex post, when the catastrophic consequences of the initial minimum cause have already occurred. Any action, however small, such as a rumor or a whisper, could be considered as potentially dangerous; such strange forms of anticipation are the stories of nightmares or stereotypical disaster movies.

Frame of anticipation: The third definition is built in opposition to the notion of ordinary risk as defined above. One of the prerequisites of this definition is the existence of a frame of reference enabling events to be anticipated. The probability and the value of events anticipated depend on the ability to maintain this frame of reference during the evaluated duration of the risk.

"Major risk," then, can be defined as the anticipation of the breakdown of one's own frame of anticipation. This definition of risk defies common sense.[5] However, it is possible to find examples that show how this surprising definition applies to everyday life. Since the emergence of "mad cow disease," or bovine spongioform encephalopathy (BSE), it has become possible to consider eating a steak as a form of hazardous behavior. For French citizens, for whom eating a *"steak frites"* used to represent the most comforting behavior one could imagine, this corresponds without a doubt to a breakdown of one's frame of anticipation. Similarly, rumors about the dangers linked to the use of mobile phones (suspected of being at the origin of brain cancer) may serve as another example of the way in which both our senses and our common sense may, at times, be of little guidance in matters of daily life.

In spite of these examples and others,[6] it comes as no surprise that this definition of "major risk" elicits criticism. Some will see in it the expression of a negative, sick, and overimaginative mind, lacking in measure and common sense. Others will reject the attempt to reduce the complexities and specificities of concrete experience to a single, simple formula. Still others will object that, while it may serve as an adequate formal description of the state of mind of people involved in a crisis, the definition falls short of answering the key issue of why uncertainty is no longer what it used to be.

Let us consider each of these objections one by one.

To those who consider this definition as lacking in measure and common sense, one could answer as follows:

1. Let us not forget that this definition corresponds to the difference between the uncertainties managers are used to facing (positive and hopeful) and those which characterize crisis management (negative and fearful).

2. It also corresponds to the difficulties encountered by risk managers in firms when they try to address the issue of "major risk." When interviewed, they often describe their role as being similar

to that of Cassandra, the soothsayer Agamemnon brought as a slave from Troy to his kingdom, a woman given the gift of foresight by the god Apollo, yet condemned by him never to be believed.[7] Their position is akin to that of "whistle blowers," albeit "official whistle blowers."

3. Finally, "a sick mind" hearkens back to the original definition of the word "krisis," the origins of which lie in the medical vocabulary of ancient Greece.

To those who tend to reject the abstract and general character of this definition on the basis that it does not give due respect to the complexities of concrete experience, one could quote Patrick Lagadec, a researcher devoted to the empirical study of crises: "In each and every case, one sees powerlessness in the face of complexity, delay in the face of urgency, a gap between available solutions and the problems at hand, the incomprehension of ordinary citizens and the helplessness of specialists. Each situation is unique, and one person's experience is of no help to others" (Lagadec, 1988, pp. 397–398).

This leaves us with the question of determining how to show that risk—now defined as a subjective evaluation of a given state of the world—has changed to the point of requiring a new name, "major risk," and new managerial approaches, such as crisis management.

Actually, many would question such an endeavor on the basis that risk and uncertainty have always existed, that they have always characterized human life and that history is full of such experiences, be it the great fire of London, Lisbon's earthquake, or the Great Depression of 1929, not to mention wars and the "slings and arrows of outrageous fortune," which have never been in short supply. It is very difficult to argue that the world is more dangerous and risky than it used to be. Actually, some will maintain that, on the contrary, the development of health care in the Western world has led to a spectacular increase in life expectancy; that, especially in the Western world, the development of nuclear energy, for example, has reduced casualties associated with the mining industry and its hazardous firedamp explosions. Some will even argue that the world is becoming less dangerous precisely because we are becoming more aware of the dangers that threaten it. This last argument is in line with Karl Weick's proposed models of organization, HROs.

To answer the objection concerning the evolving nature of risk throughout history, we shall argue, in the lineage of British anthropologist Mary Douglas, that one should not ask whether the world is more or less risky than it used to be, but rather why it is perceived as being so. This can only be achieved by addressing our attention to the institutions that determine the social acceptability of risk (Douglas, 1986). At this level, risk and uncertainty are no longer defined as an individual and subjective experience but as a social phenomenon that equally affects all members of a given society:

> Certainty is not a mood, or a feeling, it is an institution: this is my thesis. Certainty is only possible because doubt is blocked institutionally: most individual decisions about risk are taken under pressure of institutions. If we recognize more uncertainty now, it will be because of things that have happened to the institutional underpinning of our beliefs. And that is what we ought to be studying. (Douglas, 2001, p. 146)

Only once the "institutional underpinning of our beliefs" has been defined will it be possible to understand the changes contributing to the emergence of "major risk." Only then will it be possible, in the third section of the present chapter, to address the principles guiding the management of "major risks" (of which crisis management is only one dimension).

What Has Changed in "The Social Underpinning of Our Beliefs"

To define what has changed in "the social underpinning of our beliefs" it is necessary to show that it is possible to define this notion formally and to account for its history. However, given the complexity of the arguments implied in such a definition, we shall deal with it in two parts. In the present section we shall restrict ourselves to the statements required to understand the principles of the management of major risk, which will be described in the third section. A more detailed theoretical presentation of the argument will be left for the last sections. As we know, the last is not necessarily the least. In fact, in this section it will be shown that the ultimate paradox in the long list of paradoxes that characterize major risks and crisis management could well be that they correspond to situations that are so radically pragmatic that they can only be characterized theoretically. This is what Mary Douglas's article "Dealing With Uncertainty" allows us to understand. Let us follow her arguments through the following five quotations.

> *We need certainty as a basis for settling disputes. It is not for intellectual satisfaction, nor for accuracy of prediction for its own sake, but for political and forensic reasons.*

The question of certainty is to be defined and discussed in the context of conflict resolution.

Let us consider someone (anyone) who acts in our society. Either it goes well (there is no conflict, nobody objects to the act) or it does not (there is a conflict, somebody objects). If it goes well there is no more to say. If someone objects, the actor will address an objection in the form of a question such as "Why have you done that?" The answer to this question, which is intended to override the objection and consequently state why the action was acceptable, is what we propose to call *the system of legitimacy* of the actor.

We may note that this scenario is compulsory in our society: Given that people are not allowed to use violence to settle their conflicts, they have to resort to words. This necessity is in accordance with the fact that the state, according to Max Weber, is defined as having a monopoly on the exercise of legitimate violence.

To evaluate the legitimacy of a given answer we can consider it (in its turn) as an act: Either it goes well (the answer is accepted) or it does not (the answer is rejected). If it goes well there is nothing more to say other than the fact that it proved effective as a legitimate answer. If it does not, if the answer is rejected, the actor tries another one, and in this manner enters a process of negotiation. If after a certain number of trials the actor does not find a satisfactory answer, the conflict will be brought in front of a judge, as, once again, direct use of violence is prohibited. The role of the judge is to look at a special text (the law) to state which sentence (the question or the answer) conforms to the legal rule and is consequently legitimate.

Lawyers have invented a principle according to which nobody can be excused on the ground that he ignores the law. This makes two things clear: One, that the system just described is compulsory, and two, that to produce a legitimate answer, one must anticipate the statement of the judge.

It can easily be seen that in accordance with the above quotation from Mary Douglas, certainty is provided "for political and forensic reasons": The state has a monopoly on legitimate violence, and consequently, conflicts must be solved having in mind what would happen in court.

The problem is not knowledge but agreement.

What this sentence implies is that we live in a society in which knowledge plays a central role when we deal with the issue of certainty. This can be related to the fact that modern societies are dominated by what Max Weber has called the legal-rational type of legitimate authority: an authority that relies on the laws produced by reason, be they those of society (the legal system) or those of nature (scientific knowledge).

What Mary Douglas tells us concerning the status of knowledge in a situation of conflict resolution is that it must be considered not so much from the point of view of its truth value (its actual correspondence with the state of the world) as from the point of view of its performative

(Austin, 1962) value (its ability to produce a consensus relative to the state of the world).

By definition, this performative value is dependent upon the submission of the institutions of the society being considered to the legal-rational system of legitimacy. This implies that the domain of validity of the analysis proposed be restricted to modern Western democracies.

A liberal democracy (. . .) needs authority to back interpretation and control dissent.

Since, in a liberal democracy, everyone is entitled to express freely his or her own opinion, conflicts may arise that cannot be solved by direct negotiation. Central to our argument is the fact that the production of a consensus on a common representation of the state of the world is so important for conflict resolution that it is made compulsory by law. In the last section of the present chapter we shall see how knowledge, under the definitions of epistemological paradigms and "official" scientific propositions, is intimately linked to the legal system that institutes its legal authority. This allows us to distinguish action as it is defined at a local level (i.e., by the actor himself or by consensus between an actor and his objector if the conflict considered is solved without direct reference to the legal norm) and action defined at a social or global level (i.e., according to the way it would be defined in front of a judge). We may note that conventional agreements, agreements defined at a local level, are always possible and legitimate in a democratic society as long as they do not consciously contravene the legal rule. In cases in which they contravene the legal rule *unconsciously* (by error or lack of knowledge), their illegitimacy would only become manifest at an ulterior point if a new conflict arises.

As a consequence, it is possible to define a *social system of legitimacy* as the system of social norms that allow social actors to define with certainty the legitimacy of their actions.

Commitment to open enquiry is part of the constitution. This will be part of the reason why certainty raises itself as a problem.

This premise allows us to understand the dynamic of social systems of legitimacy: When an established system is open to questions, a time may come when the answers provided by the social system of legitimacy are no longer convincing. Agreements required for the settling of disputes may require a change in the system of legitimacy. This manifests itself quite obviously each time a central principle of the legal system of a given society undergoes a deep change. The history of such norms being the history of compulsory principles is, in and of itself, a compulsory history. It will be shown in the last section of the present chapter that this history can be described as following three stages: from 1800 to 1880/1900, from 1880/1900 to 1945/1960, and finally from 1945/1960 to the present.

... we have definitely entered a period where uncertainty is formally recognized. This very esoteric aspect of our culture might have some theoretical interest for risk analysis. For the present argument what is important is that it would inevitably have arrived in some form or other in an open democracy. The form it takes with us is mathematical, analytical, the result of pushing to extreme the forensic aspects of certainty, and trying to extend the certainty-seeking practice of science. (Douglas, 2001, p. 147)

That our times are characterized by a "formal recognition of uncertainty" is precisely linked to the emergence of the notion of "major risk."

It will be shown in the last section of the present chapter that it corresponds to the fact that since 1945/1960, society has been undergoing what we propose to call a *crisis of the social system of legitimacy.*

This text constitutes a precious springboard for developing a conceptual framework for crisis management as it tells us that one should not relinquish the effort implied in "pushing to the extreme the forensic aspect of certainty" if one is to get a clear understanding of the modern aspect of risk analysis. However, such an endeavor, which implies the exploration of "esoteric aspects of our culture" under the form of some "analytical" or "mathematical" approach, is somewhat complex. This is why we shall limit ourselves to what is required to describe the methods involved in the management of major risks. We shall limit ourselves to the statement of a few propositions. They represent a summary of a theoretical argument, the detailed development of which will be left for the last section of the present chapter.

Proposition 1: The history of the social system of legitimacy of Western democracies follows three periods.

Proposition 2: The first period (from 1800 to 1880/1900) corresponds to the "garrison state." The legitimacy of actions lies in the *origin of power;* that is, on the legal status of the actor. Central to the social system of legitimacy is the opposition between the realm of nature and the realm of culture, nature being strictly separated from culture. The "official" form of scientific knowledge that corresponds to this period is characterized by the fact that laws of nature are expressed by a single science: Newtonian physics in the realm of natural phenomena and the Smithian model of classical economic theory in the realm of cultural phenomena. In both domains science is deterministic; that is, the social system of legitimacy is characterized by the presence of certainty.

Proposition 3: The second period (from 1880/1900 to 1945/1960) corresponds to the "welfare state." The legitimacy of actions lies on the "*finality of power*"; that is, on the function of the actor as it is defined by scientific knowledge. The official form of scientific knowledge that corresponds to this period is *positivism.* It is characterized by the fact that the laws of nature are expressed through the existence of several mutually exclusive scientific disciplines: astronomy, physics, chemistry, biology, and social physics. Each of them is developed by a group of specialized scientists. The knowledge thus developed is characterized by two major traits: the notion of *closed systems* and the notion of *progress.* The notion of closed systems implies that the world can always be described as a set of mutually exclusive, well-defined components; thus, the complexity of the world represented—which corresponds to the fact that it is composed of several parts—is limited, as these parts are clearly specified by well-defined borders. Progress guarantees that in a world that is now considered as following a process of continuous transformation resulting from the development of human knowledge, the situations that result from these actions are always good. In each domain of specialized knowledge, scientific laws are deterministic; that is, once again the social system of legitimacy is characterized by the presence of certainty.

Proposition 4: The third period (since 1880/1900 to 1945/1960) is characterized by the crisis of the social system of legitimacy. The legitimacy of action now lies in *the methods of power.*

The situation is now characterized by two major traits: the notion of open systems and the nondeterministic nature of knowledge. The existence of open systems means that while the world can still be described as being made of different parts, these parts are no longer well defined as their borders can no longer be specified unequivocally. It is now impossible to separate nature from culture. The complete confusion of nature and culture is the artificial. The science that corresponds to it is the "science of the artificial"; that is, according to Herbert Simon, system analysis. System analysis can be defined as the fact of representing the world with "circles" and "arrows" (more often called "entities" and "flows"). The knowledge produced by system analysis is no longer deterministic. This corresponds to the fact that, as Mary Douglas tells us, *"we have definitely entered a period where uncertainty is formally recognized."* According to Herbert Simon, the criterion for assigning legitimacy to the models produced by system analysis is that it be considered satisfying by those to whom they are submitted. Henceforth, opinion becomes the ultimate criterion of the legitimacy of actions.

This allows us to readily describe some important of characteristics of major risk:

1. "Major risk" characterizes a situation in which complexity and uncertainty exist in their most radical form. Complexity reaches such a level that the world cannot be described and uncertainty cannot be predicted.

Crisis Management and Legitimacy 41

2. The management of "major risk" can thus be defined as the management of uncertainty. This is in agreement with the fact that the title of Karl Weick's book on crisis management is *Managing the Unexpected* (2001).

3. The paradoxes inherent in this definition of "major risk" are, as we have shown, a common characteristic of the new type of risks organizations must face. They express tensions resulting from the changes undergone by the "institutional underpinning of our beliefs."

Let us consider this last point in some detail, for we are now in a position to account for the fact that the new forms of uncertainty confronting managers are associated with the proliferation of paradoxes. We have seen that social action can be defined at two levels: a "local" level (that of the goal, knowledge, and power of a given actor) and a "global" or "social" level (that of the institutional system that guarantees the social legitimacy of a given action). Legitimization ensures *certainty* at the second level. When a system of legitimacy is well-defined, a given action—to the extent that it complies with the conditions imposed by institutions—is a priori socially legitimate. Compliance with these institutions opens the horizon for free, pragmatic endeavors at the "local level" and the types of risks that go with them. However, in a situation of crisis of social system of legitimacy, the legitimacy of a given actor is no longer guaranteed a priori by legal rules or scientific knowledge. Legitimacy is defined a posteriori; that is, either by the fact that no objections are brought against the action or, should there be objections, that the counterarguments provided are readily accepted. In such a situation, paradoxes may arise from the fact that statements relative to one level of action (the local level) contradict statements relative to the other level (the institutional level). At the first level, management requires producing a description of one's actions. This description must be acceptable to all who participate in the action or are affected by it. At the institutional level, however, the crisis of the system of legitimacy implies that actors be confronted with complexity in its most radical form: the indescribable. What seems necessary at one level appears impossible at another[8] (Weick & Sutcliffe, 2001). This paradox means that "things" (e.g., actions and descriptions of actions) may be both necessary and impossible. We are thus confronted with the need to know how it is possible to manage what is both necessary and impossible. Since the paradoxes confronting us result from conflicts between the demands of two types of symbolic representations (local representations and institutional representations), it is possible to state that the necessary and the impossible can only be managed symbolically. Before turning to a description of how to manage "major risk," one must answer three possible objections to our definition of major risk and of the management of major risks:

First objection: How is it possible to anticipate the breakdown of one's own frame of anticipation?

Reply: In line with the paradoxes we have just considered, one has to distinguish between "local" representations and "institutional" representations. Systems of legitimacy have been undergoing a crisis since 1945/1960. Logically, a social actor could be aware that his frame of reference is no longer guaranteed at the "institutional level," while continuing to act and to produce descriptions of his actions at a "local level."

But this answer leads to another objection.

Second objection: If "major risks" are rooted in a crisis of legitimacy that dates back to the years 1945/1960, why have the managements of "major risk" in general and crisis management in particular developed only recently?

Reply: To answer this question, we may turn to the relationship between society and "the idea of certain knowledge" as defined by Mary Douglas:

> The most fundamental idea which upholds the possibility of society, more fundamental even than the idea of God, is the idea that there can be certain knowledge. And this turns out to be extraordinarily robust, passionately defended by law and taboo in ancient and modern civilizations.[9]

The time lag between the beginning of the crisis of the system of legitimacy and the emergence of crisis management can be interpreted as the result of the efforts made by society to resist the idea of crisis of legitimacy.

Third objection: Why is "major risk" management of any use if, by definition, it cannot ward off a crisis?

Reply: The management of "major risk" is necessary to compensate for the legitimacy that managers can no longer derive from the established system, even if it is not sufficient to prevent, with certainty, the occurrence of a crisis. This is why crisis management can be defined as the ultimate manifestation of "major risk" management.

The Management of "Major Risk"

Having defined "major risk" and having analyzed the institutional changes that have given rise to the feeling that the world is more uncertain than it used to be, it is now time to consider the management of "major risk" in general and crisis management in particular.

The dimensions and methods of the management of major risk result from the following three characteristics: It is the management of *uncertainty*, it is the management of an uncertainty that can only be defined at an *institutional* level, and it can only be managed *symbolically*. Thus, we shall rely on the analysis of the consequences of these three characteristics of the management of "major risk" to describe the methods of the management of "major risk."

THE CHARACTERISTICS OF THE MANAGEMENT OF "MAJOR RISK"

We shall consider successively how the notions of uncertainty, of institutional level, and of symbolic methods can be related to the structure of the field of the management of "major risk."

1. Uncertainty

It is to Frank H. Knight, one of the founders of the Chicago School of Economics, that we owe the first rigorous definition of uncertainty. In his seminal book *Risk, Uncertainty and Profit,* he writes:

> Uncertainty must be taken in a sense radically distinct from the familiar notion of Risk, from which it has never been properly separated ... The essential fact is that "risk" means in some cases a quantity susceptible of measurement, while at other times it is something distinctly not of this character ... we shall accordingly restrict the term "uncertainty" to cases of the non-quantitative type. (Knight, 1922/1972, pp. 19–20)

This allows us to distinguish between three dimensions of the management of "major risk": the management of the probable, the management of the improbable, and the management of the impossible.

a. The management of the probable

If uncertainty is that which follows no laws, the management of uncertainty is the management of that which follows no laws. At least that would be the case had modern science not provided the laws of chance; that is, the laws of the absence of laws. These laws allow us to define a first dimension of the management of the uncertain: *the management of the probable.* This applies to all cases when it is possible (conventionally) to consider a series of events as being described by independent and limited random variables.

b. The management of the improbable

But this does not apply to most business decisions. As Knight tells us, there are instances that are

> so entirely unique that they are no others or not a sufficient number to make it possible to tabulate enough like it to form a basis for any inference

of value about any real probability in the case we are interested in.... Yet it is true, and the fact can hardly be over-emphasized, that a judgment of probability is actually made in such cases. The businessman himself not merely forms the best estimate he can of the outcome of his actions, but he is likely to estimate the probability that his estimate is correct. The "degree" of certainty or of confidence felt in the conclusion after it is reached cannot be ignored, for it is of a greater practical significance. (Knight, 1922/1972, pp. 226–227)

Evaluating risk in such a context of uncertainty is a two-step process. Step one consists of building a model of the situation to be managed. From the preceding section, we know that this can be done symbolically through system analysis; that is, by describing the world with "circles" and "arrows." It is then possible to produce judgments in the form of (subjective) probability statements. In step two, the decision maker produces "an estimate of the chances that his estimate of the chance of an event is a correct estimate" (Knight, 1922/1972, p. 227). This estimate can be defined as *the trust* the decision-maker has in the model he or she has constructed.[10]

Determining the value of such an evaluation in the face of uncertainty remains an open question. This is the way in which Knight addresses the issue:

The ultimate logic, or psychology, of these deliberations is obscure, a part of the unfathomable mystery of life and mind.... We are so built that what seems to us reasonable is likely to be confirmed by experience, or we would not live in the world at all. (Knight, 1922/1972, p. 227)

Mary Douglas, at the end of the text she devoted to the question of "dealing with uncertainty," allows us to interpret this requirement from an institutional point of view: "There have to be promises, guarantees and justifications, claims of secure knowledge, which work well." This need for "certain knowledge" is so important that it is "passionately defended by laws and taboos in ancient and modern civilizations."

This allows us to understand why, in spite of crises that go back to 1945/1960, crisis management was recognized only much later as a new field of management. As long as it is possible for managers to behave "as if" certain knowledge is available, they will continue to rely on the confidence they have in their own best estimate of the probabilities involved in the evaluation of the state of affairs they have to manage. This corresponds to what we propose to call the reign of "quasi-positivism." Managers behave with a nonpositivistic form of knowledge (system analysis) "as if" it were certain knowledge. We know that one of the major features of system analysis is the importance given to the notion of feedback. Any positive feedback reinforces the trust one has in the model used. Any negative feedback decreases that same trust. As long as negative feedback does not affect the trust a manager has in "the chances that his estimate of the chance of an event is a correct estimate," he may modify his model of action and thus remain within the realm of the associated "quasi-positivist" epistemology characterizing the management of the improbable.

This gives a new meaning to the emergence of crisis management: It is what happens when the confidence managers have in their own ability to construct good estimates of the situation they are facing breaks down; that is, when the management of the improbable appears impossible.

c. The management of the impossible

It is because the anticipation of the breakdown of one's own frame of anticipation appears impossible—Mary Douglas tells us that at a social level it goes against "laws and taboos," while Frank Knight tells us that at a logical or psychological level it goes against any reasonable idea of what it means "to live in the world at all"—that the idea of major risk tends to be discovered after the fact, after one has experienced directly or indirectly the actual occurrence of a crisis. Hence, "major risk" tends to be discovered after the fact, after one has directly or indirectly experienced the actual occurrence of a crisis. However, when a crisis occurs, things go so fast that it is too late to prepare an adequate response to the many questions and objections raised by such an occurrence. This is why firms gradually learn that it is worthwhile to devote attention to the question, "what should one do while waiting for the unexpected?" Such a paradoxical question can only lead to paradoxical answers; these constitute what we propose to call the management of the impossible.

2. Institutions

In order to develop "preventive" management, one must try to anticipate the questions and objections to which one may be submitted should a crisis occur. Given that anticipating the unexpected is impossible, one must rely on a kind of "retrospective anticipation"; that is, on the consequences drawn from past crises. Gradually, one becomes conscious of the uncertainty that affects our institutions. This is why one of the major sources of "retrospective anticipation" comes from a careful scrutiny of postcrisis analysis.

Given that these specific crises take place in the larger historical context of the crisis of the legal-rational system of legitimacy, they will have to focus on the three major dimensions that characterize this institutional system; that is, the legal foundations of actions, the scientific foundations of actions, and the communication processes justifying actions in the event legal and scientific arguments are not readily accepted. It is thus possible to define three levels of the management of the impossible:

a. The level of the rule of law

Firms are submitted to complex movement of regulations and deregulations, revealing how difficult it is to define on the one hand the limit between the public sector and the private sector (which corresponds to the crisis of the welfare state) and on the other hand, from the point of view of the private sector, what constitutes an efficient economic system. Sometimes a crisis occurs that leads to the emergence of new laws and regulations. These laws and regulations develop in areas where the economic model of the firm is threatened: Issues relative to good governance develop to ensure that all stakeholders are treated fairly; prohibition of insider-trading is instituted to ensure that competition on the stock market is not distorted. In each case, it is possible to underline the contradictions and paradoxes that characterize these regulations and tend to destabilize them. Good governance requires that members of boards be both competent (i.e., familiar with the business considered) and independent (i.e., have no personal interest in the business considered). Inside trading requires that financial experts whose task it is to know as much as they can about the firms they are dealing with refrain from crossing the line between the outside and the inside of the firm, in spite of the fact that defining such a line cannot be easily defined in a world described by system analysis, as system analysis implies that the world is described by "open systems."

b. The level of science

Firms are confronted with a lack of consensus among specialists as to the consequences of their actions. This is due to the fact that the guarantees that were associated with positivism do not hold anymore. As a consequence, major fears develop as to the consequences of the use of new technologies; for example, nuclear energy, genetic engineering, and electronic data processing. What characterizes these postwar technologies is that they do not conform to two of the major traits of positivism: the subordination of technique to science (they are called "techno-sciences") and the existence of closed system. Actually it could be said that they correspond to three "missions impossible": making nuclear energy safe, using computers without curbing freedom, and developing genetics without affecting natural reproductive processes (Laufer & Paradeise, 1990, pp. 262–265).

Another consequence of the lack of confidence in the models proposed by scientists and experts is the fact that all risks, however small, tend to be considered unacceptable. This is evidenced by the fears raised by the multiplication of trials involving issues of medical malpractice or the deleterious side effects of several pharmaceutical "blockbusters" (for instance, Merck's Vioxx[11]).

c. The level of communication processes

As we know, the outcome of a crisis ultimately depends on the ability of managers to give acceptable answers to all forthcoming objections. This is why so much depends on what happens at *the level of communication processes*. We know that the firm will have to confront public opinion, either because it is too large to be considered as having no autonomous effect on society or because the consequences of its actions are so complex that they cannot be circumscribed on any a priori basis. In such a situation, mass media play a central role insofar as they symbolize the freedom of opinion characteristic of democracies. Actually, a crisis may start as a result of a mere rumor and develop through media amplification. This danger is increased by the development of information technologies, in particular the Internet. Ultimately, the ability of the firm to restore its own legitimacy will depend—beyond the credibility of its arguments—on its own credibility as a source of arguments.

3. Symbolic methods

We have stated that major risks corresponding to symbolic disorders could only be dealt with symbolically, that is, by symbolic methods that allow us to reestablish a common normative system. These methods can be organized in three categories: laws and norms, independent third parties, and communication processes.[12]

a. Laws and norms

Antitrust laws are a good example of the way in which a law can serve as a symbolic "solution" to a crisis of legitimacy. Before these laws, firms were becoming so big that many were suspected of being *too* big; once the laws prohibiting firms from becoming too big were instated, all firms were assumed to be small enough; those deemed too big were exceptions to be brought to court. We shall call this symbolic "solution" a kind of law that "authorizes." Applied each time a symbolic dimension of the system of legitimacy appears to have been transgressed, it allows the reversal of the burden of proof. Information technologies, a threat to the fundamental principle of individual freedom, could not develop without the enactment of laws intended to limit the abusive use of personal data. Similarly, genetic engineering could not develop without the introduction of this type of legal regulation. This explains why a moratorium was decided by scientists themselves at Asilomar in 1975. To allow development to proceed, a law was required that stated that researchers in the field of genetics were bound to a system of laws and regulations. Paradoxically, a law intended to limit and prohibit an activity actually serves to authorize it. This is what had been noted by Thurman Arnold, a former antitrust judge (Arnold, 1937).

Similarly there is a strong demand for precise norms and officially defined standards in all areas that are likely to be considered dangerous: nuclear radiation, chemical waste, intensity of electromagnetic fields, and so on. Compliance with such norms and standards is a necessary, albeit not sufficient, justification for the action taken by a firm.

b. Third-party intervention

When the issue under consideration becomes too complex, however, it is no longer possible to define precise norms and standards. It is then necessary to resort to another mechanism: The action under consideration has to be submitted to the advice of an officially established third party. Such is the case with the multiplication of ethical committees, independent controlling agencies, and ad hoc committees.

Sometimes, a single, well-qualified person will be given the task of keeping watch over a defined danger. For instance, in the United States, it has been deemed necessary to name a "Drug Czar" who is supposed to be in charge of the control of a particularly complex nexus of illegal behaviors. Publicly naming someone for such an office expresses in and of itself the fact that the nature of the danger is recognized and that actions are being taken. The multiplication of ombudspersons in firms and administrations is an implicit recognition that the legitimacy within these organizations is an issue that must be negotiated.

c. Social communication and social negotiation

Legal and scientific norms can no longer be defined a priori. They result from a permanent process of social negotiations. Henceforth, any social and economic actor must participate, within the limits of his or her power, in the process of defining the norms to which actions will be submitted. Thus, lobbying has become an essential part of business activity. Moreover, success will depend not only on the network of relations established between a given interest group and legislators but also on the degree to which legislators think their decisions will be accepted by their constituency, as their legitimacy ultimately relies upon public opinion. This is why *lobbying* is increasingly associated with opinion campaigns in mass media.

The complexity and uncertainties linked to the social and economic use of science and technology have spawned "consensus conferences," a specific process of social communication and a proxy for generalized public debate. These are public hearings organized by an official institution (for instance, a national legislative body) that confronts a panel of, say, 10 to 15 people chosen from the general public (by a polling firm) with a panel constituted by a similar number of experts representing the scientific community. The debate between scientists and the public is organized over several days. First, scientists are supposed to communicate to the chosen members of the general public what one should know in order to be able to discuss the issue under consideration. Then, representatives of public opinion are allowed to address questions to the scientists' results. The following debate is then summarized in a report meant to express the opinions and recommendations of the general public. The report is then submitted to legislators or to the regulating institutions so that they be able to include these points of view in their deliberations. Such conferences have actually been organized in Denmark and in France.

Having given an overview of the major characteristics of the methods of the management of major risk, we may now turn to the description of the scope and methods of the management of major risk.

THE SCOPE AND METHODS OF THE MANAGEMENT OF MAJOR RISK

We have seen that any managerial action can be defined at two levels: the "local level," where it is defined conventionally between the economic and social actors involved, and the "global level," where it is defined institutionally by the social system of legitimacy that expresses what Mary Douglas calls the "institutional underpinning of our beliefs." If major risk is what results from the crisis of the social system of legitimacy, we can say that all management in such a period can be considered under the category of the management of major risk. This is not merely a theoretical proposition; at the practical level, it implies that all actions occurring in a context of institutional uncertainty must be considered as having the potential to generate a managerial crisis. This may be the reason why the notion of "zero fault," however unrealistic it is, has become a common slogan for industrial production, as if a single fault had the potential to destroy the "image" of the product considered. Moreover, in a situation of crisis, as the respect of limits and subordinations can no longer be guaranteed, it is impossible to consider that crisis management be delegated to a group of specialists; however disturbing it may appear, crisis management implies that everyone be prepared, to some extent, to act in a destabilized environment. This is best exemplified by the way in which it is considered normal for anyone working in an office building to participate regularly in drills required to react adequately in case of a fire alarm.

Consequently, what we have defined above as the management of the probable and the management of the improbable must be considered as dimensions of the management of major risk defined *lato sensu*: It corresponds to the way in which management faces uncertainty at a "local level." The specificity of the symbolic nature of this type of management is best defined by the way in which Karl Weick defines organizations as being *enacted* through the interactions of its members. By the choice of a word that belongs to the vocabulary of law (when one enacts a *bill*) on the one hand and one which belongs to the vocabulary of performance (when one assumes a *role*) on the other, it could be said that Karl Weick tends to consider organizations as a quasi-legal structures constructed conventionally by a process of rhetorical interactions[13] (Weick, 1969, 2001). As long at this approach succeeds, we may say that we remain within the limits of what we have proposed to call a quasi-positivist approach, given that it deals with the definition of action at the "local level" *as if* it could be isolated from the same action considered at the "global level" (or to the extent that it may be considered in such a manner at a pragmatic level). It is only when management is directly and explicitly confronted with uncertainty at the "global level" ("that of the social underpinning of our beliefs") that the management of major risk can be defined, *stricto sensu*, as the management of the impossible. Thus, it is to the methods of the management of the impossible that we shall now turn our attention.

The very task of describing the methods of the management of the impossible cannot help but fall itself under the category of the management of the impossible. In principle, the very notion of major risk implies that everything is connected to everything else in a somewhat confusing manner, so the pretension to establish some order in such a situation can only be accomplished symbolically; that is, by falling back on what we know of the structure of the institutional underpinning of our beliefs. This is why we shall consider successively each of the three institutional dimensions of the management of the impossible as they concern, respectively, the legal system, the scientific system, and the communication system, which together characterize "the ideological underpinning of our beliefs." In the two first instances, the presentations of the methods of the management of the impossible will be organized according to the three types of symbolic methods that we have identified above: laws and norms, third-party guarantee, and communication processes. As for the presentations of the methods concerning the communication processes themselves, they will have to be analyzed according to the way in which they are supposed to be organized hierarchically between the "local level" (the level of managerial action) and the "global level" (the "societal level," the level at which institutional laws and norms are supposed to be established). For each subcategory, we shall give definitions of the methods considered and give one or two concrete examples.

1. *Legal system*

The legal rational system of legitimacy assumes that the legitimacy of social actions be defined by their conformity to a legal system. The crisis of the legal-rational system of legitimacy implies that such a system of legal rules and norms cannot be defined unambiguously. This contradiction generates a very high level of activity among lawyers and lawmakers.

a. At the level of laws and norms

We have already considered how antitrust laws could be considered as authorizing what they are supposed to prohibit: abuses of dominant positions. Recent evolution in the application of these laws tends to confirm the complexities and the ambiguities that characterize these types of laws, as they are confronted with the task of trying to limit a power that is ever more difficult to define or control. This can be seen when considering the heated debates that have developed since the 1960s as to the very meaning of the Sherman Antitrust Act, which opposes those who think that U.S. Congress intended to protect free and fair competition or trade by acting on market structures and those who think that they were meant to promote the welfare of consumers by all appropriate means; that is, without attacking monopolies as long as they benefited the consumer (Grandy, 1993). This debate is at the center of the mutation of the way in which antitrust laws are applied in the United States. More complexity arises when one considers the fact that firms are now global. Legal control traditionally relied on the sovereign power of the state and the way in which it could be defined as having a monopoly on legitimate violence. Nowadays, competition and its consequences must be evaluated at the international level, where standards are often conflicting and where the power required to enforce the law is not readily warranted. The way in which Microsoft is submitted to the conflicting views of American and European courts is a good example of the fact that it is difficult for a firm to know in advance what behaviors will be considered legitimate.

Whatever is thought of the merit of the doctrine that links antitrust laws to the welfare of consumers, it must have fallen short of succeeding completely, as is shown in the development of class actions as a way of defending the consumer against the power of large corporations. The cost of legal procedures is such that they are not worth the trouble unless the amounts at stake are important enough. Consequently, consumers have no efficient way of defending themselves against abuses in most instances. This is why consumers have been granted the ability to act collectively, all consumers potentially being victims of the same abuse being represented by a group. Given the time required for due process of law to take place and given the huge amount of punitive damage that can be claimed, firms are often led to reach a settlement out of court even when they do not consider themselves responsible, lest the impending trial affect their public image and the value of their stock. Thus, firms are submitted in permanence to a threat that some compare to what amounts to the king of blackmail.[14] Consequently, class action can be considered as one of these symbolic solutions that prove both necessary (to the extent that the legitimacy of the power of large organizations is questioned) and impossible (inasmuch as it submits business firms to the attacks of lawyers who specialize in this type of litigation).

An analysis similar to the one regarding antitrust laws could apply to the question of the preservation of information privacy. The issue is to know how it is possible to reconcile the development of ever more powerful means of gathering, circulating, and accessing information with the principle of the autonomy of the will that lies at the foundations of modern Western democracies. Laws pertaining to information privacy have developed everywhere, and everywhere the efficiency of such measures has been questioned.

The Sarbanes-Oxley Act is another example of a law with a value best analyzed at the symbolic level. The necessity for such a law resulted from the crisis that followed the Enron bankruptcy at the end of 2001. Trust in the value of the data provided by auditing companies (such as Arthur Andersen, which disappeared in the process) and in the management of public firms was deeply affected, endangering the very workings of the stock market. However, since then, protests have arisen regarding the fact that the costs and constraints resulting from this new regulation were excessive and thus negative from the point of view of economic efficiency. It is to the point at which some firms may prefer to avoid registering in the New York Stock Exchange so as to escape requirements that are deemed excessive. A movement toward a modification of the Sarbanes-Oxley Act was mounting after less than 2 years, which might have succeeded if another large financial scandal, the REFCO bankruptcy (October 2005), had not recalled that this law was required to maintain trust among shareholders.

Another example of the necessity and the impossibility of such a control mechanism is given by the very fact that with Arthur Andersen's bankruptcy, the big five became the big four, which means that if another auditing firm were to be confronted with a similar situation, the nature of the competition between auditing firms would become an issue.

The emergence of the notion of transparency can be considered a symptom of the difficulties raised by issues of dissymmetry of information in times of uncertainty. Transparency as a demand addressed to any power expresses the fact that one is not satisfied with the way in which it presents itself publicly. It seems that this demand knows no limit, as no consensus can be reached as to what constitutes a good representation of the actor considered. Actually, social and economic actors, however official and public they are, are likely to be addressed with the same suspicion as if they were unofficial entities potentially involved in illegitimate activities. The universal success of the *Da Vinci Code* (Brown, 2003) seems to correspond to the fact that populations seem to be attracted by the ideas that the world is dominated by plots developed by secret organizations.

The way in which major risk can be a source of norms and regulations is exemplified by the way in which the regulations known as "Basel 2," in 2004, instituted the principle that firms had to establish a "continuity plan" that would identify the potential crisis that could disrupt its operations and specify the provisions required to be able to overcome them. The control of these plans was to be delegated to auditing firms.

b. Intervention of third party

The very complexity of the tasks involved in the control of the legality of business firms led to the development of independent agencies. These agencies consist of experts delegated the task of regulating aspects of market behavior. For instance, the Sarbanes-Oxley Act of 2002 instituted a "Public Company Accounting Oversight Board." One of the difficulties of such institutions is the way in which they succeed in reconciling two requirements that tend to be conflicting: expertise and independence. If the experts are the best experts in the field considered, it is likely that they are familiar with the people and organizations that compose it (Morrison, 1988).

Similarly, the laws on information privacy have led to the development of independent agencies such as the CNIL (*Commission Nationale Informatique et Liberté*) in France and the ICO *(The Information Commissioner's Office)* in Great Britain. It is left to anyone to evaluate the difficulty of their task, given the limits of their means and the fact that they must reconcile the conflicting demands of economic efficiency and individual freedom.

To solve these contradictory demands, the best way may be in some circumstance to rely on the charisma of some individual who seems able to embody the dual characteristic of being perfectly expert in his domain and completely independent of external influences. This is best exemplified by the role played by Alan Greenspan as head of the Federal Reserve Board and by the way in which the financial markets tend to overreact to the speeches of his successor, Ben Bernanke. Henceforth, it seems that the smooth workings of stock markets require that a talented guru be at the helm of the FED.

c. Communication processes

The very complexity and uncertainty that characterize laws and norms tend to lead to a movement of permanent change. This situation is very favorable to the development of processes of communication and persuasion intended to influence lawmakers (i.e., lobbying). Two traits characterize lobbying in a situation of crisis of legitimacy: One, it tends to develop its activities beyond the limits of the lobbies that have given its name to this activity, and two, it tends to become popular where it was rejected and rejected where it was popular. On the first point, in a time when public opinion tends to become the ultimate criterion of legitimacy, the activities of lobbyists will depend on their ability to argue that the proposed regulation is supported by public opinion, which is why they often have to rely on the efficiency of media campaigns. On the second point, it is worth noting that lobbying is becoming official in countries such as France where it was once considered illegitimate (lobbying at the level of the European commission and parliament has become an essential component of the strategies of large organizations), while it is increasingly coming under criticism in countries such as the United States, where it was considered a normal way of informing members of Congress, as shown by the Abramoff scandal in the United States in 2006.

2. Scientific system

a. At the level of laws and norms

Since the explosion of the first atomic bomb, the issue of knowing whether some limits should be imposed on the scope of scientific research has become an issue that scientists have to confront each time they extend their inquiry to brand-new domains. This type of questioning, which contradicts the epistemological optimism of positivism, occurs each time it is felt that some symbolic limit is going to be transgressed. We have already described the way in which specialists of genetics decided that they were to stop all research until a law was promulgated to rule this new, uncharted land. Similar debates are being staged on the issue of cloning, as is exemplified by the debate on the use of stem cells to develop medical knowledge and cures.

The definition of safety norms is another occasion of witnessing the uncertainties related to the limits of scientific knowledge. Nuclear radiation, asbestos, dioxin, intensity of electromagnetic fields, and the share of genetically manipulated products contained in food products are examples, among so many others, of occurrences where even very small quantities of some component can be considered potentially hazardous to our health. Consequently, they have to be subjected to the publication of safety norms. Without such norms to be respected, any presence of such a substance would immediately generate complaints and even panic. Uncertainty tends to generate a conflict between a desire to overestimate the danger so as to minimize the health risk, and a desire to establish realistic norms so as to allow economic development to take place.

Among the norms imposed on scientific development, the most paradoxical may be what has come to be known as the *precaution principle.*

To understand the meaning of the development of the *precaution principle* it is necessary to start from the closely related notion of prudence. Prudence, or practical wisdom, is not defined as some stable reference to which people would be able to conform their choices; on the contrary, it is people by their very choices who manifest their capacity to make good choices. This is why Aristotle advises us to look for prudence by looking for the prudent: "One way of grasping the nature of prudence is to characterize which are the persons which we call prudent.... That is to say able to deliberate correctly on what is good and advantageous for himself, not on a limited point... but in a general manner in such way that for instance things may lead to a happy life."[15] We may note that this description seems to echo Frank Knight when he tells us, "The ultimate logic, or psychology, of these deliberations is obscure, a part of the unfathomable mystery of life and mind..." (Knight, 1922/1972 p. 227).

It remains to be seen what it is that makes the existence of prudence possible, or rather, as it is the prudent who is the warrant of prudence, what it is that makes the existence of the prudent possible. Aristotle (Barnes, 1984) states clearly that all men are not equally capable of becoming prudent. The prudent is first, the one who is endowed at birth with a good nature; second, the one who has benefited from a good education; and last, but not least, the one who has benefited from a good experience of sufficient length in a favorable context, for it is by the fact of having the experience of choosing in a suitably well-governed family or city (i.e., family and cities governed by prudent men) that man learns to make the good choices. A kind of circle establishes itself between the prudent and the city, with each requiring the existence of the other. But this circle starts with the city: "Prudence presupposes the city, thus it does not allow by itself to built it even if it allows a well constituted state to last thanks to the good sense of its Leaders" (Weil, 1991). From the point of view of our framework, we could say the definition of the prudent and the very possibility of prudence require the existence of a stable system of legitimacy inasmuch as it constitutes the type of favorable context that is likely to provide the prudent with the experience the development of prudence requires. From that point of view, the emergence of the notion of precaution may thus be considered as the expression of the fact that henceforth prudence is both necessary—as Knight points out when he says that "We are so built that what seems to us reasonable is likely to be confirmed by experience, or we would not live in the world at all" (Knight, 1922/1972)—and impossible as the crisis of the system of legitimacy implies that the conditions for the emergence of prudence are no longer satisfied. The paradoxes implied in the notion of precaution principle have already been discussed in this chapter.

b. Independent third parties

Given the complexity of these norms, independent agencies are established to define and control the norms that are deemed acceptable. The U.S. Food and Drug Administration (FDA) is thus in charge of defining the protocols and criterion for the authorization of new medicines as well as for the establishment of norms to which the production of food must be submitted.

In all fields of industrial activities, normalization processes are developed by agencies such as AFNOR in France (French Association for Normalization).

The development of modern technology in medicine, especially in the domain of artificial procreation, results in situations that can no longer be left to scientists or specialists to decide. This has given rise to the development of ethics committees at the national level to give advice on legislation or at the level of local hospitals to give advice on specific decisions.

Beyond these institutions, it can be seen that some individual experts tend to play a determining role in discussions relating to the use and abuse of new technologies.

c. Level of communication processes

With the role of experts we have already entered the realm of communication processes. It reminds us that the legitimacy of judgments in the field of science, as in all other fields, now lies ultimately in public opinion.

This can be seen using three examples: *consensus conferences* (such as the one organized in Denmark to generate legislation on genetic manipulations), *the referendum* organized in Sweden to decide on the future of the development of nuclear energy, and the *precaution principle* that has been included in France or in Europe as a constitutional principle.

What is interesting about consensus conferences as organized in Denmark by the Environmental Assessment Institute is the way in which they try to symbolically integrate all potential sources of legitimacy (Lomborg, 2004) by involving scientists, social scientists, thinkers and journalists, etc. The debate opposes scientific experts and an equal number of individuals selected at random from the general population. The results of the debate are then submitted as suggestions for potential regulations.

The fact that the Swedish government organized a referendum on the development of nuclear energy in 1980 shows that such a decision can no longer be delegated to experts or to political representatives of the people.

3. Communication system

Ultimately, all conflicts that cannot be solved at the level of the legal system or the scientific system will have to be solved at the level of the communication system. What is at stake is the ability of management to survive the destabilization that results from a crisis at the "local level" in a situation characterized by the type of institutional uncertainty we have just described at the level of the legal and scientific systems. We shall consider successively communication processes at the local, intermediate, and global (or societal) levels.

a. Communication process at the local level

In such a situation, the first thing that is likely to be destroyed is its legitimacy as a social and economic actor. This implies that all of its actions will be questioned and that all of its answers will be received with distrust. In such a situation, management is paralyzed: It cannot act, it cannot speak. This is what happened to Union Carbide, the 37th-largest American corporation and the third-largest in the chemical industry, in 1984 after the catastrophe at Bhopal, India. The first condition for management to be able to survive a catastrophe is precisely its ability to appear a legitimate speaker in a situation when its responsibility may be involved. This will depend entirely on the way it is perceived by the public; that is, the way in which it has been able to acquire a positive image before the crisis: Institutional communication is a major dimension of the management of major risk, as it constitutes a central component of what management should do while it waits for the unexpected.

The development of institutional communication assumes that answers to the following three questions be given: Why should the firm communicate? What should the firm communicate? How should a firm communicate?

The first question we have already answered: A firm should communicate because its system of legitimacy is undergoing a crisis. If it wants to be listened to, trusted, and believed, and thus able to act, in a situation of crisis it must have developed a favorable image in the public's opinion.

If a firm must develop and manage its public image, it is because it can no longer rely on the ability of legal and scientific systems to produce an acceptable representation of its actions. Consequently, what must be communicated is nothing other than the management of the firm. The first condition for such a communication to be successful is the very communicability of the management it tries to communicate. This condition, however obvious or tautological it may seem, is far from being easy to fulfill in practice. What this condition implies is that the management of the firm be constructed in such a way as to be able to comply with the constraints imposed by the process of communication to a large and diverse audience. It has to be understandable, it has to be credible, and it has to be acceptable. To be understandable, it must be simple, identifiable, delimited, and readable.

Thus emerges one of the most interesting paradoxes of all the paradoxes that characterize the management of major risk—that communication often considered secondary is becoming a strategic dimension of business. Henceforth, it defines the constraints any management must comply with if it wants to have a chance to survive a crisis.

Far from being superficial, the requirements of communication may imply a deep transformation in the management of the firm. We shall give several examples at the operational and strategic levels.

At the operational level all firms know that they must be able to track with precision the products they stock, transport, and sell. When in 1986 the warehouse of the Sandoz factory near Basel caught fire, people realized that they had no precise description of the quantity and the nature of the chemicals that were at risk. Similarly, producers—be they makers of cars or makers of cheese—know that they must establish a system of tracking sales so that they are able to recall products that belong to a given batch and thus limit strictly the consequences of an accident that otherwise could destabilize the perception of all its production.

The way in which Perrier water removed all of their products from the shelves of supermarkets is a good example of what one may have to do to make visible and credible the idea that the firm is doing all it can to ensure the quality of its production.

At a more strategic level, nowadays management is required to show that it is doing all it can to contribute to the welfare of society (as this is no longer guaranteed by legal and scientific norms, as has been stated previously and as will be demonstrated further in this chapter). This is what is demonstrated by the development of strategies in the realm of corporate social responsibility and in the area of sustainable development (Aggeri et al., 2005).

However, whatever the quality of the management, it must recognize that it may have to face a crisis. This is expressed directly by the development of risk management and of crisis management.

Risk management developed some 40 years ago as a consequence of recognition of the need to better manage the growing cost of insurance. More recently, some 25 years ago, this function underwent a deep transformation: Besides the management of insurance, a new preoccupation emerged concerning the need to manage major risk and the threat it represents.

The continuity plans of the Basel 2 regulation described above correspond to an institutionalization of this preoccupation.

Among the tasks of risk managers is the organization of crisis-management structures and routines, which have to be developed in advance if one wants to be able to react in a timely fashion to the extremely disturbed environment that might result from an accident of some kind.

b. Communication processes at an intermediate level

By definition, the management of major risk cannot be limited to the local level. It implies necessarily the participation of, and cooperation with, other organizations. Let us give three examples.

Crisis management, in the case of an industrial or ecological catastrophe, will require the participation of all the organizations, public or private, belonging to the community directly affected by their consequences. Thus it will be necessary to prepare the type of cooperation required in case of emergency. Hurricane Katrina has shown the difficulties that can be involved in such a process and the consequences that can result from a lack of preparation. The role of the U.S. Federal Emergency Management Agency (FEMA) during this crisis perfectly exemplifies this point.

After a crisis such as the Sandoz catastrophe, the question of the legitimacy of management is not limited to the firm. The fear generated by the catastrophe is readily associated with the whole chemical industry. Thus, crisis management requires that each business organize at the level of its profession the argumentation and the managerial standards required for its activity to be considered acceptable. This process takes place in front of the public; that is, governments and political representatives as well as nongovernmental organizations that assume the task of defending the interests of the public. These organizations may at times become important players in the development of a crisis as well as in the elaboration of acceptable standards of action. As the President of Sandoz declared, "We know now that the chemical industry must rely on nothing else but itself."

One of the major obstacles to the development of a management that can be communicated is the very fact that major risk implies that society is deprived of an adequate system for symbolically representing social actions. This is why third parties may intervene to elaborate and propose some acceptable measure of acceptable standards of behavior. It is the function of rating agencies to try to overcome the pervasive asymmetry of information that characterizes such a situation and to bring some "transparency" to the system. By the way in which they evaluate firms from the point of view of governance, ethical behavior, social responsibility, and so on, they contribute to their public image, their reputation. Satisfying this requirement has become a determining (necessary and not sufficient) element of the strategies of modern organizations at the beginning of the 21st century.

c. Communication processes at the global level

It is in the nature of major risk that no a priori limit can be imposed on the development of a crisis. Whatever the efficiency of the methods of managing the impossible developed at organizational-level and interorganizational-level crises, affecting communication processes has the potential to become global. We could even say that these crises reveal their nature by the way in which they demonstrate that no acceptable common language exists that is able to justify a priori the course of action taken by social and economic actors.

The way in which such a situation is intimately linked to the development of modernity is best shown by the way in which Auguste Comte, the founder of positivism in the first half of the 19th century, had already considered how communication processes were threatened by scientific progress. He pointed to the fact that "the excessive specialization of individual research" could end in disorder and anarchy.[16] Actually, it could be argued that it is precisely to prevent such a negative outcome that he developed an epistemology wherein the principle of the division of labor among scientists was strictly controlled by special kinds of specialists, the "specialists of generalities," whose role was to submit the realm of science to a system of common rules and methods. It seems logical from that point of view that the crisis of positivism that characterizes the present be associated with a threat to communication process that recalls the story of the Tower of Babel, when the efforts of men to extend the reach of their power resulted in a complete breakdown of communication because of the excessive diversity of the languages in use. Thus the management of major risk must develop at the level of global systems of communication. It will consist of trying to impose some common language so as to bring some organization and coordination in a world threatened by chaos. Four examples will allow us to show the various ways in which this can be achieved in practice.

One is struck by the way in which the World Wide Web, which is supposed to allow anyone to communicate freely with whomever he or she wishes, is governed by a highly organized and centralized system of protocols and addresses. This stresses the degree to which free communication can only be reached at the cost of extremely stringent constraints. The panic that was associated with the threat of the Y2000 bug shows that the very rigor of common practices can, by itself, be the source of major uncertainty.

To avoid the chaos that may result from the existence of conflicting views on the dangers associated with some aspect of human behavior (be it global warming, genetic manipulations, the development of nuclear energy, information processing, nanotechnologies, etc.), it is necessary to create the conditions for the organization of an orderly debate. This can be done by developing specialized media and forums where the issues, opinions, and doctrines can be discussed. Such systems of social communication must be established each time a topic becomes the source of major fear. While it cannot ensure the production of a consensus about what is to be done, it at least provides the components of a symbolic representation of what is at stake, thus allowing the transformation of panic into a debate.[17]

A good example of such a global effort to formalize the fears that threaten social cooperation can be seen in the way the United Nations Organization declared the years 1990–2000 "the decade of catastrophic risks," generating all kinds of occasions to study and discuss the fact that the world was actually becoming more and more uncertain.

A last example of the type of process through which discussion about major risk, forecasting of catastrophes, and prevention measures against the consequences of a catastrophes can be organized lies in what we propose to call "specific major risks." These correspond to the construction of models of action that conform to the logic of quasi-positivism; that is, models that consider situations of major risk *as if* positivism were still "the name of the game."

The first requirement of such a system is that it be possible to define a limited number of major risks, each of them having their own well-defined characteristics. We know that this contradicts the fact that the number of major risks is potentially infinite and that what characterizes them is that they are likely to behave in an unexpected manner. To understand the construction of a limited number of "specific major risks," it is necessary to take into consideration the existence of the media and the way in which they determine the historical destiny of social fears.

At a given time, the media can deal efficiently with only a very small number of topics; thus, the list of specialized major risks will be limited by this constraint. Once this is understood, it is possible to define the product life cycle of a major risk. First a new fear appears, be it as the result of a catastrophe (as with the tsunami that destroyed vast regions in the Indian Ocean in 2004), from the actual emergence of a new, unknown, and devastating illness (such as AIDS), or from some form of symbolic breakdown (the "mad cow disease" that destabilized the production and consumption of meat and the "avian flu" that raised the fear of a pandemic similar to the one that killed nearly 50 million people in 1918). In the second stage, the fear becomes a major topic in the media. A collective debate is generated, and the issue appears in the political agenda of governments. Each social actor in front of the new situation develops a strategy. Conflicts between experts develop. At a third stage, measures of regulation, prevention, and information intended to lead to the control of the "specific major risk considered" are developed by political authorities in conjunction with NGOs. The fourth stage corresponds to the decline of the major risk as new "specific major risks" take their place in the attention of the media. The old "specific major risk" survives, then, through the regulatory, scientific, and organizational mechanisms and devices established in the preceding period.[18]

So far, we have proposed an organized description of the methods of the management of major risk, but we have not developed the theoretical justification of this organization. There are at least three reasons why we should not avoid confronting this theoretical justification directly.

First, and this is obvious enough, it is required to be able to reply to those who would like to know how the hypotheses proposed earlier have been established and to the various objections that could be raised against them.

Second, a full development of the theory is required to reply to those who do not accept that so many practical consequences can be derived from a theoretical argument.

What we propose to show is that major risk corresponds best to the situation where the proverb "there is nothing more practical than a good theory" applies. The demonstration of the existence of a good theory that allows us to confront chaotic situations can be considered itself as belonging to the methods of the management of the impossible.

But there is a last reason why a more precise exploration of the structure of our arguments may be of use. The notion of a system of legitimacy as discussed so far constitutes but one out of the three types that Max Weber allows us to consider: legal-rational, traditional, and charismatic. This may allow us to understand why a crisis of the legal-rational system of legitimacy will tend to give more weight to arguments related to tradition and charisma.

Systems of Legitimacy and the History of the Social Acceptability of Risks

In the following section, we shall explore notions of *systems of legitimacy, the history of systems of legitimacy,* and *the crisis of legitimacy as a way of formalizing* "standardized ideas about justice," which, according to Mary Douglas, determine *"the public reception of any policy for risk"* (Douglas, 1986).

In previous works over the years, we have utilized the notion of "systems of legitimacy" as a framework for analyzing many different social and managerial issues.[19] Given the limits and the aim of the present chapter, we shall only present a summarized, albeit complete, version of this conceptual framework.

SYSTEMS OF LEGITIMACY AND CONFLICT RESOLUTION IN MODERN SOCIETIES

Our analysis will rely on a theoretical model of modern Western democracies. Let us define society as a system of conflict resolution. On the one hand, modern society can be characterized by the presence of bureaucracies (i.e., large organizations) and on the other hand by the principle of individual freedom (the right to question the legitimacy of the actions of any other individual belonging to a given society).

In a free society, freedom of expression presupposes that any individual may question—and so confront—any other individual. If a bureaucratic organization is defined as a large number of people (say 10,000) who deal with an even larger number of people (say 10 million), the potential total number of interactions between all these individuals turns out to be more than 100 billion. If each potential interaction were to give rise to a conflict, let alone a simple objection, we could assume that the activity of the organization would stop immediately because of the cost (in time and money) of solving these conflicts. That any collective action whatsoever does take place appears as a kind of "miracle" (or at least a very unlikely event). It must be assumed that, for collective action to be possible, there are stringent mechanisms in place constraining the freedom of action (and of inquiry) of those involved. Let us consider the conditions for this type of action.

We shall propose that the first condition for collective action is that, in 99% of the cases, no conflict (not even an objection) occurs. The required institutional conditions for this are quite difficult to study insofar as they remain implicit. Such cases fall outside of the scope of direct empirical scrutiny[20] (Laufer, 2002). Let us simply note that if this first precondition for collective action is met, we are still left with 1 billion objections, which is probably more than enough to threaten the development of any collective action.

It is more productive to turn to cases where conflicts exist. Not that the interactions considered in this second case are more easily treated because they are less numerous—1 billion conflicts could prove costly enough to prevent any collective action. More to the point, conflicts are explicit, observable phenomena. They can be the object of scientific inquiry.[21]

For any cooperative action to take place, it is necessary that the interactions in each case be very brief, so as not to be too costly. They must be reduced to an exchange of the type: "Why? . . . Because," predicated on the fact that a readily acceptable answer exists. This leaves us with the task of determining what allows millions of people, in millions of situations, to recognize an answer as legitimate (i.e., acceptable). What makes an answer legitimate must include not only a common accord on the description of the conflict (or the actions under scrutiny) but agreement on the definition of who is right and who is wrong. This is the certainty that Mary Douglas refers to when she says that it is "not a mood but an institution."

To answer this question, we shall refer to the work of Chester Barnard (Barnard, 1938), one of the major authors of managerial literature. His analysis of authority claims that "authority does not lie in the person of authority but in the person who receives the order." This means that, for an answer to be accepted, it must immediately be recognized as valid by the person who asked the question. For this to happen it is necessary that

1. This answer be already present in the mind of the person to whom it is addressed. We could say that it belongs to his or her "ideology."
2. The answer be recognized immediately as fitting the situation under scrutiny.
3. This be true for millions of people, in millions of situations.

For these conditions to be fulfilled, it is necessary to hypothesize the existence of *a very simple system of shared symbols,* considered by most members of a given society as providing a satisfactory description of most of the actions that are likely to be the source of conflicts or objections. *This system of shared symbols constitutes by definition an important part of the "ideology" of the society under scrutiny and will be considered as constituting its system of legitimacy.*

For the remaining conflicts we can assume that the biggest part will be solved through a more or less extensive process of negotiation, while the rest will require court action.

Let us draw some consequences from this analysis:

- To assume that conflicts that cannot be solved by negotiation end up in court ultimately implies that they fall within the jurisdiction of modern nation-states.
- The *system of shared symbols* determining which actions are readily acceptable in a given society—its *system of legitimacy*—constitutes what we propose to call a *normative phenomenology of common sense* of the society under consideration. It provides a description of *how* things pertaining to a given society *should appear to any one of its members.*

From an epistemological point of view, it is interesting to note that the value of this theory does not lie so much in the fact that it is true—i.e., that it provides an accurate representation of reality—but in the fact that it is a necessary precondition for fruitful social interactions. The social importance of such a precondition explains its compulsory nature. The fact that law represents a *normative phenomenology of common sense* is expressed in the famous and compelling dictum that "ignorance of the law is no excuse." This means that, in case of conflict, even if you did not in fact consider things from a legal point of view, the mere fact that you are a member of society means that you cannot escape the constraints of the law (whether you were aware of them or not).

The empirical value of this theoretical approach relies on the role played by *performative statements*"[22] (Austin, 1962); that is, statements whose value depends on the degree to which they are actually accepted, such as those of the legal system. Law is, by definition, a compulsory normative phenomenology of common sense. It is what allows us to give a precise operational definition of the notion "*system of legitimacy*" with precision, thus linking theory and practice. The link between words (theory) and things (actions) is ensured by the ability of the state to enforce it thanks to the exercise of legitimate violence. We may recall that Max Weber characterizes the state by the very fact that it is endowed the monopoly of legitimate violence (through the actions of justice and police).

SYSTEMS OF LEGITIMACY AND MAX WEBER'S TYPES OF LEGITIMATE AUTHORITY

We are left with the task of finding the systems of shared symbols that characterize modern, democratic, and bureaucratic societies. For this we shall turn our attention toward Max Weber, who defines three types of legitimate authority: charismatic authority, traditional authority, and legal-rational authority (Weber, 1961). One might wonder if this list is pragmatic—i.e., opened to modification and completion, or if it is theoretical—in which case no other categories of legitimate authority can be defined. In the latter case, they would meet the requirements of simple systems of shared symbols.

A first argument for the completeness of this list could be that no one has proposed a fourth system since Weber's seminal writings. However, such an argument remains quite pragmatic. A more theoretical argument consists of stating that in order to define what we shall call a "well-formed" system of legitimacy, one must start with a "cosmos" in which a dichotomy is specified between two points: the locus at the origin of legitimate authority and that which concerns the application of legitimate authority.

We must add that to see such a dichotomy, it is necessary to look at it through special "glasses." This allows us to make the following definitions:

Crisis Management and Legitimacy

Charismatic authority is characterized by a dichotomy between the *sacred*, as seen through the lenses of *faith*, and the *profane*, the *profane* being submitted to the *sacred*.

Traditional authority is characterized by a dichotomy between *culture*, as seen through the lenses of respect, and *nature*, *nature* being submitted to (traditional) *culture*.

Legal-rational authority is characterized by a dichotomy between *nature*, as seen through the lenses of *science* and *culture*, *culture* being submitted to *nature*.

In sum, two dichotomies (sacred/profane and nature/culture) define three systems of legitimacy. Whereas with nature/culture it was possible to elaborate two systems, it was not possible to do so with sacred/profane, insofar as the sacred can never legitimately be submitted to profane.

Given that for more than 2,500 years, Western culture has only been able to produce these two dichotomies, we can argue that unless one comes up with a new cosmos (defined by a new dichotomy), one is limited to the three types of legitimate authority listed above.

The History of Systems of Legitimacy

Systems of legitimacy can evolve in three ways:

1. A revolution—The French Revolution can be seen, for example, as a move to replace the charismatic and traditional system, characteristic of the *Ancien Regime*, with a legal-rational system. As we have seen above, this system of legitimacy is founded on the way science articulates the relationship between nature and culture. Epistemology, a mode of discourse that legitimizes science, is therefore a central element of this system.

Let us consider an example of how science can be said to allow the laws of nature to govern men. The legal-rational system of legitimacy institutes free-market democracies. At its heart lies the science of classical microeconomic theory. This science states that if economic actors are small enough with respect to the market (i.e., if the conditions of pure and perfect competition are met), they may act as they please as long as they respect the *right of property*. In such a situation, the ("natural") laws of market equilibrium guarantee that, whatever they do, the market will reach a *social optimum* provided that all economic actors are "profit maximizers."

2. A crisis—We need to distinguish between "local crises" that occur within the limits of a system of legitimacy (i.e., any conflict resulting from the behavior of a social actor) and "global, unlimited crises," which affect the system of legitimacy itself as a whole. *The latter imply that the clear dichotomies that characterize the system of legitimacy are in a state of confusion.*

Local and limited crises—each affecting one of the above systems of legitimacy—can be associated with a specific denomination. These denominations fit within the logic of each system and constitute an integral part of the institutions considered. For instance, according to the French dictionary, the word "danger" (which dates back to the 12th century) is the state of someone at the mercy of some power (the word comes from "dominarium," power to dominate, or "dominus," master). It corresponds, in effect, to a local crisis within the charismatic system of legitimacy. Similarly, the word "transgression" (also from the 12th century) expresses disregard for a set of well-defined rules. It corresponds to a traditional system of legitimacy that, at its core, distinguishes between a right path of action and a wrong path of action. Finally, the word "risk" (which dates back to 1557 and the development of merchant capitalism[23]) is the key word that corresponds to a local crisis in our own legal-rational system of legitimacy. As we have seen, "risk" is defined as something that can be calculated.

This could lead us to a new definition of the term "major risk": It is what results from a global, unlimited crisis of the legal-rational system of legitimacy.[24] To demonstrate that uncertainty is not what it used to be requires defining, rigorously, how this system of legitimacy was structured since it has come into being and showing how it has evolved throughout history.

In the following developments, particular attention will be devoted to the notion of risk and the way in which it has been associated with the notion of insurance.

The History of the Legal-Rational System of Legitimacy

To analyze the precise workings of a system of legitimacy, we must consider the institutional systems of specific nation-states. In what follows, we shall deal with France and the United States. These two countries are two extreme instances of the legal-rational system of legitimacy: In the first, the state and public administration are dominant, and in the second, civil society and private enterprise prevail.

In both cases, it is important to understand how science, law, and actions are articulated in such a way as to constitute an efficient system of conflict resolution. For this purpose, we shall give a more developed description of the way in which the kernel of the legal-rational system of legitimacy was established by the French Revolution.[25]

The Kernel of the Legal-Rational System of Legitimacy

The minimum number of symbols required to define the legal-rational system of legitimacy instituted by the French Revolution can be described as follows:

Crisis Management and Legitimacy

- At a first level—the level of the "cosmos"—one finds the dichotomy between nature and culture. Nature is contemplated through the "lenses" of Newtonian and Galilean science. This model, by analogy, engenders another model, describing social interactions. We may note that the economic theories of Adam Smith and Jean-Baptiste Say were developed according the model of Newtonian physics.

- At a second level, one finds law and the dichotomy between the public and the private sectors. The private sector is defined as what can be governed directly by the laws of nature; that is, the laws of political economy (according to Adam Smith or Jean-Baptiste Say). The public sector is composed of the institutions required to discover the laws of nature (the legislative body), to promulgate them (the executive body), and to control and enforce them (through the existence of the judicial body and police). The various components of public administration bring together all of the preconditions required for the effective and efficient functioning of market mechanisms. This is why—in addition to the Police and the Justice Departments—the Army, the Department of Foreign Affairs (guaranteeing the peace required for doing business), and the Department of Transportation (allowing for merchandise produced in different places to be exchanged in a single market) all belong to the public sector.

- At a third level, there are pragmatic processes developed by various administrative authorities. The legitimacy of an administrative action depends on two conditions: compliance with the rule of law, in turn subject to compliance with the laws of nature as defined by science.

The possibility of defining in a precise manner the history of the legal-rational system of legitimization is linked to the status of the rule of law in such a system. Actually, the legal-rational system of legitimization is characterized by the fact that problems of legitimacy (and their attendant conflicts) are reduced to problems of legality.[26] Law constitutes a central and compulsory element of the system of legitimacy. As a result, the evolution of the rule of law is in itself tightly bound to the history of the system of legitimacy.

This description of the three levels of the legal-rational system of legitimacy allows one to associate the evolution of the rule of law, the history of science, and epistemology. Associated with the history of the rule of law, the legal-rational system of legitimacy can also be related to the history of science and epistemology, as well as to the history of administrative action (i.e., management).

We shall first consider the history of the public sector in France and the history of the private sector in the United States. This will allow us, in turn, to describe the corresponding history of epistemological paradigms. In the process, we shall give a more detailed definition of the notion of risk and a historical account of the emergence of management within the system of legitimization.

The History of the Symbolic Definition of the Public Sector in France

The analysis of the French public sector will allow us to precisely define the crisis of a system of legitimacy.

In France, in order to guarantee the separation of powers (especially between the judicial and executive branches), a special body of judges has been created to monitor the public sector. Thus, courts have to decide explicitly what should and should not fall under either of the two branches of government. They do so by defining the "criterion of administrative law." The evolution of this criterion corresponds to the history of the legitimacy of decisions and actions made within the public sector. According to all textbooks on the topic, this history develops in three stages, separated by two transitional periods.

The first stage (from 1800 to 1880/1900) corresponds to the criterion of Public Power: All activities carried out by civil servants are considered to fall in the domain of public law. In a Garrison State, the *origin of power* determines the legitimacy of an action.

The second stage (from 1880/1900 to 1945/1960) corresponds to the primacy of Public Service: Anything done to render a public service falls in the domain of public law. In the Welfare State, legitimacy lies in the *finality of power*.

The third stage (from 1945/1960 to the present) corresponds to what is known as *the crisis of administrative law*; that is, to the confusion concerning the limit between the public and the private sectors. Inasmuch as this limit constitutes an essential dimension of the system *of shared symbols* required by the system of conflict resolution, it indicates a *crisis of the system of legitimacy*.

There are three possible ways to justify an action: the power at its source, its finality, or its modalities. As we have seen above, it has become impossible today to justify an action only on the basis of its source (first stage) or its finality (second stage). We shall therefore argue that today, actions have to be justified (legitimized) by the methods used. With management by definition being a method of action, it has emerged as an essential and official component of social institutions.

Given the confusion between the public and the private, a given social actor no longer knows with which set of rules he or she must comply. Here, then, is a possible explanation for why certainty, characteristic of institutions (and provided by them) in the two preceding periods, has been replaced by uncertainty. This may be said to correspond to the emergence of the notion of "major risk": Henceforth, any citizen can "anticipate" (consciously or unconsciously) the collapse of the frame of reference that once allowed him or her to distinguish between legitimate and illegitimate acts.

The tardy emergence of "major risk" and crisis management can be explained by the tendency of society and its citizens to avoid acknowledging a state of affairs that is threatening and, as such, dysfunctional. It is only when experience forces us to confront the uncertainties that have characterized institutions since 1945/1960 that certainty manifests itself in the form of a problem (Douglas, 2001).[27]

Having shown that the public sector has been undergoing a crisis in a country were it was the most legitimate, France, we shall turn to the United States, where the private sector, always a stalwart of legitimacy, is also undergoing a crisis.

The History of the Symbolic Definition of the Private Sector in the United States

The history of the legitimization of private enterprise in the United States can be divided into three stages. It is interesting to observe that these periods correspond to those found in France, a fact which gives some weight to the idea that the history of the legal-rational system of legitimacy develops in parallel patterns throughout Western society.

For each stage, we shall consider the way in which market theory has been institutionalized. This will allow us to follow the evolution of the status of the notions of risk and of management in the institutional settings considered.

a. Stage 1—From 1800 to 1880/1900: The Reign of the Invisible Hand

We shall start by considering the basic principle underlying the legitimization of "classic" free-market theory, predicated on the submission of all to the law, be it scientific (the law of the market) or legal (the right to private property).

In its pure form, as it was supposed to work in the 19th century, "classical" free-market theory implies the following four conditions:

- *Pure and perfect competition.* Business enterprises are very small; as a result, they do not have the power to influence market prices and quantities; they can therefore exert "freely" whatever power they have.
- *Profit maximization.* Each entrepreneur seeks to maximize his profit; according to Pareto's definition[28] and market theory, a "Social Optimum" is reached.
- *Risk of the entrepreneur.* Insofar as an entrepreneur risks losses, he is entitled to profits when there are some.
- *Property rights.* These guarantee the principle under which authority can be exerted within the firm (the "atomistic" firm).

Two conclusions can now be drawn concerning management and risk.

The atomistic nature of firms inhibits the formal (institutional) recognition of management as a discipline in the United States. Business schools, for example, did not develop in the United States until the end of the 19th century. Institutionalizing management assumes that firms are big enough to allow complex interpersonal processes to take place within them. Management, defined as the concrete behavior of entrepreneurs within a "free-market" economy, is associated with "freedom" and thus must remain "secret" (i.e., private). The techniques used by entrepreneurs are legitimate to the extent that the entrepreneur is legitimate as a social actor; that is, as long as he respects the legal rules that ensure his submission to the laws of the market.

To understand what Mary Douglas meant when she said that "certainty is not a mood but an institution," it will be useful to consider that the entrepreneur is confronted with two types of risks: risk in terms of legitimacy (risk linked to the social acceptability of his actions) and pragmatic risks ("speculative risk"). This distinction allows us to understand how it is possible for an entrepreneur to face both uncertainty at the pragmatic level (if his business fails) and certainty at the institutional level (that of the limits imposed on his actions by the rule of law).[29] Here, processes of legitimization depend entirely on being submitted to the "invisible hand of the market."

b. Stage 2—From 1880/1900 to 1945/1960: Antitrust Laws

As corporations grow, it becomes impossible to pretend that their size does not alter the terms of competition within the market as a whole. This constitutes a "crisis of legitimacy." At the end of the 19th century, antitrust laws stated that "firms should not be too big, lest they be broken up into sufficiently small corporations." These symbolic stopgap measures maintained free-market principles.

A special court was given the task of deciding whether a firm was "too big" or "sufficiently small." This required the intervention of a specialist in the measurement of the sizes of firms considered (i.e., an antitrust judge).[30] The fact that certain firms could be suspected of being too big was a tacit recognition that they were big; that is, big enough to include events and processes requiring the development of management processes. Management could be officially recognized and business schools set up. It should come as no surprise that official management first developed in business school was named "*scientific management*," for as we know, scientific knowledge is the source of legitimate power in the legal-rational system of legitimacy. A scientific manager is a specialist whose knowledge of the measures of time and movement allows him to define the "one best way" in which production must be organized. The legitimacy of the antitrust judge and the scientific manager lies in their ability to measure. This implies a reference to a common epistemological paradigm, which allows us to define precisely the finality of actions.

As a result, the risks undertaken by the scientific manager and the antitrust judge can be characterized in the following manner:

1. Pragmatic risk and risk in terms of legitimacy can no longer be distinguished.

2. The antitrust judge and the scientific manager actually undergo no risks as long as they obey the methodological and epistemological rules that guarantee their expertise and the existence of a "one best way." This much said, the social acceptability of risks taken on by an entrepreneur is not limited to the guarantees afforded by "the rule of law" and the mechanisms of "perfect competition." He also has to consider the specific situation of his employees, who run risks of accidents at work.

The social acceptability of work-related accidents in a legal-rational system of legitimacy depends on the degree to which the cause of the accident is considered as "natural." By definition, a work-related accident that results either from the way work is organized or from the details of a specific setting cannot be considered to have resulted from a "natural" physical cause. Similarly, it cannot be considered to have resulted from a "natural" social cause, such as the laws of the market: The "autonomy of the will" of the worker is restricted by his subordinate status in the organization. If the possibility of a work-related accident is a risk a worker takes on consciously, it is not a risk he takes on willingly (i.e., it is a risk he would prefer to avoid). This type of risk cannot be considered socially acceptable. Systems of compensation have to be established. Given its cost, the financial weight of an accident is too heavy to be borne by either the entrepreneur or the employee. It has to be mutualized, thanks to a sophisticated system implying economics, mathematics, and innovative legal principles, called "insurance."

From an economic standpoint, this implies distinguishing between *pure risk* (a risk that one suffers unwillingly and that is the result of pure chance phenomena) and *speculative risk*. Mathematics allows the mutualization of pure risk: The central-limit theorem states that the average value of the sum of a number of independent and limited random variables that follow the same probability distribution converge rapidly toward a Gaussian law. The amount of money required to cover the cost of accidents can be calculated in advance and very precisely. The mutualization of costs is made possible by a radical legal innovation in the field of tort law: the dissociation of responsibility and fault[31] (Ewald, 1986).

   c. Stage 3—From 1945/1960 to the Present: The Reign of the Very Large Firm

If pure competition could be symbolically prorogated with antitrust laws, other problems led to a deepening of the crisis of legitimacy.

The question of whether owners or managers should govern a firm was initially solved by stating that the owner defined the objectives of the firm, whereas the manager applied his or her know-how to their implementation within the firm. This model, however, left open potential contradictions that manifested themselves later. The relationship between owners and managers could not be organized in a stable manner. As Frank Knight put it in 1922, "in more recent times . . . the accumulation of capital and the perfection of financial institutions and the growth of competition brought the center of interest to business ability . . . [It became] easy or at least possible for ability to secure capital when not in possession of it by direct ownership, and made common the carrying-on of business predominantly with borrowed resources" (Knight, 1922/1972, p. 23).

This reversal of hierarchical power between owners and managers became obvious after the Great Depression of 1929. A renowned study by Adolf Berle and Gardiner Means brought to light the emerging separation of responsibilities between managers and owners (Berle & Means, 1932), contrary to the principle that a decision-maker must bear the consequences of his or her own decisions. This impasse was soon resolved by new regulations instated by the Securities and Exchange Commission (SEC), ensuring that shareholders be kept regularly informed of the decisions taken by managers.

However, just as antitrust laws could not stop the ever-increasing concentration of firms (Arnold, 1937). SEC regulations could not stem the emerging power of managers over that of shareholders. In the 1960s, this led to a reappraisal of the principle of maximization of profit itself, as can be seen in the economic literature dealing with the managerial theory of the firm. Maximization of sales could be shown to become the objective of an organization over and above maximization of profit (Baumol, 1959).[32]

Finally, the risk of bankruptcy itself disappears in certain cases. This is what happens when a firm is considered essential for national independence or when it employs too many people to be allowed to disappear overnight. It has become too big to fail.[33] The fact that Chrysler had to be bailed out by a loan from the federal government in 1979 revealed the contradictions inherent to the application of U.S. antitrust laws at the time.[34]

Since then, some have argued that competition should be measured and regulated at a global level. This can be considered another expression of the crisis of the legal-rational system of legitimacy; that is, the crisis of the principle of national sovereignty. According to Max Weber, a nation-state is defined as having a monopoly on legitimate violence; it alone can enforce the rule of law. Today, the legitimization of market mechanisms lies in an efficient international legal system. In spite of the progress of the World Trade Organization, we cannot claim that such a system is actually in place. This new situation has led to a crisis of antitrust laws, as evidenced by the Microsoft antitrust saga, the conflicts between European and American approaches to antitrust law, and the differences in the political agendas of the Clinton and Bush administrations in this area. This has led to a general feeling that the power of firms is no longer submitted to the laws of the market. "The visible hand" of managers is seen as having replaced "the invisible hand of the market" (Chandler, 1977).

This crisis of legitimacy expresses itself in many different forms. Since the 1960s, criticism of corporations has given birth to consumer and ecological movements; conflicts of interest between owners and managers have given rise to legal battles (such as the one concerning insider trading) or political fights (such as the one which opposed "Raiders" and "Managers" during the 1980s), the development of legal "class actions" has submitted an increasing number of large firms to the growing threat of huge punitive damages. Increasingly important governance issues reflect how difficult it has become to determine who governs, or, for that matter, who should govern, a firm. (To understand how this translates in the area of management and insurance, it is necessary to examine the transformation undergone by science. This requires that we devote more attention to the epistemological foundations of the system of legitimacy; see below.)

With these facts in mind, it is possible to begin to determine when a big risk becomes so big that it deserves to be called a "major risk." We defined "major risk" as occurring when a firm becomes so big that it cannot be said to be submitted to the laws of the market. The social acceptability of its actions can no longer be guaranteed a priori by its submission to legal rules. This explains why a crisis may result from a minimal event (e.g., a rumor) and reveals how risks involving questions of legitimacy (e.g., suspicions concerning a firm's conformity to legal norms) or pragmatic risks overlap to the point of interfering with each other. On the one hand, suspicions of illegitimate behavior will affect a firm's performance; on the other hand, bad performance is readily interpreted as a symptom of illegitimate management rather than as a normal consequence of market uncertainties. Before turning to the management of "major risks," it is important to consider the evolution of the epistemological paradigms characteristic of the rational-legal system.

The History of Epistemological Paradigms and Their Symbolic Structures

An action can be defined, phenomenologically, in the following manner: a change in appearances inasmuch as it is attributed to a cause.

It is possible to show that there are logically only three manners of legitimizing an action thus defined. They correspond to the three periods in the history of the rule of law described above, reinforcing the hypothesis that each modification of the rule of law corresponds to a modification of the associated underlying scientific paradigm and consequently (as the legitimacy of management lies in its submission to the legal rule on one hand and to scientific knowledge on the other) to a modification of the status of management. For each period, we shall describe the corresponding epistemological paradigm and devote some attention to the status of certainty and complexity.

1. *If the cause is legitimate, the action is legitimate.*

The first case we have to consider corresponds to the case when the legitimacy of an action relies on the origin of power.

This situation corresponds to an epistemology where nature is strictly separated from culture. Here, legitimacy *is not pragmatic* to the extent that the process of legitimization is not related to "the change in appearances." This corresponds to the first stage of the history described above. This paradigm, in its fully developed form, corresponds to Kant's epistemology; as a matter of fact, *The Critique of Pure Reason* is devoted to an epistemological account of Newton's theory. Both Adam Smith and Jean-Baptiste Say consider their own approaches to the science of the market as "Newtonian," and to this extent it can be said that they share the same epistemological principles (Laufer, 1990). From the point of view of the notion of certainty, it is worth noting that the laws of science are considered deterministic.

The status of the notion of complexity can be traced in the following two ways:

- by the number of scientific fields of knowledge defined within the epistemological paradigm;
- by the degree of confusion between the laws governing nature and those governing culture. The name of the confusion between nature and culture being the artificial, this confusion is measured by the part played by the artificial in the epistemology. The notion of art from which is derived the notion of artificial comes from "ars," which is the Latin translation of the Greek "techne." Consequently, the confusion of nature and culture can also be measured by the role played by technique in the epistemology.

On the one hand, the epistemology considered here corresponds to a single science (mathematical physics in the realm of the science of nature, market economics in the realm of the science of society). On the other hand, nature is, by definition, strictly separated from culture. Thus technique plays no role in this epistemology and consequently in the system of legitimacy.

In addition, we may note that opinion plays no role in this epistemological paradigm, as everybody has equal access to the "glasses" of science. Consequently, rhetoric—a technique that deals with opinion—does not play any role in it either.

2. The relation between nature and culture becomes somewhat confused, however much a consensus on measurement is guaranteed.

If the limits between nature and culture are no longer well defined, one can no longer legitimize an action by its cause (as it is no longer clearly defined). One must now rely on a measurement of the change in appearances. Legitimacy becomes pragmatic. Two cases may then be distinguished according to whether it can be assumed that a consensus on measurement will necessarily be reached (moderate pragmatism) or not (radical pragmatism).

This corresponds to a *positivistic* epistemology. Legitimacy now lies in the finality of action; that is, the measure of the change in appearances on which, by definition, there is a consensus. This corresponds to the second stage of the history of the rule of law described above.

The major characteristics of the epistemological model discussed here are taken from the work of Auguste Comte, one of the major proponents of positivism.[35] He considered the world to be divided into various domains, each corresponding to a field of specialized scientific knowledge. Limits between sciences had to be strictly respected; "*multidisciplinarity*" was, as a result, strictly prohibited.

Given the confusion between nature and culture, the processes of legitimization of action require the existence of a principle that guarantees the positive inherent social value of the consequences of scientific knowledge (i.e., a belief in progress).

One of the central aspects of this epistemology is the status it gives to descriptions of *closed systems*. This implies a certain degree of complexity as the world is now composed of multiple entities. Borders—be they those of a country, those of an organization, or those that separate the various specialized functional components of an organization (according to the principles of the division of labor)—play a central role in the symbolic system that allows us to describe legitimate actions.

Certainty is a central characteristic of scientific knowledge, which is deterministic. It is the combination of determinism, division of labor, and the belief in progress that lends its force to the notion of the "one best way" central to scientific management.

Given that we have hypothesized a certain degree of confusion between nature and culture, the artificial now plays a role in the epistemology, and technique can be attributed a status. (Auguste Comte says that mathematics are less important as a special science than as an "artifact" useful to all other sciences.)

At this juncture, opinion plays a role in the epistemological paradigm. Those who have direct access to knowledge (specialists of a given, specialized field of knowledge) and those who do not (the others) have a different relationship to knowledge. Rhetoric, the technique of shaping opinion, now has a role in the realm of science. In the name of "pedagogy," those who know communicate their knowledge to those who do not.

3. If there is no more a priori consensus on the measurement of "the change in appearances," the consensus must be produced pragmatically.

The confusion between nature and culture leads to the radicalization of complexity and to the generalization of the category that corresponds to it (i.e., to the confusion between nature and culture): the artificial. Science becomes the science of the artificial, the architecture of complexity; that is, the science of systems as defined by Herbert Simon. The products of science are descriptions, *simulations* of the world via "entities and flows"— in pragmatic terms, charts made of "circles" and "arrows." The validity of these simulations depends entirely on the conformity of the depicted behavior to the phenomena considered. No longer does anything guarantee the determinism characteristic of the processes inherent to the natural sciences defined by Kant and Comte.

How can one measure the legitimacy of an action; that is, how it is possible, under these circumstances, to reach a consensus on the ways of measuring "the change in appearances"? The answer is quite pragmatic: One need only consider measurement itself as an action. *A measurement becomes legitimate insofar as people consider it so.* The legitimacy of science lies now in *the methods used* to measure. These methods are legitimate to the extent that they are considered to be so.

The crisis of the system of legitimacy—evidenced by the fact that determinism is no longer guaranteed—corresponds to the development of "major risk." Humanity's horizon has become uncertain.

The science of the artificial is characterized by descriptions of the world as composed of open systems. This implies that limits and borders are no longer defined in a clear, precise, and unambiguous way. The crisis of the system of legitimacy corresponds to the crisis of the ability to have a stable consensus on the description provided by scientific knowledge. Multidisciplinarity is the name of the new knowledge game.

Science is no longer deterministic. The "one best way"—which once ensured the legitimacy of the scientific manager—is replaced by unexpected outcomes and perverse side effects. With open systems, it is no longer possible to define causal chains in an unambiguous manner. The "circles" and "arrows" that describe a given situation can always be redefined. The world is not only more uncertain than it used to be but has also become complex; not only is it composed of parts (subsystems) but these subsystems are "open systems," making it impossible to define their number or borders with any certainty. As a consequence, not only do different models lead to different results, but different results can be interpreted in different ways. In this light, "major risk" can be defined as a consequence of the indetermination of causal chains.

Indeed, opinion and science can no longer be clearly separated. Rhetoric, the technique of opinion management, now plays a central role in the production and reception of scientific knowledge[36] (Toulmin, 1958). According to Aristotle, rhetoric is characterized by the fact that it conjointly uses arguments from three sources: *pathos, ethos,* and *logos.* This can be related to the fact that the crisis of the legal-rational system of legitimacy implies that henceforth the underpinning of the beliefs of public opinion may be found in any of the three types of legitimate authority defined by Max Weber: charisma (which corresponds to *pathos*), tradition (which corresponds to *ethos*), and reason (which corresponds to *logos*).

It is increasingly difficult to distinguish between science and technique. Nuclear energy, genetic engineering, and information processing are known as "techno-sciences." At the symbolic level, this corresponds to the fact that there is complete confusion between nature and culture. The crisis of legitimacy corresponds to the reign of the artificial, which itself corresponds to the supremacy of technique, as is revealed by the etymology of the word "artificial," which comes from "art," the Latin translation of "techne."

We are now in a position to better understand the mutation undergone by the principle of "insurance." The fact that limits and borders and causal chains can no longer be defined in a clear, unambiguous way leads to a degree of confusion between the notions of speculative risk and pure risk: It becomes more and more difficult to distinguish between the risks one takes willingly and those that are the result of an unexpected sequence of events. For insurance companies, the effects of moral hazard, adverse selection, and the size of risks are among the many challenges they have to face. Kenneth Arrow writes: "the insurer cannot define completely its risks, in most cases he can only observe a result which is a mix of the unavoidable risk he is ready to ensure and of human decisions" (Arrow, 1970). Thus, the differences between banking and insurance tend to be blurred. Deregulation allows these two types of activities to mix; new financial instruments are invented that link the logic of finance with that of insurance. Insurance is developed for areas such as "product liability," ever closer to the primary objectives of the firm itself. The question of the limits of insurability become central to the insurance industry.[37]

Conclusion

In order to understand the historical transformations that have led to the development of "major risk," it has been necessary to devote our attention to the institutions that determine the social acceptability of managerial actions. These institutions are constituted by a system of shared symbols, of which scientific knowledge and legal norms are key elements. Social actors can rely on these symbols to justify their actions.

It has been shown that today, legal norms and scientific knowledge no longer provide the social legitimacy of actions a priori. Thus, it has become necessary to produce, alongside any given action, the conditions that will ensure its legitimacy. Henceforth, the legitimacy of a firm depends on its ability to produce a socially acceptable, symbolic representation of its actions. This new requirement implies a deep—strategic—mutation within management, of which crisis management is but one of the most noteworthy and visible symptoms.

The symbolic disorders undergone by social institutions are reflected in the many paradoxes that characterize the notions of "major risk" and crisis management. The fact of not having devoted any time to the question of how to manage specific crises in and of themselves may be considered yet another expression of these paradoxes. The success of crisis management depends in very large part on what is done before and after a crisis actually occurs. Focusing on these two moments is an essential prerequisite for establishing an efficient system of crisis management. Before the occurrence of a crisis, the structure of the firm's activities and processes must be developed according to the principles of "the management of the impossible," which corresponds to what firms must (and can) do while waiting for the unexpected. It is only after the occurrence of a crisis that one can reap the lessons of experience through postcrisis analysis and derive from this analysis new insights that can be brought to bear on the way in which the firm, as well as all the other social actors involved, will prepare for the unexpected in the future.

Notes

1. This is the opinion expressed by Judge Richard Posner (Seventh Circuit U.S. Court of Appeals) in the ruling in *Matter of Rhone-Poulenc Rorer, Inc.*, 51 F 3d 1293 (7th Cir. 1995).

2. *Oxford Dictionary*, 10th edition, 1999.

3. Freud's example is the following: "A borrows a cauldron from B. After A has restituted it to B, B complains that there is a hole in the cauldron. The defense of A goes then as follows: first I never borrowed the cauldron, then it already had a hole when I borrowed it, and anyway when I gave it back it had no hole in it" (Freud, 1916, New York, Moffat, Yard and Company).

4. First moment: expectation is defined as $ei = \Sigma$ i from 1 to n $(piVi)$. Second moment: variance is defined as $vi = \Sigma$ i from 1 to n, pi $(Vi-V)$ square were V is the mean of the Vi's.

5. It may noted that this is coherent with the fact that "major risk" has been defined as corresponding to the breakdown of common sense.

6. For instance, the way in which eating fast food in the United States is increasingly considered a health hazard to the point of leading to the development of legal class actions may be given as another similar example.

7. This reference to Cassandra was made by several respondents in an unpublished study of risk management conducted in large French firms.

8. To better understand the nature of these paradoxes, it may be useful to refer to Watzlawick's works (Watzlawick et al., 1967; Watzlawick, 1990).

9. Douglas, M., *Dealing With Uncertainty*, op. cit. p. 154.

10. Knight notes that this definition is opposed to "Irving Fisher's contention that there is only one estimate, the subjective feeling of probability itself" (Knight, 1922/1972, p. 227).

11. Approved by Health Canada in 1999 as a treatment for osteoarthritis, it was voluntarily withdrawn from the market in 2004, when it was discovered that it could increase the risk of cardiovascular events (www.merchantlaw.com/vioxx.html).

12. This way of organizing the topic can be justified conceptually. The two first categories correspond to the ways in which Hans Kelsen (1967) and Alexandre Kojeve (1981) respectively define a legal system. For Kelsen, law is a system of norms. For Kojeve, a legal system is characterized by the intervention of independent third parties. The third category can be considered as what results from the breakdown of the two preceding definitions.

13. We may note that the empirical analysis of the social psychology of organizing assumes that there is a space, defined at the local level, where it is possible to observe the interactions that participate in the construction of the organization. This leaves open the question of knowing how this place (or commonplace, as it is what allows the possibility of constructive rhetorical interactions) itself has been built, and ultimately on which institutional underpinning its enacting is made possible in a given context. The fact that a crisis tends to destabilize the very limits that allowed the observation of organizational process is what requires a shift from the level of conventional interactions to the level of the analysis of the institutional presuppositions that govern any social action.

14. Posner R., op.cit.

15. Aristotle, *Nicomachean Ethics*, 1140–23–25.

16. Auguste Comte, *Cours de Philosophie Positive*, pp. 31–32, quoted in Laufer and Paradeise, 1990, p. 178.

17. Among the productions linked to this effort of codification of chaotic situations, see Leben and Caron (2001). In the work of Habermas and more recently that of Latour and Callon, one may find theoretical justifications for this types of negotiation processes (Callon et al., 2001; Habermas, 1986; Latour, 1999).

18. The system of fire prevention can be considered as one of the oldest and the most enduring organizations resulting from the need to manage a "specific major risk."

19. See above, note 2.

20. However, recently, a method has been developed that allows us to analyze this component of the system of legitimacy of Western countries (Laufer, 2002). Given that its development is not required to develop the general principles of the management of "major risks," it will not be dealt with here any further.

21. This line of reasoning is in accordance with the distinction made by Kant between the *noumenon*, the thing in itself, which cannot be the object of scientific knowledge, and the *phenomenon*, that which can be perceived, which can, given the existence of categories of perception that allow us to give a precise status to its measure.

22. This refers to the work of Austin in the field of the philosophy of language.

23. The various dates quoted above can be found in *Le Robert: Dictionnaire Historique de la Langue Française*, Paris, 1998.

24. Whereas the global crisis of the system of legitimacy affecting charisma could be called the *unspeakable* ("l'innomable") or the horrid, and the global

crisis of the system of legitimacy affecting tradition the *indescribable* (which imply that one can speak but cannot finds words to describe the situation).

25. From a methodological point of view, the approach proposed here is an application of Max Weber ideal-type theory. The extension is that it will be proposed that it is possible to define an ideal-typical description of history, which Max Weber would have opposed, in spite of the fact that his description of the routinization of charisma can be considered an example of such an ideal-typical description of historical processes (Weber, 1961).

26. This may be considered one of the reasons why the notion of legitimacy developed by Max Weber has been all but forgotten by social scientists for so many years: In the legal-rational system of legitimacy, the notion of legitimacy is not legitimate; at the institutional level, all that counts is what is defined as legal.

27. That this argument is not just an ex post facto analysis can be shown by the fact that the analysis of the crisis of legitimacy was already elaborated during the 1970s (Laufer, 1977). However, at that time, this crisis was not linked to the notion of the management of "major risk" or even to crisis management, but to public management (Laufer & Berlaud, 1980). It was only at the end of the 1980s that a demand made by the French Ministry of Environment led to an analysis of the attitude of firms faced with "major risks." "Major risk" appeared, then, as being nothing but an expression, albeit the most extreme expression, of the crisis of legitimacy (Laufer, 1993). Another indication of the accuracy of this historical hypothesis is the emergence of sociological and philosophical approaches of the notion of legitimacy, which had been somewhat left aside since Max Weber's time (Boltanski & Thevenot, 1991; Habermas, 1975). Similarly, in economics, this period witnessed the development of institutional economics (Williamson, 1975).

28. We may note that profit maximization implies also the existence of an anthropological hypothesis relative to the fact that economic actors do wish to maximize profit: This hypothesis has been developed in Max Weber's major opus, *Capitalism and the Spirit of Capitalism*. To this issue is linked all the literature that developed on what has been called the achievement motive (McClelland, 1961).

29. This distinction between pragmatic risk and risk in terms of legitimacy can be exemplified also by the way François, the first King of France, described his situation after a terrible defeat at Pavie: "All is lost, but for the honor," honor being, according to Montesquieu, the principle of Aristocracy.

30. The fact that this corresponds to a crisis in the system of legitimacy can be seen by studying the legal and social conflicts that resulted in and from the establishment of antitrust laws in the United States. However, after a transition period, this crisis was ultimately resolved within the framework of the free-market principle.

31. On the history that led to this innovation (Ewald, 1986).

32. William J. Baumol developed a model in which the firms were supposed to maximize sales (a measure of the power of managers) under the constraint of a given level of profit (corresponding to what the shareholders would consider satisfactory).

33. The fact that the present period is characterized by the return of bankruptcy of huge firms such as Enron or Andersen Consulting must be analyzed in this context. Is it a sign of crisis of legitimacy, or, as some have said in American economic newspapers, proof that the system is working well? One should also take into account the actual meaning of bankruptcy as defined by Chapter 11.

34. The antitrust judge had stated that competition required the existence of four competitors: GM, Ford, Chrysler, and American Motors.

35. This summary of some of the major characteristics of this epistemological model is taken from the work of Auguste Comte, which can be considered as one of its most elaborate presentations. A more detailed presentation of this paradigm may be found in Laufer and Paradeise (1990, pp. 175–182). While it is argued that this model has a general value, as can be seen in the description of Taylorism (legitimation by the finality of action, the principle of specialization and division of labor, the central role of measurement), it must be acknowledged that other versions exist (as that represented by the work of John Stuart Mill, who had, for a while, been in direct contact with Auguste Comte). From our point of view here the major difference might lie in the status of probability. But probability is not uncertainty, as we have seen above when dealing with the issue of the establishment of insurance systems.

36. For a parallel analysis of the role of rhetoric in Law, see Perelman, 1977.

37. *Limits of Insurability of Risks,* Geneva Papers no. 39, April 1986.

Bibliography

Aggeri, F., Pezet, E., Abrassart, C., & Acquier, A. (2005). *Organiser le développement durable, expériences des entreprises pionnières et formation des règles d'action collective.* Paris: Vuibert.

Arnold, T. (1937). *The folklore of capitalism.* New Haven, CT: Yale University Press.

Arrow, K. (1970). *Essays on risk bearing.* Amsterdam: North Holland.

Austin, J. L. (1962). *How to do things with words.* Oxford, UK: Clarendon Press.

Barnard, C. (1938). *The function of the executive.* Cambridge, MA: Harvard University Press.

Barnes, J. (Ed.). (1984). *The complete works of Aristotle: The revised Oxford translation.* Princeton, NJ: Princeton University Press.

Baumol, W. J. (1959). *Business behavior, value and growth.* New York: Macmillan.

Beardon, C., Berleur, J., & Laufer, R. (1993). *Facing the challenges of risks and vulnerability of an information society.* Amsterdam: North-Holland.

Berle, A. A., & Means, G. C. (1932). *The modern corporation and private property.* New York: Macmillan.

Boltanski, L., & Thevenot, L. (1991). *De la justification: Les economies de la grandeurs.* Paris: Gallimard.

Brown, D. (2003). *The Da Vinci code.* New York: Random House.

Callon, M., Lascoumes, P., & Barthes, Y. (2001). *Agir dans un monde incertain, essai sur la démocratie technique.* Paris: Le Seuil.

Chandler, A. D. (1977). *The visible hand: The managerial revolution in American business.* Cambridge, MA: Harvard Belknap.

Douglas, M. (1986). *Risk acceptability according to the social sciences.* London: Routledge and Kegan Paul.

Douglas, M. (2001). Dealing with uncertainty. *Ethical Perspectives, 8*(3), 145–155.

Ewald, F. (1986). *L'Etat providence.* Paris: Fayard.

Freud, S. (1916). *Wit and its relationship to the unconscious.* New York: Moffat, Yard and Company.

Grandy, C. (1993). Original intent and the Sherman Act: A re-examination of the Consumer-Welfare hypothesis. *The Journal of Economic History, 53*(2), 359–376.

Habermas, J. (1975). *Legitimacy crisis.* Boston: Beacon Press.

Habermas, J. (1986). *Morale et communication: Conscience morale et action communicationnelle.* Paris: CERF.

Kelsen, H. (1967). *Pure theory of law.* Berkeley: University of California Press.

Knight, F. H. (1972). *Risk, uncertainty and profit.* Chicago: University of Chicago Press. (Original work published 1922)

Kojeve, A. (1981). *Esquisse d'une phénoménologie du droit.* Paris: Gallimard.

Lagadec, P. (1988). *Etat d'urgence: Défaillance technologique et déstabilisation sociale.* Paris: Seuil.

Laufer, R. (1977). Crise de légitimité dans les grandes organisations. *Revue Française de Gestion, 9.*

Laufer, R. (1993). *L'Entreprise face aux risques majeurs: A propos de l'incertitude des normes sociales.* Paris: L'Harmattan, coll. Logiques sociales.

Laufer, R. (2002). Les figures de l'espoir. In R. Laufer & A. Hatchuel, *Le libéralisme, l'innovation et la question des limites.* Paris: L'Harmattan, coll. Ouverture Philosophique.

Laufer, R., & Burlaud, A. (1980). *Management public: Gestion et légitimité.* Paris: Dalloz.

Laufer, R., & Paradeise, C. (1990). *Marketing democracy: Public opinion and media formation in democratic society.* New Brunswick, NJ: Transaction.

Latour, B. (1999). *La politique de la nature: Comment faire entrer les sciences en démocratie.* Paris: La Découverte.

Leben, C., & Caron, D. D. (2001). *The international aspects of natural and industrial catastrophes.* Leiden: Martinus Nijhoff.

Lomborg, B. (2004). *Global crisis, global solution.* Cambridge, UK: Cambridge University Press.

McClelland, D. C. (1961). *The achieving society.* Princeton, NJ: D. Van Nostrand.

Means, G., & Berle, A. (1991). *Modern corporation and private property.* New Brunswick, NJ: Transaction. (Original work published 1938)

Morrison, A. B. (1988). How independent are independent regulatory agencies? *Duke Law Review,* pp. 252–256.

Nader, R. (1965). *Unsafe at any speed: The designed-in dangers of the American automobile.* New York: Grossman.

Perelman, C. (1977). *Logique juridique.* Paris: Dalloz.

Perrow, C. (1999). *Normal accident: Living with high risk technologies.* Princeton, NJ: Princeton University Press.

Posner, R. *In the Matter of Rhone-Poulenc Rorer, Inc.,* 51 F 3d 1293 (7th Cir. 1995).

Toulmin, S. (1958). *The uses of argument.* Cambridge, UK: Cambridge University Press.

Watzlawick, P. (1990). *Münchhausen's pigtail, or psychotherapy and reality.* New York: W. W. Norton.

Watzlawick, P., Beavin, J. H., & Jackson, D. D. (1967). *Pragmatics of human communications: A study of interactional patterns, pathologies and paradoxes.* New York: W. W. Norton.

Weber, M. (1961). *The three types of legitimate rule* (H. Gerth, Trans.). In A. Etzioni (Ed.), *Complex organizations.* New York: Holt, Rinehart and Winston.

Weick, K. (1969). *Social psychology of organizing.* Reading, MA: Addison-Wesley.
Weick, K. (2001). *Managing the unexpected.* San Francisco: Jossey-Bass.
Weick, K. E., & Sutcliffe, K. M. (2001). *Managing the unexpected: Assuring high performance in an age of complexity.* San Francisco: Jossey-Bass.
Weil, E. (1991). L'Anthropologie d'Aristote. In *Essais et conférences* (Vol. 1, p. 29). Paris: Vrin.
Williamson, O. (1975). *Markets and hierarchy, analysis and antitrust implications.* New York: Free Press.

Understanding and Managing Crises in an "Online World"

3

Sarah Kovoor-Misra
and Manavendra Misra

Given the pervasive use of online technology in conducting business today, it is important to understand the threats inherent in the online environment. The academic literature on crisis management has not sufficiently studied online forms of crises and their implications for crisis management. This paper discusses why the online environment creates vulnerabilities for organizations, the various forms of crises that may threaten organizations, strategies for crisis management, and implications for future research.

After the Bhopal and *Challenger* disasters in the 1980s, we have seen increased interest in the academic literature on the subject of crisis management. Crises are events, situations, or trends that can threaten the survival or goals of an organization (Nystrom & Starbuck, 1984). Researchers have provided key insights into the causes of crises and their manifestations, and have prescribed strategies for crisis management (Pearson & Mitroff, 1993).

The last 20 years have also seen radical changes in the business environment, particularly as it pertains to crisis management. The Internet has transformed business communications and operations and new forms of threats have emerged. In February 2000, for instance, a 14-year-old hacker from Montreal, Canada, using the screen name "MafiaBoy," launched denial-of-service attacks on some of the most prominent Web sites. He singlehandedly brought down the Web sites of companies such as Yahoo!, Amazon, eBay, Buy.com, E*Trade, Datek Online, and CNN. It is estimated that the resulting downtime at these companies caused more than $1.7 billion in damages.[1] At approximately the same time, a hacker named "Curador" claimed to have hacked into at least eight e-commerce sites and stole over 23,000 credit card numbers. He then proceeded to post these stolen numbers on his Web site (Borland, 2000).

These new threats are not only relevant for "pure play" online organizations (those that are totally reliant on the online medium for the delivery of their product or service) but also provide an avenue for attacking more traditional companies that may have an online presence (i.e., either a Web site or an online distribution channel). Today, many traditional brick-and-mortar organizations in banking, retailing, and education have established online operations. With the maturing of the Internet as a medium for conducting business, it is important to take stock of and understand the threats inherent in the online environment and how organizations can be better prepared to manage them.

The academic literature on crisis management, however, has not kept abreast with some of these changes. Relatively little attention has been paid to understanding the threats inherent in the online environment, the forms these threats may take, how they fit into existing categorizations of crises, and their implications for crisis management. In this chapter we seek to fill some of these gaps in the literature. The chapter examines why the online environment creates vulnerabilities for organizations. We discuss the various forms of online crises that have emerged and where they fit in existing crisis frameworks, and then suggest strategies for crisis management and directions for future research.

Threats in the Online Environment

Organizations differ in their reliance on the online environment for their business operations. There are "pure play" organizations such as Amazon.com that are totally reliant on the online medium for the delivery of their product or service. Other organizations may be "bricks and clicks" such as banks and stores that have traditional brick-and-mortar outlets but also use the Internet for offering their product or service. However, most organizations use online technology to communicate information and conduct day-to-day operations. In this section, we discuss some of the attributes of the online environment that create crisis vulnerability for organizations.

EASY ACCESSIBILITY, A DOUBLE-EDGED SWORD

The World Wide Web allows users anywhere in the world to have access to a company's Web site 24 hours a day. Geography and time are therefore not significant constraints to reaching customers. However, the same attribute that allows an organization to reach a worldwide audience also allows a malicious attack to be launched from geographically distant points at any time of the day. For example, the Mafiaboy attacks described before originated in Canada but overwhelmed a number of U.S.-based companies. In another case, May Day 2001 saw a number of attacks from Chinese activists against a number of U.S. government sites in order to protest the U.S. handling of the spy-plane-collision crisis. Furthermore, the cross-border nature of these incidents makes it very difficult for authorities in one country to pursue the perpetrators in another. For instance, the creator of the "Love Bug" virus could not be indicted, as there were no laws addressing computer attacks in the Philippines.[2] In contrast, for individuals to shut down all outlets of a large brick-and-mortar company, a significant amount of organization is needed to bring people to each physical location. Thus, geography can be a deterrent to physical threats for brick-and-mortar organizations. Organizations that rely on the online medium lack this deterrent.

CENTRALIZED OPERATIONS

Exacerbating the vulnerability of these organizations is the fact that online operations tend to be centralized. The Web sites run off servers located in one data center, which creates a single point of failure that may be exploited either inadvertently or maliciously. Even those companies that can afford multiple data centers typically have no more than a few. This means that any kind of an outage, whether a systems outage or a malicious attack, has the potential to prevent the company from generating any revenue from its online operations.

THE ARCHITECTURE OF THE INTERNET

In addition to centralized operations, many organizations with an online presence are vulnerable because of the architecture of the Internet itself. Since the Internet was designed as a research collaboration tool, it lacks significant security mechanisms built into it. Unlike the telephone network, where it is extremely difficult for an end-user to get access to the control components of the network, the Internet has both the transport and the control on a single network. All the control devices, such as routers and switches, are accessible by the same Internet Protocol (IP) addressing mechanism that a user uses to access Web servers. This means that a hacker could access devices on the Internet infrastructure and cause them to crash, in turn preventing a number of Web sites from being accessed.

HIGH VOLUMES OF CUSTOMER DATA

Unlike a brick-and-mortar retail store, where a customer can come in and anonymously buy products, the very nature of e-commerce results in Internet-based companies collecting a large volume of data on customers such as names, credit card numbers, and addresses. A large database of personal information that is also accessible to potential saboteurs anywhere in the world creates a vulnerability to crises. In January 2000, a hacker calling himself "Maxus" claimed to have stolen 350,000 credit card numbers from online store CD Universe and demanded $100,000 from the company in return for these numbers (Borland, 2000). Loss of sensitive customer data makes these organizations vulnerable to economic losses, a negative image, and potential legal liability.

24/7 OPERATION

Further compounding these problems is the fact that Internet-based organizations have little down time to solve problems that may occur in their systems. They are open to their customers 24 hours a day, 7 days a week. As a result, problem-solving becomes difficult as it is most often done while being operational. Brick-and-mortar companies, on the other hand, often have the luxury of addressing problems during off-hours.

HIGH VISIBILITY

Exacerbating all of these issues is the fact that operational problems in online organizations are also highly visible. If a site is down, for instance, that information is available to anyone tracking the site. In addition, the hype that has surrounded the Internet has resulted in inordinate media coverage of the "dot-coms." This has made it more attractive for hackers that are seeking attention or notoriety to make such companies targets of their attacks. The high visibility also affects how the investment community perceives the company. A major crisis can cause a severe drop in market capitalization for these organizations. For example, a June 1999 outage at eBay caused its stock price to drop by 20%.[3]

QUICK DISSEMINATION OF INFORMATION AND A WELL-CONNECTED CLIENTELE

The Internet medium also allows for the quick dissemination of information and the spread of rumors. Through mass mailings, chat groups, and fraudulent Web sites, rumors can be spread quickly and persist.

Caribou Coffee, for example, had to dispel a two-year-old rumor that it was linked to Islamic terrorists. This rumor cost them sales in the Jewish community. Procter and Gamble has also had to battle rumors that it is linked to Satan, as some individuals believed they saw the number 666 in the company's logo. Procter and Gamble subsequently changed its logo (Schmeltzer, 2004).

Furthermore, Internet organizations need to be vigilant as their consumers tend to be highly connected through e-mail as well as discussion and chat groups and dissatisfaction can spread quickly between them. To organize a grassroots boycott campaign against a major brick-and-mortar chain requires significant organizing capability and considerable time and resources. The connectedness of consumers in online organizations enables dissatisfied consumers to quickly put pressure on the organization to respond. In 1999, for instance, a lawsuit was filed by eToys against a group of artists who owned the etoy.com domain name. These artists, lacking the resources of the larger organization, launched a counterattack through the Internet called Toywar. Using e-mail, discussion groups, and Web sites, the small organization was able to mobilize thousands of activists from many countries in a concerted boycott and public-relations campaign against eToys. Finally, eToys was forced to drop the lawsuit.[4] The Toywar was a successful campaign because eToys was able to recruit numerous activists over the online medium.

HIGHLY MOTIVATED HACKER COMMUNITY

Unlike other industries, the online sector has associated with it a hacker community that is technologically savvy and motivated to identify flaws in the technology of these firms. These hackers are often driven by the need to gain attention or notoriety, or simply by the challenge of beating a well-designed technology system. Easy accessibility enables these individuals to demonstrate their technological expertise by bringing down a site. Unlike the brick-and-mortar world, where an organized group is often needed to do any harm, these hackers can single-handedly cause major damage. Most physical retail stores budget for a small amount of petty theft in the form of shoplifting, or "shrinkage" of inventory, but the damage here is akin to having shoplifters who can shut down the whole company on their own! The examples of Mafiaboy, Curador, and Maxus described above highlight these dangers.

To summarize, easy accessibility, centralized operations, insufficient built-in security in the Internet architecture, being open 24 hours a day and 7 days a week, high visibility, the quick dissemination of rumors, a connected Internet community, and motivated hackers all contribute to the crisis vulnerability of online organizations. In the next section, we examine various forms of crises that organizations with an online presence may experience, and we discuss those that are specific to online organizations and those that are shared with traditional organizations.

Forms of Online Crises

Crises may be caused by a combination of individual and organizational failures or by changes in an organization's environment that put pressure on the organization to respond (Hambrick & D'Aveni, 1988; Kovoor-Misra, Clair, & Bettenhausen, 2001; Pauchant & Mitroff, 1992; Shrivastava, 1987; Turner, 1976). For example, crises such as denial-of-service attacks can be attributed to insufficient security in the current technology of online organizations to differentiate between spurious and legitimate customer requests and individuals with malicious intent interested in attacking the organization. As another example, the deaths of many dot-coms, such as mvp.com, garden.com, and WebVan.com, can be attributed to their inability to compete in an increasingly resource-scarce environment.

Crises also tend to be multidimensional, with multiple crises present in the same situation, often with one crisis triggering others (Kovoor-Misra, 1995; Pearson & Mitroff, 1993). In the Napster crisis, for example, where the organization was being sued by the recording industry, the economic survival of the company was at stake, the organization's reputation was threatened, and the organization had to deal with the ensuing legal issues. When hackers attack an organization, it has to protect its technology and its reputation and minimize economic losses that could ensue. Thus, an organization is very often confronted with multiple crises that require attention.

Crises may take various forms. Researchers in crisis management have categorized the forms of crises that threaten traditional companies (Fink, 1986; Pearson & Mitroff, 1993). For example, crises may be classified based on whether they are technical-economic or human and social on one axis, and severe versus normal on another (Pearson & Mitroff, 1993). Another way of classifying crises is to categorize them by the dimension of the organization where their triggering causes originate or the dimension that they primarily impact (Kovoor-Misra, 1995). Thus, an organization may face technical, economic, human and social, legal, and political crises.

This same categorization scheme can be used to classify online crises. However, the examples of crises within each category may be different from those experienced by traditional organizations. Table 3.1 uses this scheme to highlight some general crises that online organizations share with traditional companies, and crises that are specific to them.

Below, we describe five of these crises: Web site failures, denial-of-service attacks, virtual blackmail and sabotage, virtual boycotts, and copyright and privacy issues that we believe are currently most salient to online

Table 3.1 Some Types of Crises for Online Organizations

Category	General Crises (shared with traditional organizations)	Online Crises (specific to online organizations)
1. Technical Crises (Caused by failures in the technology core or may impact it)	Loss of database	Web site failure
2. Human and Social Crises (Caused by people-related dysfunctions or may have serious consequences for individuals' psychological or physical health)	Workplace violence Strikes Bomb threats	Denial-of-service attacks Virtual blackmail
3. Public Relations Crises (Adversely affects the organizational reputation and relationship with external stakeholders)	Negative publicity	Negative publicity associated with online-specific crises
4. Legal Crises (Caused by perceived violation of the law)	Violations of relevant laws	Copyright and privacy violations (not specific to online organizations but currently salient)

organizations. We also describe how these crises trigger other crises. The extent to which any of these situations would rise to crisis potential would depend on their scope and impact. Crises, as we have indicated, are those situations that could threaten the survival or goals of an organization; hence, if these situations have serious economic, human, and social or reputational costs to the organization, they would be considered a crisis.

WEB SITE FAILURES

Web site failures are technical crises as failures occur in the technical core of online organizations. These failures may be due to a number of reasons, such as glitches in software or a poor system architectural design. Web sites in Internet-based organizations are also vulnerable to high volumes of traffic and problems with their external networks. Web traffic to the sites of online organizations tends to be highly cyclical and often unpredictable. There are cycles with well-defined peaks during the day, as well as cycles during the year. Since a number of e-commerce companies serve the gift market, they have significant peaks around gift-giving occasions. Toy sites, for instance, see tenfold jumps in traffic during the 6 weeks preceding Christmas. In 1999, almost every major e-commerce site had problems because they under-estimated the volume of traffic that they would receive. Toysrus.com, for instance, was overwhelmed by traffic generated by the mailing of their "big-book" of coupons that promised discounts to shoppers on the Web site. Most companies had to throttle traffic coming to their sites, resulting in large numbers of customers either not being able to access their site or seeing extremely slow page download times.[5] This resulted in the maturing of an industry niche in 2000. Service companies such as Mercury Interactive developed technologies to provide realistic load-testing of sites so that e-commerce sites could better prepare themselves for the upcoming peak season.

In addition, Web site problems for online organizations may also be precipitated because of problems in external networks that prevent customers from getting to their sites. In March 2001, for instance, the Yahoo! advanced services (Instant Messaging, Mail, MyYahoo) were unavailable for a day to a large section of the population because of a problem with a global-crossing router in Denver.

Web site outages for the prominent Internet-based organizations result in tremendous media scrutiny. Thus, the organization also must deal with the related public-relations issues and maintain customer confidence. In addition, inability to access Web sites also results in a loss of revenue and in some cases can significantly hurt the market valuation of a public company, as experienced by eBay and discussed earlier in the chapter.

DENIAL-OF-SERVICE ATTACKS

A denial-of-service attack is an example of a crisis in the human and social category. These crises are caused by individuals with malicious intent who bring down a company's Web site. As we have noted, the accessibility of online organizations makes it relatively easy to attack a company's Web servers from multiple machines that all generate spurious requests for Web pages. It is hard for the Web site to distinguish real requests from spurious requests. Real customers, therefore, start seeing slow response times, and eventually the servers crash. Companies with a single point of failure in any piece of their systems architecture are particularly susceptible to accidental or maliciously caused shutdowns at this "Achilles' heel."

In June 2004, Akamai, whose servers provide content distribution for the Web sites of Microsoft Corp., Google Inc., and Yahoo! Inc., experienced a denial-of-service attack that slowed down the Web sites of these companies (Associated Press, 2004). Denial-of-service attacks trigger Web site failures and public-relations issues as an organization's technical vulnerabilities are exposed. Also, there may be a loss of revenue if customers are unable to access the Web site. The organization in these cases also has to work with law-enforcement agencies such as the FBI to track down these hackers.

VIRTUAL BLACKMAIL AND SABOTAGE BY HACKERS

This is another example of a human and social crisis where saboteurs may steal information from a company's databases by locating security holes in their software. In 2001, the FBI informed e-commerce companies about an extortion racket wherein hackers claim to break into the credit-card databases of e-commerce companies. They then contact the management and demand large sums of money to not misuse these numbers or reveal the break-in.[6]

Another crisis situation involves hackers breaking in and stealing customer information. In December 2000, for instance, hackers penetrated Egghead.com's customer databases and had access to information about their 3.7 million customers. A similar attack in September 2000 allowed a hacker to steal approximately 15,700 credit card numbers from the Western Union site. The FBI also indicted a Russian thief who stole more than 300,000 credit card numbers from CD Universe, an online music seller (Lemos & Charny, 2000; Musil, 2000).

Such incidents bring negative publicity to the organization and erode customer confidence in trusting these organizations to maintain their confidential information. There is the threat that customers may leave and opt for sites that they perceive to be more secure.

VIRTUAL BOYCOTTS OF PRODUCTS OR SERVICES

This is an example of a public-relations crisis that Internet-based organizations may experience. These crises bring negative publicity to the focal organization. Online organizations are vulnerable to these crises, as their highly connected, activist community can quickly initiate and spread the word of a boycott and shut down a site. The eToys example described earlier highlights the vulnerability of online organizations to such activities. Although there have been no well-publicized events so far, it is likely that the online presence of click-and-mortar companies will be the target of activists who want to campaign against the larger companies. Once again, easy accessibility and high visibility will make these companies desirable targets. Another variation of this kind of crisis is when the online medium is used as the means to organize boycotts and protests against companies. Large companies whose policies or business practices are seen as controversial by some groups are often the target of such mobilization. For instance, Web sites abound that help provide a forum for discussion and organization against Wal-Mart (see http://www.walmartwatch.com) and

Microsoft (the Microsoft Boycott Campaign, http://www.msboycott.com, lists over 160 anti-Microsoft sites and discussion forums). Some of the anti-Wal-Mart sites have been used effectively to oppose new Wal-Mart superstores in communities such as Inglewood, California. Such boycotts bring negative publicity to the company, and if not quickly contained can have serious negative economic consequences for the organization.

COPYRIGHT AND PRIVACY ISSUES

Online organizations are also vulnerable to particular legal crises. The Napster case highlights some of the copyright issues that the online medium has precipitated. Napster provided its consumers free access to music through a peer-to-peer online medium. The recording industry, however, felt that Napster was infringing on its copyright and that it was losing revenue. It sued Napster, which was subsequently forced to stop providing this free service. Despite the demise of Napster, a number of other peer-to-peer networks have persisted and a variety of copyrighted material is distributed through these networks. In August 2004, the federal government cracked down on some of these networks in an effort to reduce the sharing of copyrighted material.[7] Educational institutions offering classes online are also forced to grapple with copyright issues. A number of universities are looking at online learning as a new way of educating students while providing a new revenue source for the university. Typically, faculty members retain copyright of the material they develop in order to teach a course. They can therefore use that material to teach at other universities as well. The copyright ownership is less clear for a course that a university puts online.

Copyright issues as illustrated by the Napster crisis can seriously threaten the survival of an organization. The organization also finds itself in the media spotlight and has to fight to justify its legitimacy and reputation. The economic costs of these efforts itself can weaken the viability of the organization.

The privacy of customer information has also become a major concern. Legal issues related to companies selling this information have been highlighted in the media. Another situation that is getting media and legal attention is what happens to customer data when a company shuts down or is acquired. When Toysmart.com shut down, Disney paid $50,000 to have the customer data destroyed after initial attempts to sell this information created a huge controversy (Sandoval, 2001). Attorneys general of a number of states also made sure that the eToys customer data could not be sold directly as part of bankruptcy proceedings.

Public-relations crises ensue when a company has deliberately or unknowingly violated privacy laws by sending customer data to other companies. Such incidents also have serious economic and legal implications for organizations.

In April 2001, for instance, Alexa, an online subsidiary of Amazon.com, paid $1.9 million to its customers as settlement of a class-action lawsuit. The suit claimed Alexa had sent confidential customer information to Amazon.com in violation of its privacy policy. Alexa, however, did not admit to any wrongdoing as part of the settlement.[8]

Strategies for Crisis Management

Researchers have categorized the phases of effective crisis management as

1. crisis prevention,
2. preparedness,
3. containment,
4. recovery,
5. learning (Kovoor-Misra, Zammuto, & Mitroff, 2000; Pearson & Mitroff, 1993).

Thus, organizations must be able to prevent crises if possible, but they must also have the preparedness capability to contain, recover, and learn from them if they do occur. However, most online organizations are still developing their capabilities in the area of crisis management. As new forms of crises emerge, organizations are making incremental strides in learning from and avoiding them. The occurrence of various online crises has generated awareness among these organizations and has resulted in business opportunities for infrastructure and service companies. For instance, after the inability of a number of e-tailers to adequately prepare for the holiday traffic surge in 1999, a number of companies such as Mercury Interactive now offer services that will test e-commerce sites with artificially generated traffic. Also, a number of security companies have emerged that either provide products or services to help online companies identify vulnerabilities through security audits or help monitor their systems on an ongoing basis.

Online organizations could benefit from the crisis-management literature, where a plethora of strategies are prescribed for organizations in general (Barton, 1993; Fink, 1986; Kovoor-Misra, 1995; Pauchant & Mitroff, 1992; Pearson & Mitroff, 1993). For example, strategies such as having in place crisis plans and teams, instituting a control room, the use of a learning audit, and managing the psychological stress of employees are all valuable crisis-management strategies for online organizations.

In this paper, we suggest seven strategies that we believe are particularly important for leaders of Internet-based organizations to better manage crises. Table 3.2 maps these strategies across the phases of crisis management.

Table 3.2 Crisis Management Strategies for Online Organizations by Phases

Recommended Strategy	Phase of Crisis Management				
	Preparedness	Prevention	Containment	Recovery	Learning
Monitor technology and chat groups		■	■		
Identify key online stakeholders		■	■		
Develop online crisis portfolio	■	■	■	■	■
Institute secondary data centers	■	■	■	■	
Address nontechnical aspects of online crises	■	■	■	■	
Customer relationship management		■	■	■	
Share crisis learning across online organizations					■

NOTE: Shaded cells indicate phases that each strategy addresses.

MONITOR TECHNOLOGY AND CHAT GROUPS

Top managers must detect threats from external stakeholders, primarily hackers, by monitoring signals in technology and chat groups. One of the most severe threats to an Internet-based organization is to its Web site. Organizations need to be able to differentiate between denial-of-service attacks and increased volume of legitimate customers. They also need to have the necessary security systems in place that will inform them of attacks to their customer data. While there is work underway to create intrusion detection systems that provide early-warning signals to an organization, the technology is still in its infancy. The fact that the nature of these attacks keeps changing also complicates the problem of developing a foolproof security system. External monitoring services such as Keynote and Mercury Interactive are examples of organizations that provide an early-warning system for potential problems on the Web site.

Chat groups that allow consumers to connect with each other are also accessible to members of the focal organization. Chat groups relevant to the organization can be continuously monitored to determine the focus and tone of discussions. Security specialists are often able to gain valuable insights by monitoring hacker chat rooms and notice boards. Financial sites like Yahoo! Finance and Quicken also provide discussion boards that can provide useful information. The Computer Emergency Response Team (CERT) also maintains a database of known vulnerabilities and attacks and should be monitored regularly by the information-technology staff.

IDENTIFY KEY STAKEHOLDERS IN AN ONLINE ENVIRONMENT

A second strategy that can be used to prevent and contain crises is a stakeholder audit that identifies stakeholders who play a critical role in an online environment. Stakeholders are those individuals or groups who can affect or be affected by an organization (Freeman, 1984). Other than the traditional stakeholders of an organization, such as customers, employees, investors, competitors, suppliers, and the media, other stakeholders must be considered, such as the hacking community, online service providers, data center operators, or the Computer Emergency Response Team (CERT).

Stakeholder audits can also be used to determine stakeholder attitudes—whether they are antagonistic or cooperative, and whether they are allies, enemies, or neutral toward the organization. Their power in terms of their ability to harm the organization should also be assessed (Savage, Nix, Whitehead, & Blair, 1991). The organization may find that they have both antagonistic and cooperative stakeholders with high power over the organization. These two groups may indicate who the salient stakeholders are and which groups would be allies versus which would be threats. For example, an organization may have antagonistic investors if it is slow to show a return on the investors' investment. It may also find that it is the target of particular hackers. On the positive side, its employees may be loyal and supportive or the local media may be inclined to give it positive press, as it is the dominant online firm in the community. Efforts need to be made to defuse antagonistic stakeholders and strengthen relationships with cooperative stakeholders. Stakeholder audits prior to a crisis could shed light on and defuse a situation that has the potential to escalate to a crisis. During a crisis, the results of an audit could help an organization plan its crisis-containment strategies.

DEVELOP A CRISIS PORTFOLIO FOR ONLINE CRISES

Crisis-management researchers have suggested the importance of preparing for a portfolio of crises. It is assumed that if organizations prepare for a particular type of crisis, the capability to respond to that crisis can be translated to other similar crises (Pearson & Mitroff, 1993). In this chapter we have described various crises that Internet-based organizations could experience. Thus, we suggest that they prepare for the possibility of Web site failures (technical), sabotage and blackmail (human and social), virtual boycotts (public relations), and copyright and privacy issues (legal).

Threats in the online world are also characterized by constant evolution. After Microsoft reacted to a denial-of-service attack on its DNS servers by distributing its DNS servers across Akamai's content-distribution network, hackers then targeted Akamai's network with a similar attack. It is therefore a challenge to try and stay one step ahead and anticipate the nature of potential attacks. Some security companies have started offering an "ethical hacking" service that attempts to attack a company's network and computers the same way malicious hackers may attack. This often helps identify potential vulnerabilities and new types of attacks that emerge. Similarly, security companies offer intrusion-detection services that detect network intrusions and automatically keep up-to-date with the latest types of intrusions being practiced by hackers. It is important to realize that the nature and form of online crises changes rapidly, and it is critical for an organization to keep updating its crisis preparedness to be prepared for new kinds of online crises.

INSTITUTE SECONDARY DATA CENTERS

Since Internet-based organizations are highly dependent on their Web sites for revenue, it is critical that they build redundancy into their systems architecture in order to be able to recover if there is a fire or a malicious hacker attack against them. While building full redundancy with automatic failover is an expensive proposition, the goal of the technology team should be to eliminate all single points of failure in the system. Even if the organization cannot afford a full secondary data center, it should have crisis-response plans in place that allow the site to be up and running in a matter of hours out of a secondary facility should the primary data center have a catastrophic failure. The company should also carry an adequate insurance policy to ensure that it can survive a temporary outage. Such preparedness enables the organization to minimize losses and quickly recover from a crisis.

ADDRESS THE NONTECHNICAL ASPECTS OF THE ONLINE CRISIS

Internet organizations have a strong technology core. Therefore, there may be a tendency to focus on the technical aspects of a crisis and ignore some of the nontechnical aspects such as the negative media attention, customer relationships, or the psychological burnout of their employees. For example, even though not an Internet crisis, the response from Intel to the floating-point unit bug in the Pentium processor exemplifies this problem. Once the technical problem in its processor was highlighted in the press, Intel focused on arguing the technical issues such as the low impact of the bug in most day-to-day operations. It was slow to recognize and address the public-relations aspects of this problem. This caused a backlash, and Intel was finally forced to recall the processor at an economic cost and with damage to its reputation.

It is important for online organizations to realize that the nontechnical aspects of the crisis often have a significant impact as well. For instance, after a denial-of-service attack, in addition to the technical issue of bringing the Web site back, executives must pay attention to repairing customer relationships (we discuss this further below). They must also project the company's point of view in the media, and address employee burnout once the crisis is past. It is therefore critical that the organization assign high-level executives to manage these nontechnical issues.

CUSTOMER RELATIONSHIP MANAGEMENT

We focus attention on the issue of customer relationship management (CRM) here as many organizations with an online presence are still building their brand and loyalty with their customers. Thus, loss of trust because of an unreliable Web site or an inability to deliver products or services can severely damage the possibility of a longer-term relationship with consumers, and impede an organization's recovery from a crisis.

For online retailers, it is extremely important that the three bases on which customer loyalty is built—a fast and stable Web site, fast and reliable order fulfillment, and excellent customer service—are given the highest priority. Special attention needs to be given to customer-relationship management so that the organization can understand its customers and meet their needs effectively. Efforts need to be made to demonstrate that these relationships are important. For example, after toysrus.com was unable to deliver all orders in time for Christmas during the 1999 season, it attempted to repair the damage by sending customers $100 gift certificates.[9] In addition, evidence that the organization has learned from the crisis and made changes goes a long way in rebuilding trust with stakeholders.

SHARE CRISIS LEARNING ACROSS ONLINE ORGANIZATIONS

Crises are important sources of learning as they highlight organizational strengths and weaknesses, and challenge existing assumptions. Organizations may learn from direct experience or vicariously if they perceive the crisis of another organization as having a high probability of happening to them (Kovoor-Misra, 1996). To effectively learn from a crisis, researchers suggest that top managers create a positive learning climate, conduct a learning audit, use multifunctional learning teams, reward learning behaviors, and follow through with the necessary changes (Kovoor-Misra & Nathan, 2000). We believe these strategies are all relevant for online organizations as well. We suggest, however, that there is a need to share learning across online organizations. We see such shared learning in more mature industries, such as the chemical and airline industries. Given the threat to the industry as a whole, when one organization has a crisis such as a gas leak or airline crash, they make it possible for other members of the industry to learn from each other. For online organizations, crises such as denial-of-service attacks, virtual boycotts, blackmail, and sabotage can severely erode consumer confidence in all online organizations. Thus, we suggest that organizations focus not only on their own learning but share information to build capability in the industry as a whole as well.

Future Directions for Crisis-Management Research

The onset of online crises also has implications for academic research on crisis management. First, additional dimensions need to be added to existing models of crisis typologies. Current models categorize crises by variables such as crisis severity, the source of the primary cause of the crisis, or the area of its impact. Online forms of crises highlight other dimensions, such as geographical scope and speed of escalation, that must be considered in crisis classification schemes.

Online forms of crises often transcend national boundaries. Crises such as fires and explosions may have a local boundary, whereas online crises such as virtual boycotts or sabotage may have international boundaries. Similarly, stakeholders in these online crises may be located in other countries. In some of the examples we discussed, hackers were based in China, the Philippines, and Canada. The geographical scope of a crisis is an important variable to be considered because of its implications on the scope and reach of crisis planning and management activities.

The speed of escalation after a crisis has manifested itself is another dimension that needs to be added to crisis typologies. Crises vary in their speed of escalation. For instance, crises such as virtual boycotts may escalate more quickly than other forms of boycotts because the online medium provides accessibility and visibility of information on the Internet. The faster the escalation, the greater the urgency to minimize the crisis. Thus, models of types of crises should include this variable to classify crises.

Second, the accessibility of organizations to threats and the visibility of a crisis are other variables that must be considered in estimating crisis vulnerability. These factors make online organizations more prone to crises. Typically, models of crisis causation have focused on organizational variables such as structure, culture, technology, and lack of processes such as plans and procedures. The online medium provides greater access to organizations. Organizational Web sites and databases can become targets of malicious individuals at any time of the day or night, from individuals anywhere in the world. In addition, when a Web site fails or a denial-of-service attack is in progress, it becomes visible to other interested observers based anywhere in the world and creates awareness that an organization is in trouble. Accessibility and visibility are important factors and should be considered in estimating the vulnerability of an organization to crisis.

Finally, brick-and-mortar organizations that move to online operations are a rich context for studying how top managers adapt to changes in their crisis environments and prepare for crises. Online divisions typically have different cultures than more established companies by virtue of their environment and the kinds of individuals they attract as employees and as attackers such as hackers. There is often a difference in values and language. The extent to which top managers are able to transcend their more traditional cultures, be open to these new forms of crises, and create greater crisis preparedness provides us with deeper insights as to how top managers respond to potential threats and the crisis-preparation process.

To conclude, the Internet as a medium of conducting business is here to stay. As we become more and more dependent on this medium, it is important to understand the threats inherent in the Internet and the kinds of crises that may ensue. This chapter has sought to shed light on these issues, suggest strategies for top managers to better manage them, and extend academic research to capture some of the complexities of crises that exist in an "online world."

Notes

1. MafiaBoy pleads guilty in hacker case, http://news.cnet.com/news/0-1005-200-4523277.html.

2. Global hacker agreement could affect bug hunters, http://news.cnet.com/news/0-1005-200-3314003.html.

3. Outages plague eBay again, http://news.cnet.com/news/0-1007-200-344247.html.

4. See www.toywar.com and eToys settles net name dispute with etoy, http://news.cnet.com/news/0-1007-200-1531854.html.

5. See Toysrus.com's net congestion continues, http://news.cnet.com/news/0-1006-200-1435578.html.

6. See FBI probes extortion case at CD store, http://news.cnet.com/news/0-1007-200-1519088.html; Borland, op. cit.

7. http://www.cnn.com/2004/TECH/08/26/cybercrime.probe.

8. Amazon unit settles privacy lawsuit, http://news.cnet.com/news/0-1007-200-5754965.html.

9. See Toys "R" Us falling short on Christmas deliveries, http://news.cnet.com/news/0-1007-200-1503101.html.

Bibliography

Akamai says Internet attack disrupted major Web sites. (June 15, 2004). Associated Press.

Barton, L. (1993). *Crisis in organizations: Managing and communicating in the heat of chaos.* Cincinnati, OH: South-Western Publishing.

Borland, J. (2000, March 2). Hacker attack latest in string of online credit card thefts. Retrieved December 29, 2006, from http://news.com.com/2100-1017-237553.html

Fink, S. L. (1986). *Crisis management: Planning for the inevitable.* New York: AMACOM.

Freeman, R. E. (1984). *Strategic management: A stakeholder approach.* Englewood Cliffs, NJ: Prentice Hall.

Hambrick, D. C., & D'Aveni, R. A. (1988). Large corporate failures as downward spirals. *Administrative Science Quarterly, 33,* 1–23.

Kovoor-Misra, S. (1995). A multi-dimensional approach to crisis preparation for technical organizations: Some critical factors. *Technological Forecasting and Social Change, 48,* 143–160.

Kovoor-Misra, S. (1996). Moving towards crisis preparedness: Factors that motivate organizations. *Technological Forecasting and Social Change, 53,* 69–183.

Kovoor-Misra, S., Clair, J. A., & Bettenhausen, K. L. (2001). Clarifying the attributes of organizational crises. *Technological Forecasting and Social Change, 67,* 77–91.

Kovoor-Misra, S., & Nathan, M. (1999). Crisis causation re-framed. *Central Business Review, 18*(2), 29–35.

Kovoor-Misra, S., & Nathan, M. L. (2000). Timing is everything: The optimal time to learn from crises. *Review of Business, 21*(3), 31–36.

Kovoor-Misra, S., Zammuto, R. F., & Mitroff, I. I. (2000). Crisis preparation in organizations: Prescription versus reality. *Technological Forecasting and Social Change, 63,* 43–62.

Lemos, R., & Charny, B. (2000, December 22). Hackers crack Egghead.com. Retrieved December 29, 2006, from http://news.com.com/2009-1017-250262.html

Musil, S. (2000, September 10). Western Union Web site hacked. Retrieved December 29, 2006, from http://news.com.com/2100-1023-245525.html

Nystrom, P. C., & Starbuck, W. H. (1984). To avoid organizational crises, unlearn. *Organizational Dynamics, 12*(4), 53–65.

Pauchant, T. C., & Mitroff, I. I. (1992). *Transforming the crisis-prone organization.* San Francisco: Jossey-Bass.

Pearson, C. M., & Clair, J. A. (1998). Crisis management re-framed. *Academy of Management Review, 23,* 59–78.

Pearson, C. M., & Mitroff, I. I. (1993). From crisis prone to crisis prepared: A framework for crisis management. *The Academy of Management Executive, 7*(1), 48–59.

Sandoval, G. (2001, January 31). Judge OKs destruction of Toysmart list. CNET News.Com. Retrieved December 29, 2006, from http://news.com.com/2104-1017_3-251893.html

Savage, G. T., Nix, T. W., Whitehead, C. J., & Blair, J.D. (1991). Strategies for assessing and managing organizational stakeholders. *Academy of Management Executive, 5*(2), 61–75.

Schmeltzer, J. (2004, May 20). Caribou grinds away at rumor. Chicago Tribune.com. Retrieved December 29, 2006, from http://www.kellogg.northwestern.edu/news/hits/040520ct.htm

Shrivastava, P. (1987). *Bhopal: Anatomy of a crisis.* Cambridge, MA: Ballinger.

Turner, B. A. (1976). The organizational and interorganizational development of disasters. *Administrative Science Quarterly, 21,* 378–397.

Part II

New Crises, New Meaning

Organizational Sensemaking During Crisis[1]

Karlene H. Roberts, Peter Madsen, and Vinit Desai

At 9:40 A.M. on the morning of Saturday, June 15, 1996, the Greater Manchester Police Department operated under seemingly normal conditions. At 9:41, a bomb warning reported by a local television station dramatically altered those conditions. Suddenly, the Greater Manchester Police faced a major crisis situation. Groups of police officers immediately set out in search of the alleged bomb while others worked with store security personnel to evacuate the roughly 80,000 people in the center of downtown Manchester that morning. The bomb was found in a truck parked in front of a major shopping mall at 10:00. Evacuation continued as a bomb squad was called to the scene. The bomb squad arrived at 10:05, about 15 minutes before the bomb was set to detonate, but was unable to disable the 1,500-kilo bomb. Its explosion created a 40-foot-wide by 15-foot-deep crater, damaged several skyscrapers (six of which were later demolished because of irreparable structural damage), blew out windows over a radius of more than half a kilometer, and created shockwaves that were felt over 8 kilometers away. Miraculously, no one was killed by the blast, but 220 people were injured and an estimated £700 million of damage was done to the city center.

Although Manchester Police were unable to prevent the detonation of the bomb, they succeeded in evacuating 80,000 people from a major metropolitan area in very little time. That no one was killed in the explosion of such a massive bomb is a testament to the effectiveness of police response to the crisis. The Manchester Police were able to act quickly and decisively in response to the bomb warning largely because they were rapidly able to effectively integrate information from two seemingly unrelated sources. The local television station received a telephone call warning of a bomb in downtown Manchester (but not giving its location) less than an hour before the bomb was set to go off. Police received no warning until the television news story aired about 40 minutes before the detonation.

However, police officers had issued an illegal parking ticket to the truck containing the bomb more than 2 hours before the detonation. The officers issuing the ticket noted that the truck's placement was unusual. Consequently, when police officers on the street were informed of the bomb warning, they were immediately suspicious of the truck and were able to connect the truck with the bomb quickly. Only 20 minutes after first receiving word of the possible presence of a bomb somewhere in downtown Manchester, police pinpointed its exact location. Despite the rapid location of the bomb, the bomb squad was left with only 15 minutes to deal with it. This period of time was not long enough to allow the bomb squad to defuse explosives, but it was enough time for police to focus their evacuation efforts on the buildings that would feel the brunt of the blast. The combination of two pieces of seemingly unrelated information allowed the Greater Manchester Police Department to make sense of the nature of the crisis they faced and to prevent any loss of life.

Crisis situations force organizations to swiftly make sense of turbulent environments that are often unlike anything they have previously experienced. Organizational routines and understandings that work well under normal conditions usually fail during crises. Business-as-usual approaches are inadequate for dealing with crises, in large part because successful crisis resolution requires the quick combination and comprehension of large amounts of new information, while normal operations only require attention to a few familiar information sources. To successfully manage crises, organizations must develop the capability to rapidly assimilate information from many disparate sources into a coherent picture of the developing situation.

Developing the capability to make sense of crisis situations is difficult because most organizations only rarely experience crises and thus have little opportunity for trial-and-error learning of effective sensemaking methods. However, emergency-response organizations, such as police and fire departments and paramedic organizations, by nature deal with crises on a frequent basis. Because of their unique experience bases, many emergency-response organizations have developed well-refined sensemaking capabilities. However, these capabilities are rarely discussed (for an exception see Hutchins, 1995). Moreover, how people in groups, rather than as individuals, develop such cognitions is also given short shrift in the organizational literature (again, for an exception see Weick & Roberts, 1993).

The purpose of this chapter is to describe sensemaking routines developed by one large police department, which we will call Big City Police

Department (BCPD). In this police department we focus on how people bring their cognitions together. We approach this issue inductively through an archival review of a sample of 32 adjudicated homicide cases. In the following sections, after briefly reviewing the relevant literature, we will describe the sensemaking methods we observed at BCPD and suggest how these methods could be adopted as part of a crisis-management strategy by other organizations.

Crisis Management

Interest in crisis management is growing as it becomes clear that in many modern organizations, a crisis can have devastating results for the organization and for surrounding communities (Perrow, 1984). A crisis is defined as a low-probability, high-consequence event that develops very rapidly and involves ambiguous situations with unknown causes and effects (Aguilera, 1990; Dutton, 1986; Quarantelli, 1988). Crisis management focuses on how to avert crisis situations when possible and how to minimize the damage caused when crises are unavoidable (Pearson & Clair, 1998). A growing number of organizations recognize the catastrophic potential of low-probability, high-consequence events (Jackson & Dutton, 1987; Shrivastava et al., 1988). The Manchester bombing is one example of destruction caused by such an event. Low-probability, high-consequence events by definition occur so rarely that they cannot be anticipated and prepared for based on past experience. For example, before June 15, 1996, the city of Manchester had never experienced a large-scale terrorist bombing. Nevertheless, the Greater Manchester Police were required to respond quickly and effectively in order to save lives and limit damage.

One major difficulty in dealing with an emergency is making sense of what is happening. Maintaining proper situational awareness is crucial to crisis resolution (e.g., Bigley & Roberts, 2001). During the 40 minutes in which Greater Manchester Police were aware of the bomb in the city center, they were able to respond to the situation by evacuating surrounding buildings and locating the vehicle containing the bomb. If they had become aware of the situation earlier, their response could have been even more effective.

Sensemaking

Different authors have defined organizational sensemaking in many different ways. However, central to all of these definitions is the notion that sensemaking is the process through which members of organizations subjectively construct the reality in which they operate (Weick, 1979). The sensemaking perspective argues that people do not live in a concrete, objective world. Rather, they create internal images of an objective world based on their perceptions and experiences (Morgan, Frost, & Pondy, 1983). Thus, people are constantly in the process of constructing reality based on cues from their environments. Sensemaking is often retrospective, as people try to make their actions and experiences fit logically into their understanding of the world (Weick, 1995). For this reason, sensemaking can be a self-reinforcing process. Because people take actions that are consistent with their views of the world, these actions are likely to produce results that fit with their worldviews.

In organizations, reality is constructed by organizational members as they develop shared understandings of the world and of the organization (Weick, 1995). Thus, organizational sensemaking is the process by which organizational members build mental models of the organization and its surroundings. All members of an organization are unlikely to hold precisely the same mental model of the organization. But because organizational members develop their mental models largely through interactions with others in the organizational setting, their individual mental models are likely to be similar and compatible. These similar, or overlapping, mental models allow organization members to work together in the pursuit of organizational goals. Organizational activities and outcomes are then subjected to collective sensemaking processes through which organizational reality is constructed.

Sensemaking During Crises

The mental models held by organizational members are products of sensemaking in response to an organization's interaction with its environment. Thus, organizational members' overlapping mental models of the organizational environment are adapted to fit well with the conditions under which the organization normally operates (Weick, 1995). Minor or slow changes in the organizational environment can be reconciled with these mental models. Organizational members ignore such environmental changes if they are minor, or gradually adjust their understandings of the environment to take the changes into account. Crises involve rapid and unfamiliar changes in the organizational environment that cannot be reconciled with existing mental models (Weick, 1993). For this reason, organizational members experience crises as stunning, frightening, and completely incomprehensible (Perrow, 1984).

Effective response to the developing crisis requires organizational members to quickly construct new mental models of the crisis situation. But doing so is extremely difficult. Rather than build new mental models, organizational members typically cling to existing models as long as possible, ignoring information that cannot be reconciled with them (Louis & Sutton, 1991; Weick, 1995). When information about the impending crisis becomes impossible to ignore and forces people to abandon existing mental models, they often give up hope of understanding the crisis and (sometimes literally) run for their lives (Weick, 1993).

Similarly, one of the characteristics of organizations and individuals that successfully contend with crises is the ability to recognize anomalies or cues that may help recognize or manage the crisis. Although post hoc investigations of critical incidents with disastrous outcomes frequently reveal that there were timely warnings or telltale signals that all was not right, the individuals and organizations overlooked the warnings or made sense of them by reconciling them with their benign mental models of the situations. Organizations that manage critical incidents more effectively recognize the anomalies and reconsider or revise their understanding of the organizational environment. In the Manchester bombing, the police had a separate and discrete warning that caused them to revise their understanding of the environment. Members of the organization then reexamined their understanding of the anomalous illegally parked van. In the context of a pending bombing, the officers recognized the sinister implications of a car parked differently than most they observed. These related abilities—to more closely examine anomalous events in routine context, and to reexamine one's observations in a changed context—are special kinds of heedful sensemaking that help organizations and members avert or manage crises.

Despite the importance of organizational sensemaking in crisis management, most organizations are poorly equipped to locate and utilize information about developing crises (Weick, 1995). Over time, organizations adapt to the requirements of their environments. As part of this process, organizational members learn which sources of information about their environments are most useful in performing their daily functions. When useful information sources are known, organizational members tend to monitor them closely while ignoring other sources of information. This process is adaptive because monitoring information sources is costly and organizations can become more efficient by paying attention only to those information sources that are most useful under normal conditions (Starbuck & Milliken, 1988). Over time, organizational members become habituated to ignore most information about the organizational environment.

While selective attention may be efficient under normal conditions, it is highly ineffective when dealing with crises. By definition, crises occur rarely but may have very serious consequences. The low-probability, high-consequence events that cause crisis situations push organizations outside of their normal environments into conditions with which they are not familiar (Dutton, 1986). When that happens, the highly refined information-gathering routines that bring high efficiency under normal conditions fail to provide organizations with sufficient information to make sense of the crisis. The environmental turbulence that accompanies crisis makes organizational sensemaking very difficult.

During crises, organizational members must not only build new mental models to accommodate the crisis conditions, they must also find ways to integrate their individual mental models in such a way that coordinated action is possible (Roth, 1997). Furthermore, since crisis situations are highly ambiguous, organizational members are often forced to abandon one model in favor of another as conditions change or new information is discovered (Bigley & Roberts, 2001). Weick and Roberts (1993) develop a concept of collective mind to explain how some organizations are able to successfully maintain shared mental models in very dangerous and quickly changing conditions. Collective mind involves heedful interrelation, such that organizational members understand that their actions are connected and construct their mental models and choose their actions with this connectedness in mind. Successful heedful interaction allows organizational members to resolve crises. As Weick and Roberts note, "As heedful interrelating and mindful comprehension increases organizational errors decrease" (1993, p. 357). Collective mind and heedful interrelating contribute to elasticity and to interpreting how redundancy operates.

While sensemaking is usually an unconscious process, Weick (1995) suggests that leaders can structure their organizations and train their employees in such a way that rapid sensemaking in crisis is possible. Emergency response organizations are especially likely to have well-developed methods for sensemaking during crisis because they deal with crises on a regular basis (Bigley & Roberts, 2001). The remainder of this chapter is devoted to describing the methods used by one police department to facilitate sensemaking in emergencies.

Research Setting

Police departments are designed to protect citizen safety and detain criminals. Because of this, an attempted homicide is one of the most significant crises to which they must respond. We chose to study police responses to homicide cases in order to understand how police officers respond to very severe emergencies.

Big City Police Department (BCPD) serves a large urban city with a population of approximately 380,000 people. BCPD investigates in excess of 100 homicides annually, one of the highest totals per capita in the United States. Furthermore, in 2000 each of this department's emergency response phone line (#911) operators answered an average of 17,000 calls. This was the highest level of emergency operator activity of any large U.S.

city surveyed. BCPD monitors its environment in several different ways. Police officers walking or driving city streets watch for unusual activities. Citizens may approach police officers to report criminal activities they witness. Furthermore, officers frequently know which members of a community are likely to have information about a given crime.

In spite of the importance of these information-gathering methods, the vast majority of BCPD's information about its city comes in the form of phone calls from citizens. BCPD maintains a large communication center staffed with trained civilian 911 dispatchers, supervised by civilian supervisors and police sergeants. BCPD's communication center answers both emergency (911) and nonemergency calls from anywhere in the city, exchanges information, coordinates with the state highway patrol, and maintains contact with police officers in the field. In large communication centers such as BCPD's, the same personnel do not answer 911 calls and dispatch police units at the same time. The center is divided into three stations, each with its own responsibilities. In this system, personnel rotate across the three stations in any one shift, doing a different job at each station. These jobs are complaint operator, dispatcher, and service operator. Complaint operators answer the emergency and non-emergency phone lines. Dispatchers gather information from complaint operators, assign police officers to respond when needed, and maintain radio communications with officers in the field. Service operators communicate additional information to officers such as outstanding warrants and driver's license and vehicle registration data.

Information coming into the communication center passes across at least four different individuals. Citizens make emergency calls to report a crime or to request police assistance. Complaint operators answer and evaluate citizen calls. If they determine that a call requires police response, they record pertinent details in a computerized format and electronically transmit important information to dispatchers. Included in this information is the complaint operator's assessment of the level of urgency with which the call should be handled. Such assessments are made by assigning the call one of four different priority levels: A, B, C, or D. A priority calls are time-sensitive emergencies where failure to respond immediately could result in serious injury or death. B priority calls are emergencies that must be attended to quickly but do not involve immediate threat to citizen health. C priority calls are non-emergencies that are handled when time permits. And D priority calls are calls that are not eligible for service.

After receiving the computerized information from complaint operators, dispatchers again evaluate the calls and may change a call's priority level if they feel it is appropriate. Dispatchers also assign available police units to handle the calls. Dispatchers communicate with officers through primary police radio channels to make assignments and monitor police response to calls. In emergency situations, complaint operators send preliminary information to dispatchers while continuing to question callers for additional information. Thus, complaint operators and dispatchers maintain contact through the communication center's computer system. Dispatchers also remain in contact with police officers through the duration of the event. One of the principal responsibilities of call-takers and dispatchers is to make sense of incoming 911 calls and let police officers know what to expect when they arrive at the scene.

Roughly 85% of the 911 calls made to the BCPD communication center are either nonemergencies or straightforward emergencies. Such calls require very little sensemaking effort. It is likely that call-takers apply an initial filter by asking themselves whether this call is routine or nonroutine. The roughly 15% of calls that report nonroutine emergencies require call-takers and dispatchers to make sense of incomplete or conflicting information and to keep pace with rapidly changing situations. Such emergencies also require integration of information from several different sources. Significant emergencies, such as homicides, are usually reported by several different callers, each of whom has a unique vantage point and offers unique information. In dealing with such emergencies, complaint operators, dispatchers, and police officers must construct overlapping mental models of the situation so they can effectively share information and best make sense of the situation.

BCPD is a paramilitary organization and structures itself along bureaucratic military lines. However, emergency dispatchers and police officers are granted a great deal of flexibility in dealing with emergencies in order to facilitate communication and sensemaking. The two overriding goals at BCPD are citizen and police safety. Consequently, BCPD has developed methods that allow emergency dispatchers and police officers to make the best possible sense of dangerous situations so that police officers can respond quickly to protect citizen safety without placing themselves at excessive risk.

Homicides

As part of a larger research program to understand sensemaking in emergency response organizations, we examined police records of a sample of 32 adjudicated homicide cases investigated by BCPD. The sample of homicide files was not randomly selected. Homicide files were placed in the sample at the discretion of a BCPD homicide investigator who was asked to provide us with files that would illustrate sensemaking under difficult conditions and whose review by researchers would not imperil confidentiality or the prosecution of active cases. Thus, the sample was not representative of the population of all homicides investigated by BCPD, but it was representative of ambiguous homicide cases investigated by the department. BCPD selected these cases from their archives. Since many years are often required to fully adjudicate cases, this sample size is fairly large.

The homicide case files included audio tapes of all 911 calls received by the communication center in connection with each case, printouts of all computerized communications between emergency operators and dispatchers, audio tapes of all radio communication between dispatchers and police officers, and copies of all police reports dealing with the case (including all statements made by witnesses). For each case file, we first listened to the audio tapes of the 911 calls, read the printouts of emergency operator notes, and listened to the tapes of radio communication between dispatchers and police officers. Finally, we read witnesses' statements and homicide investigators' notes. We were assisted in this process by a veteran BCPD police officer who interpreted police codes for us and provided background on the different parts of the city in which the homicides occurred.

All the data handling was done within the confines of BCPD Headquarters. The researchers were not allowed to remove data from these premises. They could, however, take their own notes from the premises. Understanding the data required close cooperation with the BCPD senior officer, who often could make optimal sense of the interactions on the tapes.

Sensemaking Practices

We went through the cases one by one, looking for similarities in how police personnel handled difficult and ambiguous situations. As we listened to the tapes, we tried to understand how dispatchers used the information provided by 911 callers and police officers on the scene to make sense of each situation. Afterwards, we read witnesses' statements and homicide investigators' notes to get a sense of how well dispatchers' mental models mapped onto the reality experienced by witnesses. We paid particular attention to cases in which dispatchers correctly made sense of what was going on at the scene before police officers arrived. We also noted cases where dispatchers failed to make correct interpretations. The process of listening to the taped 911 calls was darkly fascinating. On more than one occasion, we heard the voices of people who would be dead shortly after hanging up the phone.

The complexity of the call-takers' job was illustrated by cases in which callers minimized or withheld information for a variety of reasons. Other callers simply reported their understandings of the calls based on incomplete information; these callers often gave accounts that made sense of what they saw or heard, but did not suggest that a homicide had taken place. Reports of the same incident by a variety of people each with a different perspective, the changing nature of the situation over time, and the addition of an increasing number of first responders can also make the call-takers' jobs more complex.

Through all of this, we observed several regularities in how police officers and dispatchers communicated and interacted that seemed to facilitate sensemaking. Some of these practices reflected police department written policies and others were informal practices developed at the department over years of responding to emergencies. We focus here on three practices that appear to significantly aid the sensemaking process. We label these three practices early model adoption, model migration and resetting, and having the bubble. We will discuss each of these practices in the following sections using different homicide cases to illustrate each.

Early Model Adoption

As discussed previously, most organizations find crisis response difficult because during crisis situations, people's shared understandings break down, preventing effective coordination. BCPD dispatchers and officers avoid this difficulty through early model adoption. As soon as a 911 call is received, it is assigned a priority code and an identifying code (a numerical code represents each type of eligible request for service: homicide, kidnapping, burglary, and so on). The combination of the priority code and the identifying code functions as a unifying framework that police personnel use to coordinate information and understandings. The practice of assigning codes to calls very early means that dispatchers and officers always have a working shared mental model of the situation to which they are responding. In this situation the incident is unambiguous.

Most of the homicide cases we reviewed were first reported by citizens who had not seen any crime but heard gunshots. When gunshots are fired in a large city, they are usually heard by many people, at least several of whom report hearing shots to the police. Using the locations of the citizens who call, dispatchers are usually able to identify the particular city street or building where the shots were fired. Using this information, dispatchers direct officers to the location of a possible crime and put them on alert for armed suspects. Through the use of early model adoption, dispatchers and police officers are able to quickly form and share initial impressions regarding events. There are few other kinds of incidents that fit the early adoption strategy unless it is done incorrectly.

The downside of early model adoption occurs when the initial model is incorrect but adopters retain it beyond its usefulness. While early model adoption is usually a shortcut to problem solving, it can be misleading if it leads observers to generate inaccurate conclusions about their situation. This may occur if initial evidence is highly ambiguous or misinterpreted. When call-takers form early mental models regarding particular situations, they rely primarily on auditory evidence. Speech patterns, pauses, inflections, and tones of callers become substantially meaningful given the absence of visual and other descriptive cues. This evidence is combined with information learned through experience to form early mental models. As information regarding an objective event is initially incomplete and ambiguous, these models may form around incorrect assumptions and potentially lead to inaccurate sensemaking.

This occurred when BCPD received a call from a bar during which the caller calmly announced that the disc jockey was dead. The calmness of the caller led the call-taker to strongly suspect the call was a joke. Based on this auditory evidence, the complaint operator formed an early mental model and initially interpreted this situation as a low priority. However, despite this initial model, she sent help and discovered the call was not a hoax. Her mental model changed and expanded as new evidence was incorporated and processed, leading her to feel increasingly uncertain about the initial interpretation. Mechanisms to update mental models based on new information, and to share updated understandings of situations, are required. These mechanisms are discussed below.

Model Migration and Resetting

Many people are involved in the police response to any given homicide, including citizen callers, emergency operators, dispatchers, officers, and witnesses. Although the adoption of a model allows all of these people to share information and coordinate actions, they each have unique information that can facilitate sensemaking. Model migration is the process through which each individual involved with a case adds her information to the working mental model and then passes it to others who may be able to integrate that information with their own to further refine situational awareness.[2] Early model adoption is useful because it provides a base of shared interpretations on which to plan emergency response. However, as suggested above, they may actually detract from this effort if they are incorrectly formed. Thus, as models migrate across different people, everyone recognizes that the working model will probably be reset when more information is available. Model resetting is the process through which working mental models are updated or abandoned in favor of new models when new information necessitates such a change.

Very few of the homicide cases we examined were first reported as homicides. They are often first reported as fights or as gunshots. Initial mental models formed regarding these calls may be quite accurate because the majority of calls received by BCPD are routine in nature. Most fights end with minor injuries; callers may falsely believe backfiring cars or other loud sounds to be gunshots. However, some cases reported as minor incidents turn into serious crises. A false presumption that a potential homicide will not escalate into an actual homicide can be costly. When in doubt of an initial model's accuracy, therefore, BCPD personnel actively search for new information.

An example demonstrates model migration and resetting. In one homicide case a female citizen placed a 911 call. She told the emergency operator that a man in her apartment was bleeding and she thought he needed medical attention. When asked how he was injured, she responded that she didn't know. The 911 operator asked if she could speak with the man. When he took the phone, he said he was fine and didn't want police service, and hung up. The complaint operator called back (complaint operators always call back people who hang up). The female caller answered the phone and this time she hesitated about whether she needed service and ultimately said she was wrong and didn't need help. By this time, the complaint operator had determined that something was seriously wrong and started transmitting information through the computer link to the dispatcher. The call was labeled as a medical emergency with a B priority. The complaint operator or dispatcher can change these labels of the incident's type or seriousness at any time. At this point, the meaning of this incident was still very unclear to the complaint operator and dispatcher and possibly to the caller. Nevertheless, a working mental model was adopted and 911 personnel used it to prepare their response.

The dispatcher radioed a police car on patrol in the area of the call with the details of the incident and the address of the caller. The emergency operator and dispatcher treated the call as a possible medical emergency, but nothing else. However, the police officer radioed back that he had responded to calls at the address several times in the past and suspected this was an issue of domestic violence. The woman who made the 911 call had used a knife to make her point in arguments with her boyfriend on several previous occasions. After receiving the working model of the incident from the dispatcher, the officer altered it based on his unique information. He saw the situation not as a possible medical emergency but as a possible case of domestic violence and passed his interpretation back to the dispatcher through the radio.

The dispatcher immediately changed the incident's label to domestic violence and possible assault with a knife, changed the incident's priority to an A, called for an ambulance, and radioed additional police units to provide backup to the first responder. When police arrived on the scene, they found a man at the apartment with a massive knife wound to the neck. Paramedics who arrived shortly after police officers attended to the man, who had lost too much blood and died. Police took the woman into custody.

No one involved in this case knew that it would turn out to be a homicide when it was first reported to police. Even the suspect thought that it would turn out to be a minor medical emergency, which was why she called police to begin with. Based on the information that was known to the dispatcher, this was not a particularly serious emergency. However, as the police model of the incident was passed from one person to another, someone was able to provide a different interpretation based on uniquely held information. This interpretation turned out to be correct and was the basis for an effective police response.

Another example of revising a model did not work out as well as this one and has served as a basis for police training in this department. Here the call-takers, the dispatcher, and the police failed to comprehend the number of intruders in a situation. They ordered a victim to come out of a house and she was killed by an intruder. They failed to reset the model as conditions changed.

Having the Bubble

In any organizational crisis, each organizational member has a unique view of what the crisis is and how it is changing. These local views are important, but they must be integrated by someone who can see the big picture. During crises, the environment changes so rapidly that it is usually impossible for everyone in the organization to be kept up to date on every new development. At least one person needs to able to see the big picture in order to facilitate coordination. On aircraft carriers, someone who is in a position to see the big picture is said to "have the bubble."

At BCPD the dispatchers are expected to have the bubble. The dispatcher is the hub of communication during the course of any emergency. In the case of a serious emergency, 911 calls are usually made by many different callers and answered by many different emergency operators. Such emergencies are responded to by many police officers and sometimes by other emergency response agencies (e.g., fire departments and paramedics). However, except for very large emergencies (e.g., major fires or riots), an incident is coordinated by only one dispatcher. This is done deliberately. BCPD dispatchers are trained to keep track of large amounts of information and to keep everyone involved in an incident up to speed. In fact, dispatchers are so good at doing this that they may be sent to the scene of a hostage situation to help the hostage negotiators keep track of everything that is going on.

In one homicide case we reviewed, a man was shot as he drove along one of the city's biggest streets. The shooter, who was also in a car, turned a corner and speeded off before other drivers knew what was happening. The victim's car rolled into a busy intersection and was hit by oncoming cars. The first 911 calls of the incident reported it merely as a large traffic accident. However, when officers arrived at the scene, they found the victim dead and were told by witnesses that the shooter had fled the scene. The incident quickly became a high-speed chase as BCPD officers and highway-patrol officers blocked off roads to try to stop the fleeing suspect.

As the suspect tried to get away, 911 calls reporting a dangerously reckless driver started pouring in. While these calls were handled by many different operators, the whole incident was handled by one dispatcher who integrated information from callers with reports from police and highway patrol officers. The dispatcher eventually got police officers to block the suspect's escape route and the man surrendered and was taken into custody.

Effective police response in this case would not have been possible without someone who could see the big picture. Because the dispatcher had the bubble, she was able to direct officers to the right place. No one officer on the ground could have kept up with the torrent of information about the case that passed over the radio waves and telephone lines, but officers were able to take necessary steps to resolve the situation under the direction of the dispatcher.

If model migration is done correctly, "having the bubble" may ultimately occur. In our example of the female caller, the person who had the bubble was the police officer because he could put disparate pieces together to come up with a true picture.

Conclusion

Crises are very rare events for most organizations, but they can have devastating results. Effective crisis management can significantly reduce the damage caused by a crisis, but good crisis management is difficult. One thing that makes crisis response so difficult is that crises thrust organizations into new and rapidly changing environments where old individual mental models and shared understandings no longer apply and need to be updated. Organizational sensemaking breaks down during crisis because people cannot effectively gather and integrate information about the emergency.

Police organizations, such as BCPD, respond to crisis frequently and have developed methods to facilitate sensemaking during crisis. The processes of early model adoption, model migration and resetting, and having the bubble allow BCPD to respond effectively to serious emergencies while protecting officer and citizen safety. Police members at BCPD and other similar urban police departments might be able to refine the ways they think about crisis response by adopting and developing these response categories. Previous research on reliability-enhancing organizations finds that implementation strategies developed from the research conceptual findings improve organizational performance (Madsen, Desai, Roberts, & Wong, 2006). Training strategies can be developed that focus on these processes. Other organizations could also adopt these practices as part of a crisis-management strategy to facilitate organizational sensemaking during crisis.

Future research needs to be more concerned with how individual-level processes translate into organizational sense-making. Recent work illustrates the importance of examining those places where organizational processes come together: the interstices in organizations or the space between processes (Bradbury & Lichtenstein, 2000; Roberts, Madsen, & Desai, 2005). Examples of interstices include shift changes, moving patients from intensive care units to wards, the coordination of marketing and production groups, and certainly interactions among various kinds of emergency responders. While we are fairly certain that the probability of error is high at interstices, we know little beyond that. Finally, future research needs to develop and compare implementation strategies drawn from these findings and those of others concerned with crisis response.

Notes

1. This work was supported by National Science Foundation Grant SES-0105402.
2. The overwhelming number of 911 personnel are women.

Bibliography

Aguilera, D. C. (1990). *Crisis intervention: Theory and methodology* (6th ed.). New York: Mosby.

Bigley, G., & Roberts, K. (2001). The incident commands: High-reliability organizing for complex and volatile task environments. *Academy of Management Journal, 46,* 1281–1299.

Bradbury, H., & Lichtenstein, B. B. B. (2000). Relationality in organizational research: Exploring the space between. *Organization Science, 11,* 551–564.

Dutton, J. E. (1986). The processing of crisis and non-crisis strategic issues. *Journal of Management Studies, 23,* 501–517.

Fiske, S., & Taylor, S. (1991). *Social cognition* (2nd ed.). New York: McGraw-Hill.

Grabowski, M., & Roberts, K. (1996). Human and organizational error in large scale systems. *IEEE Transactions on Systems, Man, and Cybernetics—Part A: Systems and Humans, 26,* 2–16.

Hermann, C. F. (1963). Some consequences of crisis which limit the viability of organizations. *Administrative Science Quarterly, 8,* 61–82.

Hutchins, E. (1995). *Cognition in the wild.* Cambridge: MIT Press.

Jackson, S., & Dutton, J. (1987). Categorizing strategic issues—links to organizational action. *Academy of Management Review, 12,* 76–90.

Louis, M., & Sutton, R. (1991). Switching cognitive gears: From habits of mind to active thinking. *Human Relations, 44,* 55–76.

Madsen, P., Desai, V., Roberts, K. H., & Wong, D. (2006). Designing for high reliability: The birth and evolution of a pediatric intensive care unit. *Organization Science, 17,* 239–248.

Morgan, G., Frost, P. J., & Pondy, L. R. (1983). Organizational symbolism. In L. R. Pondy, P. J. Frost, G. Morgan, & T. C. Dandridge (Eds.), *Organizational symbolism* (pp. 3–38). Greenwich, CT: JAI.

Pearson, C., & Clair, J. (1998). Reframing crisis management. *Academy of Management Review, 23,* 59–76.

Pearson, C., & Mitroff, I. (1993). From crisis-prone to crisis-prepared. *Academy of Management Executive, 7,* 48–59.

Perrow, C. (1984). *Normal accidents: Living with high-risk technologies.* New York: Basic Books.

Quarantelli, E. L. (1988). Disaster crisis management: A summary of research findings. *Journal of Management Studies, 25,* 373–385.

Roberts, K. (1989). New challenges in organizational research: High reliability organizations. *Industrial Crisis Quarterly, 3,* 111–125.

Roberts, K., Madsen, P. M., & Desai, V. (2005). The space between in space transportation: A relational analysis of the failure of STS 107. In W. H. Starbuck & M. Farjoun (Eds.), *Organization at the limit: Lessons from the* Columbia *disaster* (pp. 81–98). Malden, MA: Blackwell.

Roth, R. J. (1997). Insurable risks, regulation, and the changing insurance environment. In H. F. Diaz & R. S. Pulwarthy (Eds.), *Hurricanes: Climate and socioeconomic impacts* (pp. 261–272). Berlin: Springer.

Shrivastava, P. (1987). *Bhopal: Anatomy of a crisis.* New York: Ballinger.

Shrivastava, P., Mitroff, I., Miller, D., & Miglani, A. (1988). Understanding industrial crisis. *Journal of Management Studies, 25,* 285–303.

Starbuck, W., & Milliken, F. (1988). Executives' perceptual filters: What they notice and how they make sense. In D. C. Hambrick (Ed.), *The executive effect: Concepts and methods for studying top managers* (pp. 35–66). Greenwich, CT: JAI.

Weick, K. E. (1979). *The social psychology of organizing.* Reading, MA: Addison-Wesley.

Weick, K. (1988). Enacted sensemaking in crisis situations. *Journal of Management Studies, 25,* 305–317.

Weick, K. (1989). Mental models of high reliability systems. *Industrial Crisis Quarterly, 3,* 127–142.

Weick, K. (1993). The collapse of sensemaking organizations: The Mann Gulch disaster. *Administrative Science Quarterly, 38,* 628–652.

Weick, K. (1995). *Sensemaking in organizations.* Thousand Oaks, CA: Sage.

Weick, K., & Roberts, K. (1993). Collective mind in organizations: Heedful interrelating on flight decks. *Administrative Science Quarterly, 38,* 357–381.

Weick, K., Sutcliffe, K., & Obstfeld, D. (1999). Organizing for high reliability: Processes of collective mindfulness. *Research in Organizational Behavior, 21,* 81–123.

Crisis Sensemaking and the Public Inquiry

5

Robert P. Gephart, Jr.

Public inquiries and hearings are investigations conducted by governmentally mandated bodies to assess important social issues or technologies (Salter & Slaco, 1981). Public hearings and inquiries are important aspects of the life history of many organizationally based crises, and sensemaking about technological risks and crises is an important feature of inquiry discourse and documents. The purpose of this chapter is to provide insights into the central role that sensemaking plays during public inquiries and hearings into crises. The chapter also discusses the important role that public inquiries play in the crisis-management process. To accomplish these objectives, the chapter reviews key features of public inquiries that have been documented in the scholarly literature. Next, the chapter discusses the different perspectives or approaches that have been used to study crisis sensemaking during public inquiries. The chapter also describes the findings that this research has produced. Next, the chapter indicates important issues in crisis sensemaking during public inquiries that could be fruitfully explored in future investigations. The chapter concludes by addressing practical implications for managers that this research provides regarding crisis sensemaking.

Crisis Sensemaking

Sensemaking is the process by which people construct a sense of shared meanings for society and its key institutions (Gephart, 1993, p. 1469). In sensemaking, people generate a social world and then interpret it (Weick,

1995, p. 13). Sensemaking thus involves constructing features of the world that then become available to perception (Gephart, 1997, p. 588; Weick, 1995, p. 14). Sensemaking includes the invention process that precedes interpretation as well as the interpretation process itself (Weick, 1995, p. 14). Interpretation is accomplished by providing explanations and accounts of sensed features or phenomena that make the phenomena meaningful (Weick, 1995, p. 588). Sensemaking thus involves verbally interpreting actions and events (Gephart, 1992, p. 118; Weick, 1977, p. 271), producing shared or intersubjective interpretations for events, and creating assumedly shared or collective, cultural meanings for important phenomena.

Two explicit conceptions of sensemaking frame the present discussion. The first perspective is Weick's (1995, 2001) cognitive psychology. For Weick, sensemaking involves environmental scanning, interpretation, and associated responses (Weick, 1995, p. 5). The concept highlights the action, activity, and creation of meaning that results when people interpret what they have generated (Weick, 1995, p. 13). Weick's conception of sensemaking emphasizes the invention processes by which stimuli are placed in some kind of frame of reference (1995, p. 4). Weick (1995) conceives sensemaking as grounded in identity construction (p. 17); retrospective (p. 24); enactive of sensible environments (p. 30); social (p. 38); ongoing (p. 43); based on cues (p. 49); and driven by plausibility rather than accuracy (p. 55).

Sensemaking tends to occur in situations where ambiguity and uncertainty are high (Weick, 1995, pp. 91–100). Ambiguity refers to an ongoing stream of cues that support several different interpretations at the same time, as commonly occurs during jury trials (Weick, 1995, p. 91). Uncertainty refers to imprecision in estimates of future consequences that are conditional on present activities (March, 1994, in Weick, 1995, p. 95). Two types of interruptions trigger sensemaking and changes in cognition: (1) a new event that is not expected and (2) an expected event that does not occur. Weick (1995) assumes that unusual events (e.g., crises) can disrupt sensemaking and lead to further sensemaking to create a meaningful understanding of events. This view highlights the construction and bracketing of cues that are interpreted and de-emphasizes the interpretations that are produced (Weick, 1995, p. 8). Although this chapter uses Weick's perspective as a general perspective on sensemaking, his research is not explored in detail here because this research explores the initial sensemaking accomplished during crises and does not explore inquiry sensemaking per se.

The second explicit perspective on sensemaking used in the chapter is provided by ethnomethodology, which conceives sensemaking as practical reasoning (Handel, 1982; Leiter, 1980) that differs from the rational practices associated with scientific thinking (Weick, 1995, p. 12). Ethnomethodologists emphasize the role of the interpretive process in sensemaking. Ethnomethodology assumes that sensemaking practices create a world of sensible objects and processes (Gephart, 1997, p. 588; see also Garfinkel,

1967; Gephart, 1993, 2004; Leiter, 1980). Sensemaking is manifest in natural language use and texts, including conversations and documents. Ethnomethodology has identified sensemaking practices that make speech acts comprehensible and sustain a sense of shared meaning during interaction (Gephart, 1992, p. 118). For ethnomethodology, conversations and interaction become confusing or senseless when these sensemaking practices are disrupted. Thus, when sensemaking practices are disrupted or their effective use is prevented, senselessness emerges and sensemaking is undertaken to restore meaning and a sense of social order to a setting. Ethnomethodology, including conversational analysis, is used in this chapter to address the interpretive practices that produce a sensible world during crisis inquiry sensemaking.

The chapter also addresses insights into crisis sensemaking provided by narrative methods (Boje, 2001; Riessman, 1993), rhetorical analysis (Brown, 2000) and Habermasian critical theory (Gephart & Pitter, 1993; Habermas, 1973, 1979). Although these approaches were not developed as explicit frameworks for analysis of sensemaking, they do provide insights into the substance of crisis sensemaking and the processes through which crisis sensemaking occurs. Narrative methods examine stories told about crises. Rhetorical analysis examines how texts and discourse including narratives and figures of speech are used to persuade the reader about the truthfulness of claims that are made. Habermasian critical-theory-based research has explored how sensemaking during public inquiries challenges or reproduces legitimacy of key organizations including state agencies and private companies. Habermasian critical theory is used in this chapter to understand how crisis sensemaking is constrained by institutional features and how sensemaking is directed at legitimating or delegitimating key social institutions.

Crises

Crisis is defined in this chapter as a major, unpredictable event that may produce negative outcomes including substantial damage to an organization and its employees (Barton, 1993, p. 2). Crises involve negative events of sufficient magnitude that it may take time to comprehend them (Barton, 1993). Crises result from a serious breakdown or malfunction in the relationship among people, organizations, and technologies (Mitroff, 2004, p. 3). This breakdown invalidates critical assumptions humans make about people, organizations, and technologies (Mitroff, 2004).

An industrial crisis is a crisis that results from industrial activities (Shrivastava, Mitroff, Miller, & Miglani, 1988, p. 287). Industrial crises are a major source of damage to humans and the environment (Shrivastava et al., 1988). Four key features that define industrial crises are (1) crisis types—there are different types of crises, (2) crisis mechanisms—signals of crises, (3) crisis systems—organizational structures, and (4) crisis stakeholders—parties including institutions and groups that are affected by crises (Mitroff, 2004, pp. 4–5). The difference between crisis management and crisis leadership is that crisis leadership addresses these four factors before, during, and after crises. Crisis leadership can be initiated by taking precrisis audits, enacting previously developed key capabilities during the crisis, and reassessing crisis performance after the crisis ends. Another model of industrial crises is provided by Shrivastava et al. (1988) who note eight key aspects of industrial crises: (1) triggering events that initiate a crisis and become a reference point for identifying crises; (2) large-scale damage is produced; (3) large economic costs emerge; (4) large capital costs accrue; (5) specific causes emerge from human, organizational, and technological factors that trigger the event and lead to regulatory, infrastructure, and preparedness failures; (6) multiple stakeholder involvement and conflict (Shrivastava et al., 1988, p. 291) since multiple stakeholders are invariably involved; (7) responses to crises including mitigation and efforts to prevent future crises; and (8) crisis resolution and extension.

Crises can also be characterized and understood in terms of an unfolding life history or sequence of events (Turner, 1976, 1978). This sequence commences in Stage 1 at a "notionally normal starting point" (Turner, 1976, p. 381) with accepted beliefs about the world and its hazards. Stage 2 involves an incubation period when unnoticed events accumulate but are ignored because they do not accord with prevailing beliefs. Stage 3 involves emergence of a precipitating event that forces recognition of a hazard or emerging crisis. For example, a large fire ball or cloud of gas may be noted in the vicinity of a pipeline, thus indicating a leak is occurring. Stage 4 is the onset of impacts where the immediate effect of the failure of cultural precautions is evident. This is followed by stage 5, rescue and salvage. Stage 6 involves cultural adjustment that is often accomplished in part by holding a governmentally organized public inquiry into the crisis. Based on information and recommendations at the inquiry, regulations and work practices are often adjusted to address the newly acquired understanding of risks and dangers that the crisis produced.

Crises thus clearly require sensing and sensemaking if they are to exist as meaningful phenomena to members of society. Indeed, a crisis exists only when certain events or cues are sensed or noticed and then interpreted as crises by sensemaking. It often takes time to detect or notice important events, or to interpret these as relevant to crises, particularly in cases of "crescive" troubles that accumulate slowly and over time (Beamish, 2002, p. 4). Also, there may be divergent views of the meaning of cues and other events. Indeed, differences among stakeholders, complex situational and communication dynamics, and conflicts in sensemaking can lead to failure to develop shared interpretations of crisis events and to the emergence of incorrect interpretations.

The public inquiry phase in the life history of a crisis is relevant to crisis management and crisis leadership. Public inquiries related to crises and potential crises can occur at two points in the crisis process—prior to industrial development and after crises. Predevelopment hearings are frequently conducted to assess and prevent risks of large-scale technological developments before the developments are constructed and hence before crises emerge. Postcrisis inquiries that inquire into the causes, consequences, and means to prevent crises are common after the crisis. Hearings and inquiries are thus important settings where sensemaking is done prospectively to anticipate crises, and retrospectively to prevent, manage, or mitigate crises. Crises occur when sensemaking is deficient or problematic regarding human, organizational, and technological factors that could potentially cause crises.

Further, crises have two important dimensions: meaningfulness and rhetorical aspects. Events need to be conceived or labelled as crises if they are to be reacted to and addressed as crises. Otherwise, events will be interpreted as isolated events unconnected to other events. Or, crisis events and signs may even go unnoticed and their serious nature may not be understood (Beamish, 2002). Labelling or conceiving events as a crisis releases additional social processes, including efforts to avoid or escape the crisis situation, government action and funding to mitigate the crisis, and legal action. Effective crisis management also requires rhetoric because people have to be persuaded that certain actions need to be undertaken to prevent or control the crisis. Constructing events as a crisis thus requires sensemaking, communicative interaction, and persuasive communication—one or more persons or group needs to convince others that seemingly isolated and benign cues are harbingers of crisis. The rhetorical dimension of crises does not imply that crises do not "really" exist or that they are "merely" rhetorical and exist only in language (McCloskey, 1985). Rather, the research evidence shows that without persuasive communication—rhetorical sensemaking—many events would not be quickly recognized as crises and would be treated as isolated problems or ignored. Indeed, sensemaking is used at many inquiries to expose false or misleading rhetoric, specious claims, and facades that impedes recognition and control of crises.

Following this, we can define crisis sensemaking as the processes through which events and phenomena are noticed, interpreted, and reacted to as crisis events. Through crisis sensemaking, one notices certain events, interprets these events as crises, and responds to these events and phenomena as crises. Organizational crises are important events or phenomena that disrupt or threaten ongoing organizational processes and settings. Sensemaking is a central and fundamental aspect of crises. Public hearings and inquiries thus provide an important setting for crisis sensemaking.

Crisis Management

Crisis management can be defined as the activities and resources that organizational actors use to prevent, control, mitigate, recover from, and resolve crises. Crisis management involves processes of thinking about many different crises and how they occur; anticipating systems where failures can cause crises; and planning for stakeholder actions related to crises (Mitroff, 2005, p. 205). Crisis management can thus involve preplanning for crises, although Mitroff tends to regard preplanning as crisis leadership given the rarity of preplanning and crisis preparation in organizations. Inquiry sensemaking is relevant to the crisis-management process in several ways. At a general level, inquiry discourse often investigates key topics related to the crisis such as how it was noticed, how it occurred, and how it was handled or contained and resolved. This discourse involves sensemaking oriented to assessment of past actions that can be used in planning for future crises.

Mitroff and Pearson (1993, pp. 10–11) and Mitroff (2005, p. 205) have also identified the phases or mechanisms of crisis management: (1) signal detection or sensing of early warning signals, (2) preparedness and prevention, (3) damage containment, (4) business recovery, (5) learning, and (6) redesign. Inquiry testimony and discourse usually address many of these topics, including how the event was detected, the preparations that had been undertaken, actions needed to contain damage, steps taken to get the business operating again, what was learned, and how the company has altered its practices based on what was learned through the crisis. Hence inquiry testimony and transcripts provide important insights into crises, and organizations and managers can learn from this information.

Further, Mitroff (2005) offers seven lessons for crisis management that highlight the importance of inquiry sensemaking and information provision in crisis survival. First, one needs to prepare emotionally before the crisis. Inquiry testimony reveals the emotional nature of crisis events and sensemaking. Having personnel attend an inquiry into a serious incident involving harm to persons could potentially facilitate emotional learning and encourage crisis preparation by managers and workers. Second, one needs to think critically. Critical thinking is an inherent feature of inquiry discourse. It is also a process that is stimulated and encouraged by observing or reading inquiry testimony given the extent to which conflicting facts are offered and challenged during inquiry testimony—for example, through processes of interrogation of witnesses. Third, one needs to use social and political skills. These skills are topical and visible in inquiries; hence, managers can gain insights into key social and political skills for crisis management by examining inquiry testimony and documents. Fourth, one needs to address and expect uncertainty and complexity in crisis events. These are key features of crisis events that one learns about through inquiries. Fifth, inquiry testimony often reveals denial among managers and workers—and other stakeholders—as well as revealing the consequences of such denial. Denial can be addressed and overcome by learning to think unethically and learning to view the world as a sociopath. Involvement in inquiry testimony and other processes can encourage critical thinking that can help to overcome denial. Sixth, one needs to redesign organizations to overcome the image of an organization where parts can be added without disrupting the organization. That is, one needs to redesign organizations for crisis leadership. Inquiry testimony, questions, and reports are often oriented to understanding design defects and encouraging design improvements; hence, they are a source for learning about improved designs. Finally, Mitroff (2005) notes the importance of using existential and spiritual dimensions of life to restore meaning and purpose after a crisis. Existential and spiritual reactions are triggered by crisis events and inquiry participation, including reflection. Thus, managers and others can prepare emotionally for crises by attending inquiries into emotionally charged crises involving other organizations or personnel, by reflecting on crisis events, and by considering the existential and spiritual needs of people faced with crisis.

Crisis management is thus a process of learning and acting effectively as outlined by Mitroff and colleagues (Mitroff, 2005; Mitroff & Pearson, 1993). This chapter emphasizes communication-based issues including story-telling, rhetoric, sensemaking practices, conversations, and valid communication. It assumes that communication is fundamental to crisis management, and that all inquiries and crises involve processes of communication. Effective crisis management is aimed at preventing, managing, and controlling crises. Crisis management is not mere rhetorical legitimization of organizational action.

The Nature of the Public Inquiry

Public hearings and inquiries can be defined as investigations conducted by governmentally mandated bodies to assess important social issues or technologies (Salter & Slaco, 1981, p. 26). They are state-organized face-to-face ceremonial occasions that assemble legitimating and critical institutions for purposes of investigating the causes and consequences of critical social events such as organizational crises (Gephart, 1992). During public hearings and inquiries, inquiry participants seek to describe and understand important features of the events of concern. Generally these persons engage in extensive sensemaking about the events of concern. Public hearings and inquiries are similar to one another (Salter & Slaco, 1981); hence, the present chapter does not further distinguish public inquiries from public hearings.

The public hearing or inquiry process emerged in Great Britain in the 18th to 19th centuries (Kemp, 1985, pp. 178–182) when public meetings were held to draw up petitions for Parliament to endorse a proposed enclosure of public lands and to settle objections to enclosure proposals. Since that time, a large number of public inquiries have been conducted. However, "No two inquiries are alike" (Salter & Slaco, 1981, p. 22). Thus, while it is not possible to specify a set of features common to all inquiries, there are important political and legal characteristics of inquiries that can be noted. First, public inquiries can be either informal or formal in terms of their structure and procedures (Boyer, 1960). An informal inquiry is similar to the town hall meeting (Boyer, 1960). The informal inquiry format allows the convenors great latitude in how to proceed. In contrast, the formal inquiry is a hearing that is similar to courtroom proceedings (Boyer, 1960; Salter & Slaco, 1981). It is conducted by a government appointed hearing board that solicits testimony under oath from witnesses who may be subpoenaed. Cross-examination of witnesses may be undertaken, formal exhibits can be provided, legal counsel may represent key parties to the hearing, and rules of evidence may be employed. The outcomes of formal public hearings and inquiries are commonly a transcript of the actual testimony—the proceedings—and also a hearing report that is provided to government agencies.

Both formal and informal inquiries differ from courtroom proceedings since inquiries have more flexibility regarding evidence than courts and they differ from courts in the way evidence is used (Salter & Slaco, 1981, pp. 191, 194). For example, formal and informal inquiries lack established provisions for disclosing information or for evaluating and weighing evidence. In terms of hearing and using evidence effectively, inquiries are highly dependent on the sensitivity and good will of inquiry commissioners (Salter & Slaco, 1981, p. 195). Nonetheless, inquiry testimony can be used in a court of law or can be the basis for later legal investigations. Inquiry testimony and evidence are therefore not freed from legal processes.

Second, inquiries attempt to bring the public into the planning process (Salter & Slaco, 1981, p. 21). Inquiries are one of three general means for public participation in policy making (Boyer, 1960). Inquiries thus allow public deliberation and input into policy-making about important social issues. Public deliberation involves debate and discussion undertaken in public that aims to produce reasonable, well-formed opinions. In public deliberation, people share or express views, understand others, revise their opinions, and reach agreement on matters of public concern (Delli Carpini, Cook, & Jacobs, 2004, p. 318). Public deliberation is a form of discursive participation that is considered the cornerstone of participatory democracy and representative government (Delli Carpini et al., 2004, p. 315).

An inquiry is thus a temporary forum that involves groups or individuals directly in discursive participation, deliberation, and public policymaking. These groups or individuals are often "active" and "noisy" advocates of an issue or position (Salter & Slaco, 1981, p. 21). By bringing these varied interests together, inquiries facilitate assessment of critical issues and enlarge and extend discussion of these issues (Salter & Slaco, 1981, p. 22). Further, accountability based on discursive participation has replaced consent as the conceptual core of legitimacy in contemporary society (Delli Carpini et al., 2004). Accountability means giving an account that publicly explains and justifies public policy. Following this, we can see that sensemaking defined as the giving of accounts that justify and legitimate public policy is central to public inquiries and hearings.

Third, public hearings tend to emerge at two points in the crisis life cycle as noted above: prior to construction of a technological system, and after an accident or crisis. Predevelopment hearings and inquiries conducted prior to development of large-scale technological systems can be used to assess benefits and problems with such systems. Predevelopment hearings seek to uncover problems that could potentially emerge during the life of a technological development (Kemp, O'Riordan, & Purdue, 1984). The "big public inquiry" is an important type of pre-development hearing. For example, the Sizewell B Inquiry in the United Kingdom was convened by the Secretary of State for Energy to examine a proposal to construct Britain's first pressurized water-based nuclear reactor (Kemp et al., 1984, p. 478). The big public inquiry commonly reflects four characteristics (Kemp et al., 1984, p. 480). First, it is held regarding proposals with national significance when the proposal is one of a series of proposals that can be expected. Second, the proposal is politically contentious and different groups have established positions that differ from one another. Third, the proposal proponent is not independent of the governmental officials or agencies that make the final decision on the proposal, and the proposal is consistent with existing priorities. Fourth, the proposal proponent can use financial, legal, and technical resources that are significantly more substantial than those of objectors to the proposal. Predevelopment inquiries thus assess potential risks and dangers of a proposed development and seek to provide strategies and policies to avoid risks from evolving into crises.

Inquiries are also commonly held following crises. Postcrisis inquiries are a "major instrument" in the cultural adjustment process that occurs subsequent to the onset and initial resolution of organizational crises (Turner, 1976, 1978). In the cultural-adjustment stage of accidents (Turner, 1976, 1978), individuals and agencies review problematic events to determine what happened. They seek to discover how culturally approved precautions could have turned out to be so inadequate (Turner, 1978, p. 91). In this process, inquiry tribunals and participants address the adjustments that need to be made to beliefs and assumptions about risks, as well as the adjustments that need to be made to laws and statutes, to prevent or avoid accidents in the future. These adjustments are based on the new understanding of the world that the crisis has provided. Postaccident inquiries are thus "a major social mechanism for adjusting to the revelations that disasters always provide, and for trying to accommodate the lessons of these revelations into collective experience" (Turner, 1978, p. 201).

The features of public inquiries demonstrate that public inquiries are heavily composed of efforts by social actors to interpret and make sense of crises (e.g., Gephart, 1993). Given that it is often difficult and dangerous for researchers to directly observe crisis events as they unfold in real time, inquiries often provide the best available evidence concerning crisis events and crisis sensemaking despite the retrospective and reconstructed nature of inquiry accounts. They also provide direct evidence of organizational and interorganizational practices used to interpret, manage, and prevent crises and to learn from them. Further, although inquiries are often physically and temporally distant from the crisis and risk events they purport to address, inquiry sensemaking provides a window into how people and organizations undertake sensemaking about risks and crises. In addition, ideas and actions from past crises and inquiries often play a role in efforts to control a current crisis. Also, crisis actions can be selected so as to address anticipated interests and concerns of a future inquiry panel. Thus, by examining public inquiry sensemaking, we can learn how people interpret risks and threats before and after they occur. We can also learn how sensemaking is relevant to organizational adjustment and change that is intended to prevent future risks and accidents.

Public Inquiry Sensemaking

Public inquiry sensemaking has been investigated using five perspectives or approaches: narrative analysis, rhetoric, ethnomethodology, conversation analysis, and critical theory. This section describes these approaches, reviews research done using each approach, and illustrates the approaches using this research.

NARRATIVE ANALYSIS

Narrative can be defined as a first-person account of events or experiences (Riessman, 1993). Narratives are used by social actors to communicate and understand rich details of experiences (Riessman, 1993) and are a key means by which people give voice to their experiences and concerns (Riessman, 1993). Public inquiries are composed in large part of testimony that narrates experiences people have had with crises. Past research that has examined public inquiry narratives has been concerned to describe and understand people's narratives and stories of crises, as recounted at inquiries, as well as their stories of participation in inquiries. Narrative oriented research on public inquiries into crises thus explores the substantive or content dimension of narratives (Gephart, in press) and stories that communicate the nature of crisis events and their implications.

Narratives and stories frame experience by emphasizing certain features of the world and de-emphasizing other features. Narrative analysis thus examines the substance of people's stories, how stories are assembled or "put together" (Riessman, 1993, p. 2), and the cultural resources that stories use. Narrative analysis reveals how individuals and groups understand and interpret events, and how they create meaning by using narratives to make sense of experience (Barry & Elmes, 1997, p. 432).

Narratives of public inquiries into crises are uncommon in the scholarly literature. Narratives of legal action and courtroom experiences related to crises are more common. For example, Ridington (1982, 1990) has described how the Dunne-za aboriginal people from the Blueberry Reserve in northern British Columbia, Canada, used legal processes to resist sour gas wells and processing facilities on their lands following an uncontrolled blowout of highly toxic hydrogen sulfide (sour) gas. One elegant narrative of inquiry sensemaking is found in Brody's (1981) discussion of how the Dunne-za people experienced a hearing into a proposal for construction of an oil and gas pipeline.

The native people were informed of the inquiry by an announcement fixed to their community hall door stating dates, terms, and conditions. The hearing was characterized by the Northern Pipeline Agency as an opportunity for aboriginals to respond to draft conditions and terms for the pipeline even though the terms of the pipeline had already been established. The announcement was written in "tortured bureaucratese" that obscured the meaning of documents and made the pipeline a "vast and distant enigma" to the people affected.

The hearing was held on a good day to hunt—the weather was cold and clear, and a bear den had just been discovered. People talked about whether to hunt or to attend the hearing. They decided to attend the hearing and to hunt the next morning. Brody chronicles the lengthy hearing, the room arrangements, and the atmosphere. Two separate events emerged. The formal hearing was conducted by the Chair. Pipeline personnel spoke in English, using professional terms and jargon. The hearing was a business trip for these people and they were ready to leave when the hearing adjourned at 2 p.m. In contrast, Blueberry Reserve residents spoke in Beaver that required translation to English. Once the formal hearing ended, the aboriginals provided a feast and urged the visitors to stay. The aboriginals had more to say once the whites were feasting on their food and the hearing formality had dissipated. As the feast progressed, a band member brought out a dream map unpacked only on very special occasions. The people then spoke about what they wanted and needed. But the discussion ended when the white officials hurried to their buses. This puzzled the natives who expect someone to drum and chant once the dream map—a map to heaven—is unpacked.

The narrative shows how the rhetoric of economic development was used to deprive the Blueberry people of their economic future (Brody, 1981). Each group held an understanding of events that differed from that of the other culture. The two different accounts produce an ironic contrast that reveals the power effects that formal institutional logics have on the public.

RHETORICAL ANALYSIS

Rhetorical analysis is complimentary to narrative analysis and is often applied to narratives. Rhetoric is the art of speaking and the study of how people understand (McCloskey, 1985, p. 29). It is "the art of discovering warrantable beliefs and improving those beliefs in shared discourse" (Booth, 1974, in McCloskey, 1985, p. 29). Building on this definition, rhetorical analysis addresses how stories and narratives persuade readers and hearers of their authenticity, and how story features such as omissions shape interpretations (Brown, 2000). The focus in rhetorical analysis is often texts, since rhetorical analysis conceives organizational documents as a form of discourse designed to persuade readers of their truthfulness rather than as true accounts (Brown, 2000; Gephart, in press).

Sensemaking, from the view of scholars of narrative and rhetoric, is conceived as a narrative process involving interpretation and meaning production that produces intersubjective accounts (Brown, 2000, pp. 45–46). Sensemaking is accomplished through narratives that (1) make the unexpected expectable (Robinson, 1981, in Brown, 2000, p. 47); (2) allow comprehension of causal relationships so they can be predicted, understood, and potentially controlled; and (3) assist organizational participants in mapping reality (Brown, 2000, p. 47).

The rhetorical analysis of organizational texts is a craft exercise that requires creativity. There is no single accepted approach to rhetorical analysis (Brown, 2000). The rhetorical analysis of organizational documents conceives texts as an exercise in universalizing, essentializing, and panoptic control (Brown, 2000, p. 50); hence, nonuniversal, inessential, and uncontrollable features of texts and accounts are investigated (Gephart, in press). The rhetorician examines authorial strategies that construct a consistent text, legitimate professions, and avoid questioning the legitimacy of governments. Rhetorical studies of public inquiry sensemaking seek to understand how inquiry reports support the legitimacy of social institutions and extend prevailing ideologies (Brown, 2000, p. 48). Inquiry reports are considered to be texts that are designed to persuade us to accept contestable ideas (Brown, 2000, p. 48). Rhetorical analysis of organizational texts, including public inquiry reports, assumes that (1) authors embed interpretations in their texts, (2) texts are derived from and acquire meaning in relation to other texts, and (3) texts are power effects that incorporate and reflect institutional and ideological circumstances (Brown, 2000, p. 49).

The rhetorical approach to crisis inquiry sensemaking was used by Brown (2000) to analyze the Allitt Inquiry report on attacks on children in Ward 4 of the Grantham and Kesteven Hospital in the United Kingdom. The inquiry sought to explain how a nurse could commit crimes including murder against young patients and how these crimes could go undetected if institutions and professionals were acting effectively. To explain this situation, the report constructed a narrative consistent with prevailing institutional logics and expectations (Brown, 2000). The first rhetorical theme Brown (2000) surfaced and analyzed was normalizing and demonizing. The inquiry team constructed a narrative of nurse Allitt as apparently free of disorder; for example, by recounting her normal babysitting experiences. Abnormalities such as her tendency to exhibit injuries were considered unexceptional. The sole plausible interpretation of the evidence was that Allitt went unnoticed because she did nothing unusual. However, an alternative narrative could have been created to show Allitt as demonizing: "The inquiry team deliberately made sense of ambiguous and sometimes contradictory information to construct one sort of narrative (normalizing) rather than another (demonizing), and that this represented a contestable choice, an invention not a discovery" (Brown, 2000, p. 55).

A second rhetorical practice contrasted the observation of events with the discernment of causes. Each incident was noticed individually but the pattern was only detected after lengthy police investigation. This process is plausible and resonates with people's sensemaking proclivities because people often notice events but fail to discern a pattern. Disease, limited resources, and accidental harm were plausible alternative explanations for the deaths and injuries. Third, the report uses blaming and absolving strategies to allocate responsibility for detection. Things appeared normal, the pattern was complex and only clear retrospectively, the events were unique, and the small number of previous medical homicides occurred in North America where similar detection delays occurred. Thus, institutions were absolved of blame for failure to rapidly detect the source of harm to children.

The Allitt inquiry thus shows inquiry reports are contrived rhetorical products—artefacts created to persuade us to accept a contestable interpretation of events (Brown, 2000). Inquiry sensemaking produced novel plot lines that linked events and provided explanations of events in ways previously only inchoately realized. And the report sought to close down rather than open competing plot lines and questions. The final report thus ameliorated anxiety by providing a sensible account of why Allitt went undetected, thereby increasing the public's sense of control. More specifically, inquiry sensemaking involves deployment of arguments with the intent to influence others' interpretations and meanings (Brown, 2000, p. 67). Public inquiry sensemaking as encoded in rhetorical products such as final reports is thus an exercise in power used to support the legitimacy of social institutions and to extend the hegemony of prevailing ideologies (Brown, 2000). The inquiry can be viewed as a cathartic ceremony that produced a mythical report to help society enact fantasies of control to cope with mysterious events.

ETHNOMETHODOLOGY

Ethnomethodology (Garfinkel, 1967) investigates accounts and the accountability of the social world by studying the sensemaking that occurs in descriptive accounts (Leiter, 1980, p. 160). Accounts are any intentional communications between two or more people that reveal features of a social setting and serve the pragmatic interests of participants (Leiter, 1980, p. 162). Accounts are descriptive accounts because they organize and render observable the features of society (Leiter, 1980, pp. 161–162); they communicate understanding; and they assist people in finding meaning in objects and events. The focus in ethnomethodology is how people depict the world—the work people do in talk and text to make the world observable (Leiter, 1980, pp. 236, 240). Ethnomethodology's interest in accounts addresses accounting or sensemaking practices members use to create intersubjective objects (Leiter, 1980, p. 163), not the content of accounts per se. The only place to find sensemaking practices is in people's talk and behavior (Leiter, 1980, p. 240).

Ethnomethodology has also been depicted as the science of sensemaking (Heap, 1979) that studies the methods or procedures of practical reasoning individuals use to give sense to the world at the same time they accomplish daily actions (Coulon, 1995). Sensemaking is "the genesis of meaning which social phenomena have for us as well as for the actors" (Schutz, 1964, p. 7, in Leiter, 1980, p. 52). Two core concepts of ethnomethodology refer to properties of social phenomena that are foundational to sensemaking are reflexivity and indexicality. Reflexivity refers to the self-constituting property of social phenomena including accounts and conversations (Garfinkel, 1967; Handel, 1982; Leiter, 1980). "Accounts establish what is accountable in a setting. At the same time, the setting is made up of those accounts" (Handel, 1982, p. 39). For example, public hearings are reflexive because crisis accounts produced during hearings produce descriptions of crises that are assumed to be external to accounts as well as constitute the setting as a hearing concerning a crisis. Indexicality refers to the natural incompleteness of words and language. Words, terms, and expressions have a fringe of incompleteness such that the meaning of terms can be clarified only by referring to the context of use of the word or term (Garfinkel, 1967; Handel, 1982, p. 40; Leiter, 1980). Thus, the meaning of a word or term depends on its context of use. There is no absolute meaning of a word independent of context. This concept or property suggests that negotiation of meaning is an ongoing task in settings where sensemaking occurs.

The focus in ethnomethodology is the ways or methods by which members of society assemble settings and behaviors so as to create and sustain a sense of social order (Leiter, 1980, p. 159). These interpretive methods or sensemaking practices provide members with the ongoing sense that the social order is an objective fact independent of perception (Leiter, 1980,

p. 160) and that the meaning of this world is shared by members of society. Four interpretive or sensemaking practices that are central to the ethnomethodological perspective (Cicourel, 1973; Garfinkel, 1967; Gephart, in press; Leiter, 1980) have been used to analyze inquiry accounts and sensemaking (Gephart, 1992, 1993, p. 1470). The *reciprocity of perspectives* is a practice where each party to a conversation assumes that they could exchange places with others in the conversation and experience the same perspective on the world. This practice is evident in discourse, for example, when one person makes gestures acknowledging they have heard what the other said. The second practice, using *normal forms,* refers to use of recognizable words and terms to refer to conventional or common (normal) features of the world. People attempt to use normal forms and expect others to do so as well. The third practice is the *etcetera principle.* This practice assumes that the often vague and incomplete aspects of conversation will be clarified or filled in later in the conversation. The final practice, *using descriptive vocabularies as indexical expressions,* refers to the assumption made in conversation that general background knowledge and knowledge of context will be used to interpret statements or actions.

The interpretive practices are promissory and do not settle the factual nature of the world once and for all (Leiter, 1980, p. 55) since interaction is an ongoing process of interpretation and reinterpretation. Thus, ethnomethodology views social actors as actively engaged in sensemaking through conversations, textual accounts, explanations, and discourse (Gephart, 1993, p. 1470). Further, ethnomethodology has established that when sensemaking practices are disrupted, meaning begins to dissolve and members can demand and engage in remedial practices intended to restore a sense of social order. The basic concepts of ethnomethodology suggest that meaning is not inherent in events (Gephart, 1988). An event becomes a disaster when it is socially interpreted and given meaning as a disaster; hence, events become disasters through sensemaking (Gephart, 1988). For ethnomethodology, a disaster thus exists in the interpretations, narratives, and accounts of members. In contrast, members assume that disasters are events external to accounts. The meaning of events that are constructed as disasters is actively managed by groups that offer competing or divergent claims about events. Multiple and differing accounts can be produced for ostensibly the same event (Gephart, 1988). The ethnomethodological perspective thus focuses on the production of accounts and interpretations of disaster rather than treating disasters as reified events that are external to accounts.

Analysis of Sensemaking Practices

Gephart (1988, 1993) provides an analysis of crisis sensemaking using ethnomethodological sensemaking practices. This research examined sensemaking during a federal energy board public inquiry into a pipeline accident. The accident occurred in western Canada in February 1985 and involved a fireball that erupted during efforts to repair a leak of natural gas liquids from a pipeline. Two workers died as a result of the burns they received from the fire and several other workers were seriously burned. Phase 1 of the inquiry was held in March 1985 and lasted six days. Phase 2 was held in October 1985 and lasted three days. The major participants in the hearing were the federal energy board, the company, and legal counsel for the widow of the pipeline foreman who was fatally burned and who had been the on-site supervisor of the repair effort. The board heard testimony from workers and managers involved in the repair effort, including workers who were seriously burned.

The research compared and contrasted views of the government board, company managers, and workers as a means to pose and answer the following four questions related to inquiry sensemaking. First, what were the important terms, concepts, and vocabularies used in sensemaking about the accident that occurred during the hearing? The study found that the key themes used in sensemaking were responsibility, risk, and safety. Second, how did participants use risk and blame concepts to interpret the event? Here, the study found that the board's policies and mandate prevented explicit blaming of persons. Instead, actors sought to assign responsibility and control to specific others. Organizational schemes that addressed authority, responsibility, rules, and policies were used in this process. Third, how were sensemaking practices used to interpret disasters? In this case, all witnesses, legal counsel, and board members used sensemaking practices to produce coherent accounts of events and to challenge aspects of such accounts. The district manager was found responsible for a critical decision that led to the unplanned fire and injuries. Basically, the district manager failed to order the work crew to flare or voluntarily ignite the leaking gas early in the event, an act that would have incinerated the residue and prevented an unplanned fire from occurring. The district manager was shown to have breached sensemaking practices and to have construed the meaning of events in a manner different from that of other participants in the hearing, including in particular other managers of the company, and the inquiry board.

The fourth question asked: What social entities—organizations, persons, selves—were constructed as interpretive schemes during disaster sensemaking, and what role did the schemes play in interpretation? This question addresses how key resources for sensemaking—members' conceptions of personal selves and of organizations—were used to interpret and allocate responsibility for the critical decision. In this case, the district manager's use of the organizational scheme as an interpretive resource differed greatly from the conceptions of others. For example, the board emphasized public safety as a key goal for the pipeline organization and workers emphasized and discussed personal safety. In contrast, the district manager emphasized financial risk from flaring and the relative safety that emerged from voluntary ignition. The board and workers also constructed the pipeline organization as a clear hierarchy of authority with the district manager in the key position of authority to decide how to control the leak. In contrast, the district manager argued that on-site personnel had discretion over key decisions. The board thus viewed the company as a clear hierarchy of authority and a clear set of rules for flaring that, if followed, would have prevented the accidental fire. They held the district manager responsible for the accident because he was located in a key position of authority and because he interpreted organizational rules, policies, and general features in a problematic manner.

This study thus reveals several features of public inquiry sensemaking, summarized as propositions (Gephart, 1993, pp. 1506–1508) that may be evident in inquiries in general. First, sensemaking practices are used by inquiry participants to describe features of critical events. Second, inquiry participants use organizational schemes to interpret and explain organizational actions and identify actors who are responsible for events. Third, individual and organizational actions are interpreted using risks, hazards, and dangers as interpretive schemes. Fourth, the effectiveness of organizational and individual risk-management actions will be interpreted using organizational schemes. Fifth, actors will be assigned responsibility for events when (a) they are shown to have misunderstood procedures or behaved in a way inconsistent with organizational schemes, (b) the actors are constructed as ineffective at managing risks, and (c) actors are constructed as generally problematic selves in terms of organizational schemes. In contrast, actors will be credited with contributing to the prevention or resolution of critical events where their actions are interpreted as being consistent with organizational schemes.

Quantitative Sensemaking

Gephart (1997) used sensemaking practices to examine the neglected topic of quantitative sensemaking during hearings. This study examined the discourse that occurred at an Alberta Energy Resources Conservation Board hearing into an uncontrolled flow of toxic hydrogen sulfide gas from an exploratory well being drilled near Lodgepole, Alberta, in 1977–1978. The well flowed uncontrolled for 28 days during which it released approximately sixteen million cubic meters of gas with a hydrogen sulfide content estimated at 25%. The hearing lasted two days and produced a 217-page official proceedings and a 16-page final report.

The study posed three research questions. First, what quantitative practices and terms were used in sensemaking about organizational crises, and how? Second, how were quantitative practices and measures related to management of risks and hazards? Third, what variations in quantitative sensemaking occurred across different stakeholder groups, and what were the action implications? In terms of the first and second questions, the study found that quantitative terms were used extensively as descriptors of features of the uncontrolled flow. Detecting and affirming the existence of an uncontrolled flow was stated to have been accomplished through measurement of the flow, although the measures were estimated and were inexact. As reported in testimony, quantitative terms and measurement practices transformed subjective perceptions (e.g., odors) into objective factual hazards and led personnel to assess and interpret these hazards using mathematical and engineering practices. Quantification of hazards made hazards amenable to management although inquiry testimony also revealed that many of the measures were inexact estimates based on subjective criteria. Thus, the plausibility of claimed measures was important given the problems of accuracy of measurement. In terms of the third question, the study found that quantified hazards were basic to the rationale for the inquiry and for subsequent actions taken by the energy board. The energy board focused on procedural measures for protecting groups, on manual methods of measuring features of the flow, and on the accuracy of measures of the hazard. The board's goal was to assess hazards, separate real from other hazards, and to assess attempts by the company to mitigate the hazards. In contrast, the company's view was that individual perceptions were a primary means to detect and assess the flow and measures of the flow were supplements to perception. The major action taken by the company was thus to monitor the flow to insure that the flow did not create a hazard. From the company view, the flow was a risk but not a hazard since local conditions, e.g., wind, prevented it from becoming a hazard.

The study thus showed that quantification is important in sensemaking about the causes of oil and gas accidents. Perceptual cues such as unusual odors suggest that an uncontrolled flow of hydrocarbons may be occurring—for example, a well blowout. However, quantitative measures of the gases being released are needed to interpret perceptual cues and to transform them into facts.

Quantification and measurement are therefore sensemaking tools that allow phenomena to be identified, treated as real, and monitored. That is, quantitative sensemaking plays an important role in determining the nature, causes, and consequences of accidents (Gephart, 1997, pp. 589–590). Quantification and measurement also provide grounds for subsequent actions taken in regard to risks and hazards. Further, different groups and stakeholders used quantitative terms and sensemaking differently and there is some evidence that these differences relate to the institutional settings, frameworks, and interpretive logics of these groups. Finally, quantitative sensemaking is particularly important in inquiry sensemaking because quantification is an important tool with which professionals describe and analyze the world. Inquiries provide important occasions for professional interpretation of accident causes.

Cultural Rationalities

One study of crisis sensemaking based in ethnomethodology and symbolic anthropology investigated differing cultural rationalities used by different stakeholders during an inquiry to interpret crisis events (Gephart, Steier, & Lawrence, 1990). This research hypothesized that each distinct group or subculture at an inquiry may have its own distinctive form of organization and its own interpretive scheme (Gephart et al., 1990) or "rationality" (Douglas & Wildavsky, 1982). These rationalities are used in sensemaking and the management of meaning. Each rationality can be conceived as a distinctive interpretive scheme or framework used to produce a distinctive interpretation of events. The rationalities investigated were hierarchical rationality, market rationality, and sectarian rationality (Douglas & Wildavsky, 1982).

The study found the three rationalities were evident at the inquiry and were used by different groups. The National Energy Board of Canada used hierarchical rationality to interpret events. *Hierarchical rationality* assumes tightly knit and clearly stratified groups that use rules and standard operating procedures to understand and control behavior (Gephart et al., 1990, p. 31). Events that threaten the hierarchy are conceived as risks. In *market rationality*, clear individual goals or proclivities are assumed to exist and group boundaries are weak. This is an individualistic culture. Achievement is evaluated in terms of some currency, and events and behaviors are interpreted in terms of rules of fair exchange (Gephart et al., 1990, p. 32). Events that produce losses in terms of some currency or that change market rules are interpreted as risks. Sectarian rationality occurs in tightly knit groups with limited stratification and high value placed on individuals and equality. Behaviors and events are interpreted in terms of individual proclivities toward goodness and evil, rather than rules. Events that threaten group integrity are conceived as risks (Gephart et al., 1990, p. 33).

CONVERSATION ANALYSIS

Conversation analysis is based in ethnomethodology and assumes that speakers produce "sensible and precise communication" (Lynch, 1993, p. 25) by placing words and utterances within situationally coordinated action sequences. Conversation analysis seeks to understand the underlying properties of conversation that influence how speakers coordinate their actions to create coherent sequences of talk. It investigates "the demonstrably rational properties of indexical expressions by describing recurrent sequential actions in conversation and specifying formal rules for generating their organizational features" (Lynch, 1993, p. 25). The conversation-analysis view of language contrasts with the views of philosophers and linguists who assume words and utterances are "inherently meaningful" (Lynch, 1993, p. 25).

Michael Lynch and David Bogen (Bogen & Lynch, 1989; Lynch & Bogen, 1996) used concepts from ethnomethodology and conversation analysis to analyze testimony at the Iran-Contra congressional hearings. The Iran-Contra affair posed the potential for a crisis of confidence in the Reagan presidential administration because of the sales of antitank and ground-to-air missiles to Iran. A central feature of the Iran-Contra affair, the transactions threatened the credibility of the administration. The arms sale was authorized by neither Congress nor its intelligence oversight committees, and it violated U.S. policies against aiding terrorist nations. The sale was presumably intended as a means to free hostages, which also violated U.S. policies against paying ransom for hostages. The hearings addressed the legitimacy of the sale of arms to Iran.

Bogen and Lynch (1989) were interested in the methods by which official histories get assembled, and in how the social production of testimony at the Iran-Contra hearings gave rise to the irresolute features of the Iran-Contra affair (Lynch & Bogen, 1996, p. 5). They argue that the conventional methods for producing history are an important topic for social research, and further, that the public record of the Iran-Contra hearings provides a rich documentary source for studying methods by which plausible, coherent accounts of historical events get assembled.

In their research, Lynch and Bogen (1996) depict the Iran-Contra hearing as an example of the discourse of a public tribunal and the history-producing work done by parties to an official investigation (Lynch & Bogen, 1996, p. 1). Lynch and Bogen (1996) sought to develop insights into situated practices through which historical events are assembled and decomposed. In particular, they examined how documentary evidence was used by committees, along with details of testimonial discourse, to construct conventional history from documentary evidence at hand. They focused on procedures through which testimony was "solicited, verified, challenged and equivocated" (Lynch & Bogen, 1996, p. 5). In this process, they examined how written documents were used at the hearing and the practical methods through which the event was assembled, contested, and stabilized (Lynch & Bogen, 1996, p. 7). Their research thus addressed the practical, discursive methods that the interrogators at hearings used to assimilate witnesses' stories into a conventional history, and the methods that witnesses used to resist having their narratives assimilated into conventional history. This is an important domain for investigation by crisis researchers because the production of a conventional history of crisis events is a central focus and preoccupation of crisis hearings and inquiries in general. Here, I outline the findings Bogen and Lynch (1989) and Lynch and Bogen (1996) produced in relation to three important issues: (1) the production of conventional history from narratives, (2) the interrogation process at inquiries, and (3) the production of plausible deniability.

The Production of Conventional History

Bogen and Lynch investigated the conventional methods by which official histories get assembled (Bogen & Lynch, 1989, p. 197). Public hearings are oriented to producing a report that provides an official, conventional history of an event of significance—an event that is prominent in media and popular imagination (Bogen & Lynch, 1989, p. 199). Hearings are a fact-finding operation that seeks to produce a specific product—a conventional history in the form of a final report that definitively states a chronology of dates, times, events, agents, and actions (Bogen & Lynch, 1989) related to a significant event. A conventional history is a realistic account of an event presented as a "singular, cogent and univocal historical narrative" (Lynch & Bogen, 1996, p. 58). Bogen and Lynch (1989) assume that official histories are assembled using conventional, pragmatic features of social discourse that extend beyond the context of hearing testimony. Bogen and Lynch also assume that conventional methods are an important topic for discourse analyses of social issues.

Lynch and Bogen found that the Iran-Contra hearings were viewed by investigating committee members as a fact-finding mission to produce a committee report containing a classical style history—a master narrative transcending individual narratives of witnesses produced during the hearing. The report was a product of investigators charged to write an official history and the testimony of witnesses questioned on relevant matters. As a conventional history, the report had a plain organization consisting of dates, times, and ordinary methods of reasoning and writing about events that was indifferent to issues in professional history writing (Lynch & Bogen, 1996, p. 58). It provided a linear chronology of events (p. 59) and arranged stories of events in chronological order (p. 158). The account of events provided was stated to be factual, and no disclaimers were included in the account (p. 59). The factual account produced ironic contrasts between actors' narratives and matters of fact. And the account often included quotations from testimony and hearing documents (p. 158).

The researchers found that a conventional history is a narrative written in an anonymous (Bogen & Lynch, 1989, p. 59) and impersonal voice (Lynch & Bogen, 1996, p. 158). A conventional history does not provide an explicit standpoint from which the narrator came to know events, and the narrator does not play a role in the key events. Rather, the narrator's voice frames events, interprets them, and comments on them from the perspective of a "virtual" or "superwitness" with no concrete place in the world (Lynch & Bogen, 1996, p. 158). The narrator attempts to rise above limits imposed by "partisan interests, hidden motives, organizational divisions of labor, and temporal and spatial localities" (Lynch & Bogen, 1996,

p. 159). The questioning, answering, and use of documents that occurs in testimony on which a conventional history is based are all done with an "eye to the place" occupied by the testimony in the accumulating record on which the conventional history will be based (Lynch & Bogen, 1996, p. 58). Thus, a detailed orientation to the production of conventional history is basic to the very constitution of the record of inquiry testimony that is produced.

Interrogation of Witnesses

A second important feature of hearings is the process of producing testimony by posing questions to witnesses. Lynch and Bogen (1996) describe this as a process of interrogation based on the idea that under the right conditions, a sequence of questions can compel a reluctant witness to disclose the truth (Lynch & Bogen, 1996, p. 128). The interrogator thus seeks to produce truthful testimony by means of discursive examination rather than by using coercion or torture, since a coerced confession is considered suspect. Interrogation can be defined as "a form of dialogue that instantiates the possibility of an immanent, logical analysis of its own contingent performance" (Lynch & Bogen, 1996, p. 128).

The basic rule of interrogation is that the interrogator poses questions and the witness answers them. A question requests information (Lynch & Bogen, 1996, p. 130) although "questions may be scarcely recognizable as requests for information" (Lynch & Bogen, 1996, p. 131). Questions in transcripts of hearings are statements by interrogators punctuated by question marks. An answer is a response or statement subsequent to a question. The identity of an utterance as an answer is based on the contingent relevance of the answer in relation to a prior question (Lynch & Bogen, 1996, p. 131). Thus, the in situ identity of an utterance is based on contextual rules and relevancies and the formal speech act identity of an utterance may not correspond to how the utterance is interpreted in actual discourse (Lynch & Bogen, 1996, p. 131). Indeed, questions from interrogators often request more than a yes or no response. For example, open-ended questions solicit stories and invite reactions (Lynch & Bogen, 1996, p. 135). Questions can also be posed in a restrictive manner that compels a binary choice, and by using this approach one can "press" a witness into making an admission that would otherwise be avoided.

Lynch and Bogen (1996) outline seven features of interrogation they found in the Iran-Contra hearings that can also be expected in other crisis-related hearings. First, questions often take the form of assertions or descriptions that inform a witness about particular issues about which they are accountable (Lynch & Bogen, 1996, p. 140). Second, these assertions and descriptions are presented as formulations of facts. Third, the sequential design of questioning allows the witness an opportunity to respond after each question. Fourth, questions strongly prefigure witness confirmation and if the question is disconfirmed, the witness is burdened with the work of explaining why the question is disconfirmed. Fifth, questions are designed and understood as being linked both progressively and in sequence to a line of argument that is unfolding (Lynch & Bogen, 1996, p. 141). Sixth, witnesses and questioners are held accountable for organizing their actions in accordance with the scheme of interrogation. Finally, interrogation places witnesses in a dilemma. In an adversarial dialogue, questions can carry or lead up to accusations and the impugning of witnesses (Lynch & Bogen, 1996, p. 141). Given that witnesses are often asked to confirm a series of statements or questions leading up to a key question, the witness can then deny the key question or contradict it only at the cost of contradicting prior testimony. Or, the witness can accept the accusations being offered and the impugning of the person to whom the accusations are addressed.

The structure of interrogation makes the tribunal a "liminal space" where the different accounts of events confront one another in a "vivid and potentially hostile forum" (Lynch & Bogen, 1996, p. 177). For witnesses, an important issue becomes how to resist the accusations and impugning statements of the "truth-finding engine" (p. 152).

The Production of Plausible Deniability

Bogen and Lynch (1989) therefore examined how witnesses can resist having their testimony interpreted in ways that undermine their credibility. They focused on practices of story-telling and the construction of plausible deniability during the hearing. Plausible deniability is the documentary practice through which parties to an event anticipate the significance of the event and use available records and practices to facilitate denials of their activities if the record of events comes under hostile scrutiny in the future. People can be hostile natives during testimony if they were party to creating documents under consideration and did so in anticipation of hostile scrutiny. The veracity of these native accounts then becomes topical at the hearing and is resolved through discourse that addresses and reveals story-telling entitlements.

The analysis revealed how the unfolding record of testimony was put to use in situations that reflexively constituted the record. To undertake the analysis, Bogen and Lynch (1989) examined select segments of testimony at the Iran-Contra hearings given by Oliver North. The conduct of testimony relied on organizational properties of conversational story-telling—methods people use to tell plausible and coherent stories about past events. Bogen and Lynch (1989) used conversational analysis concepts to examine problems that the properties of narrative raise for the task of assembling conventional histories. That is, they examined conflicting features of narrative history and conventional history. Narratives or stories typically report experience in which the teller plays a role and they are organized around the story-teller's experiences. The plausibility and other features of the story depend on how the teller experienced or witnessed the events retold—their unique access to events and their entitlements to tell the story from a particular perspective. The unfolding story establishes how speakers came to be in a position to know about the story and how they happen to care; that is, their local identity and story entitlements. For witnesses, the display of their entitlements is important to establishing the plausibility of the story and its objectivity. Yet conventional history presupposes objective events that are not influenced by the local character of stories and incidental observations of witnesses. Hence witnesses face a problem of providing testimony that is adequate from a conventional history perspective but which protects the respondent's entitlements as a teller of, and party to, events in question.

For example, hostile native witnesses such as Oliver North could give testimony that preserved the equivocal features of records that were products of effort to establish plausible deniability. They could deny evidence of this prior effort and provide claims consistent with equivocal features. In this case, North was questioned about efforts to enlist Central Intelligence Agency support during a shipment of HAWK missiles. Counsel sought to learn whether Mr. Clarridge, a CIA official, knew the planes carried arms and not oil-drilling parts. In reply, North said, "I did at some point confirm to him that it was not oil-drilling equipment but that it was HAWKS. As w-wuz very obvious to almost everybody out there at that point because they were reading the same sensitive intelligence that I was" (North, in Bogen & Lynch, 1989, p. 217).

North worked to disentitle himself as teller and character from Clarridge's knowledge. The temporal formulation of "point" is specifically vague and not readily placed chronologically, but fits the narrative. North confirmed to the counsel what Clarridge already knew, and indicated he did not thus "inform" Clarridge, but merely confirmed the shipment based on information from an impersonal source also available to Clarridge and others—"sensitive intelligence." North thus disentitles himself from any claim to be the source of Clarridge's original knowledge of the shipment. North told a story in which he, as a character, is placed somewhere distant from the scene. The relationship between the shipment and CIA involvement remains indeterminate and plausible deniability is produced.

This example shows how witnesses use the differing practices of conversational story-telling and doing conventional history to build a plausible basis to deny implications of the record and to create narratives that cannot be readily compared to the record. Witnesses can thereby provide accounts at hearings that resist translation into generalized narratives, thereby constraining the goal of producing a conventional history of the event.

HABERMASIAN CRITICAL THEORY

Habermas' critical theory (Alvesson & Wilmott, 1992; Gephart & Pitter, 1993; Habermas, 1973, 1979, 1989; Offe, 1984, 1985) offers an integrated micro- and macro-level perspective on the production and reproduction of social order. At the macro level, critical theory posits a theory of successive crises that can occur in capitalist societies and can culminate in a legitimation crisis—a breakdown of society that emerges when the state fails to secure the loyalty of citizens. At the micro level, critical theory posits and examines how four types of speech acts that compose the ideal speech situation are enacted in social settings such that truly legitimate and democratic decisions are reached in society. The two levels of analysis are integrated insofar as speech acts in specific settings can be examined to understand how these speech acts legitimate or delegitimate macro structures such as government agencies and key social institutions (Gephart & Pitter, 1993). Critical theory is relevant to understanding crisis sensemaking because it provides an understanding of the conditions under which public hearings will be conducted by key social institutions. It also provides insights into how discourse at public hearings produces valid decisions that address broad interests, or alternatively, how communication and sensemaking are distorted to serve particular interests of capitalists. This section reviews the key features of critical theory that inform our understanding of crisis sensemaking during public inquiries.

One basic assumption of critical theory is that contradictions arise during social reproduction, where a contradiction is a tendency in a specific mode of production to destroy the very preconditions on which the mode of production depends (Gephart & Pitter, 1993; Offe, 1984, p. 132). The fundamental contradiction in advanced capitalism is the contradiction between the desire for profit and the available profit, since the desire for profit exceeds that which is available. This contradiction leads to steering problems for governments that must keep the economy vital while preserving the legitimacy of state institutions. Steering problems result in crises if they cannot be resolved. Large distributive injustices emerge in capitalist society given that in capitalism there is a tendency for profits to fall, and given that capitalists skim profit by appropriating the surplus value of labor. That is, there is an irrational basis for social distribution. This leads the state to intervene with policies that seek to defuse political conflict and to mask problems and contradictions through ideology. Ideology systematically distorts communication (Habermas, 1979; Kemp, 1985) and thus hides contradictions and conflicts.

The Crisis Cycle

Economic crises emerge because exploitation of nature requires continuous and costly increases in technical rationality to offset market forces, and there are real limits to resources that can be extracted from given ecosystems. Thus, the state tends to intervene in the economy by means of markets and planning to preserve adequate profits. *Political crises* then arise in the administrative subsystem of society when government fails to accomplish economic imperatives (e.g., the desired rate of profit) or when capitalist interests that are served by the state become visible. *Motivational crises* arise when state-required motivations for people (e.g., the motivation to work for given wages) become discrepant from motivations supplied by the socio-cultural system. This can arise when the role of the state in protecting the hidden interests of capitalists at the expense of labor is revealed or where the demand for rewards to labor exceeds the available supply of rewards and workers interpret their share as unfair. This perceived unfairness leads people to be estranged from standard social motivations and produces a failure of what Habermas (1973) terms action-motivating meanings. These crises can thus lead in turn to legitimation crises where the state fails to secure mass loyalty. Legitimation crises carry the risks that (1) the state is threatened with disintegration, (2) the basic organizing principles of society will change, or (3) social control will be accomplished through authoritarian repression (Habermas, 1973).

The crisis potential of advanced capitalism, and the simultaneous role of the state as steering agent for the economy and legitimating agent for society, puts pressure on the state to make the legitimation system as independent of the administrative system as possible (Habermas, 1973). The result is that legitimating institutions emerge in society. These are organizations that are expert in legitimation (Berger & Luckmann, 1966) and that bestow legitimacy on other institutions as a means to legitimate themselves. Crisis inquiry boards and agencies are examples of legitimating institutions that respond to industrial crises by providing interpretations of events that legitimate key state agencies (Gephart & Pitter, 1993). Industrial crises also create the potential for critical institutions to emerge and to provide delegitimating interpretations of the actions and policies of legitimating institutions (Gephart & Pitter, 1993). The public inquiry tends to emerge where critical institutions can mobilize critical interpretations and where legitimating institutions exist and have a mandate and the resources to undertake inquiry. Inquiries thus engage in sensemaking about institutional legitimacy challenges that emerge from crises.

The goal of inquiry boards is generally to relegitimate key institutions and to assign responsibility for the incidents (Gephart & Pitter, 1993). Thus, inquiry discourse is oriented to interpreting events, and both legitimating and critical interpretations are commonly produced. During inquiries, multiple and competing interpretations and rationalities become visible. To preserve governmental legitimacy, the inquiry board must resolve these inconsistencies in a manner that isolates the critical event from the authority of the legitimating institution. Inquiries can thereby be viewed as a mechanism whereby state policy-makers channel demands they find difficult or impossible to accommodate owing to lack of fiscal and institutional resources at their disposal.

Speech Acts and the Ideal Speech Situation

True legitimation as well as rational agreements and decisions require that governmental policies be developed in a democratic manner using valid speech acts that are free from institutional constraints (Habermas, 1979; Kemp, 1985). Four types of speech acts constitute the ideal speech situation and each type of speech act is related to a specific type or form of validity. Communicatives claim to be comprehensible and they function to produce a speech situation where recognizable utterances are present. Representatives claim to be sincere or truthful and they disclose the subjectivity of a speaker. Regulatives claim to be normatively correct and appropriate in a given context, and they function to establish legitimate interpersonal relations. Constatives claim that an utterance is valid or truthful. They are grounded in experiential claims and theoretical discourse and function to represent facts. Critical theory assumes these ideal features of speech acts operate as a taken-for-granted background consensus or framework used by participants to produce, recognize, and assess the rational features of actual speech acts and the extent to which they are free from institutional constraints. Speech is rational and free of constraints if all participants to a conversation have the same chance to employ each of the speech acts.

Kemp (1985) and Gephart (1992) have applied this framework and perspective to understand discourse at public hearings. Kemp (1985) illustrates the model by examining a 100-day public local inquiry into a proposal to construct a nuclear waste fuel reprocessing plant at Windscale, England in 1977. Kemp analyzes how the inquiry process systematically distorted communication and how the subsequent parliamentary decision to allow construction of the facility failed to reflect genuine consensus and was not reached solely due to a better argument.

Critical institutions (e.g., Friends of the Earth) faced constraints on the use of constatives. They had limited funds to develop their arguments and to hire counsel, and did not receive financial support from government. Thus, objectors had difficulty presenting their cases in an appropriate way and faced difficulty in conducting cross-examination. Further, the chair of the hearing ruled economic arguments could count in favor of the development but not against it; hence, critics could not present financial arguments. External constraints on representative speech acts that sincerely expressed views included problems finding expert witnesses with knowledge of nuclear fuel reprocessing who would have been willing to testify. Most such witnesses were already involved in the industry. And the nuclear lobby provided accounts at the inquiry that were not wholly truthful accounts

(Kemp, 1985, pp. 192–193). Regulative speech acts used to command, oppose, permit, or forbid arguments were also not equally distributed. The Official Secrets Act prevented much evidence from being made public. Confidentiality was used as a reason to limit information disclosed to the public. Finally, constative speech acts allowing participants to offer and criticize arguments were institutionally constrained, in part due to the Official Secrets Act that prevented discussion of issues. In addition, inquiry procedure exempted government policy from discussion although the purpose of the inquiry was to develop government policy. And several arguments were omitted or misrepresented in the official report (Kemp, 1985, p. 196).

Kemp (1985) shows "the truthful grounding of arguments both at the inquiry itself and in subsequent parliamentary debate was hindered through misrepresentation and distortion" (Kemp, 1985, p. 196). Each of the four features of distortion-free communication was undermined; hence, any emergent consensus was a false one. Legitimacy for the decision was thus achieved through systematic distortion of communication that allowed the interests of state and capital to prevail. Public hearings may be less open, impartial, and rational than they are claimed to be. The legitimacy of the inquiry may be questioned if distorted communication allows particular interests to dominate general interests.

Gephart (1992) integrated critical theory and sensemaking practices into a framework used to understand discourse at a hearing into a fatal pipeline accident. Different groups were hypothesized to use different criteria to validate claims and to use sensemaking practices to contest the claims and interpretations of other groups. This research explored the question of how sensemaking practices were used to transform various interpretations of events into culturally rational, sensible, and standardized interpretations shared by participants. The research found that sensemaking practices transformed the situated safety logics that workers used to explain crisis actions into top-down safety logics used by regulatory agencies. Situated safety logics are the actual logics of work in action, and these allow for workers to develop ad hoc tactics or practices highly related to specific objects of concern (Baccus, 1986; Gephart, 1992). Top-down safety logics are formal safety logics that specify logical conditions that could deductively prevent accidents by formulating overriding safety mechanisms—e.g., rules and regulations that specify particular equipment and actions—necessary to prevent accidents (Baccus, 1986; Gephart, 1992). Such logics often specify a series of sequential steps or actions necessary to work safely. By transforming situated safety logics into top-down safety logics, the inquiry board was able to show how the situated logic actually used by workers was problematic, and how top-down logic that was specified in regulations would have been more effective but was not used. This process of communicative distortion allowed government legitimating institutions to allocate responsibility for the accident to workers and managers who failed to use formal, top-down safety logic. By showing how top-down logic would have been effective had it been used, the legitimating institution showed that it is capable of preventing or mitigating critical incidents, and that defective actors have intervened in ways the institution could not prevent to pre-empt institutional control.

Summary

The five approaches to understanding crisis sensemaking that are addressed in this chapter are summarized in Table 5.1. The narrative approach addresses stories and narratives that are produced in verbal discourse and in texts. Sensemaking is addressed in terms of coherent narration of experiences that makes events meaningful and comprehensible. Narratives and narrative analysis contribute to understanding crises by providing thick, detailed descriptions of crisis events as these are experienced by participants. Rhetorical analysis builds on narrative to address how accounts given in texts and talk persuade readers that the accounts are themselves truthful representations of events. Contested or conflicting stories are also investigated and insights are developed regarding the operation of power in and through texts. Sensemaking is conceived or addressed as persuasive communication practices that allow one to expect the unexpected, understand crisis causes, and map reality. Counternarratives that seek to disrupt persuasive claims are also used for sensemaking. Rhetorical analysis contributes to understanding crisis sensemaking by showing how persuasive communication is accomplished or undermined. It also shows how crisis documents, including reports, are selectively composed or contrived.

Ethnomethodology focuses on sensemaking practices used in practical reasoning about crises that create shared meaning and a sense of social order or disorder during conversation. Ethnomethodology conceives sensemaking as the basis for meaning. Sensemaking is done using sensemaking practices to detect and understand crises. Ethnomethodology contributes a framework to crisis management that outlines sensemaking practices needed for sensible crisis communication and explains breakdowns or failures of communication. Ethnomethodology also provides insights into the allocation of responsibility and blame during crises.

Conversational analysis addresses structures and processes that underlie conversation (coordinated speech acts) and are necessary for sensible conversations. Sensemaking is viewed as the process of using conversational rules to produce coherent conversations. Conversation analysis addresses conversational structures needed for crisis communication and shows how conversational practices are used to produce important features of inquiry testimony.

Habermasian critical theory addresses macro aspects of crisis sensemaking, including the broad institutional context of society, where the

Table 5.1 Five Approaches to Crisis Inquiry Sensemaking

Approach	Focus or Foci	Sensemaking	Contributions
Narrative	• Stories and narratives in texts and talk • How stories are assembled • Cultural resources used in storytelling	• Coherent narration of experiences that makes events meaningful and comprehensible	• Shows context of events • Provides thick descriptions of crisis events from participants' perspectives
Rhetorical Analysis	• How texts and textualized talk persuade readers of truth • Contested stories • Power behind texts	• Persuasive communication • Narrative and rhetorical practices that make unexpected expectable, allow understanding of causes and map reality • Production of counter or anti-narratives that disrupt persuasive claims and replace these with other claims	• Reveals how persuasive discourse is produced and contradicted • Surfaces key themes of persuasive communication • Uncovers contrived features of inquiry reports and documents
Ethnomethodology	• Sensemaking practices that produce a sense of shared meaning and social order in conversation • Disruptions of sensemaking that create confusion • Practical reasoning about crises	• Genesis or basis of meaning • Process of using sensemaking practices to notice, recognize, interpret, understand, and act regarding crisis events • Creation of a sense of shared meaning and social order	• Provides understanding of practices needed for sensible crisis communication • Offers a framework for understanding production of shared meaning of crises or breakdowns in meaning during conversation and communication • Provides insights into how responsibility and blame are allocated in crisis discourse

Approach	Focus or Foci	Sensemaking	Contributions
Conversational Analysis	• Sensible and coordinated speech acts • Underlying structures and processes of conversation that influence how speakers coordinate speech acts to create coherent talk	• Use of conversational rules (structures) to produce sensible, comprehensible, orderly conversations that unfold without disruption	• Provides insight into underlying structures of conversation necessary for crisis communication • Reveals practices used to create conventional histories of crises; compel witness testimony; challenge, verify, or contradict testimony
Habermasian Critical Theory	Macro • Crisis cycle in advanced capitalism • Contradictions in processes of social reproduction that lead to state intervention in economy and society • Irrational bases of social redistribution Micro • Speech acts • Conditions for valid, democratically enacted communication • Distorted communication	• Use of communicative, representative, regulative, and constative speech acts to produce rational arguments and decisions by democratic means where the decisions are free from institutional constraints	• Provides integrated macro and micro framework for understanding crises • Addresses conditions where crises threaten institutional legitimacy • Provides understanding of dynamics of re-legitimation and de-legitimation of social institutions • Uncovers constraints on "free" speech including institutional power constraints • Establishes conditions for valid, democratic communication

crisis cycle operates based in irrational social distribution and contradictions in social reproduction. It embeds micro-level speech acts in this macro context and focuses on conditions needed for truthful and valid communication. Sensemaking is conceived as the use of key speech acts to produce rational arguments and decisions. Habermasian critical theory contributes insights into crisis sensemaking by offering a framework that helps understand the social context of crises and how crises can threaten institutional legitimacy. It provides a framework for understanding constraints on speech that undermine valid communication, and it explains conditions needed for valid communication.

Discussion

This chapter shows crisis sensemaking is an explicit and often reflexive focus of testimony and evidence provided during public inquiries and hearings into crisis-related events. Although sensemaking occurs throughout the unfolding life history of crisis events, inquiries are highly visible public events that investigate what has been done or what has been decided. Sensemaking during public inquiries into crises is explicitly oriented to detecting the origins, causes, and features of crises. Inquiries use sensemaking to produce comparative data that are conducive to policy choices and recommendations that could potentially prevent recurrences of the crisis being investigated (Turner, 1978). Inquiries thus seek to ensure that some past event "must never happen again" (Turner, 1978, p. 91). To some extent, inquiries are always investigations into potential negligence or wrongdoing (Salter & Slaco, 1981, p. 191). Inquiries produce one-shot assessments of critical events (Salter & Slaco, 1981, p. 16) and often seek to allocate responsibility or blame for problematic events (Brown, 2000; Gephart, 1993).

Inquiry findings and recommendations including suggestions for regulation are often provided through final inquiry reports. Inquiry reports highlight poor practices and recommended precautions (Turner, 1978, pp. 95–96). They interpret the disaster as it is now revealed rather than as it presented itself to those involved before the disaster or during the onset and critical impacts of the disaster (Turner, 1978). As a consequence, the regulations that are created seldom meet the expectations of inquiry panels or their participants (Salter & Slaco, 1981). Often, inquiries produce regulations that call for actions that are unworkable (Turner, 1978, p. 201) or that regulatory agencies are unable to perform (Salter & Slaco, 1981, p. 21). The literature thus argues that inquiry reports are rhetorical constructions designed to elicit attributions of truthfulness from target audiences (Brown, 2000, p. 45). Inquiry reports seek to reduce public anxiety about important events, and they construct elaborate fantasies of institutional omnipotence and control (Brown, 2000, p. 45). Public inquiries and reports are centrally concerned with establishing and protecting the legitimacy of key social institutions (Brown, 2000, p. 47).

This chapter has reviewed research findings from five different scholarly approaches that provide insights into crisis sensemaking during inquiries. Narrative analysis captures, analyzes, and reports first-person accounts of crisis events. This research shows that different groups often have different conceptions or interpretations of crises. These conceptions are articulated during hearings. Rhetorical analysis analyzes how stories and narratives persuade readers to accept certain interpretations of events in the face of alternative accounts and interpretations. In particular, rhetorical analysis reveals how inquiry reports reproduce institutional power and extend the dominance of prevailing ideologies and worldviews. Ethnomethodology shows how sensemaking practices are used during inquiries to construct meaning for crisis events, and how different groups use these sensemaking practices to contest the interpretations of other groups and persons and in the allocation of responsibility and blame. Ethnomethodological research has also revealed that quantitative sensemaking is important in inquiries. This form of sensemaking transforms subjective experiences into scientific facts that become grounds for action. Conversational analysis shows that inquiries are occasions for the production of official histories of crisis events. These official histories are produced from inquiry testimony that relies on the interrogation of witnesses who may attempt to use storytelling practices to plausibly deny certain aspects of accounts that impugn their integrity or competence. Critical theory contextualizes crisis inquiry sensemaking as an attempt to resolve crises emerging from fundamental contradictions in the basic organizing principles of society. Crisis inquiries emerge to defend or restore the legitimacy of the state and key institutions. This legitimacy requires that inquiry discourse is free from institutional constraints. Yet research shows that inquiry discourse is often distorted so as to create a false sense of consensus among key stakeholders. This distortion is accomplished in part by using sensemaking practices to transform accounts of inquiry participants that reflect local safety logics into top-down logics of regulatory agencies. This transformation shows that regulatory logic would have prevented accidents if the logic had been used. Responsibility for critical events is thus allocated to those persons who were responsible for managing hazards, and who failed to use regulatory logic in this regard.

Conclusions and Implications

Crisis sensemaking during public inquiries is an important aspect of the life history of organizational crises. An examination of crisis sensemaking provides important insights into how people construct and interpret crisis events as well as how people recount crisis events they experienced on prior occasions. Several interesting research issues emerge from this literature that would benefit from further investigation. First, it would be useful to examine crises that emerged subsequent to predevelopment inquiries and to compare sensemaking practices and processes that occur in predevelopment and postaccident inquiries. This is challenging because many crises emerge in situations where predevelopment hearings were not conducted and it is thus difficult to find crisis incidents that allow for such a comparison. Second, the sensemaking that initially detects or notices key events and that conceives these as crises needs to be investigated. Researchers are unlikely to be present during the onset stage of disasters; hence, inquiry testimony is an important and critical source of information on how people do notice and initially interpret events as crises. Comparative analysis of inquiry discourse wherein different persons recount such initial detection and interpretation could be undertaken across multiple incidents, or within given incidents and across different persons involved in the same incident. Third, it would be useful to trace sensemaking across the unfolding history of crises and thus to examine sensemaking that occurs after a crisis is contained but before a public inquiry is conducted. In addition, it would be useful to investigate postinquiry sensemaking that occurs when new regulations and recommendations are implemented for purposes of preventing crises.

Crisis sensemaking in public inquiries also reveals that public inquiries are inherently organizational and interorganizational events (Gephart, 1984, 1993, 1997) that occur in complex, interorganizational contexts (Perrow, 1999) and that have organizational and interorganizational implications for government agencies, corporations, local stakeholder groups, and even environmental organizations as well as citizens acting on their own behalf. Thus, public inquiries provide an opportunity for organizational crisis researchers to study the multilevel nature of crises and the ways that micro- and macro-level practices produce challenges and solutions to macro-social problems (Brown, 2000, p. 47). Organizational scholars have examined crises in some detail. This chapter shows that beyond being important to understanding crises, public inquiries into crises are, in and of themselves, an important (if neglected) topic for organizational research.

There are also practical implications for practitioners that emerge from the ideas in this chapter. The chapter addresses different approaches to understanding crisis sensemaking in actual contexts where it is accomplished. The approaches discussed in the chapter converge around the issue of situated crisis communication but differ in terms of how talk and discourse are analyzed, interpreted, and understood. At a general level, the chapter shows that inquiries have recurrent processes or patterns grounded in the features of communication and sensemaking addressed in the chapter. The chapter can thus help practitioners anticipate and prepare for crisis management and for inquiry participation by directing attention to important features of crises and of inquiry sensemaking and participation, and by demystifying these features.

More specifically, each approach offers useful practical insights and implications. Narrative and rhetoric encourage practitioners to listen to and understand narratives that describe events and to be aware of the rhetorical practices that construct narratives. It is important for crisis management that stories of all impacted stakeholders be heard, not just self-serving stories or stories of dominant leaders. Understanding narrative and rhetoric can help to improve discourse at inquiries by encouraging truthful and meaningful narratives that provide richer information. It can also help identify and overcome self-serving or misleading rhetoric and can thus help managers distinguish meaningful statements from misleading statements and distortions. Ethnomethodology highlights practices of sensible, shared communication and helps practitioners recognize important features of shared meanings and agreements. It provides insights into the dynamics of sensemaking that may help managers create and sustain shared meaning during crisis communication, and recognize signs of impending breakdowns in shared meaning. Further, it encourages crisis managers to monitor the views of a range of crisis stakeholders' views of crisis issues. And it teaches crisis managers to anticipate differences of opinion among stakeholders in their views of crises.

Conversational analysis assists managers in understanding how accounts, conversations, and inquiry talk are controlled, directed, or constrained by situational features and underlying rules of conversation. Conversational analysis can thus help managers participate more effectively in inquiries by allowing them to anticipate and address or deal with these constraints during testimony and inquiry participation. Conversational analysis also facilitates an understanding of the role conversational structures play in effective communication during the active phases of crises. Further, conversational analysis has identified tactics such as plausible deniability that can be used by managers and others to resist institutional power.

Habermasian critical theory provides insights into how legitimation challenges are created and resisted by organizations, institutions, and people through use of speech acts. It also offers a practical framework that identifies features necessary for truthful and valid communication that creates a true democratic consensus in society. Habermasian critical theory could be used by managers and others to develop crisis and inquiry communication that is free from institutional constraints that distort the communication. It could also be used by institutions to redesign and improve inquiries to allow all stakeholders and participants equal access to all types of speech acts.

Taken together, the five approaches to understanding crisis sensemaking suggest that crisis management can be strengthened by enhancing crisis sensemaking. Enhanced sensemaking during discursive participation by stakeholders at inquiries is also likely to produce better inquiry outcomes. Improved crisis sensemaking is thus important for preventing and managing crises. It is also important for sustaining and advancing democratic decision making in society at large, since public participation in deliberation about pressing social issues such as crises is essential to democratic governance and the reinstantiation of democracy in contemporary society.

Bibliography

Alvesson, M., & Wilmott, H. (1992). *Critical management studies.* Newbury Park, CA: Sage.

Baccus, M. D. (1986). Multi-piece truck wheel accidents and their regulation. In H. Garfinkel (Ed.), *Ethnomethodological studies of work* (pp. 20–59). New York: Routledge & Kegan Paul.

Barry, D., & Elmes, M. (1997). Strategy retold: Toward a narrative view of strategic discourse. *Academy of Management Review, 22*(2), 429–452.

Barton, L. (1993). *Crisis in organizations: Managing and communicating in the heat of chaos.* Cincinnati, OH: South-Western.

Beamish, T. D. (2002). *Silent spill: The organization of an industrial crisis.* Cambridge: MIT Press.

Berger, P., & Luckmann, T. (1966). *The social construction of reality.* New York: Anchor.

Bogen, D., & Lynch, M. (1989). Taking account of the hostile native: Plausible deniability and the production of conventional history. *Social Problems, 36,* 197–224.

Boje, D. (2001). *Narrative methods for organizational & communication research.* London: Sage.

Boyer, W. W. (1960). Policy making by government agencies. *Midwest Journal of Political Science, 4,* 267–288.

Brody, H. (1981). *Maps and dreams.* New York: Pantheon Books.

Brown, A. D. (2000). Making sense of inquiry sensemaking. *Journal of Management Studies, 37,* 45–76.

Cicourel, A. V. (1973). *Cognitive sociology: Language and meaning in social interaction.* Hammondsworth, UK: Penguin Education.

Coulon, A. (1995). *Ethnomethodology.* Thousand Oaks, CA: Sage.

Delli Carpini, M. X., Cook, F. L., & Jacobs, L. R. (2004). Public deliberation, discursive participation, and citizen engagement: A review of the empirical literature. *Annual Review of Political Science, 7*(1), 315–345.

Douglas, M., & Wildavsky, A, (1982). *Risk and culture.* Berkeley: University of California Press.

Garfinkel, H. (1967). *Studies in ethnomethodology.* Englewood Cliffs, NJ: Prentice Hall.

Gephart, R. P. (1984). Making sense of organizationally based environmental disasters. *Journal of Management, 10,* 205–225.

Gephart, R. P. (1988). Managing the meaning of a sour gas well blowout: The public culture of organizational disasters. *Industrial Crisis Quarterly, 2,* 17–32.

Gephart, R. P. (1992). Sensemaking, communicative distortion and the logic of public inquiry legitimation. *Industrial and Environmental Crisis Quarterly, 6,* 115–135.

Gephart, R. P. (1993). The textual approach: Risk and blame in disaster sensemaking. *Academy of Management Journal, 38*(6), 1465–1514.

Gephart, R. P. (1997). Hazardous measures: An interpretive textual analysis of quantitative sensemaking during crises. *Journal of Organizational Behavior, 18*, 583–622.

Gephart, R. P. (2004). Sensemaking and new media at work. *American Behavioral Scientist, 48*(4), 1–17.

Gephart, R. P. (in press). Hearing discourse. In M. Zachry & C. Thralls (Eds.), *The cultural turn: Perspectives on communicative practices in the workplace and the professions.* Amity, NY: Baywood Press.

Gephart, R. P., & Pitter, R. (1993). The organizational basis of industrial accidents in Canada. *Journal of Management Inquiry, 2*(3), 238–252.

Gephart, R. P., Steier, L., & Lawrence, T. (1990). Cultural rationalities in crisis sensemaking. *Industrial Crisis Quarterly, 4*, 27–48.

Habermas, J. (1973). *Legitimation crisis.* Boston: Beacon Press.

Habermas, J. (1979). *Communication and the evolution of society.* London: Heinemann.

Habermas, J. (1989). *Structural transformation of the public sphere: An inquiry into a category of bourgeois society.* Cambridge: MIT Press.

Handel, W. H. (1982). *Ethnomethodology: How people make sense.* Englewood Cliffs, NJ: Prentice Hall.

Heap, J. (1979). What are sensemaking practices? *Sociological Inquiry, 46*, 107–115.

Kemp, R. (1985). Planning, public hearings, and the politics of discourse. In J. Forester (Ed.), *Critical theory and public life* (pp. 177–201). Cambridge: MIT Press.

Kemp, R., O'Riordan, T., & Purdue, M. (1984). Investigation as legitimacy: The maturing of the big public inquiry. *Geoforum, 15*, 477–488.

Leiter, K. (1980). *A primer on ethnomethodology.* New York: Oxford University Press.

Lynch, M. (1993). *Scientific practice and ordinary action: Ethnomethodology and social studies of science.* Cambridge, UK: Cambridge University Press.

Lynch, M., & Bogen, D. (1996). *The spectacle of history: Speech, text, and memory at the Iran-contra hearings.* Durham, NC: Duke University Press.

McCloskey, D. N. (1985). *The rhetoric of economics.* Madison: University of Wisconsin Press.

Mitroff, I. (2004). *Crisis leadership: Planning for the unthinkable.* Hoboken, NJ: John Wiley & Sons.

Mitroff, I. (2005). *Why some companies emerge stronger and better from a crisis: 7 essential lessons for surviving disaster.* New York: American Management Association.

Mitroff, I., & Pearson, C. (1993). *Crisis management: A diagnostic guide for improving your organization's crisis-preparedness.* San Francisco: Jossey-Bass.

Offe, C. (1984). *Contradictions of the welfare state.* Cambridge: MIT Press.

Offe, C. (1985). *Disorganized capitalism: Contemporary transformations of work and politics.* Cambridge, UK: Polity Press.

Perrow, C. (1999). *Normal accidents: Living with high risk technologies* (with a new Afterword). Princeton, NJ: Princeton University Press.

Ridington, R. (1982). When poison comes down like a fog: A native community's response to cultural disaster. *Human Organization, 41*, 36–42.

Ridington, R. (1990). *Little bit know something: Stories in a language of anthropology.* Vancouver, BC: Douglas & McIntyre.

Riessman, C. K. (1993). *Narrative analysis.* Newbury Park, CA: Sage.

Salter, L., & Slaco, D. (1981). *Public inquiries in Canada.* Ottawa: Science Council of Canada.

Shrivastava, P., Mitroff, I., Miller, D., & Miglani, A. (1988). Understanding industrial crises. *Journal of Management Studies, 25,* 285–303.

Turner, B. A. (1976). The organizational and interorganizational development of disasters. *Administrative Science Quarterly, 21,* 378–397.

Turner, B. A. (1978). *Man-made disasters.* New York: Crane, Russack.

Weick, K. (1977). Enactment processes in organizations. In B. M. Staw & G. R. Salancik (Eds.), *New directions in organizational behaviour* (pp. 267–300). Chicago: St. Clair.

Weick, K. (1995). *Sensemaking in organizations.* Thousand Oaks, CA: Sage.

Weick, K. (2001). *Making sense of the organization.* Cambridge, UK: Blackwell Business.

A Cognitive Approach to Crisis Management in Organizations

6

Jean-Marie Jacques,
Laurent Gatot, and Anne Wallemacq

The goal of this chapter is to gain insight into the sociocognitive analysis of organizational crises using a crisis perception model. Using complementary cognitive mapping to elicit collective and individual cognition, we intend to understand why and how perception, cognition, and semantics play an important role in understanding organizational crises. The first part of the chapter defines the characteristics of organizational crises, the second presents the theoretical foundations of the sociocognitive roots, and the third explores crisis empirical data using cognitive mapping software. We embed our research in organizational theory viewing organization in three dimensions: the "*structures in which actors' games take place,*" the "*relations between actors who set in motion these structures, contributing to change these structures by their game-actions towards new organizational arrangements,*" and finally the dimension that "*takes into account the principles of legitimacy through which actors give meaning to and justify their games and the new structures created*" (Jacques et al., 2004a). This framework is constructivist because it takes into consideration the dualities of certain structures that are at the same time products but also processes. This perspective is intended to identify the production and permanent reproduction of psychosocial realities in the interaction between individuals.

Crisis: A Galaxy of Concepts and Characteristics

CRISIS DEFINITION

Defining crisis is not easy. The topic of crises has not been a favorite research field in organization science (Roux-Dufort, 1996), but it has recently become one (Preble, 1997) and thus the theorization is still developing (Forgues & Roux-Dufort, 1998; Gatot, 2000; Preble, 1997), even polemical (Pauchant & Mitroff, 1990). Definitions and characteristics of crisis vary according to the context. We concentrate on organizational crises, and consequences of human, technological, or natural causes. The multidimensional character of crises should be mentioned (Forgues, 1991; Kovoor-Misra, 1995; Shrivastava et al., 1988). The determining factors, the consequences, and the types of crises are rooted in different dimensions of organizations themselves (human, social, technical, economical, legal, and ethical). The integration of these dimensions constitutes an obstacle to a unified theory of crises. In this chapter we consider crisis as a cognitive phenomenon. The event itself, the processes that lead up to it and the consequences of the crisis can be interpreted differently depending on the interpreter. Different interpreters may characterize a phenomenon as normal, minor, major, an incident, or a catastrophe, depending on their perception and cognition. Perception (of crises) is influenced by cultural, social (Laufer, 1993), psychological, or biological conditions (Edelman & Tononi, 2000). The importance attributed to the crisis depends also upon its media coverage (Laufer, 1993). We define a crisis as *a process perceived as complex, dynamic, out-of-control, allowing little time for reaction, representing a menace to the survival of the organization, and transforming the organization* (Jacques et al., 2003).

CHARACTERISTICS OF A CRISIS

Whereas the event approach focuses on the nature and consequences of crises, the process approach insists on elements referring to the dynamics of crises (Forgues & Roux-Dufort, 1998). It suggests that crises must be studied in an extended span of space and time. The process approach complements the event approach to the extent that crises are seen as being the result of an incubation period that suddenly erupts because of the influence of a triggering event (Shrivastava, 1987). The process perspective is based on the idea that crises evolve in phases (Fink, 1986). The crises are the final stage of a continuous cumulative process of human and organizational failures. The complexity of the process that leads to a crisis is linked to the complexity of the organization itself, or to the multidimensional nature of the crisis. Perrow (1984) constructed a typology of organizational systems in regard to risk of crisis. His typology compares systems in terms of their complexity, the interaction that exists between the components of a system, and the manner in which they are connected. Many researchers have been influenced by Perrow's work in interpreting the relationship between the complexity of organizational systems and the occurrence of crises. Wahlström (1992) indicates that complexity is not merely a factor related to the technical systems of an organization but is also related to the socioeconomic aspects of the system, while Shrivastava (1994) attributes the occurrence of crises to the presence of contradictions within systems, generating vicious circles. The causes, consequences, and types of crises vary according to the dimensions of the organization (Kovoor-Misra, 1995; Mitroff, 1988). The diversity of these dimensions and their interactions generate degrees of complexity for crisis managers, whose decisions must integrate matters relative to psychology, sociology, law, finance, technology, politics, anthropology, medicine, and natural science. Some models of crisis management also take into account the external dimensions of the organization. As an organization is a puzzle of atomized individuals and groups in charge of specific activities within the system, the coordination of group of actors, with their different functions and objectives, is a source of complexity (Forgues, 1991; Stubbart, 1987). A crisis constitutes a threat to the survival of the organization: In a crisis, decision-makers are faced with unknown situations (Goetschin, 1975) that they do not control, and are forced to make emergency decisions (Hermann, 1963; Smart & Vertinsky, 1977). Emergencies are ambiguous (Holsti, 1978; Weick, 1988), complex, uncertain, and stress-filled (Dutton, 1986; Forgues, 1991; Hermann, 1963; Holsti, 1978; Shrivastava, 1994; Smart & Vertinsky, 1977; Stubbart, 1987; Weick, 1988). The process of a crisis generates two types of transformations: one of direct consequences (pollution, fire, cost of intervention, etc.) or indirect consequences (changes in the law, loss of identity image, etc.). Crises also constitute a unique opportunity to learn and to make changes within an organization (Nystrom & Starbuck, 1984). Roux-Dufort and Metais (1998) think that a crisis can even generate a competitive advantage if it is accompanied by a high degree of organizational learning. Nevertheless, experience does show that postcrisis organizational learning is often not satisfactory owing to failure to acquire all of the necessary information, or other defects in interpretation, storage, or distribution of the requisite information (Gatot et al., 1999; Kletz, 1993; Roux-Dufort, 1996, 1997). The sociocognitive approach of crisis and the related consequences in terms of behavior have been translated into a management model of anticipatory crises management.

THE MODEL

To take into account the above-mentioned constraints and characteristics, we worked up a model of anticipatory crisis management. This model identifies five stages in the development of a crisis. The first one is *the prodrome stage:* warnings (Mitroff, 1988), indications (Lagadec, 1992; Roux-Dufort, 1996), prodromes (Fink, 1986), and early warnings (Jacques & Wybo, in press) indicate that a crisis is latent. The *incident stage* is the event that in retrospect appears to have been the beginning of the crisis. The *catastrophe stage* is the point at which an incident is out of control and a disaster has already caused damage. The *resolution stage* is the end of the catastrophe. Finally, the *adaptation stage* is the period during which investigations are conducted, damage is assessed, legal actions occur, and in general a new equilibrium is established. The hypothesis of the model is that "aggravating factors" (Jacques & Gatot, 1997) constitute the main elements of crisis evolution. In the study of aggravating factors, emphasis has been concentrated on human and organizational elements, taking the roots in cognition.

Inside the Inside

> ... one of the keys to the strategic process, perhaps the only one, resides in the thinking of the managers, in the content of that thinking, and its mechanism. (Laroche & Nioche, 1994, p. 65)

Simon's work (1959, 1986) states that the information used by the decision-maker is often uncertain, that his environment is complex and his cognitive capacities often limited. In the case of complex decisions or behavior, the difference between the real environment and the environment perceived by the agent may be important, due to omissions or distortions in the processes of perception and inference (Simon, 1959, 1978). Numerous studies (Laroche & Nioche, 1994; Schwenk, 1989; Smart & Vertinsky, 1977; Stubbart, 1987; Taylor & Crocker, 1981; Tversky & Kahneman, 1974) showed that the thoughts of actors could generate distortions in the acquisition and handling of information, particularly during a crisis. Human and organizational "aggravating factors" (Jacques & Gatot, 1997) are seen as elements of crisis dynamics. We used cognitive perspective to analyze crisis and aggravating factors. Cognitive sciences are a galaxy of epistemologies, paradigms, models, and methods, but for the purpose of this research we selected two different paradigms: a cognitivist one and a structuralist one.

TWO PARADIGMS TO ANALYZE COGNITION

1. A Cognitivist Paradigm

In complex situations, the individual needs criteria and rules in order to select, structure, and interpret information (Vidaillet, 1996). Cognitive schemas (Gioia & Manz, 1985) are used to interpret sensory information, to retrieve information stored in memory, to organize actions, and to fix objectives (Rumelhart, 1980). Schemas guide, sometimes unconsciously, expectations and actions and even the interpretation and storage of information (Augoustinos & Walker, 1995; Lord & Foti, 1986; Schneider & Angelmar, 1993; Taylor & Crocker, 1981). The repeated use of a schema leads to a lack of reflection and an increasing myopia when it comes to detecting contradictory information (Stubbart & Ramaprasad, 1990). Schemas contribute to the production of a mental representation of a stimulus; on the basis of such representations, individuals make decisions (Rumelhart, 1980; Stubbart & Ramaprasad, 1990). Mental representations contain all of an individual's knowledge about himself and the world (Cottraux, 1988). It is almost universally admitted that cognitive behavior is only understandable if we assume that an individual acts "*through representing to himself the pertinent elements of situations in which he finds himself*" (Varela, 1989, p. 37). The effectiveness of the agent's behavior thus depends on the adequacy of his mental representation to the situation (Varela, 1989). The theory of schemas is particularly appropriate for the analysis of decisions made in a crisis context. In fact, crises can generate two kinds of cognitive processes: processes of cognitive elaboration (Nystrom & Starbuck, 1984; Stubbart, 1987), which are phenomena linked to the crisis and the objects of a perception and an interpretation on the part of different individuals; and processes of cognitive reduction (Nystrom & Starbuck, 1984; Stubbart, 1987); that is, the crisis causes a weakening of cognitive capacities on the part of individuals, and leads to simplifications at the level of representations and of information handling. These two processes can affect the capacity of individuals to manage a crisis, as shown in many studies. The prodromes of a crisis may not be perceived or may be transformed, because they do not correspond to the expectations of the individual, or the individual thinks that nothing is going to happen (Turner, 1976). Inadequate hypotheses (Turner, 1976, 1994) and fear of doing something wrong or fear of change (Slatter, 1984) can lead to the nonperception of a crisis; the limited cognitive capabilities of individuals can generate vicious circles that are themselves sources of crises (Masuch, 1985). Emergency status and hurrying (Hermann, 1963; Smart & Vertinsky, 1977), ambiguity (Holsti, 1978; Weick, 1988), stress and uncertainty (Dutton, 1986; Forgues, 1991; Hermann, 1963; Holsti, 1978; Shrivastava, 1994; Weick, 1988)—all of these cognitive limitations lower the quality of decisions made during a crisis (Stubbart, 1987). In a crisis, the members of a group tend to adopt group attitudes in order to preserve an internal order, the "groupthink" phenomenon (Nystrom & Starbuck, 1984; Smart & Vertinsky, 1977). An information overload during a crisis can cause things to be forgotten or can cause delays and filtering of information (Smart & Vertinsky, 1977). Fear of failure and doubts about one's ability to meet a crisis successfully can cause agents to flee their responsibilities (Dutton, 1986; Slatter, 1984). The never-seen-before aspect of a crisis can increase feelings of insecurity and cause a "collapse of meaning" (Weick, 1988); time pressure, the great amount at stake, and stress can cause agents to use solutions that were effective in the past, but are not appropriate for the immediate crisis situation, in an abusive manner (Smart & Vertinsky, 1977; Stubbart, 1987; Turner, 1976); intervening actors interpret the crisis in different ways, sometimes in contradictory or ambiguous ways, and this causes postcrisis learning to bifurcate (Dutton, 1986; March et al., 1991).

2. A Structuralist Paradigm

Structuralists consider cognition as follows: It affirms the primacy of the structure of the phenomenon. Structuralism is characterized by its rejection of the subject and all that it is supposed to represent, in terms of a free or autonomous entity. Nevertheless it is possible to understand structuralism without this absence of the subject being felt as a lack (Jacques & Laurent, 2005). The apparent void conceals in reality a topos of symbolic exchanges—a topological landscape from which all possible subjectivity surges forth. The structuralist ambition is the following: A phenomenon does not have meaning of its own, by itself, but it acquires meaning through its relationship to other elements of a system to which it belongs. The relations that exist between elements of a system are based on combinatory logic of transformations. The system of possible transformations—that is, the *structure*—determines the meaning of the elements that make it up. Meaning thus appears as the simple product of one possible combination among others. By playing with the axes of opposition in the systems of communication, the entire culture interprets itself as a system of signs in which the signified becomes in its turn the signifier for a new signified element, whatever the system in question may be (e.g., speech, objects, merchandise, ideas, values, feelings).

Mapping Crisis Perception

To be able to elicit cognition and mental representation of actors in the two paradigms, we use two different cognitive mapping techniques.

BOX AND LINKS

Cognitive mapping in the sense of Axelrod (1976) or Eden (1988) enables representing, in a two-dimensional map, the structure and the dynamics of mental representations (Kelly, 1955) of an individual or of a group of individuals on the basis of their discourse. Cognitive maps give a clear, synthetic image of an actor's mental representation in relation to the phenomenon under examination; this image emphasizes and contextualizes the concepts and connections expressing the subject's mental representation (Jeanson & Cossette, 1996). On one hand, this approach allows the global dynamic of the phenomenon under examination to be taken into account, and on the other, it allows a given concept to be reinserted into the discourse of the subject. Thus, the meaning of a concept is enriched by its interactions with other concepts represented on the map. Cognitive mapping contributes to an improved understanding of the behavior (Cossette & Audet, 1992); a map expresses the experiences of a subject and integrates his or her own values, concepts, and meanings into that context (Eden, 1988). The analysis of cognitive maps can help the actor in resolving problems (Cossette & Audet, 1994), anticipating the consequences of an action (Axelrod, 1976), and arranging tools (Eden, 1992). Cognitive mapping also emphasizes the accent on relationships between unconscious concepts of the actor (Vidaillet, 1996). For the visualization we use the graphical form of maps, and in so doing support the validation and analysis. The objective is to identify the aggravating factors that threaten the organization, through the analysis of cognitive maps.

SEMANTIC FIELDS

Semantic mapping (Wallemacq & Jacques, 2005) is a cognitive mapping technique inspired by poststructuralism and phenomenology. Semantic fields constitute the network of evocations that gravitate around words. They structure the manner in which speakers perceive the real: *When I say "white," I am saying not only the color (denotation) but also the entire register of evocations (pure, snow, clean, blank, etc.)*. These semantic fields are important because they color the meaning aimed at by a speaker. They constitute the fields upon which a sentence takes on meaning, announces itself, and becomes heard. *When I say "white" meaning the color, its evocations are ineluctably present.* They are, in a manner of speaking, the "wake" of the word, although they have relatively little to do with the denotative meaning intended (in this case, *white*). Our interest is semantic relations. These are difficult to analyze because of their characteristics: Semantic relations are not univocal; no formal connection exists between the two semantic elements— for example, "white" and "pure"; and these relations are context-dependent.

The originality of semantic maps is that they try to grasp not so much an articulation of concepts within a chain of reasoning but rather a more basic level of semantic intention, in isolation, among the semantic fields in which the speaker is situated. Their purpose is not so much to retrace the logic behind a certain chain of reasoning as to determine the words with which one reasons (the ensemble of associations and oppositions that gravitate around words). There is another, more fundamental reason for the difficulty of the study of semantic relations: Priority is given to natural language over formal language. It is no longer a question of attempting to purify natural language in order to make it univocal. To the contrary, it is a matter of understanding the logic of development that belongs properly to natural language. The originality of this viewpoint lies in seeing language as an enlacing medium (which we represent in the form of semantic landscapes) in which an individual is immersed. These semantic fields are neither true nor false, but simply form a medium within which discourse is spoken and received. An important field of research has opened up in recent years concerning the role of language within organizations. We are in a field that is constructivist (Worf, 1956) and phenomenological: How can an organization and the individuals who make it up have their perceptions of the real organized so as to grasp it as a universe of meaning, a universe of making sense (Weick, 1993)? In this approach one traces out "cognitive maps," individual or collective, which allow decision-makers to reflect on their own biases (Wallemacq & Jacques, 2005).

Empirical Evidence

The data are drawn from a project in which the ReCCCoM has been involved over the past few years, this project concerning "human factors" in crisis management (Jacques & Gatot, 1997, 1998). To study the crisis process and particularly the role played by actors' cognition in the evolution of the crisis (mainly in the apparition of aggravating factors), we conducted a longitudinal study (1995–1999) of the Crisis Center of the province of Namur. Here, we performed 21 semidirective interviews with actors dealing with crisis management and a simulation exercise, "Chlorex '98" (a chemical spill accident in an urban area), carried out in the Namur area. For this paper, we worked on two different data sets (interview material). The first data set explores the presence of aggravating factors in the discursive material (interview) of the actors, by using cognitive mapping software (decision explorer). The second data sets explore the semantic content of the interview by using semantic mapping software, Evoq (Wallemacq & Jacques, 2005).

BOX AND LINKS: DECISION EXPLORER

In the interviews we identified and coded concepts and the links (see Figure 6.1) between concepts following the classical methodology (decision explorer). We used codes in order to limit the interpretations of the researchers during the elaboration of the map (Ackermann et al., 1995; Allard-Poesi, 1997; Gatot & Jacques, 1997; Huff et al., 1990; Wrightson, 1976). *Concepts* are words or phrases, while *links* are relationship between concepts. The identification of types of concepts and links facilitates the graphical representation, validation, and analysis. Concepts are qualified as "repeated," "problem," "solution," and combinations thereof. Most works using cognitive mapping concentrate on causal links. We have, for analytical reasons, defined other types of links. To identify aggravating factors, we analyzed the content of concepts and relations marked on cognitive maps and we cross-referenced the results obtained for different subjects. The list of concepts gives a linear representation of the cognitive map, and permits our focusing on the content of concepts, by distinguishing different categories of concepts. The list of links puts the emphasis on the structure of the cognitive map, and studies the relative importance of each type of link. The list of particular groups of concepts allows the analysis and synthesis of the bias present in subjects' discourse, and the analyzing of the repetitions. The analysis of domains measures the density of concepts as a function of entry and exit connections or relations. The graphical representation of chains of causality allows the analysis of the domain of the most important concepts and allows a deeper study of chains of argumentation (Bryant, 1983). The analysis of "clusters" concentrates the analysis on the dominant themes of the cognitive map. A cluster is a group of concepts that are all connected, usually in relation to a common theme. The list of "trailing" concepts is the repertoire of concepts that have no entry relation or connection. For validity, it is also interesting to cross-compare and validate the results of all of the analyses of the cognitive maps through an analysis of documents, observations of sites, or analyses of past incidents.

The aggravating factors are mostly individual or organizational elements contributing to the evolving of the crisis (see Figure 6.2). The aggravating factors have been grouped into six strategic actions for crisis management: emergency planning, information management between actors, management of a crisis center, management of the psychology of the actors, management of external intervention, and communication management.

We illustrate below the process of identification of aggravating factors with, for example, aggravating factor 16—*insufficient exchange between specialists in the CPC (strategic center) and the PCO (operational center)*. The identification of factors is carried out in three steps:

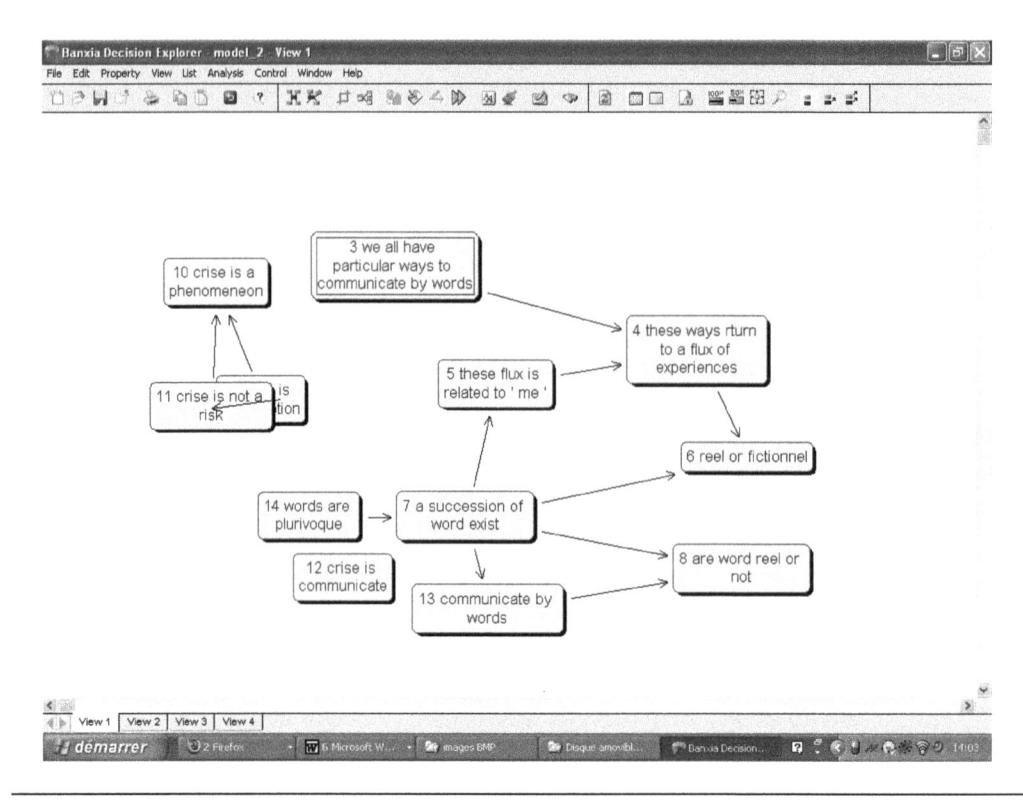

Figure 6.1 A Cognitive Mapping Identifying Aggravating Factors

1. Each cognitive map is analyzed taking into account the domains, the number of times a concept is repeated, the type of concept, and its type of links with other concepts. The causes and consequences of each aggravating factor are identified. For example, in the map of subject #10, factor 16 is present at the level of three groups of concepts:

- Concept 77, "*the leaders don't always remember to pass on information to others*" has as a consequence the concept 79, "*the section chief holds a coordination meeting regularly.*" Concepts 77 and 79 are considered as a first cluster underlining the importance of coordination, since there is to some extent a prior lack of communication between different specialists.
- Concept 204, "*there is a lack of communication between specialists of each type, and between specialists of different types*" is in conflict with concept 228, "*the job of the supervisor or his representative is to get people to communicate between themselves and to communicate with the CPC.*" These concepts designate officials who are responsible for information exchange (or the lack of same). Concept 204 is repeated by the subject " . . . *it's communication between individuals . . . between two different kinds of specialist . . . which has to be better . . .*"

The 39 aggravating factors are mostly individual or organizational elements contributing to the evolving of the crisis.	

1. Emergency plan
   AF1: Complex and voluminous emergency plans
   AF2: Uncertainty concerning the application of the emergency plans
   AF3: Multiplication and non-standardization of the emergency plans
   AF4: Overestimation of the capacities of the stakeholders
   AF5: Insufficiency of exercises and debriefings
   AF6: A too theoretical disaster medicine
2. Information
   AF7: Insufficiency of information for the stakeholders
   AF8: Problems of material, frequencies, and quality of telecommunications
   AF9: Not enough return of the field toward the CPC* and the PCO**
   AF10: Imprecise initial information
   AF11: Contradictions in information
3. Crisis teams
   AF12: Ambiguousness of functions of the CPC and the PCO
   AF13: Difficulties of co-ordination in the CPC and the PCO
   AF14: Phase of shambles during the installation
   AF15: Inadequate alert system
   AF16: Insufficient exchanges between disciplines in the CPC and the PCO
   AF17: Insufficiencies bound to the coordinator
   AF18: No priorities between the disciplines
   AF19: Problems of co-ordination within the discipline 2
	AF20: Insufficiency of the post-crisis management
	AF21: No standardization of the language between disciplines
	AF22: Difficulties of installation of the PCO
	4. Personality of the stakeholders
	   AF23: Surprise, stress, uncertainty
	   AF24: Stress of the semaphone
	   AF25: Hierarchical problems between stakeholders
	   AF26: Insufficient meetings between the stakeholders
	   AF27: Competition between stakeholders
	   AF28: Insufficient support of leaders
	5. External stakeholders
	   AF29: Delay of intervention
	   AF30: Insufficient formations of the stakeholders
	   AF31: Important disaster tourism
	   AF32: Competition between public and private stakeholders
	   AF33: Absence of an inventory of means and risks
	   AF34: Problems bound to the voluntaries
	   AF35: Insufficient knowledge of facilities and risks
	   AF36: Problems of co-ordination with non-regular stakeholders
	   AF37: Absence of a common culture of crisis management
	6. Communication
	   AF38: Insufficient relations with media
	   AF39: Insufficient preventive information to the population
	*CPC = "strategic crisis management team located at the local government"
	**PCO = "crisis team on the field"

Figure 6.2   Aggravating Factors (AF *x*) and the Related Strategic Actions (n)

- Concept 265, "*during the floods, we all kept working in shifts for three weeks,*" nuances concept 266, "*after a few days of feeling tired, we began to have problems getting information transmitted,*" and that is an example of concept 263, "*if we take breaks, the transmission of information between teams isn't complete sometimes.*" This third cluster of concepts evokes a kind of crisis, the long-term crisis, in which failure to properly transmit and distribute information can be a critical problem.

2. Then in a second step we compare the individual analyses on different maps. For example, factor 16 is present on the cognitive map for subject 7, but only through the intermediary of two clusters of concepts:

- Concept 103, "*in the CPC, some people don't tell what they know,*" leads to concept 102, "*it appears that information doesn't circulate very well at the CPC,*" notwithstanding concept 104, "*in the field, different kinds of specialists share information readily.*"
- Concept 40, "*it's hard to get the doctors a fixed meeting location,*" is the cause of concept 105, "*the doctors are the hardest to get information out of.*"
- On the other side, the aggravating factor 16 is also found in map 8, concept 160: "*some disciplines don't see that their information is of interest to others.*" This brings with it concept 158, "*in the CPC, some specialties handle their own problems and don't bother to share information, though it is necessary,*" and concept 159 is an illustration of this: "*during exercises we wanted the CPC to realize, on the basis of information coming up from the field, to understand that the (toxic) cloud had changed in some respects, but this didn't happen.*"

3. Finally, aggravating factor 16 is represented on several maps: the map of subject 21 (two concepts, one repeated twice); subject 5 (six concepts, one in domain 5 and another in domain level 3); and subject 16 (nine concepts, one in domain 3).

When we cross-reference the maps, we triangulate the information, identify the most often represented factors, associate new concepts of cause and effect with the aggravating factor under examination, and find new illustrations or likely solutions.

With the cognitive mapping, we identified the presence of aggravating factors in each of the interviews, and then we aggregate these aggravating factors in strategic action, we give an example with the strategic action "Management of the Crisis Center," where 11 aggravating factors were identified by cognitive mapping. We discuss eight of these in detail below.

1. Ambiguity of the functions of the CPC and the PCO

The two missions of the PCO are to coordinate means and operations (including individuals and groups) at the crisis site (field), and to relay information from the PCO and from actors on the field to the CPC. Unlike the actors on the field, the PCO can step back to analyze and synthesize information. The role of the CPC is strategic: It is supposed to take care of reinforcements, anticipate how the crisis might develop, and advise and inform the public and the authorities. The CPC only has a partial view of a crisis and is a coordination center. Nevertheless, the CPC does not always stick to its anticipatory and strategic role and sometimes makes operational decisions for two main reasons: The members of the CPC are often in a higher hierarchical position than the members of the PCO, and the members of the CPC regularly visit the field and are tempted to solve problems in operational terms. This ambiguity between the functions of the CPC and the PCO is made worse by the number of discipline specialists involved in the field; for example, the representatives of the medical discipline at the CPC only transmit information, with all decisions made by their counterparts at the PCO, but representatives of other disciplines (e.g., Gendarmerie) play a bigger role in CPC operations. During the simulation, operational decisions were all made by the PCO. Most specialists of the CPC only kept themselves informed of the situation; they managed volunteer workers but they did not manage the crisis proactively or strategically. Only discipline 5 (coordination), not represented at the PCO, made a real contribution to the global management of the crisis. They coordinated the management team and they kept the public, journalists, and the authorities informed. The representative of the medical discipline at the CPC also made a contribution in terms of information to the public and to victims.

2. Coordination problems between CPC and PCO

There is no hierarchy of disciplines, since the coordination of crisis teams is collegial. Decisions are made by consensus and are coordinated by discipline 5 at the CPC and by the general coordinator at the PCO. During a crisis, the disciplines work separately, and coordination meetings are regularly scheduled. These meetings allow the various disciplines to coordinate their efforts and to exchange crucial information. In order to assist the interdisciplinary meetings, the leaders of various disciplines' personnel have to stop their intradiscipline work. For this reason, meetings cannot last too long, particularly when a tense phase of the crisis is going on. The fact that the professional experts, outside of coordination meetings, keep to themselves both geographically and socioculturally slows down the circulation of information.

3. Insufficient exchanges between disciplines

The exchange of information between disciplines is insufficient. Sometimes actors working close to each other do not share information.

> ... Sometimes the leaders of one specialty ... think in terms of their people only, not about going to communicate their information to others who might need it for the good of the coordination of the whole.... (Interview 10, p. 4)

4. The ambiguity of the role of the "general coordinator"

The overall responsibility of the "general coordinator" is to coordinate the operations at the PCO, direct its effort, and make interdiscipline decisions. He or she is also in charge of collecting, digesting, and transmitting information from the PCO to the CPC. However, the general coordinators, who are "fire marshals," have hardly any specific training, and lack a written description of their function.

> ... Eventually somebody should write something down.... To put things in a fixed form on paper, what are the delegate coordinator's tasks, what is he supposed to do; you need a sort of cheat-sheet for the mission, because when you've never done it, it's hard to know how to proceed.... (Interview 15, p. 5)

The general coordinators are usually not well informed about the functions and the means of the other professional specialties involved in crisis response, the risks they may face, or the relationships of authority that exist between members of professional specialties and disciplines and that could positively or negatively affect efforts to coordinate them. Also, the general coordinator is one of the last to be alerted in a crisis, although in theory he or she should arrive at the PCO as soon as possible. Furthermore, the general coordinator is under stress as he is also part of the fire-department hierarchy. Professional specialists get information from the PCO and the CPC; the general coordinator transmits a digest of the information from both the PCO and the CPC. This duplicate path of information can lead to errors and confusion.

5. The lack of priorities concerning professional specialties and particular missions

The absence of preset priorities governing relationships between members of various professional specialties and disciplines is a source of conflict. This risk is heightened by the fact that some specialties overlap in terms of function.

> ... Today, everyone takes care of their own. Like that, well, yeah, there can be arguments over priorities to be assigned ... should the fire crews have priority, or the ambulances? If it was bad enough, I could step in and say, don't touch that because eventually I'll need it for the investigation. The investigation that always comes afterward, anyway. And so there's the problem, nobody really has any authority over anybody else.... (Interview 11, 8–9)

The absence of priorities can also cause conflicts when particular types of equipment or assistance are requested by more than one group of actors at the same time.

6. Lack of coordination in discipline 2

Medical discipline is made up of different types of actors: a hygiene inspector, a nurse, representatives of the Red Cross, a director of medical emergency services, and representatives of the SISU. Their coordination is difficult, but the main problem is the failure to integrate the Red Cross into a coherent prioritization. The hygiene inspector and the emergency services director are not especially familiar with the functioning of the Red Cross, and the Red Cross has trouble taking orders from the hygiene inspector. Also, the Red Cross has different equipment than the Service 112 personnel.

> ... In fact, there's a problem with the fact that we are volunteers and we don't have all day to wait for something to happen ... we have human and material resources, but we're always a little bit behind the regular emergency services. ... (Interview 13, p. 3)

The equipment furnished by the Red Cross is hardly ever used, while at the same time Service 112 has to claim ambulances from many areas. In the above-mentioned simulation, the Red Cross equipment was used, intradiscipline 2's coordination was satisfactory, but interdisciplinary transmission of information between the CPC and the PCO caused problems. For example, discipline 1 at the CPC alerted the hygiene inspector at 2:44 p.m. that the hospital at Auvelais was full, but the director of emergency medical services of the PCO was aware of this at 2:11 p.m.

7. Postcrisis management problems

Some people think that crisis management is over when the acute phase of the crisis is over, but the public still has to be informed about the effect of the crisis, the victims have to be informed as to the outcome (and, if necessary, directed toward crisis counselors), journalists have to be briefed, and tests for toxicity have to be performed.

8. Lack of standardization of vocabulary

Some disciplines use a specialized vocabulary.

> ... At the level of the internal functioning of the service, you use the vocabulary and the methods you are used to using, and that helps save time and avoid arguments, people getting confused, etc. But when different teams communicate, it would be better if we had a sort of common language. ... (Interview 18, p. 11)

This lack of standardization of language makes communication between teams more complicated. This phenomenon can also occur within a team. For example, within discipline 2, the Red Cross used terminology that the hygiene inspector did not always understand.

SEMANTIC FIELDS: EVOQ

In a second study (see de Saint Georges et al., 2004), our interest has been to address how, in an organizational setting, microprocesses connect to larger systems of meanings. This approach is rooted in the "organizational discourse" field. In recent years, there has been a growing interest in examining the role of text and talk in the study of work and workplace (Grant et al., 2001) and in organizational settings (Jacques, Laurent, & Wallemacq, 2004). With the "discursive turn" in the social sciences (Filliettaz, 2004; Iedema & Wodak, 1999), it has become common to view organizations as complex systems dynamically constituted in the "acts of communication between organizational members" (Iedema & Wodak, 1999, p. 7). We address the question of how, in an organizational setting, microprocesses connect to larger systems of meanings; we attempt to specify larger systems of meanings used by a specific group of professionals (crisis managers) who use this type of language; and we draw conventions and forms of expressions from this existing language. To do so, we chose to follow "webs of meanings" (Blommaert & Verschueren, 1998) intertextually woven across different institutional settings dealing with crisis management, and we examined how these webs of meaning were involved in the local discourse of the members of these various institutions (de Saint Georges et al., 2004). We took the view that meanings are meaningful in the first place because they belong to socially shared and currently used (but often subconscious) "systems of differences," and we tried to make more apparent certain patterns (recurrent cognitive images, conceptual frames, and rhetorical behaviors) prevalent in the discourse of certain individuals. Indeed, while research on crisis management has established that the representations that decision-makers form about critical situations are crucial to their decision-making processes (Gatot, 2000), there has been little empirical research done so far to understand the psychosocial, cultural, and cognitive models crisis managers use to direct their actions in both preparing for and reacting to actual crises. We thus became interested in making visible patterns in crisis management as they could be inferred from the discourse of these various individuals and seeing what these articulatory practices could teach us about the interpretative frames used by crisis managers to perform their work.

We next turn to a description and short discussion of an excerpt from our data set and show how similar distinctions are reproduced across these texts. We pay particular attention to the specific connotations the speaker is sensitive to in relation to a common distinction made recurrently in our data set: the distinction between "the crisis center" and "the center of the crises." In the course of our investigations of the data, it became clear that while aspects of the frames of references organizing individual actors' perceptions, knowledge, and actions were shaped by the codes of the organizations to which they belonged, other distinctions regarding crisis and crisis management cut across the various organizational settings and could thus be perceived as "shared codes." There were thus principles of division and distinctions that could be traced intertextually across these various interviews. They appeared notably in topical correlations and thematic overlaps in the discourses of the interviewees. Since our general interest was to contribute to the understanding of how individuals' representations about crisis management affect their reasoning about critical situations, their reactions during crises, and their relation to partners, it seemed important to us to examine empirically all of these intertextual relations. We would like here to explore one of the "common-sensical," "naturalized" ways of viewing crisis management for professionals in the field, with the hope that an analysis of these interpretative frames might help us understand crisis management from the point of view of the actors directly involved in it (de Saint Georges et al., 2004). In order to observe topic overlaps and the intertextual emergence of themes, we have chosen to use a computer software for semantic mapping, Evoq.

How does it work? Evoq works from qualitative documents (open or closed interviews, field notes, newspaper articles, archives, minutes of meetings, etc.) and the representations individual speakers construct in these texts. In contrast to other software, Evoq does not rely on a lexicometric type of coding. Evoq uses the structuralist idea that the significance of the components of a representation is always relational. In much the same way that the image of a jigsaw puzzle is reconstituted only when all of the pieces are related to one another, Evoq considers speakers' representations as organized systems of "oppositions" and "associations" and is interested in how these systems are articulated from the point of view of the speaker. The researcher is thus responsible for the informed reading of the text and the manual coding. In the coding process, the researcher is invited to code not only the meanings expressed explicitly (the "surface meanings") but also the meanings carried along implicitly (the meanings "on the rebound") in texts. This coding is not arbitrary but follows theoretical and methodological principles (we followed for this chapter the principles of structural analysis laid out in Piret et al. [1996] to ensure interreliability of the coding among the team members). The relations, once encoded, constitute a *dictionary* of relations for part of a text, a whole text, or a set of texts. This first coding thus allows the researcher to move from the level of more global, undifferentiated representations to the more precise and differentiated analytical level of showing how these representations are assembled.

The crux of the program is the intelligibility it seeks to bring to the researcher through producing visual and dynamic maps of the encoded textual relations (see Figure 6.3). The relations between explicit text and implicit subtext can be made viewed in 2-D dynamic maps that auto-organize (Figure 6.4a) and show lines of oppositions between terms (Figure 6.4b), in textured, three-dimensional semantic landscapes (Figure 6.4c), or in movable, three-dimensional, semantic constellations (not shown here). (For a discussion regarding interpretative issues linked with visual representation of a text, see Wallemacq & Jacques, 2000.)

These representations show which terms are attractors and where distinctions lie (marked by topographical boundaries in the representations).

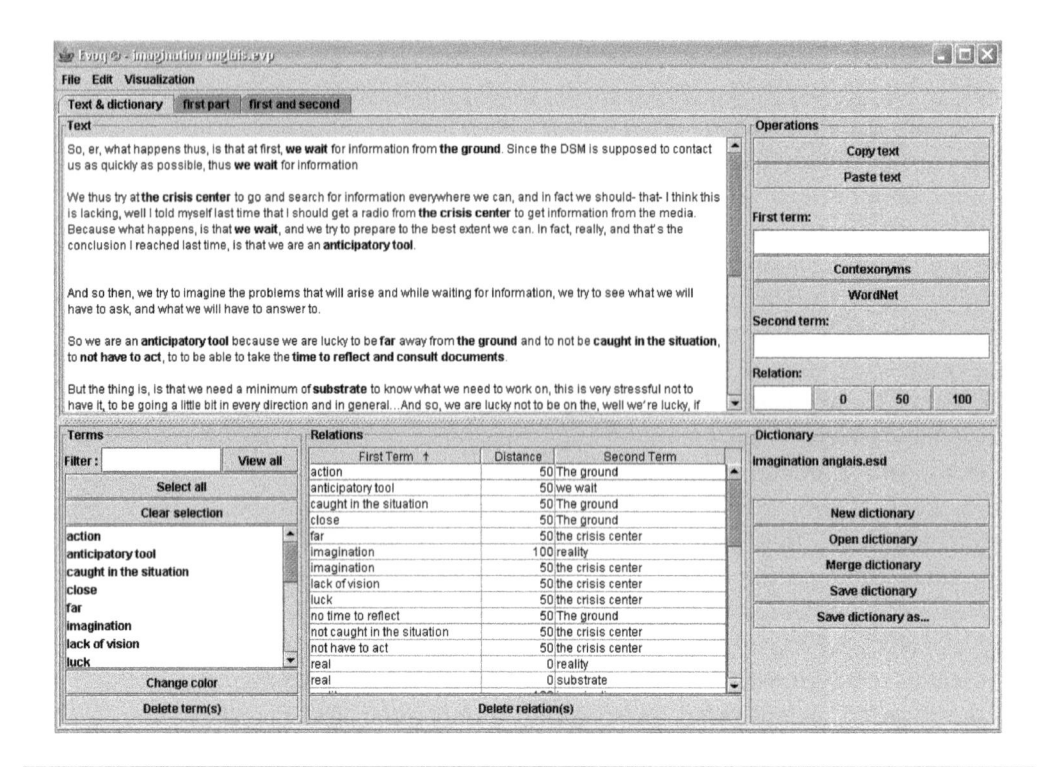

Figure 6.3 An Example of the Interface With the "Text" (Top) and "Dictionary" (Bottom) Modules

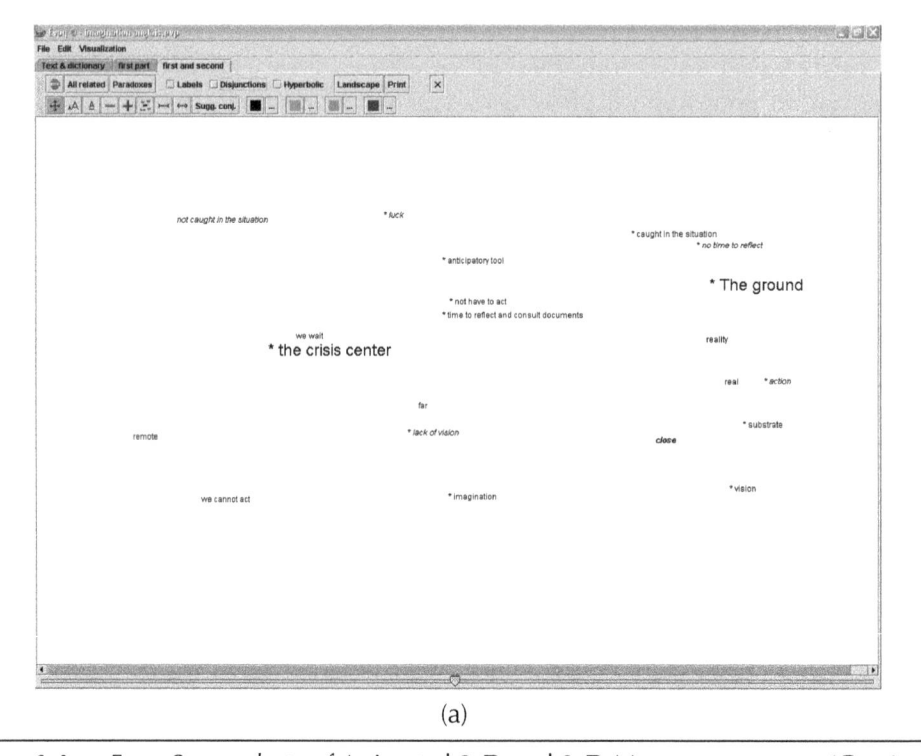

(a)

Figure 6.4 Evoq Screenshots of Animated 2-D and 3-D Maps *(Continued)*

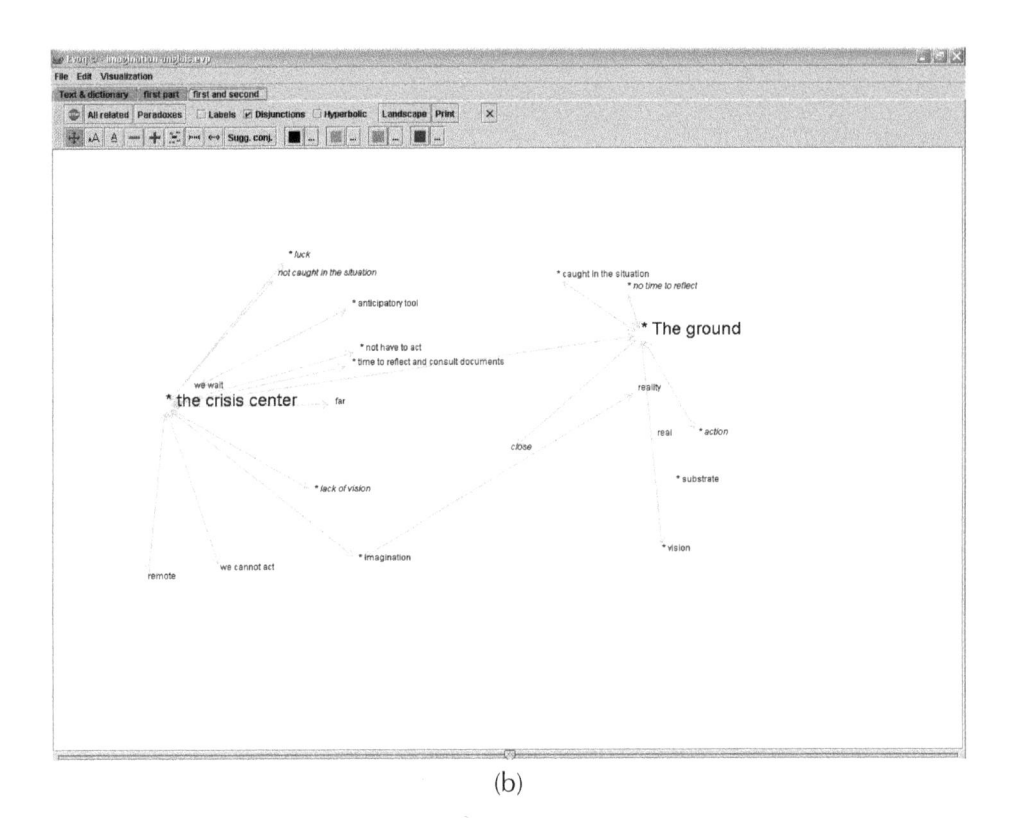

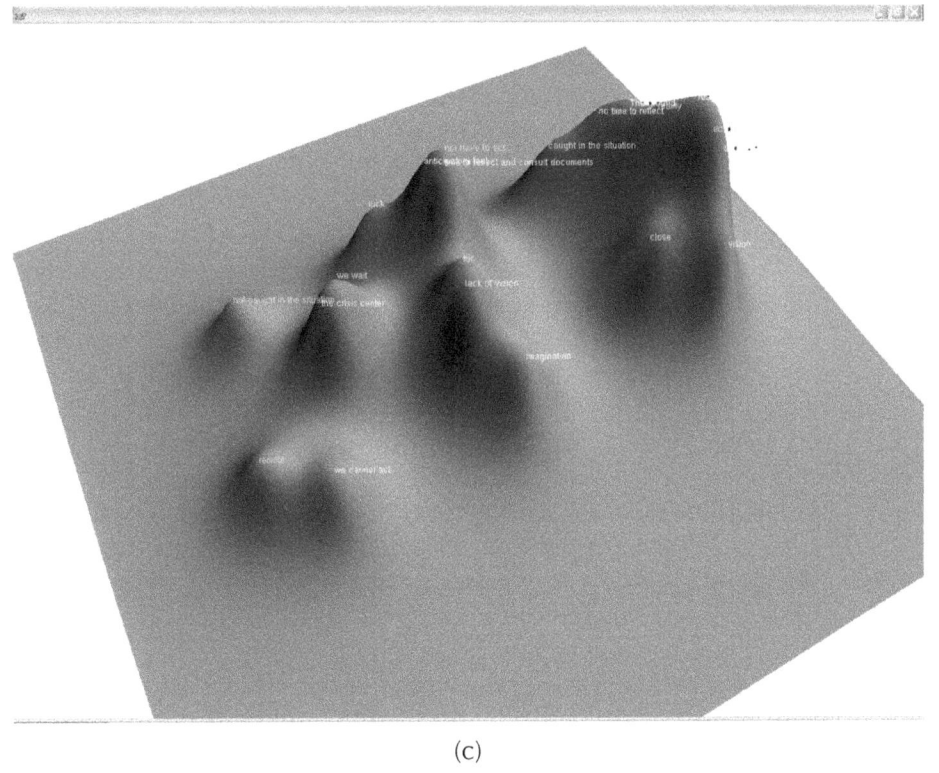

A Cognitive Approach to Crisis Management in Organizations 179

(b)

(c)

Figure 6.4 (Continued)

They also display the text, the countertext against which particular lexical choices are made, and the subtext is implicitly coded. Such graphs allow visualization of the "rhetorically and socially constructed webs of meaning" (Blommaert & Verschueren, 1998), in which an individual is immersed, from which he or she speaks, and from which he or she draws concepts, conventions, and forms of expressions. Carrying out analyses on large linguistic corpuses allows us to start seeing how some maps may follow the shape of others, assess the level of resemblance or dissonance among maps, or show how one system of meaning may invade another. In the course of exploring our data with Evoq, we were struck by a distinction that appeared regularly in the discourse of the speakers, independently from the questions we asked as part of the interviewing process, and seemed to crucially structure how the speakers viewed crisis management. This distinction, in part conceptual and in part practical, concerned the relationship between "the crisis center" as a center for decisions and the "ground" where the crisis occurred. In the next section, we begin by investigating connotations associated with the two poles of this distinction: What conceptual frames do they contribute to constitute and what do they tell us about crisis management? We do this by looking at one excerpt drawn from the data sets. Although we only discuss one example, the themes we will allude to were found repeatedly in the data, which makes us believe that they are part of a much more general frame for conceptualizing crisis management. These distinctions might not be confined solely to the domain of crisis management but may be part of a more general, archetypal order. *Sometimes imagination is worse than reality*": The material we discuss is drawn from an interview from the same data as in the first study (Jacques et al., 2003). The interviewee, a medical doctor, describes how she views the role of the crisis center. We present here the analysis of two parts of the excerpt. To the right of the text of the interview, we have represented the disjunctions encoded explicitly or implicitly "between brackets" in the text.

This transcript can be divided into two segments, which construct two different competitive interpretative frames (the contrast between these two views is encoded by the discourse marker "but," which opens the second part of the excerpt in the transcript in Figure 6.5). Let us discuss these two segments. The first part of the excerpt begins by showing how the services of emergency are organized according to a very Western frame of reference, distinguishing workers who are "on the ground" engaged in real-time action from workers located at the crisis center, who are primarily responsible for processes of decision-making. This distinction, both a conceptual one and a practical one, is probably heavily influenced by the more common divisions inherited from Taylorist principles of work organization: distinctions between conceptualization versus actualization, manual labor versus intellectual work. It is also reminiscent of military metaphors, distinguishing between agents on the front lines and agents in the back, at the

A Cognitive Approach to Crisis Management in Organizations

First part of the excerpt	**WATCH THE CORRESPONDENCE**
So, er, what happens then is that at first, we wait for information from the ground. Since the DSM is supposed to contact us as quickly as possible, we wait for information	The ground ←→ the crisis centre (they) ←→ we (they contact us to give us information) ←→ we wait for information
So we try at the crisis centre to go and search for information everywhere we can, and in fact we should do that - I think, we don't know what's going on, well I told myself last time that I should get a radio from the crisis centre to get information from the media. Because what happens, is that we wait, and we try to prepare the best we can. In fact, really, and that's the conclusion I reached last time, is that we are an anticipatory tool.	(we do not wait) ←→ we wait (we do not try to prepare to the best we can) ←→ we try to prepare to the best extent we can (action tool ?) ←→ anticipatory tool (not try to imagine) ←→ we try to imagine the problems
And so then, we try to imagine the problems that will arise and while waiting for information, we try to imagine what equipment we will have to ask for, and what we will be asked to do.	(do ?) ←→ wait (absence of luck) ←→ luck (close) ←→ far (caught in the situation) ←→ not caught in the situation
So we are an anticipatory tool because we are lucky to be far away from the ground and to not be caught in the situation, to not have to act, to be able to take the time to reflect and read a few things quickly.	(action) ←→ not have to act (no time to reflect) ←→ time to reflect and consult documents
Second part of the excerpt	
But the thing is, is that we need a minimum of information to know what we need to work on, this is very stressful not to have it, to be going a little bit in every direction and in general…And so, we are lucky not to be on the, well we're lucky, if you want,… for the sake of our state of mind, we are lucky not to be on the ground. But well, the problem is that we don't have the information and so in addition, well, I'll talk from another point of view, but it's the point of view of stress. It is very stressful, because precisely, we can't see what is happening, and so everything is based on imagination and there, we have to prepare to face the worst.	(information) ←→ lacking a minimum of information very stressful going in every direction (for the sake of our state of mind, unlucky to be on the ground) ←→ for our state of mind lucky not to be on the ground (have information) ←→ don't have information (non stress) ←→stressful (vision) ←→ lack of vision (based on reality) ←→ based on imagination

Figure 6.5 Interview Transcripts *(Continued)*

Figure 6.5 (Continued)

And so it is true that the fact that something serious has happened must draw our attention back regularly to the situation and the real problems. But in fact I realized that to a certain extent, it was maybe even more stressful than if we were on the ground. Because precisely we cannot act. We are expecting, we are trying to foresee, but we don't have the ability to react...Well, we try at least to search for the information, to consult, to look at maps, to foresee, but when the intervention team, I mean the psycho-social team, talks to intervening teams, etc. it is true that you often think about the team intervening on the ground, but we think less about those which are remote, but I tell you: imagination is sometimes worse that reality. So, it's true that . . . I think we really need to take that into account too.	know the reality of a situation ←→ to prepare to face the worst
	       for the stress ←→ for our state of mind
	
	(for stress, unlucky to be on the ground)
	
	action ←→ we cannot act, expectation, foresight intervention team ←→ (those who do not intervene)
	       (close) ←→ far
	       (reality) ←→ imagination

control room. In her discourse, "Mrs. A." endorses this system of conceptual distinctions and the attribute usually associated with them: Being located at the crisis center is considered a valued position since it is the place where decisions are made. The crisis center is located away from the crisis' epicenter and thus allows one to avoid getting caught emotionally in its turmoil. In this context, individuals at the crisis center are in a position to reason about the situation, not just react emotionally to it. The distance is constructed to make the appropriate decisions. On the other hand, "the ground" is the *locus* of action. Being on the ground means being emotionally caught in the situation, being short-sighted because of being directly involved in the situation, without the necessary distance to be able to reflect upon the situation and analyze its components. Workers on the ground thus lack the physical and psychological distance to be able to rationally analyze the situation.

In the second part of the excerpt, however, appears a countertext to this, one that threatens to destabilize the set of distinctions just established. Talking about her situation at the crisis center, Mrs. A. alludes to the fact that because she is away from the crisis location, she can only imagine how the crisis might develop. Her efforts are thus entirely oriented toward getting and finding information regarding the situation on the ground to try to form an image of it. From the point of view of what is happening on the ground, she is in fact not in a position to intervene in the course of action being performed there. Her actions of gathering information almost feel as if they are "inaction" to her. As a result, a type of anxiety arises different from the one experienced by individuals on the ground. This anxiety is "for our state of mind/from the point of view of stress": Actors at the crisis center are left to imagine the situation, but their imagination is not limited by reality anymore. Ideas follow one another, but the principle of reality is not there to frame and limit them. This situation leads Mrs. A. to state that "imagination is sometimes worse than reality." We now see how previous distinctions are restructured in relation to this new set of connotations: While the ground is still where actions take place, the crisis center is not just where decisions are made but also a place of "nonaction" or "inaction." While the crisis location is still depicted as the space "where things happen"—i.e., the domain of the "real"—the crisis center is not just the domain of rational thinking. It becomes also a place where phantasmagorical drift is likely because of the distance from reality. If actors on the ground are too close to reality, people at the crisis center are too far away; they are not in touch with what is really happening on the ground. The crisis center thus becomes constructed as a place where decisions are made while flying blind, without any means to construct an accurate picture of what is happening for real.

The field was largely devalued in the first part of the excerpt. It gains here a set of positive attributes associated with the fact that the crisis location is "real," and actors can act; they may be short-sighted but they do not grope their way as blindly as those at the crisis center. Paying attention to the text, subtext, and countertext thus allows us to show the complexities of the frames of representation organizing Mrs. A.'s perception and knowledge regarding crisis management. Figure 6.6 summarizes these relationships.

In Figure 6.6, we see that two sets of frames are in competition. In the top portion of the table, a certain number of positive values are associated with the crisis center (rationality, decision-making, time for reflection, distance) and negative values with the situation "on the ground" (emotion, short-sightedness, being caught in the action). In the bottom part of the table, the same terms are used to describe the ground, but they almost acquire on-the-rebound positive value in opposition to a new set of connotations associated with the crisis center, which are this time rather negative (inaction, stress, distance, blindness). In other words, the second game of oppositions almost requalifies the first.

Discussion and Conclusions

DISCUSSION AT THE LEVEL OF THE ARCHITECTURE OF THOUGHT

From a constructivist perspective, social realities are apprehended as historical constructions of individual and collective actors. This perspective

	On the Ground	*At the Crisis Center*
First part of the excerpt	Action Emotion Reality Close Short-Sighted −	Decision Rationality Reflection Distance Accurate Vision +
Second part of the excerpt	Action Emotion Reality Close Short-Sighted +	Inaction Stress Imagination Too Far Away Blind −

Figure 6.6 The Distinction Crisis Center/On the Ground in Mrs. A.'s Interview

consists of the production and permanent reproduction of social realities in the interaction between persons, and between observers and phenomena. For the study of crises, causal cognitive mapping software uses an interesting metaphor for the visualization of language: Language is represented as a map with box and links. It shows how an individual or group of individuals links concepts. The concepts, things, objects referred to are represented by boxes, and links are referred to by lines. Thus, we are able to determine how, for a given speaker, concepts are linked and in connection with which chain of (causal) implication one event is supposed to affect another. We can also shortcut or simplify a reasoning process, identify different reasoning processes within the same group of people, identify loop reasoning, tell which questions are central (strongly linked) and which are more tangential, and so on. This mode of visualization, however interesting, naturally carries its own built-in system of presuppositions. It stresses implication relationships (what acts on what) between relatively well-identified entities (in the boxes), such as the box contains identifiable elements (structures such as individuals, groups, tools, and spaces at the basis of actors' mental representations). This type of visualization carries with it definite biases. It implies an entire philosophy of language rooted in connexionism (see Figure 6.7).

We also presented an alternative "semantic mapping" software program, Evoq, which is inspired by a different conception of language and which thus requires another visual metaphor to be represented. We have taken a conception of natural language greatly inspired by structuralism and poststructuralism but also influenced by phenomenology. This sort of

Causal Map	Semantic Map
• Cognition	• Semantic fields
• Boxes and links	• Difference, edges
• Concepts	• Percepts
• Implication	• Associations/oppositions
• Denotation	• Evocations, connotations
• Univocity	• Plurivocity
• In front of	• Immersed
• Medium (words are in the control of the speaker)	• We have to deal with words (we are in the power of words)

Figure 6.7 The Two Conceptions of Language

thinking does not express itself in terms of boxes and links. In this conception, the emphasis is less on what language designates (what is denoted) than on what it conveys (what is connoted or evoked); less on the arrows (implication relations) than on the connections—the identity/difference system constituting the boxes (the very constitution of units, of "what we're talking about"); less on the causes and effects than on the motives, the forms (Gestalt), the patterns that organize and make intelligibility possible; less on what language lets us say and rather on what it sometimes says without our knowing it, obliquely or on the rebound. Quite simply, this conception of language seeks less to account for a form of reasoning than to account for an undoubtedly still more elementary level: the semantic field the speaker is located in and with which he or she copes and organizes his or her perceptions (see Figure 6.7).

DISCUSSION AT THE LEVEL OF THE ORGANIZATIONAL CRISIS

On the empirical level, we can also point out the remarkable complementary approach of the two methods. The identification of the concepts and links allows us to identify the presence of aggravating factors by cross-analysis of the interviews and the clustering into strategic actions. This brings us to the transposition (in crisis context) of the individual cognitive activity into collective ones, giving us a macro view of the actor's cognition in a situated position, and bringing an interpretative capacity that permits a level of validity. This macro structural level allows us to stay close to the observable action on the field; the factors and the actions are directly identifiable using an observation grid or content analysis, and the approach is a management tool that could be interfaced with the Rexao technique, which is a combination of postcrisis learning and individual or organizational learning (see the work of the multidisciplinary research team composed by Jacques, Pavard, Poumadere, Specht, and Wybo working on the development of crisis management tools based on crises exercises results organized between 1998 and 2005, http://www.rexao.org/nouveau/index.php).

In de Saint Georges et al. (2004), with semantic mapping we discover at a micro level that the job of the crisis manager, *thinking of the unthinkable and mapping the unknown,* is paradoxical and this could lead to the emergence of dysfunction. On one hand, crises are events or processes that occur as unexpected and unforeseeable events, but by definition, they "upset ideals of stability and control" (Grosz, 1999, p. 16), escape all known scenarios, in such a way that—as one speaker puts it in an excerpt not discussed in this chapter—"to foresee crises is impossible." On the other hand, the job of the crisis manager is to "be prepared for the unforeseeable." Therefore, the problem that they face can be expressed in the following terms: How do you think the unthinkable? Many strategies have been developed in the field of crisis management to seek to "eliminate the random, the wild" (Scollon & Scollon, 2001): plans, checklists, and procedures to follow when a critical situation arises, scenarios of possible crises in order to identify which unstable situations may arise in the future and the consequences these situations may produce for the population, for an organization, for a country's government, and even for scientists (Wybo & Jacques, 2006). Procedures, however, never exhaust the range of situations that may arise in certain crises (or as an interviewee said, "because procedures, you can never write everything into procedures"), and crises always end up being, as we pointed out earlier, as much material crises as they are crises of representations. Crises are crises of representations because one does not know how the crisis will develop. They are also crises of representation because crisis management is not just an intellectual exercise in foreseeing but often a matter of life and death, involving people's real lives. The nature of the critical situation can thus also contribute to annihilating the ability to think and construct a coherent representation of the situation. The roots of the representational crisis are thus both cognitive and psychological. It seems that to some extent, faced with having to construct representations of a critical situation, professionals in crisis management find themselves in a position a bit similar to that of the early cartographers who had to map a terra incognita.

The main lessons learned from this work, with the model of aggravating factors and an analysis of intertextuality between actors, are the lack of coordination and communication between actors and the plurisdisciplinarity of the various teams involved in crisis management. Plurisdisciplinarity is rooted in the concepts of both interdisciplinarity and multidisciplinarity; interdisciplinarity means the collaboration of actors who are members of different crisis specialities, and multidisciplinarity means the collaboration of professionals from different disciplines; this seems to lead to a better decision-making process, and the plurisdisciplinarity appears at the micro and macro levels of crisis management. At the macro level, aggravating factors identified are caused by failures, insufficiencies, and biases in coordination and communication along and within the continuum of crisis management, leading to a lack of integration. This lack of integration is mainly due to structural characteristics, the division of work into single-function disciplines, a separation that implies function definition, hierarchical communication, and physical communication; this means, in crisis management, the coordination between actors who nevertheless continue to recognize the differences implied by their original distinct status, their different levels of authority, their territorial responsibilities at other times, their normal structure and hierarchy of organization, their normal function, their culture, their identity, and their equipment. At a micro level we found an explanation in the relationship expressed in terms of interpersonal and inter- and intra-group relationships, in a sense making the actors submit to their individual and collective thoughts and actions. We find here the three-level model described at the beginning of the chapter. This emphasis on coordination and communication (integration) enlightens the results of Karl Weick in the area of crisis management (Weick, 1988, 1990, 1993; Weick & Roberts, 1993). Weick's approach is typical of social psychology. For Weick (1990) and Laurent and Jacques (2005), an individual error or success is usually the product of a collective error (use of language). Weick (1990) in this sense emphasizes the role played by group interaction or intersubjectivity (Laurent & Jacques, 2005) in the resolution or aggravation of crises. Interaction within a group explains why small isolated errors can become amplified in an unpredictable and incomprehensible manner, and can thus generate catastrophes (Weick, 1990). Jacques, Laurent, and Wallemacq (2004) and Laurent and Jacques (2005) explain how the use of metaphors can suppress paradoxes in the language communication, particularly in the conditions described above. Weick (1988) considers accidents as inevitable, but it is essential to analyze not only the events that lead more or less directly to a catastrophe but also the processes that cause the amplification of those events. As in Weick's work (1990), the approach developed in this chapter considers the exchange of information to be the object of a process of interpretation on the part of the agents, a process of interpretation that is itself a function of a shared language, relations, authority, and communication. For Weick, interaction can successfully reduce the ambiguity of situations (Roux-Dufort, 2000). Weick (1988), in a study of the connections between action, cognition, and crisis, places this dilemma in evidence: On one hand, "*the act of the explorer affects that which is explored*" (Weick, 1988, p. 306)—initial actions determine the trajectory of a crisis; actions are always ahead of understanding; the risk, in acting, is to aggravate the crisis (Weick, 1988). On the other hand, by acting, the actors can simplify a complex task (Weick, 1988). Action (including the act of language) that is appropriate to the situation does not appear until other actions have improved understanding (Laurent & Jacques, 2005; Weick, 1988): The agents do not understand what they are doing until they have done it, and the judgment about the adequateness of an action is partially a validation of prior reasoning (Weick, 1988). Retrospectively developed explanations are often rigid and can generate processes of selective attention and self-fulfilling prophecy (Weick, 1988). Weick considers cognition as a product of action, but Weick (1988) still mentions the preconceptions that underlie action. Depending on their preconceptions, agents undergoing a "process of enactment" select and analyze certain elements of a situation and give those a meaning. Then, the agents act, but their action tends to confirm their preconceptions (Weick, 1998). Thus preconceptions can act like self-fulfilling prophecies in the process of enactment and action. In his study on the Mann Gulch fire (August 5, 1949), Weick (1993) evokes the concept of "sensemaking": Reality is a permanent construction that emerges from efforts to create order and to give retrospective meaning to reality; reality could emerge through act of language preceding action (Laurent & Jacques, 2005).

Bibliography

Ackermann, F., Eden, C., & Cropper, S. (1995). Getting started with cognitive mapping. In M. Jones (Ed.), *Decision Explorer help file*. Strathclyde, UK: University of Strathclyde.

Allard-Poesi, F. (1997). *Nature et processus d'émergence des représentations collectives dans les groupes de travail restreints, Thèse pour l'obtention du titre de Docteur es Sciences de Gestion*. Université Paris IX Dauphine, Center de Recherche DMSP.

Augoustinos M., & Walker, I. (1995). Social schemata. In M. Augoustinos & I. Walker, *Social cognition: An integrated introduction*. London: Sage.

Axelrod, R. (Ed.). (1976). *Structure of decision: The cognitive maps of political elite*. Princeton, NJ: Princeton University Press.

Blommaert, J., & Verschueren, J. (1998). *Debating diversity: Analysing the discourse of tolerance*. London: Routledge.

Bryant, J. (1983). Hypermaps: A representation of perceptions in conflicts. *Omega, 11*(6), 576–586.

Cossette, P., & Audet, M. (1992). Mapping of an idiosyncratic schema. *Journal of Management Studies, 29*(3), 325–347.

Cossette, P., & Audet, M. (1994). Qu'est ce qu'une carte cognitive? In P. Cossette (Ed.), *Cartes cognitives et organization*. Laval, Quebec, Canada: Les presses de l'Université Laval.

Cottraux J. (1988). Modèles cognitifs de la dépression. In I. M. Blackburn & J. Cottraux, *Thérapie cognitive de la dépression*. Paris: Masson.

de Saint Georges, I., Wallemacq, A., & Jacques, J.-M. (2004). *Technologies of disinvolvement in crisis management: Objectifying, impersonalizing and desensitizing information from the ground* (pp. 162–168). London: KPMC.

Dutton, J. E. (1986). The processing of crisis and non-crisis strategic issues. *Journal of Management Studies, 23*(5), 501–517.

Edelman, G. M., & Tononi, G. (2000). *Comment la matière devient conscience*. Paris: Odile Jacob.

Eden, C. (1988). Cognitive mapping. *European Journal of Operational Research, 36,* 1–13.

Eden, C. (1992). On the nature of cognitive maps. *Journal of Management Studies, 29,* 261–265.

Filliettaz, L. (2004). The construction of requests in transactional settings: A discursive approach. In C. Gouveia et al. (Eds.), *Discourse and communication in the enterprise: Linguistic perspectives.* Lisbon: Ulices.

Fink, S. J. (1986). *Crisis management: Planning for the inevitable.* New York: American Management.

Forgues, B. (1991, November/December). La décision en situation de crise. *Revue Française de Gestion,* pp. 39–45.

Forgues, B., & Roux-Dufort, C. (1998). *Crises: Events or processes?* Paper presented at the Hazards and Sustainability Conference, Durham, UK, May 26–27.

Gatot, L. (2000). *Crise et cognition: Conception d'une gestion préventive.* Thèse de doctorat. Faculté des sciences économiques, sociales et de gestion. Département des sciences de gestion [Research Center for Crisis and Conflict Management]. Presses Universitaires de Namur.

Gatot, L., & Jacques, J. M. (1997). Cognitive maps as crises management tools. *Proceedings of the Fifth Workshop on Managerial and Organizational Cognition,* EIASM Namur, September 3–5.

Gatot, L., Roux-Dufort, C., & Jacques, J. M. (1999). *From postcrisis to preventive learning: Some empirical evidence for a preventive crisis learning management tool.* Paper presented at the National Academy of Management Meetings, Chicago, August 6–11.

Gioia, D. A., & Manz, C. C. (1985). Linking cognition and behavior: A script processing interpretation of vicarious learning. *Academy of Management Review, 10*(3), 527–539.

Goestschin, P. (1975). La planification d'urgence. *Société d'Etude de la Prévision et de la Planification,* Bulletin no. 2, pp. 27–39.

Grant, D., Keenoy, T., & Oswick, C. (2001). Organizational discourse: Key contributions and challenges. *International Studies of Management and Organization, 33*(3), 5–24.

Grosz, E. (1999). Thinking the new: Of futures yet unthought. In E. Grosz (Ed.), *Becoming: Explorations in time, memory and futures.* Ithaca and London: Cornell University Press.

Hermann, C. F. (1963). Some consequences of crisis which limit the viability of organizations. *Administrative Science Quarterly, 8,* 61–82.

Holsti, O. R. (1978). Limitations of cognitive abilities in the face of crisis. *Journal of Business Administration, 9,* 39–55.

Huff, A. S. (1990). Mapping strategic thought. In A. S. Huff (Ed.), *Mapping strategic thought.* Chichester, UK: John Wiley & Sons.

Huff, A. S., Narapereddy, V., & Fletcher, K. E. (1990). Coding the causal association of concepts. In A. S. Huff (Ed.), *Mapping strategic thought.* Chichester, UK: John Wiley and Sons.

Iedema, R., & Wodak, R. (1999). Introduction: Organizational discourses and practices. *Discourse and Society, 10*(1), 5–19.

Jacques, J. M., & Gatot, L. (1997). De l'incident à la catastrophe: Une lecture cognitive. *Urgences Médicales, 16*(1), 24–30.

Jacques, J. M., & Gatot, L. (Eds.). (1998). *Industrial risk assessment and management: A cognitive approach.* Final Report EEC Project ENV4 CT960242.

Jacques, J. M., Gatot, L., Decharneux, T., & Sepulchre, O. (1994). Les facteurs aggravants et les crises technologiques dans le secteur de la chimie. *Environnement et Société, 12,* 39–56.

Jacques, J. M., Gatot, L., & Wallemacq, A. (2003). Risk perception and crisis management: Landscape of mind, landscape of action. In K. Fabri & M. Yeroyanni (Eds.), *Natural and technological hazards* (pp. 24–34). Luxembourg: Office for Official Publications of the European Communities.

Jacques, J.-M., & Laurent, N. (2005). Expérience subjective et neurosciences, le paradoxe du "moi." In F. Goetghebeur & J.-M. Jacques (Eds.), *Regards croisés sur le moi: Traditions orientales, traditions occidentales* (pp. 185–250). Belgium: Kunchab.

Jacques, J. M., Laurent, N., & Wallemacq, A. (2004). Paradoxes, dilemmes et contradictions: Une mise en lumière au moyen du logiciel EVOQ©. In G. Purnelle, C. Fairon, & A. Dister (Eds.), *Le poids des mots* (pp. 644–649). Louvain-la-Neuve: Presses Universitaires de Louvain.

Jacques, J. M., Lobet, Cl., & Rousseau, A. (2004). *La modernisation de l'hôpital: Kaleidioscopie du changement.* Namur, Belgium: Presses Universitaires de Namur.

Jacques, J. M., & Wybo, J. L. (in press). Emergency and crisis management. *Sciences of natural risk reduction.*

Jeanson, B., & Cossette, P. (1996). Le champ des affaires immobilières: Une étude de cartographie cognitive. *Revue Internationale de Systémique, 10*(1–2), 131–155.

Kelly, G. (1955). *The psychology of personal constructs.* New York: Norton.

Kletz, T. (1993). *Lessons from disaster: How organizations have no memory and accidents recur.* Houston, TX: Gulf.

Kovoor-Misra, S. (1995). A multidimensional approach to crisis preparation for technical organizations: Some critical factors. *Technological Forecasting and Social Change, 48,* 143–160.

Lagadec, P. (1992). *La gestion des crises: Outils de réflexion à l'usage des décideurs.* Paris: McGraw-Hill.

Laroche, H., & Nioche, J. P. (1994). L'approche cognitive de la stratégie d'enterprise. *Revue Française de Gestion, 99,* 64–78.

Laufer, R. (1993). *L'enterprise face aux risques majeurs: A propos de l'incertitude des normes socials.* Paris: L'Harmattan.

Laukkanen, M. (1994). Comparative cause mapping of organizational cognitions. *Organization Science, 5*(3), 322–343.

Laurent, N., & Jacques, J. M. (2005). Semantic mapping of interpersonal communication: The case of emergency management. *Proceedings of the 11th Workshop on Managerial and Organizational Cognition, Collective Cognition.* Munich, Germany.

Lord, R .G., & Foti, R. J. (1986). Schema theories, information processing and organizational behavior. In D. A. Gioia (Ed.), *The thinking organization: Dynamics of organizational social cognition* (pp. 20–48). San Francisco: Jossey-Bass.

March, J. G., Sproull, L. S., & Tamuz, M. (1991). Learning from samples of one or fewer. *Organization Science, 2*(1), 1–13.

Masuch, M. (1985). Vicious circles in organization. *Administrative Science Quarterly, 30*(1), 14–33.

Matlin, M. W. (1998). *Cognition* (4th ed.). Orlando, FL: Harcourt Brace.

Mehan, H. (1982). Le constructivisme social en psychologie et en sociologie. *Sociologie et Société, 16*(2), 77–95.

Mitroff, I. I. (1988). Crisis management: Cutting through the confusion. *Sloan Management Review, 15,* 15–20.

Mitroff, I. I., & Pearson, C. M. (1993). *Crisis management—A diagnostic guide for improving your organization's crisis preparedness.* San Francisco: Jossey-Bass.

Nystrom, P. C., & Starbuck, W. H. (1984). To avoid organizational crises, unlearn. *Organizational Dynamics,* Spring, 53–65.

Pauchant, T. C., & Mitroff, I. I. (1990). Crisis management: managing paradox in a chaotic world. *Technological Forecasting and Social Change, 38,* 117–134.

Perrow, C. (1984). *Normal accidents: Living with high risk technologies.* New York: Basic Books.

Piret, A., Nizet, J., & Bourgeois, E. (1996). *L'analyze structurale: Une méthode d'analyze de contenu pour les sciences humaines.* Bruxelles: DeBoeck Université.

Preble, J. F. (1997). Integrating the crisis management perspective into the strategic management process. *Journal of Management Studies, 34*(5), 769–791.

Roux-Dufort, C. (1996). Crises: Des possibilités d'apprentissage pour l'enterprise. *Revue Française de Gestion, 108,* 79–89.

Roux-Dufort, C. (1997). *L'apprentissage organisationnel post-crise.* Thèse pour l'obtention du titre de Docteur en Sciences de Gestion, Université Paris IX Dauphine, Paris.

Roux-Dufort, C. (2000). *Le regard de Weick sur la fiabilité organisationnelle: Implications pour la gestion des crises.* Edhec School of Management, Département Management et Stratégie, Pôle "Transformations, ruptures et crises."

Roux-Dufort, C., & Metais, E. (1998). Building core competencies in crisis management through organizational learning—The case of the French nuclear power producer. *Technological Forecasting and Social Change, 60*(2), 113–127.

Rumelhart, D. E. (1980). Schemata: The building blocks of cognition. In R. J. Spiro, B. C. Bruce, & W. F. Brewer (Eds.), *Theoretical issues in readings comprehension* (pp. 33–58). Hillsdale, NJ: Erlbaum.

Schneider, C., & Angelmar, R. (1993). Cognition in organizational analysis: Who's minding the store? *Organization Studies, 14*(3), 347–374.

Schwenk, C. R. (1989). Linking cognitive, organizational and political factors in explaining strategic change. *Management Studies, 26*(2), 177–187.

Scollon, R., & Scollon, S. (2001). *Intercultural communication: A discourse approach.* Malden, MA: Blackwell.

Shrivastava, P. (1987). *Bhopal: Anatomy of a crisis.* Cambridge, UK: Ballinger.

Shrivastava, P. (1994). Technological and organizational roots of industrial crises: Lessons from *Exxon Valdez* and Bhopal. *Technological Forecasting and Social Change, 45,* 237–253.

Shrivastava, P., Mitroff, I. I., Miller, D., & Miglani, A. (1988). Understanding industrial crises. *Journal of Management Studies, 25*(4), 285–303.

Simon, H. A. (1959). Theories of decision-making in economics and behavioral science. *The American Economic Review, 3,* 253–283.

Simon, H. A. (1978, May). Rationality as process and as product of thought. *The American Economic Review Proceedings,* pp. 1–16.

Simon, H. A. (1986). Rationality in psychology and economics. In R. H. Hogarth & M. R. Reder (Eds.), *Rational choices: The contrast between economics and psychology* (pp. 25–40). Chicago: University of Chicago Press.

Slatter, S. P. (1984). The impact of crisis on managerial behavior. *Business Horizons, 27,* 65–68.

Smart, C., & Vertinsky, I. (1977). Designs for crisis decisions units. *Administrative Science Quarterly, 2,* 640–657.

Stubbart, C. I. (1987). Improving the quality of crisis thinking. *Columbia Journal of World Business, 22*(1), 89–99.

Stubbart, C. I., & Ramaprasad, A. (1990). Comments on the empirical articles and recommendations for future research. In A. S. Huff (Ed.), *Mapping strategic thought* (pp. 251–288). Chichester, UK: John Wiley & Sons.

Taylor, S. E., & Crocker, J. (1981). Schematic bases of social information processing. In E. T. Higgins, C. P. Herman, & M. P. Zanna (Eds.), *Social Cognition, Vol. 1* (pp. 89–134). Hillsdale, NJ: Erlbaum.

Turner, B. A. (1976). The organizational and inter-organizational development of disasters. *Administrative Science Quarterly, 21,* 378–397.

Turner, B. A. (1994). Causes of disaster: sloppy management. *British Journal of Management, 5,* 215–219.

Tversky, A., & Kahneman, D. (1974). Judgment under uncertainty: Heuristics and biases. *Science, 185,* 1124–1131.

Varela, F. J. (1989). *Connaître les sciences cognitives: Tendances et perspectives.* Paris: Seuil.

Vidaillet, B. (1996). *Complexité cognitive: Conceptualisation constructiviste et mesure par la cartographie cognitive.* Center d'Etudes et de Recherches de l'Essec, DR 96017.

Wahlström, B. (1992). Avoiding technological risks: The dilemma of complexity. *Technological Forecasting and Social Change, 42,* 351–365.

Wallemacq, A., & Jacques, J. M. (2000). Landscapes of words. In C. Combes, D. Grant, T. Keenoy, & C. Oswick, *Organizational discourse: Word-views, work-views and world-views* (pp. 275–276). London: KMPC. Proceedings of the conference held at The Management Center, King's College, University of London, 2000, July 26–28.

Wallemacq, A., & Jacques J. M. (2005). Spaces of thought, spaces for thought. In S. Linstead & A. Linstead (Eds.), *Thinking organization* (pp. 39–66). London: Routledge.

Wallemacq, A., Jacques, J. M., Bruyninckx, V. (2004). *Dans le sillage des mots . . . EVOQ, logiciel de cartographie cognitive.* Namur, Belgium: Presses Universitaires de Namur.

Weick, K. E. (1988). Enacted sensemaking in crisis situation. *Journal of Management Studies, 25*(4), 305–317.

Weick, K. E. (1990). The vulnerable system: An analysis of the Tenerife air disaster. *Journal of Management, 16*(3), 571–593.

Weick, K. E. (1993). The collapse of sensemaking in organizations: The Mann Gulch disaster. *Administrative Science Quarterly, 38,* 628–652.

Weick, K. E., & Roberts, K. H. (1993). Collective mind in organizations: Heedful interrelating on flight desks. *Administrative Science Quarterly, 38,* 357–381.

Worf, B. (1956). *Language, thought, and reality.* Cambridge: MIT Press.

Wrightson, M. T. (1976). The documentary coding method. In R. Axelrod (Ed.), *Structure of decision: The cognitive maps of political elite* (pp. 291–332). Princeton, NJ: Princeton University Press.

Wybo, J. L., & Jacques, J. M. (2006). Guest editors of the special issue: Future crisis, future agenda. *International Journal of Emergency Management, 3*(1), 1–5.

Part III

New Crises, New Barriers

The Psychological Effects of Crises 7

*Deny Denial—Grieve
Before a Crisis Occurs*

Ian I. Mitroff

The beleaguered CIA faces new criticism in an internal report submitted this week by [Richard J.] Kerr, [the former Deputy Director] who found serious fault with the agency's analysis on Iraq... [Kerr] believed intelligence officers had not come to grips with the causes or scope of the failure.

Kerr's comments were echoed by members of Congress who said they were becoming increasingly impatient with the agency's refusal to acknowledge that its assessments on Iraq were fundamentally flawed.

"They're in denial," said Rep. Jane Harman (D-Venice, California), the ranking Democrat on the House Intelligence Committee. "It's critically important for the national security challenges in the future that these problems get fixed. And I've seen no evidence that they are owning up to it."

—Greg Miller, "Insider Faults CIA on Iraq Analysis," *Los Angeles Times,* January 31, 2004, pp. A1, A8

In 1992, a French Airline company plane crashed on the Saint Odile mountain during... landing... just before reaching the Strasborg Airport. Only a dozen people survived the crash. A few months after [the] air crash, I had the opportunity to meet with one of the Vice Presidents... Beyond the technical explanations of [the] catastrophe, his analysis... struck me. He considered that the Mont Saint Odile crash was not a crisis. He even explained that he viewed it exactly as the *opposite* [italics in original] of a crisis, based on the fact that morning after the crash the level of the seats reserved in the planes... had not moved one iota. This is the perfect illustration of a complete denial of [a] crisis, where people manage major events by ignoring their very existence.

—Christophe Roux-Dufort, "Why Organizations Don't Learn From Crises: The Perverse Power of Normalization," *Review of Business,* Fall 2000, p. 25

Many organizations apportion blame by seeking out scapegoats [read: villains] for the cause of adverse events. This search for culpability can actually make subsequent failure more likely as individuals [read: potential victims] become reluctant to raise warnings about impending problems, or cover-up issues. Invariably, this will severely hinder the potential for effective communication, cultural change, and, in turn, learning. In such a setting of non trust, key managers and operators may not only contain potentially damaging information but may reconstruct their accounts of events to protect themselves from blame....

—Dominic Elliott, Denis Smith, and Martina McGuinness, "Exploring the Failure to Learn: Crises and the Barriers to Learning," *Review of Business,* Fall 2000, p. 18

It is challenging to find any crisis that does not demonstrate that those in charge of managing the crisis should have done better. Thoughtful critics must ask how people who have risen to positions of leadership lack foresight, judgment, and character in the face of crisis. The answers are not to be found in recalculating numbers or reenacting operating procedures. Rather, as discussed in this chapter, they often reside in a deeper understanding of what crises do to us, what it takes to recover from them, why they are often so traumatic, and why their effects are so long-lasting. I focus here on the psychological effects of crises, particularly as related to feelings of denial and betrayal. Although a tiny slice of organizational literature examines the causes and consequences of denial, the link between crises and deep, prolonged feelings of betrayal has not to my knowledge been made explicit before.

Many people are resistant to accepting the psychological impact of crises. Emotional forces are often the last outcomes to be planned for or recognized. But their influence on foreseeing, surviving, and thriving from crises is undeniable. Therefore, as a precursor to the case study and discussion that lie ahead, I begin with the end in mind by introducing eight important lessons that are derived from this work.

Lessons for Embracing the Psychological Effects of Crises

1. Emotional preparation for crises is the most difficult and the most important preparation of all; get beyond denial, confront it straight on.

2. Before one can work on crises, one has to spend the time and energy working on oneself. If one is not prepared emotionally, then valuable time and energy will be lost in working on the crises themselves.

3. One can survive, and even prosper, but if and only if he or she is prepared emotionally, physically, intellectually, and spiritually.

4. Hire counselors to work through the powerful emotions associated with all crises *before* they occur; get the grieving over so that you can get back living sooner and more fully.

5. Accept the painful fact that the Abnormal—i.e., intentionally evil acts such as 9/11—has become the new Normal state of affairs.

6. Accept the fact that in today's unrelenting 24/7/365 media-saturated world, there are no secrets anymore; the media can find out anything they want to about anyone, any corporation, etc.; secret documents and private conversations are exposed regularly on the six o'clock news and the front pages of major newspapers; if you do not accept this, then you will suffer an additional crisis; that is, the shock that comes from having all of one's personal and company secrets paraded before the public for all to see.

7. Understand that if you are in any way guilty of causing the crisis, or if you failed to prepare adequately for it, then you will be perceived as the villain; your own employees, the public, etc. will perceive that you have betrayed them.

8. In the end, all crises are perceived and experienced as major acts of betrayal, so if the original crisis was bad enough, the subsequent feelings of betrayal will be even worse.

A Major Crisis at Rural Books

Long before she got to her office door, Mary Douglas, CEO of Rural Books, could hear that her phone was ringing nonstop. It had a nasty and ominous sound.

As soon as she opened her office door, Mary saw that her answering machine was lit up like a Christmas tree. It was filled to capacity. She had already had 16 calls, and it was not yet even 6:30 a.m.

It was not a good omen. It was, in fact, the beginning of a long nightmare.

Headquartered in Montana, Mary had established Rural Books about 10 years ago. RB, as its loyal fans called it, produced a highly successful line of field books and guides for identifying and cooking wild fruit, nuts, berries, etc. Both the books and guides were extremely popular with rural and city folks alike.

On any weekend, thousands of people could be seen walking in the woods with their trusted RBs at their sides. The books and guides were not only lightweight but also extremely easy to carry and to use. For instance, carrying straps were attached to the bindings of the books so that they could easily be slung over a person's shoulder. They were also designed and manufactured to hold up to extreme elements. Most of all, they were organized around user-friendly pull-outs. They not only showed which things were edible and tasty but where they could be found as well.

RBs were especially known for their clear and simple pictures of the wild foods that were safe to eat versus those that were unsafe. The safe foods were clearly labeled and located on one page while those that were unsafe were located on a completely separate page. The pages even had different colors, green for safe and red for dangerous or unsafe. In this way, RB helped to ensure that there would be no confusion whatsoever. In the 10 years of its existence, no one had ever suffered any illness from following its recommendations.

Mary picked up the phone. Robert Turnbull, Senior Executive VP and the head of RB's East Coast division, was on the line. He was half shouting and mumbling at the same time. There were unmistakable signs of stress and panic in his voice. As he was typically calm and easygoing, it was a significant departure from his usual behavior. Mary had in fact never heard him sound more distressed in the 5 years that they had worked together.

"Mary, have you seen CNN this morning? They are running a story linking us to the deaths of a family of four. The parents were in their early 30s; the kids were just 2 and 3.

"CNN is also reporting that we are responsible for the serious illnesses of scores of others. At this time, no one knows the full extent of the injuries. It could be in the hundreds.

"CNN is saying that people became seriously ill after eating poisonous berries. They are claiming that we mislabeled some of the pages in our books.

"They are also saying something that makes no sense at all. They are saying that it's a case of product tampering. Hell, we don't make food or pharmaceutical products. What is there to tamper with?

"That's all I can tell you at this time. I don't know anything more myself. I have our production and security people checking into it, but what do we say and do in the meantime? I'm getting calls from CNN, the *Wall Street Journal*, the *New York Times*, our investment brokers, everyone. It's complete pandemonium here. They are asking tough questions that I don't have the answers to like, 'Was it a terrorist group, a group of disgruntled employees? Can you in fact rule out any of these possibilities at this time? Was it an intentional act of sabotage? Are the reports of labor troubles at RB true?' What do we say and do? I need help fast!"

Mary's mind was reeling. All she could do was mumble, "I'll get back."

RB was prepared for fires and explosions that could burn down its offices and ruin its production facilities, but not for anything like this. The possibility of product tampering, let alone terrorism and disgruntled employees, had never crossed Mary's mind. And yet, she recalled that radical environmental groups had recently been making claims that RB was endangering the environment because of all the people that were trampling—or as they put it, "loving to death"—pristine areas. A few had even sent threatening letters to RB, but she had quickly dismissed them as cranks. She also recollected that local militia groups were making threats as well because too many people were wandering too close to their compounds.

"Oh my God," Mary exclaimed, "what am I going to do? I don't have the foggiest clue as to where to begin."

Why RB Was Unable to Meet the Challenges of a Major Crisis

Because Mary and her top team had never received the proper training in crisis management (CM), they were unable to think outside the box. As a result, they were unable to imagine and to anticipate the particular types of product tampering that were directly applicable to their business. For instance, were the labels of the foods that were safe to eat versus those that were unsafe intentionally or accidentally reversed when the pages were typeset? Either case (i.e., intentionally or accidentally reversing the labels of the pages) is a *form* of product tampering that applies directly to the book business. Altering key information in a product when this information is crucial to the safety and the well-being of people *is* a major form of product tampering. In other words, product tampering is *not* confined solely to the alteration of food or pharmaceuticals.

In addition, if Mary and her top team had received proper training, then they would have been especially prepared for the strong and often overwhelming emotions that are a critical part of every major crisis. 9/11, Enron/Andersen, the Catholic Church, NASA, and a seemingly endless series of crises in recent years demonstrate clearly that crises exact a severe emotional toll on those who experience or are part of them.

The costs of crises are not only severe in terms of dollars but also in terms of emotional distress. Those who have been through major crises often use the exact same words to describe their experiences that soldiers who have been in battle and suffered severe trauma use to describe what they have gone through.

If Mary and her team had faced the challenges, and hence, learned the lessons that successful crisis leaders have to teach, then they would have been able to respond faster and better and would thereby have lowered substantially both the economic and the emotional costs of the crisis or crises that they are facing. This does *not* mean that RB would never experience a major crisis at all. In today's world, there are no such guarantees. On the contrary, *every* organization is virtually guaranteed to experience at least one major crisis in its history. It merely means that Mary and her top team would have recovered sooner and with far fewer costs.

Crisis Management Versus Risk Management

To understand more fully why neither Mary nor her top executives were prepared for the crisis that occurred, let us flash back in time to about a year before the crisis happened.

Mary was chairing the regular monthly meeting of her top executive team. The heads of the legal, marketing, finance, production, acquisitions, information technology, human resources, and public affairs departments were there as permanent, standing members. Robert Turnbull, Senior Executive Vice President and RB's Chief Operating Officer, was there as well. In addition, Bob Hunt, Head of Risk Management and Security, was there as a special, invited guest. In contrast to the other members, he was not a permanent member of the executive team.

Bob was invited to deliver a special report that he had prepared on the major risks facing RB. His report showed in no uncertain terms that the most probable and the most costly risks facing RB were fire and water damage owing to spring floods caused by melting snow. Either of these could do extensive damage to RB's production facilities and raw materials, mostly paper. RB's situation was complicated by the fact that what could inhibit and extinguish fires—i.e., water—could also do considerable damage to RB's basic raw materials. Water could also do extensive damage to RB's expensive production computers and graphic equipment. Therefore, Bob recommended the installation of special fire-inhibiting foam and paneling throughout RB's facilities. He also recommended the installation of special fire-retardant walls that would also prevent damage to RB's computers and graphic equipment. Sprinklers would be used, but only if they were needed to save lives.

With little fanfare, the Executive Committee quickly and unanimously approved the expenditure of $250,000 to protect and to upgrade RB's facilities.

The second part of Bob's report was, unfortunately, not as well received. It was, in fact, received quite negatively.

Bob informed the committee that he recently had attended a special three-day course on Crisis Management (CM). Without going into all of the details, he explained that CM took a much broader view of risks than traditional Risk Management (RM).

RM typically ranks risks according to their consequences multiplied by their probabilities of occurrence. According to this procedure, the risks that one should prepare for were precisely those that had high consequences should they occur (e.g., high injuries or high costs) and simultaneously high probabilities of occurring. Fires and water damage were in fact the highest-ranked risks according to this procedure.

Indeed, the procedure of multiplying the severity of a risk times its probability of occurrence has the general effect of selecting high-consequence, high-probability events for attention. In fact, high-consequence but low-probability events are almost guaranteed to be neglected; that is, not considered at all.

Of course, in order to perform RM, one has to have some way of estimating both the consequences and the probabilities of occurrence of potential risks. Usually this is done through studying historical records; that is, the frequency with which past, known events or risks have occurred.

Once again, according to RM, the risks that one should prepare for are precisely those that have high consequences (e.g., high injuries or high costs) and simultaneously high probabilities of occurring.

However, Bob also noted that the course had made him aware that there was a whole other category or type of risks that all businesses should consider, but unfortunately seldom did. These were high-consequence, low-probability risks. The premier example was 9/11. Obviously, terrorist acts directed against skyscrapers, but especially in New York City and Washington, D.C., were high-consequence crises. But at the same time, they were also judged to be of low probability, even though the intelligence and risk communities had for years suggested strongly that they should be considered. While perhaps unlikely, they were not impossible, and therefore, not completely improbable. Indeed, the intelligence and risk communities argued that there were strong reasons to believe that the probabilities of their occurrence were actually increasing.

To demonstrate why one needed to consider such events, the instructor pointed out that before 9/11 the most likely scenario for bringing down a high-rise was the placing of a bomb inside of a building by means of a suitcase. Flying a plane into a building was considered so improbable as to not even be worth considering. And yet, it was precisely because most people did not want to consider such events that they needed to be considered!

Closer to home, Bob suggested that RB ought to brainstorm how other types of crises—for instance, product tampering—might apply to their business. Unfortunately, because Bob could not suggest any specific examples of product tampering that might apply to RB, his proposal fell on deaf ears.

Mary politely but firmly led the charge: "Bob, I believe that I speak for all of us when I say how much we appreciate all of your efforts to protect RB. But, frankly, this is highly speculative. I can't imagine in my wildest dreams how RB could ever be the object of terrorists. We're not big or important enough. We're certainly not in a major metropolitan area. If anything, we're on the fringes. Terrorism, except maybe for eco-terrorism, just doesn't happen around here. As for product tampering, that is equally unlikely. I can't imagine any kind of a scenario where anybody would want to tamper with our products. I think that you need to confine your efforts strictly to the protection of RB's physical assets and our employees."

In order to understand Mary's reasoning, as well as that of the other members of the executive team, it is important to appreciate that every one of them was imaginative and highly creative. Indeed, it took a great deal of imagination and considerable risk to open RB in the first place.

It took a lot of guts to open RB. More than once and with great relish, Mary recounted the story of how she had received a C in her MBA class in business strategy where she first proposed the concept of RB. She had received a C because the idea was too outlandish. And yet, barely 10 years after its founding, RB was an enormous financial success. Mary had successfully foreseen and capitalized on the huge demand and desire for natural, organic foods that was soon to develop and to take hold nationwide.

Normal Versus Abnormal Business

To understand more of the deeper reasons why Mary and her top team were not prepared for the crisis that struck RB, one needs to understand that *the qualities that make for success in running a business in Normal times are not the same qualities that make for success in managing a major crisis, certainly not in Abnormal times*. Normal business demands for the most part that we learn to recognize and manage stress. Crises, on the other hand, demand that we confront and overcome some of humankind's deepest and darkest feelings. These are the emotions that are connected with denial, fear, betrayal, and the exposure to severely traumatic and traumatizing situations. To manage these kinds of feelings and emotions, one needs to develop a capacity for resilience (Reivich & Shatte, 2002). In turn, this necessitates that Mary and her top executive team undertake a rigorous and systematic program of *precrisis* psychological training. They need to take both a personal and an organizational audit of their psychological capacities to confront and to survive major crises.

The purpose of precrisis psychological training is not to be anxiety- or worry-free. No such things are possible. The purpose is to be better able to assess and manage the anxieties that accompany all crises. In other words, the purpose is not to be overwhelmed by fear or anxiety, but to be better able to cope with them.

Denial

Defense mechanisms are nature's extraordinarily clever way of protecting the fragile ego of the child from threats to its existence. Table 7.1 lists the major defense mechanisms discovered by Freud and his colleagues. These are shown in the left-hand column. The right-hand column shows some of the typical forms that these mechanisms take in organizations.

Table 7.1 Defense Mechanisms

Types of Defense Mechanisms	Examples
Denial	Crises only happen to others. We are invulnerable.
Disavowal	Crises happen, but their impact on our organization is small.
Idealization	Crises do not happen to good organizations in out-of-the-way places.
Grandiosity	We are so big and powerful that we will be protected from crises and we can handle anything that is thrown our way.
Projection	If a crisis happens, then it must be because someone else is bad or out to get us.
Intellectualization	We don't have to worry about crises since the probabilities of their occurrence are too small. Before a crisis can be taken seriously, one would have to measure precisely its odds of occurrence and its consequences.
Compartmentalization	Crises cannot affect our whole organization since the parts are independent of one another.

It is one thing for defense mechanisms to be used by young children to protect their fragile and developing egos or minds. It is quite another thing for these same mechanisms to be used to protect supposedly mature adults and organizations from thinking about unpleasant things that need to be confronted. It is also bad enough to hear denial expressed by a single person in an organization, but quite another to hear it voiced by a majority of the members of an organization. That is truly scary. When this happens, the denial is collective, and for this reason, it is much harder to confront and eliminate.

We have already seen the first defense mechanism, *Denial*, at work in Mary's response to Bob. Mary denied outright that terrorism and product tampering were even remote possibilities. Mary also used *Disavowal* and *Idealization* when she argued that RB was in an out-of-the-way place. She also used them when she argued that RB was not big and important enough to warrant preparation for certain kinds of crises. Thus, she unconsciously diminished the potential size and importance of a particular set of crises.

The fact that no one really challenged Mary is also evidence of the fact that there was a kind of collusion or unconscious buy-in by the group as well (Gabriel, 1999). This is not to say that no one quietly disagreed with Mary. Rather, no one raised their objections to the level of public discourse and disagreement. In this sense, there was collusion by the members of the group to not disagree openly with one another or their superiors.

Trauma

While not all crises are equally traumatizing, all crises have the potential to be traumatic. The major difference between denial and trauma is as follows: Denial involves denying the unpleasant feelings associated with potentially traumatic events *before* they occur. In contrast, trauma involves the denial of feelings *after* a traumatic event has occurred.

Denial arises *before* a traumatic event, whereas what we call a "traumatic reaction" involves the denial of painful feelings and emotions *after* a traumatic event has occurred. In the case of Denial, the mind shuts down *before* a crisis happens, whereas *in reaction to* a traumatic event, the mind shuts down *after* it has occurred.

In either case, the feelings, fears, and emotions surrounding a potential or known crisis are too painful for the conscious mind to accept. Thus, in the case of Denial, the mind prepares by denying the painful feelings, fears, and emotions associated with an event. In contrast, the reactions to a traumatic event involve the mind shutting down after the event has occurred in order to protect the mind from further damage by reliving painful events.

Both cases involve the numbing or the diminishing of the strong emotions that are associated with crises, both real and potential. Both of these reactions are not entirely negative. They have certain beneficial effects. For instance, one of the most painful emotions associated with traumatic events is guilt. After 9/11, many of the survivors asked, "Why did I survive when my best friends died?"

The feelings of guilt associated with being a survivor are often so painful that in order to spare oneself, the mind not only goes numb but shuts down entirely. This shutting-down process is never complete or successful. For example, some people who have survived traumatic events (e.g., Vietnam veterans) experience flashbacks and nightmares months and even years after the event. They also are more prone to prolonged bouts of depression.

Forgetting is never perfect or complete. For this reason alone, it is strongly recommended that those who have experienced traumatic events be seen immediately by experienced, trained counselors within 24 hours of the event. If someone postpones getting to a trained counselor or therapist for even a day, then that person is likely to go into posttraumatic denial.

Betrayal

One of the most striking and interesting features of crises is that virtually without exception they are experienced as major acts of betrayal. And yet paradoxically, this is one of the least-studied and least-discussed aspects of crises. For this reason, I not only want to discuss the phenomenon of betrayal, but describe in particular how it pertains to RB and the crisis it is facing. In all likelihood, Mary and her top team will be viewed as villains; that is, as having betrayed their employees, the surrounding community, and their customers because they had not thought about the particular crisis on their hands and hence were not adequately prepared for it. Mary and her top team will also likely view themselves as victims; that is, as having been betrayed by those individuals who made or ignored the errors.

If RB's crisis is like those that have assumed prominence in recent years (e.g., Ford-Firestone, the Catholic Church, WorldCom), then near-verbatim minutes of the CM team meeting where product tampering was first proposed will somehow be obtained, most likely from a disgruntled employee. It will then be shown as one of the lead stories on all of the major news networks. As a result, Mary and her top management team will be blamed for not having done more to protect its consumers and so on. In short, Mary and RB will be vilified even though there may have been very little, if anything, that they could have done to have prevented the crisis.

Crises are generally experienced as major acts of betrayal because people need to have someone to blame for the crisis. Unfortunately, blaming is a central feature of virtually all major crises. It is one of the principal ways in which we cope with the strong feelings and emotions that crises stir up.

A Working Definition of Betrayal

Betrayal is the failure of a person, an organization, an institution, or a society to act and behave in accordance with ways that they have promised or led us to believe that they will. Betrayal is the violation of the trust that we have placed in a person, organization, institution, or society. Thus, betrayal is profoundly rooted in our basic feelings of trust and goodness with regard to others.

The greater the expectation that a person will act and behave in the ways that were promised and the greater the consequences (seriousness) of their not doing so, the greater the resultant sense of betrayal. Sometimes the promise is stated explicitly; most of the time, it is unstated and implicit. It is implied and taken for granted.

Some acts of betrayal are conscious and deliberate. In such cases, the betrayer calculates brazenly whether betrayal is in his or her best interests. If the "benefits" exceed its "costs," then betrayal is "worth it." If the "costs" exceed the "benefits," then it is not.

Most acts of betrayal are unintentional. They are an unintended consequence of an act or behavior. Often, the person committing the act is completely unaware or unconscious of what he or she has done. By the same token, most people who betray someone else experience guilt; very few do not. Those who do not experience guilt are the really scary ones. They are also the most dangerous. In psychological terms, they are considered psychopathic or sociopathic.

In the case of Enron, there are strong reasons to believe that the top executives were in effect *behaving* like sociopaths (Cruver, 2002; Fusaro & Miller (2002). (Whether they were in fact *actually* sociopathic is of course another matter.) For instance, they exhibited little or no feelings of guilt or remorse for their behavior or actions. Even worse, there are strong reasons to believe that Enron exhibited the characteristics of a sociopathic organization. Worst of all is the fear that we have created a society that fosters and rewards sociopathic behavior. In effect, we have created a dangerous "variant" of capitalism—sociopathic capitalism!

In every case, betrayal is the violation of a basic and fundamental assumption we are making about an individual, an organization, an institution, or a society, e.g., that another person will stand up for us, act in our best interests, and protect us. When the assumption—or more commonly, a set of assumptions—have been shown to be false or invalid (e.g., regarding the vulnerability of a city in the Oklahoma City bombing, or a nation in the 9/11 attacks), we are stunned. We are left with the feeling of having been betrayed to the core.

For over 25 years, I have been studying how people and organizations react to crises. The following is a typical response. It shows the explicit and the strong connection between crises and betrayal.

> As bad as the crisis was that our organization experienced, even worse was the feeling that we had been betrayed by our CEO and top executives. Time and time again, they reassured us that there was no real need to even think about let alone prepare for crises that had already struck the other members of our very own industry. To do so was a needless waste of time, money and energy.
>
> After all, they argued, since the crises had already occurred, and to someone else, therefore, the probability of their occurring again was even smaller. In retrospect, we were playing a perverse form of Russian roulette. The more that one held a loaded gun to one's head, pulled the trigger, and it didn't fire, therefore, the odds were even lower that it would fire the next time, if ever! What nonsense! I should have known better. In this sense, I guess I blame myself as well since I was all too eager to go along.
>
> The rationale was that by not preparing for crises, we were going to be even more profitable. Of course, it turned out to be the exact opposite. We ended up losing far more money than if we had prepared. The amount of money that we would have spent on preparation would have been a tiny fraction of the cost of the entire crisis.
>
> The fact that I bought into the CEO's assumptions without challenging them was one of the worst things about the entire episode. Maybe it was because I wanted to believe them as well.
>
> What you are left with is the sickening feeling that you can't trust your own judgment. You feel that you have betrayed your own self. What could be worse than this?

Who Betrays Us the Most?

Our feelings of being betrayed by a crisis are basically attributable to our feelings that the CEO and top management should have taken better care of us. One of the most interesting aspects of crises is that they generally cause people to regress. In effect, the leaders of the organization become the parents; in turn, everyone else becomes the children. These feelings are intensified further by the fact that on a day-in and day-out basis, the persons who betray us the most often and the most regularly are our bosses, our immediate co-workers, and our subordinates. The boss is thus already in danger of being the bad "parent" to begin with.

Table 7.2 shows how being betrayed by one's boss as the result of a major crisis results in the collapse of one's major assumptions. That is, as the result of a major crisis, some of the most basic and general assumptions that we have been making about our leaders are invalidated. This is why a major crisis is often so traumatic. In effect, it violates *all* of the tenets of our basic belief system.

Despite this, nearly all of the people that I have interviewed react to betrayal and crises by merely "shrugging them off" or by "gutting it through." If they discussed the betrayal or the crisis with anyone else, it was with a close friend or spouse. The difficulty, of course, occurred when it was the close friend or spouse that was the betrayer. Nonetheless, most people do not seek treatment for any sort of betrayal or crisis.

The Effects of Betrayal: How We View Ourselves Versus Our Betrayers

One of the most striking features of betrayal, especially as it pertains to crises, is how people who have been betrayed view themselves in comparison and in contrast to those who have betrayed them (see Table 7.3 and Figure 7.1). In general, the person, organization, or society that has been betrayed—the victim—views himself, herself, or itself as optimistic, positive, generally upbeat, trusting, cheerful, calm, able to express feelings, easygoing, forgiving, happy, hopeful, warm, and reflective. On the other hand, one's betrayer—the villain—is generally viewed as pessimistic,

Table 7.2　Basic Assumptions That Result From Being Betrayed by One's Boss

1. You, the parent (the boss), <u>failed</u> to <u>make</u> the world safe.
2. You, the parent (the boss), <u>failed</u> to <u>make</u> the world good and just.
3. You, the parent (the boss), <u>failed</u> to <u>make</u> the world stable and predictable; as the result of your failures, things will never be the same again; 　a. One's world will <u>never</u> return to what it was before.
4. You, the parent (the boss), <u>failed</u> to <u>make</u> the crisis limited; therefore, you laid the foundation for mistrusting all leaders in organizations in the future.
5. You, the parent (the boss), <u>failed</u> to <u>be</u> inherently good.
6. You, the parent (the boss), <u>failed</u> to <u>make</u> me good.
7. You, the parent (the boss), <u>failed</u> to <u>make</u> it known that I was about to be betrayed by your actions/inactions.

The Psychological Effects of Crises

bitter, less upbeat, distrustful, moody, anxious, hiding feelings, sour, unforgiving, less happy, hopeless, cold, and unreflective. This contrast is even more striking if we line up the two portraits side by side.

If people are allowed to express their perceptions on a seven-point scale, where, for instance, 1 represents a "marked degree of pessimism" and 7 a "marked degree of optimism," then we can compare the two portraits numerically (see Figure 7.2). There is a highly significant statistical difference between the "degree of optimism" that those who have been betrayed feel is characteristic of themselves and the "degree of pessimism" that they feel is characteristic of their betrayer. From a statistical standpoint, the differences between the two perceptions or profiles are so far apart that it is highly unlikely that they are due to chance alone. In other words, we are looking at extreme portraits.

These differences can be summarized compactly as follows:

We demonize those who have betrayed us! This is true whether the betrayer is a single individual, an organization, a society, or even a civilization!

Demonization is one of the most important themes of this chapter. No matter the particular type of crisis with which we are dealing, demonization rears its ugly head again and again. *Someone or something is always*

Table 7.3 Characteristics of Betrayed and Betrayers From a Victim's Perspective

The Person Betrayed—The Victim	*The Betrayer—The Villain*
Optimistic	Pessimistic
Positive	Bitter
Generally upbeat	Less upbeat
Trusting	Distrustful
Cheerful	Moody
Calm	Anxious
Able to express one's feelings	Hiding one's feelings
Easy-going	Sour
Forgiving	Unforgiving
Happy	Less happy
Hopeful	Hopeless
Warm	Cold
Reflective	Unreflective

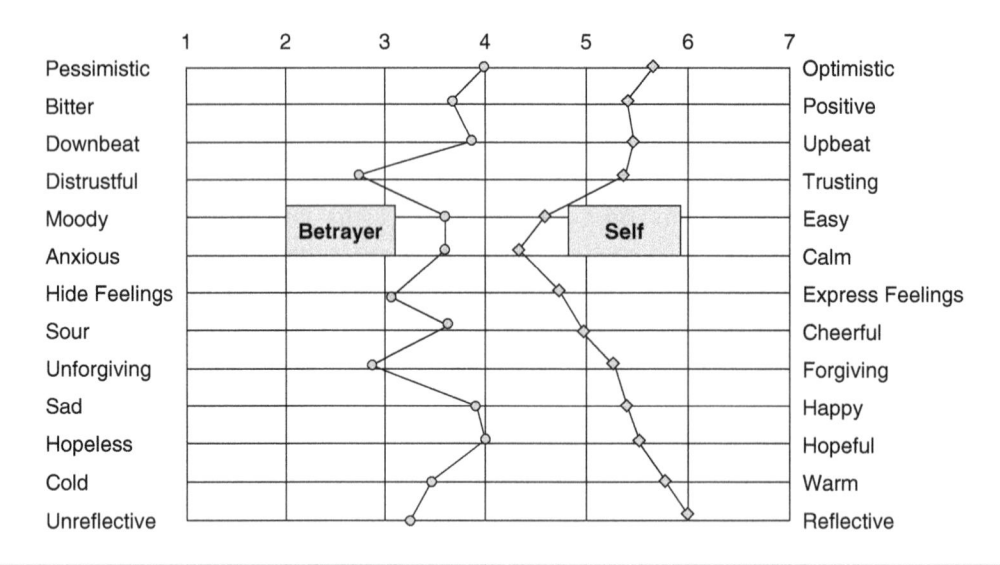

Figure 7.1 Splitting/Demonizing

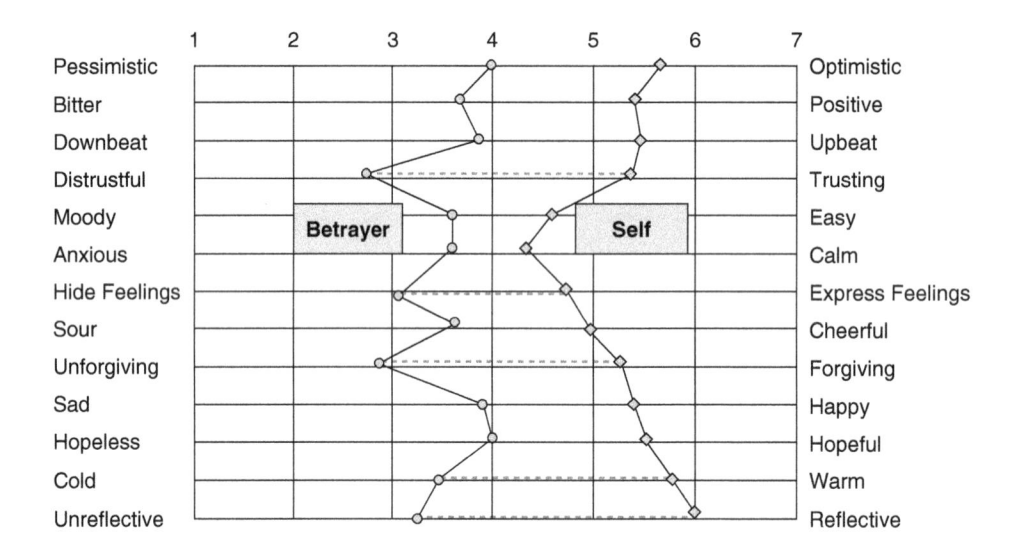

Figure 7.2 The Cold-Blooded Betrayer

demonized as a result of a major crisis. In fact, this is one of the ways of determining whether something is a "major crisis" or not. If someone or something is being demonized, then this is a very good indication that there is, has been, or is about to be a major crisis.

In this regard, I must stress that the perceptions of the "betrayer" are generally the same whether the betrayer is a single individual, an entire organization, a society, or even a civilization. In every case, the profile of the betrayer is essentially the same.

Figure 7.2 helps us understand the process of demonization even more clearly. Look at the particular scales where the greatest differences occur between the perceptions of oneself as the victim and those who have betrayed us as the villain. The betrayer is viewed as distrustful, hiding feelings, unforgiving, cold, and unreflective.

The portrait is one of a "completely cold-blooded person." This helps us to understand why it is so difficult to forgive those who have betrayed us and, no less, to accept amends from them. This also helps explain why the effects of many crises are so long-lasting and extremely difficult to overcome and to reverse.

Recovering From Crises

To recover from a major crisis, one has to go back and rebuild and readjust the perceptions of those whom one feels are responsible for causing the crisis in the first place. For instance, this means that one has to shift the perception of one's "betrayer," or the "villain," from "cold" to "warm." In other words, one has to "rehumanize" the dehumanization that has taken place with regard to his or her perception of a betrayer, be this an individual, an organization, a society, or even a whole civilization (as in perceptions following 9/11). There is little wonder why this is so difficult to accomplish. Even in the case where the betrayer, villain, or guilty party has accepted responsibility for his or her actions, has admitted it openly, and has even tried to make amends, it is still very difficult to accomplish.

Concluding Remarks

There is no doubt whatsoever that the scores of people that I have interviewed and surveyed over the years feel absolutely certain that their profile is "good" (see Figure 7.1) and that they have been victimized. There is no doubt that they feel that those who have betrayed them have the exact opposite profile, that of a villain. Nonetheless, in order for healing to take place and for forgiveness to result, there is no alternative but to adjust the portraits we have of ourselves and of others.

We have to come to realize and accept that those who have betrayed us, often unintentionally, have merely become "convenient psychological receptacles" onto which we can project (see Table 7.3) those aspects of ourselves that we do not like, and therefore, do not wish to acknowledge. Thus, as "real" as the portraits are of those who have betrayed us or caused crises for us, they also represent our own unacknowledged sides.

Addressing such realities through therapy is one of the few remedies that help to make the world, the betrayer, and the person betrayed feel whole and safe again.

At the extreme, we should also strive to value the villains—not for their decisions or deeds, but for what they can teach us about ourselves if we are truly open-minded. If we develop the capacity to empathize with the villain, our eyes may be opened to a reality at great distance from our own. Taking the villain's perspective helps us see and sense in revealing detail things which we might otherwise overlook. This perspective holds the amazing capacity to alert us to our own shortcomings before they undo us.

Of course, ideally, it would be eminently desirable if Mary and her top management team had been aware of all these forces and factors before the crisis that affected them had occurred. In addition to their training in finance and business, Mary and her top team needed to have had schooling with regard to the psychological impacts of crises. Without such training, they merely react—poorly, in most cases—to highly emotional, stressful, and traumatic situations.

If the initial crisis that Mary and RB were facing was not bad enough, then it will be compounded by all of the powerful feelings that will be unleashed in Mary, her team, RB's employees, and all of RB's innumerable other stakeholders as well. Unfortunately, Mary and her top team will most likely be blamed for the crisis owing to not having done more to have foreseen it, even if they could not have prevented it. If only for this reason, precrisis trauma and psychological training is absolutely essential. Experts in these areas can be invaluable in creating realistic simulations that give people a feel for the strong emotions that they will experience as the result of a crisis.

Once an individual or organization is in a crisis, forces are set in motion that are akin to a death spiral, especially if one is unprepared for them. If an individual or organization is not prepared, then it will lose valuable time and energy in treating its own psychological wounds instead of responding to the wounds of others.

From my experience, psychological factors are without a doubt among the most important factors, if not *the* most important ones, determining how an individual, organization, or entire society responds to major crises. One cannot overemphasize the psychological effects of major crises. To deemphasize and neglect them is merely another example and form of denial.

Crisis leaders learn one of the most valuable lessons of all: The fact that they have advanced beyond denial does not mean that everyone else in the organization has. They have also learned not to become paralyzed by their and others' fears. Indeed, people must be given time and space to vent and to work through their fears and anxieties. Above all, such responses should never be dismissed; this only makes them more intense.

Addendum

SPLITTING AND COMPARTMENTALIZATION

The findings described in this chapter pertain to psychological processes that go far beyond betrayal. They are the result of defense mechanisms known as Splitting and Compartmentalization (see Table 7.3). While important, a detailed discussion of Splitting and Compartmentalization would take us somewhat off the topic. For this reason, I have included this addendum. I recommend strongly that the reader consult it in order to gain a deeper understanding of the strong feelings and emotions that all crises unleash.

FURTHER REFLECTIONS ON THE PSYCHODYNAMICS OF CRISES

Yiannis Gabriel's important book, *Organizations in Depth* (1999), is a masterful exposition of Freudian psychoanalysis. Gabriel's book is important because he shows the direct relationship of Freudian psychoanalysis to the behavior of complex organizations.

As the following quote demonstrates, although Freud first discovered and elaborated on the phenomenon of Splitting and Compartmentalization as two of the classic defense mechanisms, Melanie Klein, one of Freud's major followers, refined it further:

> Originally a follower of Freud, Melanie Klein struck out on her own, creating theoretical links between our earliest experiences as infants and our adult responses to life's emotional challenges, one of which relates to group membership. In Klein's view, young children relate to their world through phantasy; when their emotional state is happy and contented, it experiences the world (and adults) as sustaining and nurturing. When they are distressed and angry, they can experience the world as attacking and dangerous. Klein proposed that humans at a very early age utilize two psychological defenses to cope with unpleasant emotions: Splitting and projective identification. In order to "preserve" the experience of a caring, attentive mother in those situations in which the mother is not fulfilling all the infant's needs (to eat or to feel dry, for example), the infant mentally creates two mothers: a bad one and a good mother; the first is denying and threatening, the latter all-caring and loving. The same mother that holds the infant at one moment yet refuses to pick it up the next is experienced as two separate beings, or objects (hence "object relations"). This psychological mechanism called

Splitting [italics in original], is "an action undertaken in fantasy which can be used to separate things when belong together" . . . ; Splitting allows the infant, and later the adult in stressful situations, to cope with fears about survival by separating the "self" from painful feelings. *Projective identification* [italics in original], the second mechanism, is closely related. Klein proposed that infants learned to distance themselves from their own destructive feelings by disowning them and actively "placing" those feelings in someone else. (Gabriel, 1999, p. 118)

In *The Uses of Enchantment,* the distinguished psychoanalyst Bruno Bettleheim (1985) gave a brilliant and important Freudian account of fairy tales. Bettleheim's book was especially helpful in illuminating why fairy tales have held such a grip on the human imagination for thousands of years. One of the fundamental purposes of fairy tales, and more generally of myths, is to help children cope with psychic conflicts.

A central feature of many fairy tales is the extreme conflict between two diametrically opposed female figures. On the one hand there is the "good, fairy godmother"; on the other hand, there is the "evil queen." These two contrasting female figures represent the two conflicting sides of every real mother. The "good figure" is the "good mother"; that is, the one who nurtures her child without any reservation or qualification whatsoever. The "good mother" instantly meets the child's every need, want, and wish. In contrast, the "bad mother" is the one who punishes and has to reprimand the child if he or she is to grow into a civilized, social being.

In times of major crises, the same processes operate in adults as well. For instance, consider the rhetoric of U.S. President George W. Bush following 9/11. On innumerable occasions, President Bush and the members of his administration have referred to the terrorists and their supporters as the "Axis of Evil," while presumably we and our allies, the Coalition of the Willing, are the "Axis of Good." The phenomenon of Splitting thus helps to explain the behavior of adults as well. In times of extreme crises, we are prone to divide the world into two sharp camps, evil versus good.

The purpose of Splitting is as follows: The ego of the young child, between 2 and 5 years of age, is not sufficiently developed to reconcile and integrate these two conflicting images of the mother into a single person. As a result, the mother is split into two diametrically opposed characters. Only at a later stage of human development will most people integrate and unite these two conflicting figures into a single person (see Figure 7.3).

By definition, the "good mother" is a highly idealized image of "pure goodness." On the other hand, the "bad mother" is an equally idealized image of "pure badness." Through this process, the two conflicting sides of the actual mother are compartmentalized and held apart (see Figure 7.3). The child is not yet able to deal with the fact that good and bad are aspects of every person.

Fairy tales, or in today's genre, "reality shows" (which *in reality* are fantasy shows) appeal to us precisely because they address some of the

The Psychological Effects of Crises

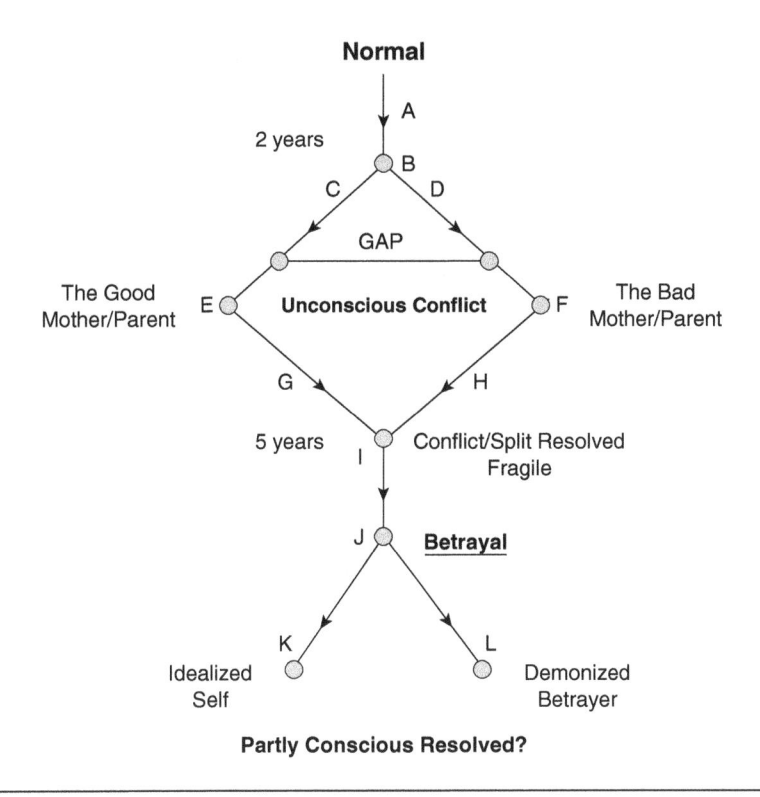

Normal

```
         A
         ↓
         B
      C / \ D
       ↙   ↘
        GAP
The Good  E      Unconscious Conflict      F  The Bad
Mother/Parent                                  Mother/Parent
       G ↘   ↙ H
     5 years  I
              ↓   Conflict/Split Resolved
                  Fragile
              J
              ● Betrayal
           K ↙  ↘ L
     Idealized      Demonized
       Self         Betrayer
```

Partly Conscious Resolved?

Figure 7.3 Normal Splitting/Demonizing

deepest issues with which we are struggling. For the most part, we are unconscious of these issues. This also helps to account for the popularity of world myths as well. Fairy tales and myths are among the most nonthreatening ways in which we can address our deepest psychic conflicts and problems. This accounts for their perennial appeal across all cultures and all ages.

It is important to understand the differences between Splitting and the related processes of Idealization and Demonization. In the case of Splitting, the conflict between the "good mother" and the "bad mother" experienced by every young child is managed by Compartmentalizing or Splitting the actual mother into two separate and distinct images. For the most part, this Compartmentalization or Splitting is unconscious (see Figure 7.3). This is in fact the psyche's enormously creative solution to the problem that "good" and "evil" cannot yet be accepted as characteristics of the same person.

Once again, the basic purpose of the various defense mechanisms is to shield the developing—and hence, extremely fragile—ego of the young child from unpleasant and traumatic experiences. Indeed, unpleasant experiences and traumatic events are serious threats to overwhelm the young ego, and hence, to send the young child back into a primitive state of fusion with the mother. If this happens, then the young child is literally not able to develop as an autonomous, separate person. The problem, of course, arises especially if Splitting persists beyond childhood.

On the other hand, those who have been betrayed at an early age by, for instance, the death of a parent carry around two completely opposite images that are in direct conflict with one another precisely because both are *partially conscious* (see Figure 7.4). (The death of a parent at an early age is experienced as one of the worst possible forms of a personal crisis. Hence, it is also experienced as one of the worst possible forms of betrayal. Interestingly, the death of the parent is experienced as a major act of betrayal by both the parent and God. By having abandoned him or her, the parent is thereby demonized; but at the same time, interestingly enough, the parent is also idealized, with the good aspects "locked in" or "frozen," often for life.) Thus, both images (the demonized parent and the idealized parent) are carried along side by side. In this way, the person who has lost a parent at an early age experiences a deep and lasting conflict. As a result, there is extreme difficulty in reconciling these two images, because each is felt intensely. The split is thereby prolonged and may well last for a

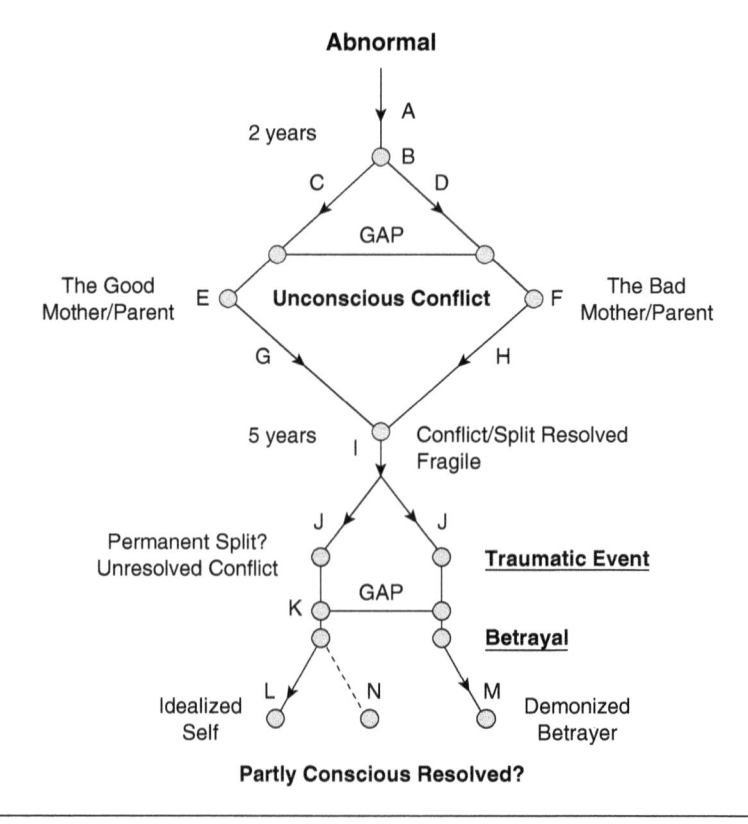

Figure 7.4 Abnormal Splitting/Demonizing

person's entire life unless the conflict is resolved through therapy. Without therapy, the person cannot be healed and the diametrically opposed images of the dead parent cannot be integrated.

A thorny problem is this question: How does one heal a society? How does one put an entire organization or society into therapy? The answer is, of course, that one does not do any of these things, at least not directly. Instead, as is so often the case, our leaders function as informal therapists to heal our suffering.

To summarize, Splitting *resolves* the conflict, at least temporarily, between good and evil that occurs by projecting complete goodness onto one character and extreme evil onto a totally distinct and separate character. But as the child matures, both of these extreme characters, or features, are seen merely as different sides of the same mother. They are thus ultimately merged into the same person. In contrast, Idealization and Demonization *perpetuate* the conflict because the same person is simultaneously idealized and demonized at the same time, often for life. That is, the images are permanently split apart.

The point of this discussion is certainly not that everyone that lives through a major crisis behaves like someone who has lost a parent at an early age. Instead, those who have lost a parent merely help us to see more clearly the processes that operate to a greater or to a lesser extent in everyone that has gone through a major crisis. In principle, everyone is subject to the phenomenon of Splitting.

The interviews I have conducted show unequivocally that those who have suffered greater stress and trauma early in life tend to suffer from the consequences of crises more intensely, more severely, and to a greater extent than those who have not. For this reason alone, it is vitally important to perform a personal *audit* of people's prior histories, especially with regard to life-stressing and traumatic events.

In this one respect, at least, those who have lost a parent at an early age fare better. They are literally forced to undergo therapy. In this sense, they are better able to recognize and deal with those individuals, organizations, and societies that have betrayed them. However, this only holds for those who have been in prolonged therapy and whose outcomes have been successful.

BASIC ASSUMPTIONS

In the beginning, one's parents *are* the world. They are not only the embodiment of society, but literally *are* society. For this reason, the death of a parent is experienced in the most intense and personal terms (see Table 7.4).

Our most basic assumptions are literally destroyed by the death of a parent, as we learn that (1) the world is *un*safe and not secure. Similarly,

Table 7.4 Basic Assumptions That Result From the Death of a Parent

1. The world, i.e., one's family, all relationships in general, is <u>not</u> safe and secure.
2. The world, i.e., God and one's parents, is <u>not</u> good and just.
3. The world, i.e., one's family, is <u>not</u> stable and predictable; things will never be the same again;   a. One's world will <u>never</u> return to what it was before.
4. Betrayal is <u>un</u>limited; the foundation for betrayal throughout one's life has been firmly laid in place.
5. The parent that died is inherently good <u>and</u> bad.
6. I am <u>not</u> good otherwise my parent wouldn't have died.
7. I should have known that I was about to have been betrayed; in other words, <u>I</u> am at fault.

(2) the world is *not* good and just. (3) The world is *not* stable and it is highly *un*predictable. One's fundamental sense of safety, security, stability, and predictability are seriously marred. In some cases, the damage is long-lasting and irreparable. With the death of a parent, the "world" is no longer experienced in abstract terms. One's "world" is literally one's "dead parent" (Harris, 1995).

The notion that betrayal or damage in general is limited in scope is also seriously marred. What has happened to one's parent is often generalized to all subsequent relationships. In an important book, *The Loss That Is Forever* (Harris, 1995), a high percentage of adults who lost a parent as a child report that they experience difficulty in establishing close, personal, and trusting relationships throughout the remainder of their lives.

Those who have been marred by the death of a parent at an early age also tend to blame themselves. They also blame themselves subsequently for all other acts of betrayal that are experienced later in life.

The assumption that "the world is *not* safe" only partially captures how the death of a parent is experienced as a form of betrayal. The anger deep down that is experienced is captured even better by the wording, "You, the parent, *failed* to *make* the world safe for me." The assumptions are not merely statements of fact about the world. Instead, they are presumptions about the moral failures of the parent (see Table 7.5). This is why the anger is so deep and long-lasting.

From my interviews over the years with people who have lived through major crises, it is clear that Tables 7.4 and 7.5 apply equally as well to those who have *not* lost a parent early in their lives (see Table 7.2). To be sure, the collapse or general invalidation of assumptions is not experienced as severely or as traumatically. Nonetheless, with the mere substitution of the word "boss" or "subordinate" for "parent," the same tables apply. Once

Table 7.5 Basic Assumptions That Result From the Death of a Parent

1.	You, the parent, <u>failed</u> to <u>make</u> the world, one's family, all relations in general safe and secure.
2.	You, the parent, <u>failed</u> to <u>make</u> the world, i.e., God and one's parents, good and just.
3.	You, the parent, <u>failed</u> to <u>make</u> the world, i.e., one's family, stable and predictable; as the result of your failures, things will never be the same again; 　a. One's world will <u>never</u> return to what it was before.
4.	You, the parent, <u>failed</u> to <u>make</u> betrayal limited; you, the parent, <u>failed</u> to <u>lay</u> the foundation for trust throughout one's life.
5.	You, the parent, <u>failed</u> to <u>be</u> inherently good.
6.	You, the parent, <u>failed</u> to <u>make</u> me good.
7.	You, the parent, <u>failed</u> to <u>make</u> it known that I was about to be betrayed by your death.

again, I must emphasize strongly that the collapse or invalidation of assumptions is not felt or experienced as severely. Nonetheless, from the interviews I have conducted, it is clear that what one feels toward one's parents is projected onto one's bosses and subordinates.

Bibliography

Bettleheim, B. (1985). *The uses of enchantment: The meaning and importance of fairy tales.* New York: Random House.
Cruver, B. (2002). *Anatomy of greed: The unshredded truth from an Enron insider.* New York: Carroll & Graph.
Fusaro, P. C., & Miller, R. (2002). *What went wrong at Enron: Everyone's guide to the largest bankruptcy in U.S. history.* New York: John Wiley & Sons.
Gabriel, Y. (1999). *Organizations in depth: The psychoanalysis of organizations.* London: Sage.
Harris, M. (1995). *The loss that is forever: The lifelong impact of the early death of a mother or father.* New York: Penguin Books.
Reivich, K., & Shatte, A. (2002). *The resilience factor.* New York: Broadway Books.

A Passion for Imperfections

8

Revisiting Crisis Management

Christophe Roux-Dufort

Risk and crisis management has become paramount for many companies, while Western societies have been more and more sensitive to risks in every domain of their development. The advent of the risk society suggested by Ulrich Beck in the mid-1980s has now come true (Beck, 1992). This tendency toward the systematic reduction of risk exerts a strong pressure upon companies. The demand for "risk zero" intensively relayed by the media is still persistent even though most authorities, governments, and companies keep explaining to consumers, shareholders, employees, and more generally citizens that it remains a myth. This demand is all the more omnipresent even though, despite continuous efforts to manage risk through regulations within and outside of companies, recurrent crises (oil spills, explosions, terrorism, food crises, climatic episodes, etc.) regularly shed light on the limits of risk and crisis management. Crises recurrently question its foundations and contribute to suspicions about the ability of companies and authorities to protect citizens against the risks of industrial and economic development. Despite regular suggestions from scholars to implement preventive crisis-management measures (Pauchant & Mitroff, 1992) companies face more difficulties to deal with; risks and shocks of all kinds may ruin part of their efforts aimed at prevention. This worrying evolution requires that we revisit our conception of crisis management and adopt a process view of crisis versus the traditional self-contained event view of crisis that has underlain research on crisis management so far (Rosenthal,

2003). The triggering event of a crisis (Shrivastava, 1992) considered as being the starting point of a crisis by most researchers and practitioners should also be viewed as the ending point of a long process of destabilization within systems and organizations. More specifically, we believe crises result from the combination of two parallel, cumulative processes. One is an undercurrent of accumulating organizational imperfections that create a favorable environment for a crisis to occur. Second is the unintentional development of a managerial ignorance or unawareness that keeps managers blind to the presence of these vulnerabilities.

The central idea of this chapter is to demonstrate that organizational imperfections are allowed to build up and grow into vulnerabilities because they are not noticed or taken into consideration by managers. They may grow to such an extent that they exceed managers' cognitive ability to control them effectively. As imperfections build up, managerial ignorance increases. Ignorance is thus primarily defined as the managers' inability to notice and take into consideration the cumulative effect of organizational imperfections. This managerial ignorance is in no way intentional. It stems from increasing cognitive narrowing as the imperfections grow into vulnerabilities. Managerial ignorance is not ignorance in the ordinary sense of not knowing; rather, it is knowledge based on erroneous cognitive beliefs shared by one or more managers about the development of anomalies and vulnerabilities and the eruption of disruptions and crises (Shamir & Shamir, 1997). Though managerial ignorance has been studied in relation to crisis management from various perspectives (Starbuck & Milliken, 1988; Vaughan, 1996; Weick, 1988, 1993; Weick & Sutcliffe, 2001), we seek to develop an alternative view where managerial ignorance is treated as a self-regulating process of managers' threatened self-esteem. We argue that imperfections entail anxiety-provoking assumptions that, as they grow, challenge and break organizational predictability and regularity. The higher the degree of imperfection, the higher the alteration of self-esteem. This increasing anxiety will cause managers to maintain a high level of self-esteem through an ongoing process of ego defense (Brown, 1997). Our argument is that imperfections that "threaten managers' self-concept will be ignored, reinterpreted, hidden or rejected in a way analogous to the methods that individual resort to defend their own self-esteem" (Brown & Starkey, 2000, p. 103). We therefore hypothesize that imperfections trigger an intense level of ego-defense mechanisms through which managers seek to insulate themselves from a growing threatening reality that allow imperfections to develop and amplify. This mitigation of threats provokes a self-nourishing retreat from reality and decreases leaders' ability to pay sufficient attention to the increasing process of accumulation of imperfections and vulnerabilities. We thus delimit the notion of managerial ignorance to the manifestation of an ongoing process of self-esteem regulation to reduce an increasing level of anxiety triggered by the production of organizational imperfections.

This chapter is structured as follows. First we discuss the limitations of crisis management that require a renewed perspective. Then we explore the theoretical foundations and differences between the event and process approaches toward crisis management. Next, we detail two dimensions along which a process view of crisis should be articulated and we expose the assumptions of our model. Finally we use these dimensions to present a four-step model of crisis development.

Renewing Crisis Management

Fifteen years ago, Lagadec (1991) defined a crisis as the result of an accident *and* of a destabilization. Since then, this equation has considerably influenced corporations, ministries, and consultants in their approach toward crisis management. Thus, crisis management has mostly consisted of quickly containing accidents or unexpected events and deploying mechanisms to handle the urgency and the destabilization. As a side effect, this equation has given to crises an exceptional, acute, urgent, and dramatic character and has emphasized how critical it is for companies not to become overwhelmed by the events. Crisis management has thus taken a significant place in organizations and to say the least, the distance between the mainstream managerial and crisis-management practices tends to diminish progressively. As such, for the last 10 years, companies have prepared themselves in this field (Rosenthal, 2003).

Yet the number of crises affecting firms, administrations, or whole sectors of activity (BSE or "mad cow disease," 1996 and 2000, asbestos, tobacco, etc.) has not dropped. Although the terrorism acts of September 11, 2001, are a symbol rather than a starting point, they represent the very type of event that forces us to recognize our inability to anticipate and the accumulation of weaknesses and ignorance that made these acts possible. Other, equally dramatic events continue to sow doubt as to our ability to anticipate and manage crises: climatic catastrophes (the heat wave of August 2003 in Europe, the storm of December 1999 in France, annual episodes of flooding), health crises (contaminated blood, dioxin, asbestos, mad cow disease), the collapse of American and European financial empires (Enron, Parmalat), and major industrial accidents (AZF, the Erika, the Prestige), and so on. These events affect companies and political and economic circles and often leave the feeling that everything has gone wrong despite the efforts of preparation that organizations regularly claim to have made. When such events occur, the limitations of crisis management, as it is currently practiced, are suddenly revealed. Whether in terms of anticipation, prevention, or management, leaders find themselves increasingly helpless in the face of these exceptional events.

Both among researchers and practitioners, there have been several streams all aimed to provide solutions to the same questions: understanding why it is so difficult to anticipate crises, setting up realistic efforts toward prevention, and regaining control in the maelstrom of a crisis. To address this issue, a number of authors (Pauchant & Mitroff, 1992; Pauchant, Mitroff, & Lagadec, 1991; Pearson & Clair, 1998; Pearson & Mitroff, 1993) have suggested that in most cases, crisis-management practices should mostly consist of carrying out prior risk analyses, implementing emergency procedures, setting up and training crisis management units, performing simulation exercises, and undergoing media training. Based on these recommendations, increasingly precise tools, simulations, exercises, and—above all—artifacts of crisis communication are multiplying in sometimes-immoderate proportions. From another perspective Dror et al. (2001) and Rosenthal (2003) suggest that the nature of crises has changed and that inconceivability has become an inner characteristic of crises. Crises today are different from what they were in the past and the practices currently used by organizations are those that were used to manage the previous generation of crises. This implies that in many cases, traditional techniques are not adapted or cannot cope. According to these authors, crises take leaders by surprise and create chaos, uncertainty, and helplessness. These profound evolutions affect the way we view the concept of anticipation up to now, and crisis teams are consequently quickly overtaken. The cases of the mad-cow crisis, anthrax, or September 11 bluntly illustrate these new forms of crisis that undermine certainties and beliefs and cause authorities and leaders to lose legitimacy in the eyes of Western countries' citizens.

Although these contributions are convincing in many respects, they do not entirely address the crucial questions they raise. They focus on an approach to crises mostly seen as events (Forgues & Roux-Dufort, 1998) as opposed to a process. As such, they concentrate on helping organizations regain control over events that by definition are inconceivable and uncontrollable. They often seek to create reflexes meant to help individuals cope with hypothetical dreaded events in which prediction models and crisis-management practices are less and less able to predict and control. We believe that the studies conducted in the past 15 years have followed a dead-end path inasmuch as they consider crises as the starting point of an exceptional event when they should also be seen as the ending point of a inherent process within organizations. In the traditional literature on crisis management, this distinction has already been surfaced through the distinction between an event view and a process view of crisis management.

From Event to Process

Early in the literature, crises have been conceptualized as an event and a process. For instance, Milburn, Schuler, and Watman (1983) proposed a conceptualization of crises that includes three major aspects arranged temporally: antecedents, both in the external and internal environment;

moderators, both of the antecedent-crisis and the crisis-response relationships; and responses, both at the individual and organizational level. In the same vein Shrivastava, Mitroff, Miller, and Miglani (1988) define crises as having transorganizational causes, involving social, political, and cultural variables. They are composed of many loosely coupled interdependent events, each of them setting the stage for the next one to occur in a chain reaction. The authors state that the crisis is triggered by a specific event identifiable according to time and place. Preconditions for this triggering event are created by organizational and environmental conditions. Finally, Shrivastava (1995) opposed clearly the event versus process approach of crisis. As he states: "Crises are not events but processes extended in times and space" (Shrivastava, 1995, p. 2). The distinction between event and process is not exclusive but complementary. Although mostly focused on one aspect or the other, some authors do hold both perspectives (Pauchant & Mitroff, 1992; Pearson & Clair, 1998; Shrivastava, 1992). But in spite of these repeated efforts to distinguish this twofold aspect of crises, what remains striking is that most of the authors understate that crises are processes and still treat them as if they were events. Doing so, crisis management scholars never achieve an integrated theory of crisis that would include both the process and the terrain in which crises take roots. Crisis management is basically a science of the event and a science of the exception. But a science of the event cannot do without a reflection on the meaning of the event itself. The triggering event is a junction point between the past and the future. The paradox and the difficulty lie in the reconciliation of the peculiar, singular, and exceptional nature of the crisis, which makes it a cosmological episode (Weick, 1993) and its revealing essence about deep-rooted structural vulnerabilities of organizations. A theory of crisis should thus reconcile singularity and regularity and should build on the exceptional nature of a disruptive event to account for more regular fragilities inherent to any organization.

THE EVENT APPROACH OF CRISIS

The event approach focuses on the notion of incidents or accidents as the unit of analysis. In this view, crises are usually defined as hazardous and harmful disruptions that threaten the very survival of the organization (Reilly, 1993). They are defined in terms of impacts and damages. Incidents or accidents are contingent events as opposed to routines, regularities, and experience. Definitions focus on the triggering properties of the event (Shrivastava, 1992). Triggering events are seen as an active constituent that puts the organization to the test. They may be isolated in space and time and have often quite distinguishable origins, which makes easier the development of classification. Typologies of crises have consequently flourished. The most influential is undoubtedly the one developed by Pauchant and Mitroff (1992). In this typology, categories of crises are displayed along two dimensions: their source (internal versus external) and their nature (social/human versus technical/economic).

In the event approach, crises are also considered as unanticipated and low-probability events (Pearson & Clair, 1998; Shrivastava, 1992) and are often associated with high impacts (Weick, 1988). The very nature of crisis is precisely defined by the inability to plan or to measure the probability of occurrence and the potential risks. The recent developments that consider inconceivability as a new characteristic of crises again fall in the category of the event approach inasmuch as they mostly put forward the increasing "unscheduled, unstructured, unplanned, unexpected" nature of crises (Rosenthal, 2003, p. 132). The surprise effect is therefore a key feature of the event view (Hermann, 1963; Phelps, 1986; Reilly, 1993; Smart & Vertinsky, 1984). Event definitions also dedicate an important role to other characteristics associated with the dynamics of the crisis and the way it develops and amplifies in the organization (Roux-Dufort & Pauchant, 1993). Time pressure, multiple stakeholders, ambiguity, and the Brownian movement of events are often mentioned to describe crises (Billings, Millburn, & Schaalman, 1980; Lagadec, 1991).

The event perspective is helpful to grasp the dynamics of a crisis in its acute phase and contributes to nourish the literature on how to react in times of crisis in order to reduce its impact and resume activity as soon as possible. In spite of this contribution, this view privileges a reactive stance among managers and is not the most adapted approach to improve prevention measures and learning capacities. In addition, even though typologies of crises are obviously useful insofar as they help managers identify dreaded events as a basis for reflection on their crisis management practices, they do not represent typologies of crises per se but rather typologies of potential triggering events. This is much more the manner or the mindset with which the organization deals with the event that may trigger the crisis. From this point of view Weick (1988) has already suggested the idea that crises are produced by the way individuals enact the unfolding event. Inadequate crisis response to small incidents may provoke a large-scale disaster. Even more well-intended responses to deal with insignificant incidents may cause counterintuitive effects.

THE PROCESS APPROACH TO CRISIS

The process approach takes a complementary perspective. It suggests that crises must be embraced in an extended span of time and space. In this view, crises are seen as being the result of a long period of incubation that bluntly occurs through the influence of a triggering event. The tenets of the process perspective mostly lie in the idea that crises manifest in phases (Fink, 1986; Mitroff & Pearson, 1993; Turner, 1976). Different stages are traditionally distinguished: warning signals, triggering event (acute phase), amplification, and resolution. This view thus goes far beyond a symptomatic approach. It suggests the existence of a genealogy of crises that may be potentially tracked long before the acute phase. The most advanced analysis of crisis viewed as a set of stages is certainly the one from Turner. Turner adopts a sociological standpoint and assumes that

> disasters in the sociological sense involves a basic disruption of the social context and a radical departure from the pattern of normal expectations for a significant portion of the community. (1976, p. 381)

According to Turner (1976) the incubation period of the crisis commonly represents the accumulation of discrepant events that develop unnoticed. The following stage is the precipitating event that arouses attention due to its acute manifestation. What is the most intriguing characteristic during this stage lies in the perception that all events in the incubation period will be transformed by offering criteria that identify the incubating network of events so that the process of transforming the ill-structured problem into a well-structured problem may begin. Many researchers have supported this view (Pauchant & Mitroff, 1992; Schwartz, 1987; Shrivastava, 1992). The process perspective thus acknowledges that crises are the ultimate moment of a continuous cumulative process of organizational failures (Bowonder & Linstone, 1987). More recently Quarantelli (1998) and Rosenthal (2003) suggested that grasping the full context of crisis from preconditions to consequences had to be the primary objective of crisis analysts reframing the analysis of crises using a process approach.

In accordance with this position, the process view of crises includes a number of definitions related to the causes of crises. An agreement has emerged that crises are characterized by the ambiguity of their causes and consequences (Pearson & Clair, 1998). Most of these works mention the need for a systemic approach to analyzing crises in order to capture their complexity and ambiguity (Kovoor-Misra, 1995). As asserted by Deschamps, Lalonde, Pauchant, and Waaub (1996), systemic management is needed to study crises because they reveal hidden systemic patterns by crystallizing different spheres that go beyond the frontiers of organizations. Systemic analysis of crises usually highlights the dynamics of a crisis, delves into their historical roots and multiple consequences, and intends to discover the many relations linking diverse stakeholders and issues. Authors who resort to this kind of analysis often minimize the contribution of pure causal and linear methods, considering they are too much restricted to embrace the dynamics of crises.

Treating crises as processes rather than as events influences the analysis of consequences. As mentioned above, in the event view, consequences are mostly treated according to their negative outcomes and threats. In a process approach, rather than considering the outcomes as entirely negative, the systemic study of crises seems particularly relevant to show that crises have revealing properties and uncover hidden factors that the organization would not have been aware of if the crises had not occurred (Morin, 1993; Shrivastava, 1995; Turner, 1976). Crises bring forth changes and transformations at different levels. These revealing and transforming properties are triggered by a sudden collapse of the basic assumptions of the organization that proves to be inefficient in coping with the crisis situation (Pauchant & Mitroff, 1992). Weick (1993) refers to a sudden collapse of sensemaking practices and talks about cosmological episodes.

The process approach to crises provides another perspective and leads us to see the triggering event as the factor that reveals a preexisting dynamic of crisis. In other words, what the event approach considers as the crisis (i.e., the triggering event), the process approach only sees as the amplifier of a process that started long before. Therefore the crisis grows more intense and visible.

The event- and process-oriented approaches are naturally complementary. Nonetheless, the crisis-management literature has mostly developed the first approach. The event perspective has the advantage of being directly operational inasmuch as it encourages individuals to develop reflexes and ways of reducing the consequences of the event. There is no doubt that a crisis seen as an event provides a clear foothold for action. The process-oriented approach has been less used and less developed, both theoretically and in practice. But when the time has come to learn from crises, the question "How did this happen?" often arouses mixed feelings: a failure to understand the reasons that have led to the situation and the guilt-filled intuition that one should have seen trouble coming. Managers may feel that something could have been done before the crisis occurred to avoid it or to reduce its impact. The process approach of crisis requires that we understand how organizational conditions build toward creating a favorable environment for crisis to be triggered.

In order to examine this issue, we draw from two joint and complementary notions: organizational imperfection and managerial ignorance. We posit that crises should be defined along three dimensions: a process of cumulating imperfections, a process of cumulating managerial ignorance, and a triggering event. These three conditions are necessary for a crisis to occur. From a practical perspective, as we put it earlier, little can be done to prevent or anticipate a triggering event. On the other hand, reducing the accumulation of prior imperfections and vulnerability or unveiling managerial ignorance about these imperfections should be considered as much more viable goals.

Organizational Imperfections

In this chapter, organizational imperfections are defined as the inherent anomalies, errors, discrepancies, negligence, deficiencies, and lacunae (holes) produced by the organization. They are defined with respect to managers' expectations (Weick & Sutcliffe, 2001), which are

> assumptions that managers hold and that guide their behavioral choices. They act as planning functions that suggest the likely course of events. As such they direct the attention of managers toward certain directions, certain type of information that are consistent with the expectations. They affect what managers notice and treat. (Weick & Sutcliffe, 2001, p. 33)

Any event is deemed an imperfection as soon as it challenges managerial expectations and threatens the expected organizational predictability and regularity. Turner (1976) would talk about the accumulation of an unnoticed set of events that are at odds with the accepted beliefs about hazards and the norms of their avoidance. These events remains unnoticed due to the presence of initially accepted beliefs about the world and associated precautionary norms set out in laws and codes of practice.

The idea of organizational imperfections contends that organizations are imperfect entities that produce an ongoing flow of dysfunctions. They are treated as a side effect of any movement of organizational growth, progress, innovation, and development (Barnard, 1938; Perrow, 1984; Thiétart & Forgues, 1995). There is a great deal of research supporting this view in the literature. Perrow (1984, 1994), for example, showed that industrial accidents are the result not only of system errors but also of a combination of serious failures occurring at the level of all components: operators, procedures, equipment, environment, and system. According to him, the probability of interactions of several local dysfunctions can prove very high and lead to major accidents. Perrow concludes that industrial systems can generate normal accidents. He points out that because of the properties of the system, failures are inevitable. Although Perrow's perceptions mostly come from the study of high reliability organizations (HROs), other authors have conceptualized organizations as both productive and counterproductive entities (Pauchant & Mitroff, 1995) and as the result of a dynamic interaction between order and disorder (Thiétart & Forgues, 1995). The manner in which organizations develop and grow produces both internal and external vulnerabilities. The external vulnerabilities reflect the side effect of production and consumption (Shrivastava, 1992). Pollution, unemployment, and sanitary crises such as asbestos or food poisoning reflect the kind of external fragilities produced by companies through their own development. Internal side effects are also critical: stress, sexual or moral harassment, workplace violence, rumors and slanders, and conflicts are part of a vast array of counterproductive side effects of certain managerial practices that may culminate in a crisis if they are not managed in a timely and efficient manner. As such, organizations are nonlinear dynamic systems driven by positive and negative feedback—that is, stability and instability—with expected and unexpected events producing both productive and counterproductive outcomes (Thiétart & Forgues, 1995). Looking at organizations as systems may also prove useful when analyzing them as generators of imperfection. The system approach has been extensively used by researchers of crisis managers to account for the complexity of crisis and to explore the multilayer nature of crisis and crisis management (Deschamps et al., 1996; Pauchant & Mitroff, 1992; Pearson & Clair, 1998). But the system approach also helps us understand organizations as a set of emergent properties produced by the interaction of their parts (O'Connor & Mc Dermott, 1997). To follow Smith (2000), "almost by definition it is the various aspects of emergence that create problems for the operator" (p. 544). Precisely because emergencies are not covered by plans, protocols, and routines, they produce unexpected reactions within the organization. Some emergencies are another manifestation of organizational imperfections because they are unexpected and overlooked. They require managers to make sense of what is happening at the point of imperfection and develop unexpected strategies to cope with them (Smith, 2000).

THE DEVELOPMENT OF CRISIS GROUNDS

Adopting a chaos and a system view of the organization is a first step toward understanding organizations as generators of imperfections. In this respect, a crisis, though not necessarily the ultimate result, is inherent to the development of firms. From this point of view crises are never extraordinary. They reflect a stage beyond which an organization can no longer function on the same basis as before. When organizations reach a saturation of imperfections, crisis conditions are created. Organizational imperfections, while accumulating, provide signs: errors, failures, incidents, near-accidents, local triggers, active failures, and unintentional deviations from a planned course of action that can be interpreted as symptoms or peaks in the development of a crisis ground. But these signals do not determine crises; rather, they build a crisis-prone environment. As Weick (1988) put it:

> what is striking is that crises can have small, volitional beginnings in human action. Small evens are carried forward, cumulate with other events, and over time systematically construct an environment that is a rare combination of unexpected simultaneous failures. (Weick, 1988, p. 309)

Knowing why minor incidents or minor failures may, in certain conditions and circumstances, turn into major crises is crucial to understanding the development of organizational imperfections. Accidents or incidents do not automatically turn into major crises. They may remain controlled, localized, and limited in scope. Literature on crisis management suggests that some conditions are needed in order to turn minor events into major ones (Gatot, Jacques, & Roux-Dufort, 1999). In this vein, Shrivastava (1992) shows how great disasters are sometimes caused and amplified by a number of historical, strategic, organizational, and human factors. Weick (1988) also proposes that hazards, accidents, and risks are put in place by human action and construction because they are caused by human invariability that cannot be planned. If we assume that risks and errors are basically inevitable in organizations, then "what is crucial is to keep errors from enlarging" (Weick, 1988, p. 308). This is why one has to apprehend crisis as an amplifying and evolving phenomenon that starts from minor incidents and moves toward a catastrophe.

DEGREES OF IMPERFECTIONS

Imperfections take different forms within organizations. Different degrees of imperfections should be distinguished depending on their evolution over time. In this chapter we have hypothesized four different degrees of imperfections: anomalies, vulnerabilities, disruptions, and ultimately crisis. These four degrees should be understood as four different manifestations of imperfections as they build up. These degrees of imperfection also feature different levels of visibility from managers' viewpoints. By definition, anomalies are less visible than vulnerabilities, while vulnerabilities are less visible than disruptions or crises.

Anomalies

These constitute the lowest level of imperfections. They take the forms of negligence, errors, or whatever unexpected events are linked to the natural movement of organizations. Anomalies can remain invisible as long as they do not threaten either the organization or part of it. They are the outcome of the natural variability of organizational and human behavior that is inherent to any structured organization. There is a constant tension between this natural invariability and the need of the organization to ensure a high degree of predictability and regularity in the activity of its members and of its stakeholders (Reason, Parker, & Lawton, 1998). In the particular example of HROs, the literature has established that reliability-enhancing organizations must be capable of both preserving unvarying routines and dealing with unexpected situations so as to prevent and avoid any undesirable and potentially catastrophic outcomes. This conflict between variability and predictability is so embedded within organizations that most of the time, anomalies remain expected and are thus viewed as part of the normal operating mode.

Vulnerabilities

These represent a second step in the development of organizational imperfections. They are produced by an accumulation and a combination of unmanaged or mismanaged organizational anomalies. Vulnerability is described in terms of a system's susceptibility to the adverse consequences of a triggering event. It relates to other well-supported notions such as incubation (Turner, 1976) or the "resident pathogen" metaphor (Reason, 1990, 1997). Researchers in "cyndinics" (science of danger) have also described vulnerabilities as a space of danger (Wybo, 1990); that is, a set of organizational conditions that make a system prone to disruptions and catastrophes. Vulnerabilities can sometimes be considered as precursors to failure or latent failure (Reason, 1990). They are rooted at different levels of the organization, namely in the HOT (Human, Organizational, Technological) components (Shrivastava, 1992). Vulnerabilities can act as aggravating and amplifying factors when a crisis hits. Organizational and individual vulnerabilities are therefore capable of making a crisis situation evolve toward more chaos and disorder.

Disruptions

These may come out when vulnerabilities have reached a level of saturation at which individuals no longer have control. Disruption relates to the notions of ultimate failure and triggering events. They should then be regarded as a crisis catalyst. In the literature on industrial accidents, disruptions are often described as unsafe acts combined with inadequate organizational defense. For Reason (1990) they result from the combination of active and latent failure, the active failure being most of the time an unsafe act that has been allowed to occur following a series of deficiencies and psychological precursors overlooked by managers. The accumulation of errors may induce an increasing probability of subsequent errors, and they can also increase the likelihood of a bad outcome. In virtually every case, a disruption or a failure cannot be attributed only to one source but rather results from a complex set of dynamic interactive factors (Smith, 2000). The analysis of a disruption to account for a crisis produces a partial view of its cause. Most of the time, disruptions take the form of unexpected events coming from inside or outside the organization that bluntly crystallize preexisting organizational vulnerabilities and precipitate the organization into crisis. A disruption is therefore a non-return point. It is the end result of a process of accumulation of vulnerabilities that have developed over time throughout the organization. A crisis should not be confused with its triggering event, and the scope of a crisis should not be related to the scope of the triggering event. What we usually deem a major crisis does not necessarily result from a major triggering event. It is the ground in which it takes root that will determine whether or not a situation will turn into a crisis.

Crises

Crises are the ultimate degree of imperfection. Whereas disruption is a catalyst, crises unveil a whole series of latent internal failures and these make a major contribution to the event both in terms of causality and consequences (Smith, 1992). In many companies, the indicator that serves most to describe a crisis is the media coverage, namely when the event goes beyond the organizational frontiers and triggers the attention of media. This external focus on crisis is critical. In a crisis, the internal vulnerabilities are abruptly made visible to a series of external stakeholders. At this point, the organizational legitimacy is endangered to the extent its ability to ensure a minimum level of predictability is overridden by the production of counterproductive and potentially harmful outcomes.

The study of the cumulative process of imperfection is not enough to convey the notion of crisis. The question is rather to determine why these vulnerabilities expand to such a point that they provoke a crisis. We thus turn to the examination of managerial ignorance.

Managerial Ignorance

Managerial ignorance has been analyzed from various perspectives and streams of research in the field of crisis management. For example, Pearson and Clair (1998) have developed a trauma approach of crisis management that sets the pace for further investigation about the relationship between crisis and managerial ignorance. They conclude that crises are caused because leaders and employees of an organization may adhere to basic assumptions about the world and themselves that make them unlikely to anticipate an organizational crisis (Pearson & Clair, 1998). Their shared beliefs veil the managers' lucidity about the potential occurrence of crisis and hinder efforts aimed toward crisis anticipation. This view is rooted in the idea that the causes of crisis should be found in managers' and employees' behavior, ineffective orientation, and other cultural limitations (Pearson & Clair, 1998).

Our assumption in this chapter is that managers structure decision situations to fit their view of the world, which is typically an "upper-echelon-theory" perspective (Finkelstein & Hambrick, 1990; Hambrick & Mason, 1984). As such, we assume that corporate elites' characteristics affect corporate strategy (Jensen & Zajac, 2004). Hence cognitively limited managers view a complex world and formulate understandings that simplify potential response sets. As a result, as Finkelstein et al. (1990) put it: "Choice is always exercised with respect to a limited, approximate, simplified 'model' of the real situation" (p. 485).

The difference between the world as it is and the lens through which managers view it is called managerial ignorance. In this view we assume that managers' actions or inactions are all derived from beliefs, knowledge, expectations, and assumptions that they bring to the organizational setting (Cyert & March, 1963; March & Simon, 1958; Weick & Sutcliffe, 2001). This behavior is particularly relevant for top executives, who are faced with high degrees of complexity and ambiguity and confronted with ongoing flows and bits of information that demand attention. Knowing how they respond and how they define what is important and what is to be discarded depends on a range of different factors. As a result, a central aim of the upper-echelon theory aims to identify the factors that direct or orient managers' attention. In the vein of the upper-echelon theory, authors have mostly emphasized the role of demography-based preferences and dispositions (age, education, functional background) and their cognitive bases and values (Wiersema & Bantel, 1992) to account for the influence elites exert on strategic decisions.

In the crisis-management literature authors also direct their attention to how corporate elites contribute to the production of crises and catastrophes. One of the premises lies in the psychological perspective of ignorance.

THE PSYCHOLOGICAL PERSPECTIVE

The psychological view of managerial ignorance has been mostly put forward by Weick (1988, 1993) where cognitive limitations and the difficulty in making sense of early warning signals mostly account for the occurrence of crisis. Limited cognitive schemes (Nystrom & Starbuck, 1984) and cognitive biases that lead to catastrophes (Halpern, 1989) are recurrent central topics that inspire this approach. Weick (1988) has been the one who extensively emphasized the importance of the individual sensemaking ability in the development or amplification of crisis (Weick, 1988). Our ability to make sense of the emergent properties associated with vulnerabilities, failures, or disruptions is of extremely high importance in dealing with crises. As Weick suggests,

> Sensemaking as a process is tested to the extreme when people encounter an event whose occurrence is so implausible that they hesitate to report it for fear they will not be believed. In essence these people think to themselves, it can't be, therefore it isn't. (Weick, 1995, p. 1)

In his analysis of the Mann Gulch disaster, Weick (1993) also demonstrates how the sudden collapse of sensemaking driven by a breakdown of the role structure of a team of firemen was at the ultimate point that precipitated the crisis within this group and caused the death of 13 of 16 firemen.

THE SOCIOPOLITICAL AND CULTURAL PERSPECTIVES

Managerial ignorance has also received a great deal of attention from a sociopolitical and cultural point of view. Starbuck and Milliken (1988) and Vaughan (1996) have described a form of managerial ignorance at NASA. They showed how the entire NASA organization had suffered from ignorance and from denial regarding the accumulating clues that could have warned the managers about the high risk of launching the space shuttle *Challenger*. The authors also illustrated how this atmosphere of complacency led engineers to turn unacceptable levels of danger into acceptable ones. As a conclusion, Starbuck and Milliken (1988) suggested that the longer dysfunctions and weaknesses are left to fester, the thicker the veil of ignorance grows. The vulnerability of an organization lies not so much in its weaknesses as in the ignorance of these weaknesses. Crises thus emerge at the intersection of a crisis-breeding ground and of an ignorance of this ground. The latter can only evolve and develop when the evolution of weaknesses and imbalances remains unseen or ignored.

THE PSYCHOANALYTICAL PERSPECTIVE

Another source of managerial ignorance has been found through the investigation of the psychoanalytical base for organizational crises. Schwartz (1987) and Pauchant and Mitroff (1992) are among the rare management scholars to have studied the relationship between mental health and the unconscious and the occurrence of crisis. Pauchant and Mitroff (1992) identified a series of existential, psychological, and cultural defense mechanisms that individuals resort to in order to justify their lack of preparation and learning regarding crisis management. Following the authors, these defense mechanisms determine a degree of psychological and cultural vulnerability within organizations. These findings were promising inasmuch as they suggested that crises mostly take root in highly defensive behavior contexts. Pauchant and Mitroff (1992) also identified how individual defensive behaviors were precursors of a defensive organizational culture built upon a series of faulty assumptions about crises and crisis management that preserved an illusory immunity to crises. Defensive behavior and faulty cultural assumptions converge toward the development of a form of deep-rooted managerial ignorance that may favor the accumulation of misjudgment and errors within organizations.

A PSYCHODYNAMIC PERSPECTIVE OF MANAGERIAL IGNORANCE

Managerial ignorance is also identifiable through the study on how managers narcissistically regulate their self-esteem (Brown, 1997; Brown & Starkey, 2000). A psychodynamic view of managerial ignorance as we seek to describe it assumes three conditions: the permanent search for self-esteem, an atmosphere of anxiety, and the use of defense mechanisms designed to regulate self-esteem. Following Brown (1997) and Cohen (1959) in this chapter, self-esteem is defined as the degree of correspondence between an individual's ideal and actual concept of himself or herself. Self-esteem has been central in management research. These researchers argue that managers are constantly seeking to maintain their concept of self and their often fragile self-esteem in contexts where their esteem is endangered as a result of competition anxiety (Watson, 1994). Most managers are dependent upon various stakeholders to validate their self-esteem (Kets de Vries, 1980). For example, the literature on self-representation suggests that managers have a high sense of their organization's identity that they attempt to protect and maintain. Managers are thus sensitive to their organizations' external reputation, which they seek to preserve by means of information disclosure (Dutton & Jackson, 1987). This need for self-esteem is regulated narcissistically. Managers engage in an ego-defensive behavior in order to perennially preserve a positive sense of self. Organizations as a whole have also been described as a means of reinforcing individual mechanisms of defense against anxiety (Jacques, 1955, quoted in Brown & Starkey, p. 103). Imperfection or controversial events for which managers are held responsible are a source of threat to self-esteem inasmuch as they may create an intolerable perceived distance between the ideal and the actual sense of self. Imperfections thus increase the level of anxiety and may arouse feelings of rejection. This situation provokes a need for self-justification and an attempt to protect a sense of self through several strategies that are called defense mechanisms necessary to preserve self-esteem as soon as it is threatened (Brown, 1997). Argyris (1982) defines defensive actions as

> Any invalid addition or subtraction from concrete reality that inhibits detection and correction of errors as well as detection of the unawareness that the actions are defensive. (Argyris, 1982, p. 230)

We believe that these defensive actions play a critical role to account for the development of organizational imperfections and to maintain managers in a state of unawareness and ignorance. Before discussing the influence of these mechanisms on the escalation of organizational imperfections, we briefly present the ones we consider the most salient to account for our model: rationalization and normalization, denial, self-aggrandizement, and escalating commitment.

Rationalization

Rationalization is an attempt to provide plausible and acceptable motives and justifications for actions in a form that is consciously tolerable and acceptable (Brown, 1997). Managers offer rationalizations for their past actions to preserve their self-esteem in a retrospective attempt to make sense of what has happened (Weick, 1995). The central idea of rationalization is that managers are prone to providing self-serving motives to justify and rationalize inadequate decisions (Janis, 1989). Rationalization is close to normalization. Normalization is an attempt to provide acceptable reasons and causes for unanticipated or unexpected events or actions or for an unusual deviation from standards (Vaughan, 1996). In psychology, the theory of attribution is also concerned with how individuals make sense of actions by attributing causes to events and how they understand, predict, and control the world around them. In psychoanalytic terms, attribution is called attributional egotism. Attribution theory describes the rules people follow to judge the causes of events, others' behavior, and their own behavior (Weiner, 1982). As far as rationalization is concerned, the actor-observer effect shows how one has a tendency to see one's own behavior as caused by situational factors while attributing others' actions to their attitude and prior actions. It thus refers to the ability of people to offer self-serving explanations for events associated with favorable outcomes to their own efforts and unfavorable outcomes to external and situational factors. Attribution thus provides a useful vehicle for self-enhancing explanations that preserve individual reputations and self-esteem (Brown, 1997). At a collective level, attributional processes enhance a form of pluralistic ignorance (Harvey, Novicevic, Buckley, & Ferris, 2001; Shamir & Shamir, 1997). Pluralistic ignorance reflects a situation wherein people evolve within a false individual inference about the state of the social world. Pluralistic ignorance can be found in contexts in which the members of a group believe that their private thoughts and behaviors differ from those of other members despite evident behavioral similarity (Harvey et al., 2001). As such, pluralistic ignorance is seen as an attributional process in which people compare their thoughts and behaviors to those of others and rationalize the differences despite obvious similarities.

Denial

Denial is "a primitive and desperate unconscious method of coping with otherwise intolerable conflict, anxiety and emotional distress or pain which can lead to increased confidence and feelings of invulnerability" (Laughlin, 1970, p. 57, quoted in Brown, 1997, p. 646). Through denial, individuals attempt to ignore the difference between an ideal self-representation and the actual self that would be intolerable otherwise. In doing so, they disclaim responsibility for failure for which they would be otherwise held responsible (Brown, 1997). Staw et al. (1983) define denial as a means to conceal unacceptable facts from themselves and from others in an unconscious attempt to preserve self-esteem. Denial is a vehicle for attenuating one's responsibility in any controversial event that could be attached to the manager. Denial takes the form of concealing negative information (Whetton, 1980) and concealing failures and faults (Sutton & Callahan, 1987) or developing counterarguments that deny the existence of an imperfection or a crisis (Starbuck, Greve, & Hedberg, 1978). Imperfections may arouse denial inasmuch as they uncover a potential inability to predict, plan, and control. When no argument can be put forward to design an acceptable accounting for the facts, denial is a way of substituting a true reality with a false one. At the collective level, denial entails a process of shared false ideas about the world wherein people deny reality despite clear evidence of this reality. Close to what we mentioned as being pluralistic ignorance, denial is similar to populist ignorance, which is concerned with the collective sharing of false ideas and false propositions about the world (Shamir & Shamir, 1997). This form of ignorance is an easily shared but false socially constructed cognitive shortcut to collective interpretation of specific information and events.

Denial gives a feeling of invulnerability. This mechanism has also been described as *self-aggrandizement*, which refers to the tendency of an individual to overestimate his or her ability to control his or her environment. Self-aggrandizement is similar to the bias of illusion of control and to the sense of omnipotence (Schwenck, 1984). As we mentioned it earlier, it could also be attached to the particular attributional mechanism in which people attribute their success to their own intrinsic qualities. Pauchant and Mitroff (1992) use the term *grandiosity* to account for such behavior. Self-aggrandizement has also received a great deal of attention in the literature on organizational uniqueness, which is concerned with the tendency to exaggerate one's ability to cope with unexpected events in pursuit of preserving a stable sense of self when confronted with potential danger (Klienfield, 1981).

Escalating Commitment

Escalating commitment has not directly been identified as an ego-defense mechanism in psychoanalysis but has been long described as a self-serving bias similar to denial. Escalating commitment refers to the tendency of decision-makers to persist in failing courses of action (Brockner, 1992). A set of research shows that escalation is determined by the managers' unwillingness to admit that their prior resource allocation to the chosen course of action was inadequate. From this standpoint, escalating commitment entails a form of denial of reality. Even though other theories account for such behavior, the view of escalating commitment has so far received a great deal of agreement within the scientific community. In escalating commitment, managers receive negative feedback showing that they have not yet reached their objective. This feedback is then used as self-serving information to persist in allowing more resources in order to reach the objective. Escalating commitment has much more to do with the investment of resources; it also deals with a strong personal investment of the decision-maker. Escalating commitment is thus a vehicle for protecting self-esteem inasmuch as the intensive resource investment made could be considered a proxy of high personal commitment and high self-esteem.

A Model of Crisis Development

Thus far, we have discussed the two major dimensions that, we think, account for a process approach of crisis and crisis management. Yet these two phenomena unfold in different stages and take different forms. The process approach of crisis requires that we consider the crisis developing over longer periods of time, and that we describe the different stages of its development. At each stage, managerial ignorance is revealed in different ways depending on whether the organization gets closer to the point of disruption. Explaining the simultaneous evolution of imperfection and managerial ignorance is therefore critical to understanding the extent to which both mechanisms foster each other. In the remainder of this chapter, we expose a model of crisis development. We propose this model in an attempt to explicitly integrate our analysis of organizational imperfections and managerial ignorance mechanisms. In Figure 8.1 we provide our version of this comprehensive descriptive model of the crisis development process. This model goes beyond the traditional view of crisis seen as an event or as a cumulative process of dysfunction by explicitly recognizing crisis as the result of both a generation of growing imperfections and increasing managerial ignorance that allows these imperfections to develop until the point of disruption is reached.

Four phases from anomalies to crises are distinguished. These phases are not mutually exclusive and do not represent a strict sequential evolution. Rather, they are intertwined and the shift from one stage to another is not as clear as the figure tends to suggest. Each stage is presented from two facets: the level of imperfections, and the associated dominant ignorance mechanism managers are most likely to resort to when faced with the imperfection. For each phase we discuss what we consider to be the most salient defense mechanism and the most expected one, but we want to emphasize that each defense action is likely to be present at each level discussed below, acting in concert with and reinforcing each other.

PHASE 1: ANOMALIES AND UNNOTICING

Small anomalies are generated into different areas of the organization. They are minimal and above all apparently insignificant. Therefore managers

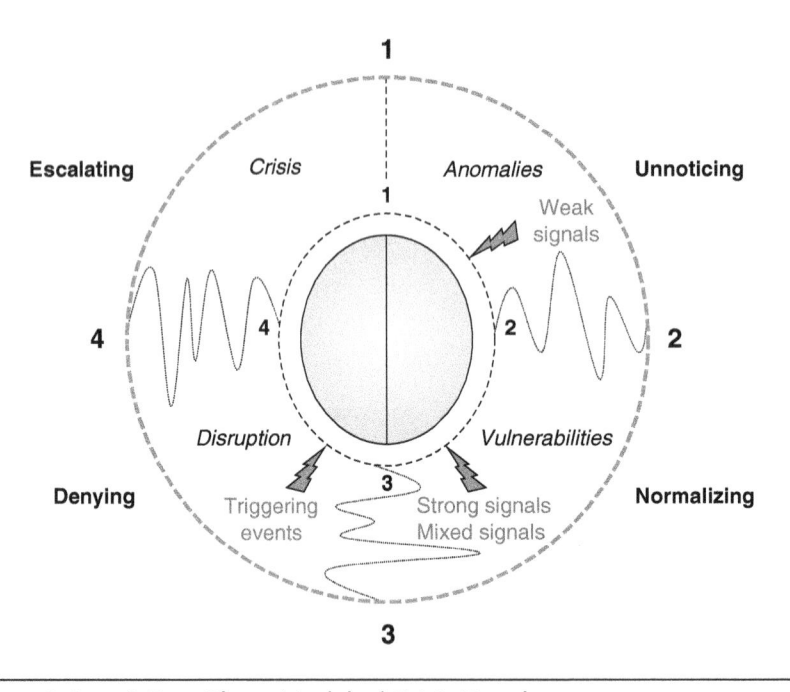

Figure 8.1 A Four-Phase Model of Crisis Development

do not automatically notice them and even when they take them into consideration they do not necessarily consider them as accurate enough to dedicate more attention to them. As managers, they have limited cognitive abilities and need to resort to several shortcuts to treat information and events. The permanent flow of information and event will cause them to take shortcuts to be able to cope with the quantity. Omission, tolerating of errors, filtering, and abstraction are all strategies used by managers to lighten this load (Weick, 1995). But these strategies are ways of dividing the experience into segments; as a result, only a minute fraction of it is retained in order to make some sense of a situation. Moreover, these organizations usually implement systems of information reporting, processing, and analysis that contribute almost automatically to the organization and selection of information. Even though anomalies can sometimes produce weak signals, they do not hold sufficient power to raise managers' awareness. As Vaughan (1996) points out in her study on the launch of the space shuttle *Challenger*: "Signals were weak: information was informal and/or ambiguous, so that the threat to flight safety was not clear" (p. 244). Phase 1 represents the way in which managers operate on a daily basis when submitted to a constant flow of information and events. In such an operating mode, managers resort to small defensive routines known as pragmatic ignorance (Harvey et al., 2001). Pragmatic ignorance is concerned with the decisions that managers have to make in situations in which certain knowledge and certain response cannot be acquired in time to make quality decisions (Dunn, 1992). In such situations, managers often act based on previous experience (i.e., expectations), and the plausible assumptions they hold about the world based on usual expectations. This is what happens in any organization where routines prevail. In such a context, a number of errors and negligence are allowed to develop in different areas of the organization. Being unnoticed, anomalies remain uncorrected, persist, and progressively grow into fragilities and vulnerabilities. On the evening when the Herald of Free Enterprise (HFE) ferry capsized in March 1987, the bow doors had been left open (anomaly #1), thus allowing the water level to rise and to rapidly penetrate into the hold of the ship (anomaly #2). However, nobody, not even the captain, was shocked by the fact that these doors had been left open, so accustomed was the crew to leaving the doors open during the crossing in order to ventilate the hold and remove the exhaust fumes of the vehicles that had just boarded the ferry. Furthermore, because the crossings are often short, the crew was convinced that closing the doors was unnecessary. Another factor is the fact that the pressure exerted on the crew to minimize turnaround time in Dover and Zebbrugge gave them very little time and room to maneuver out of port. By not closing the doors, the crew could maneuver out of the harbor more quickly. The sense of urgency prevailing during the maneuvers concentrated the attention of the managers on loading and turnaround-time priorities more than on the respect of safety maneuvers at a time the prospect of having to compete with the Channel Tunnel put pressure on the management of ferry companies to maximize crossings in order to remain competitive. Presumably exhausted by the high turnaround of the ship, the seaman in charge of checking the bow door was asleep (anomaly #3). Nobody noticed it, certainly because the fact that the door could stay open was an additional evidence that the man could stay asleep without danger for the ship. On the deck, the procedure set up to check the closing of the bow door was based on a negative information system. If the captain had no feedback from the man in charge of closing the door, he believed that the door was closed. The procedure and the information system therefore enhanced and sustained the organizational and individual expectations, keeping the organization ignorant of the development of potential imperfections and vulnerabilities.

PHASE 2: VULNERABILITIES AND NORMALIZING

As imperfections accumulate they grow into vulnerabilities. In the example of the HFE, a series of long-established anomalies made the ship more exposed to a potential wreck. In this second phase, the imperfections have built up to such a level that they cannot help but raise a certain level of awareness among managers. At least one part of the organization is disturbed or is aware of its vulnerability. Imperfections hold a higher level of visibility. By turning into vulnerabilities, anomalies often give rise to incidents, near-accidents, or near-misses (March, Sproull, & Tamuz, 1996): individual conflicts, persistent rumors, strikes, articles in newspapers, shaken titles, increase in the number of customers' complaints, loss of important contracts, recurring quality problems, higher turnover, and so on. These events act as alerts and sometimes precursors of potential further dangers (Reason, 1990). These precursors can be assimilated to surprises and unexpected events and provide stronger signals for potential risks within the organization. Vaughan (1996) distinguishes weak signals that are characteristic of phase 1 of our model from mixed and strong signals that managers are likely to find in this second phase.

> A signal of potential danger is information that deviates from expectations, contradicting the existing worldview. By definition, it is a strong signal (...) Signals were mixed: information indicating trouble was interspersed with and/or followed by information signaling that all was well. (pp. 243–244)

In phase 2 the sum of signals is more visible but still ambiguous. Most of the time they question the managers' expectations and put their self-esteem to the test, for they break the flow of organizational regularity and predictability and potentially challenge their ability to deal with specific organizational issues. The level of anxiety is higher. Based on our previous analysis, we suggest that during this phase managers resort to rationalization to reduce the increase in anxiety produced by vulnerabilities. As Weiner (1982) put it, whenever an outcome is unexpected and when desires have not been fulfilled, rationalization is likely to happen. As they tend to look for clues and evidence that confirm their expectations, they also strive to shun disconfirmation of expectations and explain away the disconfirmation of their expectations (Weick & Sutcliffe, 2001). They pay closer attention to information related to the disconfirmed expectation and try to make sense of it. They tend to use too little information compared to what is available to them and distort the sensemaking process. In doing so, they rationalize vulnerability-related incidents. Among the strategies designed to respond to the unexpected, managers attribute persistent fragilities to outside causes or more precisely to causes on which they have no influence. Miller (1993) showed the extent to which managers tend to blind their mental programming by rationalizing issues by treating them as aberrations, temporary, or beyond their control. During the first days of the heat wave that hit France in August 2003, the health authorities attributed a series of abnormal events—overloaded casualty departments, an increasing number of deaths among elderly people—to the implementation of the 35-hour working week in hospitals combined with summer vacations. Even if the explanation was a plausible one, there is no denying that, from the point of view of the authorities, it represented a useless lever on which they had little influence. Attributing an event to an outside or uncontrollable cause provides a temporary means of evasion for managers and gives them time to potentially design new responses to deal with vulnerabilities or postpone decisive action.

Rationalization takes the form of normalization when managers are faced with repeated unsolved warning signals. In the case of NASA, Vaughan (1996) illustrates how "signals were repeated, becoming routine as the frequency and predictability of erosion institutionalized the construction of risk" (p. 244). Normalization differs from rationalization in the sense that it is an acclimatization to imperfections and deviations. In the case of the HFE, the Townsend-Thrones management, the captain, and the crew made it possible for the bow doors to be left open. The fact that the bow doors remained open became so normal that it became invisible and the crew consequently expected its systematic repetition. This imperfection was even necessary for the satisfactory functioning of the organization. There was likely a tacitly accepted deviance that partly served the interests of each stakeholder. In the case of the HFE, keeping the doors open was a way for the captain to facilitate maneuvers in the harbor, for the crew in the hold to ensure a more pleasant work environment, and for the management to minimize turnaround times and thus be able to compete with the Channel Tunnel. Therefore, because all parties had something to gain from this deviance, there was no need to call it into question. In the case of the *Challenger* space shuttle, the systematic failure of the first ring and the fact of making it a normal and systematic principle become a necessary condition to proceed with the test sessions and ultimately to launch the shuttle. All parties got something out of it: Engineers saw it as a way of making progress in getting the shuttle ready for launch in time; the NASA management team saw it as an additional reason to go ahead with the launch. Anomalies and vulnerabilities are progressively considered as the conditions for the success and efficiency of a system.

Incidents or weak signals are symptoms of deeper vulnerabilities. They are the precursors of a favorable crisis ground. The alternative way of viewing phase 2 is thus to consider that managers can "fix" potential incidents linked to vulnerabilities. In HROs, for example, routines are designed to report incidents and near-misses and emergency procedures are designed to contain significant incidents. If incidents are managed successfully without dealing with the underlying vulnerability, the potential for danger will obviously persist, but managers may feel an illusion of control and a feeling of invulnerability. Here self-aggrandizement reinforces self-esteem by providing a feeling of control over unexpected events, but it is self-deceptive as it gives the feeling that if managers have succeeded in controlling the situation, then they can control any similar situation, paving the way toward further vulnerability.

PHASE 3: DISRUPTIONS AND DENYING

The third phase starts with the beginning of the crisis, its starting point being the occurrence of an event that is more acute than previous ones and that suddenly reveals the vulnerabilities that have so far accumulated and combined. Phase 3 is characterized by a collective collapse in sensemaking and role structuring (Weick, 1993). Pearson and Clair (1998) suggest that the consequence of this breakdown is a meltdown of common social order and commonly held values and beliefs. Expectations are radically disrupted and the level of visibility of imperfection is at peak. Lagadec (1991) suggests the notion of destabilization and the explosion of the traditional frames of reference. This breakdown is all the more salient in that managers and employees have adhered to basic assumptions about the world and themselves that make them unlikely to anticipate a crisis and have recurrently resorted to ego-defensive mechanisms to explain away the clues about, and signals of, potential dangers (Pauchant & Mitroff, 1992). The procedures and routines in place are usually inappropriate to provide satisfactory solutions. During phase 2, incidents are often solved through existing procedures, even emergency procedures. During phase 3, the conjunction of vulnerabilities saturates the sensemaking practices of managers and the absorptive capacity of the organization. Managers can hardly rely on known routines and practices to cope. These conditions create shock, panic, and temporary paralysis, and the feeling of loss of control prevails. The experience of such an event can cause a psychological breakdown that undermines employees' and managers' conceptual systems and self-esteem (Janoff-Bulman, 1992; Morris, 1975), upon which personal expectations about the world have been constructed. In times of disruption, the acceleration of time reduces the capacity to act. Phase 3 of the model contrasts with the first two in that it takes place over a contracted period of time. It causes managers difficulty in remaining lucid about the causes of what has happened and about the whole picture of the crisis. The experience of a disruption is short and intense. Managers often experience disillusionment, a feeling of helplessness, and confusion. They may lose their sense of worth and control. As Pearson and Clair (1998) suggest, "the result of these shattered assumptions is the need for psychic reorganization and the reconstruction of one's personal assumptive world" (Pearson & Clair, 1998, p. 63). Reconstructing new assumptions about the world takes time and managers need to act in spite of it. This context is likely to confine managers in a position of denial. Denial is a powerful ego-defense mechanism, as it prevents leaders from acknowledging what is still unacceptable and intolerable during the phase of disruptions. They may temporarily lose their sense of self and need to restore a psychological integrity that helps them deal with the unfolding events. The urgency to act, or rather, the urgency to react to the situation, prevails. This inability to detect and acknowledge the onset of a crisis is frequent (Roux-Dufort & Vidaillet, 2003). When one is overwhelmed or feels helpless, the best way out can consist of convincing oneself that there is no crisis (Lagadec, 1995). Denial is therefore frequently associated with precipitation, accusation of others, scapegoating, or even the refusal to admit any responsibility for what is happening.

In the hours before Hurricane Katrina struck, whereas officials knew that the hurricane would severely harm the coast of Louisiana and the city of New Orleans, officials were heavily criticized for their low sense of urgency at every level. Welch (2005) reports that "the federal government received hourly updates on the storm, and that the head of FEMA waited 24 hours before ordering personnel into the area. The state's governor, in her early communications with the president, mainly asked for financial aid for the city's clean-up efforts. On the local level, the mayor let a critical 12 hours elapse before ordering an evacuation of the city" (Welch, 2005). Even when faced with severe disruption, denial acts as a last resort to cope with an unbelievable reality. On December, 12, 1999, the tanker *Erika* wrecked near the coast of Brittany (France). The first oil slick hit the beaches 12 days later on December 24. During the twelve days in between, officials and authorities kept announcing that the French coasts were not endangered as the winds were pushing the slick toward the open sea. Again the officials acted as if the risk of oil pollution of the French coasts simply did not exist.

PHASE 4: CRISIS AND ESCALATION

This phase of disruption is followed by the crisis itself. Disruptions trigger the combination and amplification of internal vulnerabilities that have long incubated. The crisis triggers both internal and external vulnerabilities. In the aftermath of the shock, decision-makers slowly realize that they cannot manage their organization as they did before the crisis (Habermas, 1975). The former order has been disrupted but a new balance is still to come. In between, the legitimacy of the organization and its leaders is questioned. Crucial stakeholders may withdraw their support. The institution and structure are challenged and the situation can spiral down into a deeper human, social, managerial, and reputational crisis (Pearson & Clair, 1998). Managers no longer face a mere disturbance but a complete destabilization of the environment and organization. The management is directly called into question and its position within the organization is clearly threatened. To counteract this situation, managers are likely to engage in a form of compensation where action is supposed to fill the empty space created by the crisis. They are likely to pursue their action to exhibit a clear involvement in the resolution of the crisis. In this final phase, overwhelmed with helplessness and devoid of new solutions to address the issues raised by the crisis, managers may be tempted to resort to familiar solutions or use overlearned behaviors, and frequently put themselves in a position to reproduce already-experimented-with solutions (Weick, 1990). They engage in a form of escalating commitment in spite of recurrent negative feedback about the illegitimacy of their actions and decisions. This phase of escalating commitment is perceived as a way of restoring their self-esteem instead of remaining paralyzed by inaction.

In December 2003, a French chain of restaurants, Buffalo Grill, was the victim of an ex-employee who declared in a press article that the company had illegally imported British beef during the period of embargo. The embargo had been set up to protect the EU countries against the risk of dissemination of the Creutzfeldt-Jakob disease that was supposedly conveyed by particular sorts of beef, most of them coming from British cattle. This company had to cope with an unprecedented media crisis. They were all the more taken by surprise that during the last 20 years preceding this crisis, the company had invested most of its resources to sustain the increasing growth rates of its activity. Crisis management was thus not an issue during these golden years. Buffalo Grill was considered a success story in an industry that was tough and highly competitive. The leaders, two brothers, were self-made men. They had done everything by themselves to build this success. When the crisis hit, they decided to treat the event in the way they had been used to treating their business: by moving quickly ahead and bluntly imposing their views in complete disregard of facts. They thus immediately called a press conference and asserted publicly that Buffalo Grill had never imported British beef during the period of embargo. They did it without having checked if the employee's assumptions were right or wrong. Right after this press conference, Buffalo Grill was then heavily criticized for its arrogance and lack of professionalism.

Implications for Research and Practices

The model we present attempts to articulate a process perspective of crisis. Though each step of the model and each related proposition taken separately refer to existing literature and previous research results, we attempt to integrate these components into a coherent set of phases and using a timewise logic. We embrace crises in a large historical, structural, and psychological context. This view has different implications for research and for practice.

For research, three major implications could be put forward. First, it urges researchers of crisis management and other related areas to go beyond the acute aspect of crisis embodied in the triggering event and to look at crises as the result of three interrelated ingredients: organizational imperfection, managerial ignorance, and a triggering event. We have emphasized the role of managerial ignorance to account for the accumulation of imperfections. We are aware that the four levels of imperfections and ignorance we have hypothesized in this chapter could be refined, but they provide a promising avenue for research. Rationalization, normalization, denial, and escalating commitment can certainly take very different forms, and their identification would contribute to fine-tuning the model and make it more operational for empirical testing. Second, reframing crisis management in such a perspective should be a way to reduce even more the distance between the mainstream managerial and crisis-management research issues. Regarding crisis as the ultimate result of an accumulation of growing dysfunctions paired with a thickening managerial ignorance drives us to consider that crisis management is mostly about managing day-to-day unexpected events and imperfections rather than about managing major disruptions whenever they hit. Crisis management is not necessarily an exceptional operational mode, but an attempt to raise the usual level of managerial awareness about the small imperfections that are scattered everywhere in organizations (Roux-Dufort, in press). It is easier to adjust small dysfunctions rather than cope with a big crisis. Our model could then be a useful complement to the perspective developed by Weick and Sutcliffe (2001) where lessons to manage the unexpected are drawn from the HRO. Third, our model suggests that the distinction between external and internal crises does not hold. A crisis is more the result of how managers experience and cope with a triggering event than of the event itself. The triggering event, being external or internal, has less importance than we believe; what counts is the ground with which this event colludes. In any circumstances, organizations do hold responsibility for the occurrence of a crisis and cannot hide behind the principle of the external source of the crisis to avoid the fundamental question about how this was allowed to happen. Our model thus restores an intrinsic sense of responsibility when dealing with crises and denies the natural victimization process that may take place in organizations hit by crises.

For practitioners, this paper has other, more fundamental implications. Crisis management is not just a management of exceptions. Adjusting anomalies or vulnerabilities is less costly than coping with a disaster. The cost of ignorance is sometimes higher than the cost of fixing what appears to be of secondary importance in the day-to-day activity of an organization. Recently, the risk manager of a multinational luxury company had to deal with a consumer complaint that, at first sight from a marketing point of view, appeared totally meaningless and statistically insignificant. This customer informed the company that he had cut his finger while opening one of their most famous bottles of perfume. The complaint sounded strange to the ears of the risk manager. Its tone was unusual. As the manager was used to responding to complaints from demanding and unforgiving customers, this particular complaint sounded more an incident report rather than a real complaint with a demand for compensation or a refund. After having checked with the quality department to see that no such other problem had been reported, the risk manager called back the customer to find out more about his request. He then discovered that this customer was a professional snooker player. On the top of this, the customer had cut his finger on the very morning of the day and he had to play an internationally broadcasted competition. The risk manager finally learned that cutting one's finger could be a heavy handicap in such a sport.

He rapidly felt that the customer would be ready to put the blame on the product and the company if he happened to lose his competition on the very same evening. The risk manager then decided to find a commercial arrangement with him in order to reduce such a risk. The story does not tell how the snooker player fared in his competition, but it tells us to what extent some people may notice signs and potential anomalies that other managers just cannot see. This risk manager considers paying attention to what is perceived as being of secondary importance by other managers of this company an integral part of his job. He also has the sufficient legitimacy and power to speak up and point out these anomalies. Crisis management starts precisely at this point. In this chapter we agitate for a passion for eliminating imperfections rather than for a search for excellence. Tough excellence should drive managers and leaders to look for better performance and better value creation when an unquestioned belief turns into a strong blind spot and contributes to blinding managers' attention to their own vulnerabilities. In an age where knowledge management, learning, and excellence represent some of strongest pillars of the managerial ideology, we believe that management is also about acknowledging our ignorance and imperfection.

Bibliography

Argyris, C. (1982). *Reasoning, learning, and action: Individual and organizational.* San Francisco: Jossey-Bass.

Barnard, C. (1938). *The function of the executive.* Boston: Harvard University Press.

Beck, U. (1992). *The risk society: Towards a new modernity.* Newbury Park, CA: Sage.

Billings, R. S., Millburn, T. W., & Schaalman, M.L. (1980). A model of crisis perception: A theoretical and empirical analysis. *Administrative Science Quarterly, 25,* 300–316.

Bowonder, B., & Linstone, H. (1987). Notes on the Bhopal accident: Risk analysis and multiple perspectives. *Technological Forecasting and Social Change, 32,* 183–202.

Brockner, J. (1992). The escalation of commitment to failing course of action: Toward theoretical progress. *Academy of Management Review, 17*(1), 39–62.

Brown, A. D. (1997). Narcissism, identity, and legitimacy. *Academy of Management Review, 22*(3), 643–686.

Brown, A. D., & Starkey, K. (2000). Organizational identity and learning: A psychodynamic perspective. *Academy of Management Review, 25*(1), 102–120.

Cohen, A. R. (1959). Some implications of self-esteem for social influence. In C. I. Hovland & I. L. Janis (Eds.), *Personality and persuasibility.* New Haven, CT: Yale University Press.

Cyert, R. M., & March, J. G. (1963). *A behavioral theory of the firm.* Englewood Cliffs, NJ: Prentice Hall.

Deschamps, I., Lalonde, M., Pauchant, T. C., & Waaub, J. P. (1996). What crises could teach us about complexity and systemic management: The case of the Nestucca Oil Spill. *Technological Forecasting and Social Change, 55,* 107–129.

Dror, Y., Lagadec, P., Porfiriev, B., & Quarantelli, E. L. (2001). Crises to come. In U. Rosenthal, R. Boin, & L. K. Comfort (Eds.), *Managing crises: Threats, dilemmas, opportunities* (pp. 342–349). Springfield, IL: Charles C Thomas.

Dunn, W. N. (1992). Assessing the impact of policy analysis: The function of usable ignorance. *The International Journal of Knowledge Transfer and Utilization, 4,* 36–55.

Dutton, J. E., & Jackson, S. E. (1987). Categorizing strategic issues: Links to organization action. *Academy of Management Review, 12*(1), 76–90.

Fink, S. L. (1986). *Crisis Management: Planning for the inevitable.* New York: Amacom.

Finkelstein, S., & Hambrick. D. C. (1990). Top-management team tenure and organizational outcomes: The moderating role of managerial discretion. *Administrative Science Quarterly, 35,* 484–503.

Forgues, B., & Roux-Dufort, C. (1998). *Crises: Events or processes?* Hazards and Sustainability Conference. Durham, UK, May 26–27.

Gatot, L., Jacques, J. M., & Roux-Dufort, C. (1999). *From postcrisis learning to preventive learning: Some empirical evidence for a preventive learning management tool.* 58th Academy of Management Meetings. Chicago, August 6–11.

Habermas, J. (1975). *Legitimation crisis.* Boston: Beacon Press.

Halpern, J. (1989). Cognitive factors influencing decision-making in a highly reliable organization. *Industrial Crisis Quarterly, 3,* 143–158.

Hambrick, D. C., & Mason, P. A. (1984). Upper-echelons: The organization as a reflection of its top managers. *Academy of Management Review, 9*(2), 193–206.

Harvey, M. G., Novicevic, M. M., Buckley, M. R., & Ferris, G. R. (2001). A historic perspective on organizational ignorance. *Journal of Managerial Psychology, 16*(5/6), 449–468.

Hermann, C. F. (1963). Some consequences of crisis which limit the viability of organizations. *Administrative Science Quarterly, 8,* 61–82.

Jacques, E. (1955). Social systems as a defense against persecutory and depressive anxiety. In M. Klein, P. Heimann, & R. Money-Kyrle (Eds.), *New directions in psychoanalysis.* London: Tavistock.

Janis, I. L. (1989). *Crucial decisions, leadership in policymaking and crisis management.* New York: Free Press.

Janoff-Bulman, R. (1992). *Shattered assumptions.* New York: Free Press.

Jensen, M., & Zajac, E. J. (2004). Corporate elites and corporate strategy: How demographic preferences and structural position shape the scope of the firm. *Strategic Management Journal, 25,* 507–524.

Kets de Vries, M. F. R. (1980). *Organizational paradoxes, clinical approaches to management.* London: Tavistock.

Klienfield, S. (1981). *The biggest company on earth: A profile of AT&T.* New York: Holt, Rinehart & Winston.

Kovoor-Misra, S. (1995). A multidimensional approach to crisis preparation for technical organizations: Some critical factors. *Technological Forecasting and Social Change, 48,* 143–160.

Lagadec, P. (1991). *La gestion des crises: Outils de décision à l'usage des décideurs.* Paris: McGraw-Hill.

Lagadec, P. (1995). *Cellules de crise: Les conditions d'une conduite efficace.* Paris: Les Editions d'Organisation.

Laughlin, H. P. (1970). *The ego and its defense.* New York: Appelton-Century-Crofts.

March, J. G., & Simon, H. A. (1958). *Organizations.* New York: Wiley.

March, J. G., Sproull, L. S., & Tamuz, M. (1996). Learning from samples of one or fewer. In M. D. Cohen & L. S. Sproull (Eds.), *Organizational learning* (pp. 1–19). Thousand Oaks, CA: Sage.

Milburn, T. W., Schuler, R. S., &. Watman, K. H. (1983). Organizational crisis. Part I: Definition and conceptualization. *Human Relations, 36,* 1141–1160.

Miller, D. (1993). The architecture of simplicity. *Academy of Management Review, 18*(1), 116–139.

Mitroff, I. I., & Pearson, C. M. (1993). *Crisis management.* San Francisco: Jossey-Bass.

Morin, E. (1993). For a crisiology. *Industrial and Environmental Crisis Quarterly, 7*(1).

Morris, P. (1975). *Loss and change.* Garden City, NY: Anchor/Doubleday.

Nystrom, P. C., & Starbuck, W. (1984). To avoid organizational crises, unlearn. *Organizational Dynamics, 12,* 53–65.

O'Connor, J., & McDermott, I. (1997). *The art of system thinking: Essential skills for creativity and problem solving.* London: Thorsons.

Pauchant, T. C., & Mitroff, I. I. (1992). *Transforming the crisis-prone organization. Preventing individual, organizational and environmental tragedies.* San Francisco: Jossey-Bass.

Pauchant, T. C., & Mitroff, I. I. (1995). *La gestion des crises et des paradoxes.* Montréal: Editions Québec-Amérique.

Pauchant, T. C., Mitroff, I. I., & Lagadec, P. (1991). Toward a systemic crisis management strategy. Learning from the best examples in the US, Canada and France. *Industrial Crisis Quarterly, 5*(3), 209–232.

Pearson, C., & Clair, J. (1998). Reframing crisis management. *Academy of Management Review, 23*(1), 59–76.

Pearson, C., & Mitroff, I. I. (1993). From crisis prone to crisis prepared: A framework for crisis management. *Academy of Management Executive, 7,* 48–59.

Perrow, C. (1984). *Normal accidents: Living with high-risk technologies.* New York: Basic Books.

Perrow, C. (1994). Accidents in high risk systems. *Technology Studies, 1*(1), 1–20.

Phelps, N. L. (1986). Setting up a crisis recovery plan. *Journal of Business Strategy, 6,* 5–10.

Quarantelli, E. L. (Ed.). (1998). *What is a disaster? Perspectives on the question.* London: Routledge.

Reason, J. (1990). *Human error.* New York: Cambridge University Press.

Reason, J. (1997). *Managing the risks of organizational accidents.* London: Ashgate.

Reason, J., Parker, D., & Lawton, R. (1998). Organizational control and safety: The varieties of rule-related behavior. *Journal of Occupational and Organizational Psychology, 71,* 289–304.

Reilly, A. H. (1993). Preparing for the worst: The process of effective crisis management. *Industrial and Environmental Crisis Quarterly, 7*(2), 115–143.

Rosenthal, U. (2003). September 11: Public administration and the study of crises and crisis management. *Administration and Society, 35*(2), 129–143.

Roux-Dufort, C. (in press). Is crisis management (only) a management of exceptions? *Journal of Contingencies and Crisis Management.*

Roux-Dufort, C., & Pauchant, T. C. (1993). Rumors and crises: A case study in the banking industry. *Industrial and Environmental Crisis Quarterly, 3*(7), 231–251.

Roux-Dufort, C., & Vidaillet, B. (2003). The difficulties of improvising in a crisis situation. A case study. *International Studies in Management and Organization, 33*(1), 86–115.

Schwartz, H. S. (1987). On the psychodynamics of organizational disaster: The case of the space shuttle *Challenger. Columbia Journal of World Business, 22*, 59–67.

Schwenk, C. (1984). Cognitive simplification processes in strategic decision making. *Strategic Management Journal, 5*, 111–128.

Shamir, J., & Shamir, M. (1997). Pluralistic ignorance across and over time. Information cues and biases. *Public Opinion Quarterly, 61*(2), 227–260.

Shrivastava, P. (1992). *Bhopal: Anatomy of a crisis.* London: Paul Chapman.

Shrivastava, P. (1994). The evolution of research on technological crises in the U.S. *Journal of Contingencies and Crisis Management, 2*(1), 10–20.

Shrivastava, P. (1995). *Ecocentric management for a globally changing crisis society.* 54th Meeting of the Academy of Management, Vancouver, BC, Canada.

Shrivastava, P., Mitroff, I. I., Miller, D., & Miglani, A. (1988). Understanding industrial crises. *Journal of Management Studies, 25*(4), 285–303.

Smart, C. F., & Vertinsky, I. (1984). Strategy and environment: A study of corporate responses to crises. *Strategic Management Journal, 5*(3), 199–213.

Smith, D. (1992). The Kegworth aircrash: A crisis in three phases? *Disaster Management, 4*(2), 63–72.

Smith, D. (2000). On a wing and a prayer? Exploring the human components of technological failure. *Systems Research and Behavioral Science, 17*(6), 543–559.

Starbuck, W., Greve, A., & Hedberg, B. T. (1978). Responding to crisis. *Journal of Business Administration, 9*, 111–137.

Starbuck, W., & Milliken, F. (1988). *Challenger:* Fine-tuning the odds until something breaks. *Journal of Management Studies, 25*, 319–340.

Staw, B. M., McKechnie, P. I., & Puffer, S. M. (1983). The justification of organizational performance. *Administrative Science Quarterly, 28*, 582–600.

Sutton, R. I., & Callahan, A. L. (1987). The stigma of bankruptcy: Spoiled organization image and its management. *Academy of Management Journal, 30*, 405–436.

Thiétart, R. A., & Forgues, B. (1995). Chaos theory and organization. *Organization Science, 6*(1), 19–31.

Turner, B. A. (1976). The organizational and inter-organizational development of disasters. *Administrative Science Quarterly, 21*, 378–397.

Vaughan, D. (1996). *The* Challenger *launch decision: Risky technology, culture, and deviance at NASA.* Chicago: University of Chicago Press.

Watson, T. J. (1994). *In search of management. Culture, chaos, and control in managerial work.* London: Routledge.

Weick, K. (1988). Enacted sensemaking in crisis situations. *Journal of Management Studies, 25*, 305–317.

Weick, K. (1990). The vulnerable system: An analysis of the Tenerife air disaster. *Journal of Management Studies, 16*(3), 571–693.

Weick, K. (1993). The collapse of sensemaking in organizations: The Mann Gulch disaster. *Administrative Science Quarterly, 38*, 628–652.

Weick, K. (1995). *Sensemaking in organizations.* Thousand Oaks, CA: Sage.

Weick, K., & Sutcliffe, K. M. (2001). *Managing the unexpected. Assuring high performance in an age of complexity.* San Francisco: Jossey-Bass.

Weiner, B. (1982). The emotional consequences of causal attribution. In M. Sydor Clark & S. T. Fiske (Eds.), *Affect and cognition: The seventeenth annual Carnegie symposium on cognition* (pp. 185–186). Hillsdale, NJ: Lawrence Erlbaum.

Welch, J. (2005, September 14). The five stages of crisis management. Opinion Journal, *Wall Street Journal* Editorial Page.

Whetton, D. A. (1980). Organizational decline: A neglected topic in organizational science. *Academy of Management Review, 5,* 577–588.

Wiersema, M. F., & Bantel, K. A. (1992). Top management team demography and corporate strategic change. *Academy of Management Journal, 35,* 91–121.

Wybo, J. L. (Ed.). (1990). *Introduction aux cyndiniques.* Paris: Editions Eska.

The Eight Characteristics of Japanese Crisis-Prone Organizations

9

Toshihiko Hagiwara

Much can be learned about crisis management from the experiences of the corporate business system in Japan. Japanese organizations that are prone to crises have displayed general characteristics, each related to Japan's culture but not unique to that country's economic system. These eight general management behaviors contribute to the occurrence of crisis situations, worsen their severity, and complicate the organization's recovery. They can, however, be identified and addressed, giving hope to any organization that is thoughtful about crisis management and prevention.

Characteristics of Japanese Crisis-Prone Organizations

CHARACTERISTIC 1: REDUCTION IN THE WORKFORCE—THE EFFECTS OF RESTRUCTURING WITHIN JAPANESE ORGANIZATIONS

Management decisions of many types can contribute to the likelihood that an organization will encounter a crisis situation. One of these is the decision to make changes to the organizational structure of a company, often referred to as "restructuring," in an effort to increase efficiencies. Corporate restructuring practices in Japan lagged behind those in the United States and other Western countries by approximately 10 years. More recently, there has been a tendency in many major Japanese companies to simplify the restructuring process, from increasing efficiencies through reforming the corporate structure to merely reducing the number of employees within the organization.

It is logical that by removing any existing organizational redundancies, or any indirect departments that do not seem to add value to the business, the efficiency of the organization would increase. However, simplifying the restructuring process by merely reducing the work force may create more problems than benefits. For example, most of the general affairs departments and personnel departments in Japan's major companies had traditionally been in charge of corporate crisis-management functions, but they did not seem to add any obvious economic value to the corporate performance. Therefore, in the majority of these Japanese corporations, managers and staff members of most of the general affairs and personnel departments were not replaced after retirement or were laid off under the lengthy Japanese corporate-restructuring process. Middle managers were especially affected. The top managers of the Japanese companies thought management resources were wasted by keeping these surplus employees.

The responsibilities of corporate crisis management should have been transferred to the remaining business units after such a restructuring process, but in most cases—in part due to the traditional vertical organizational structure in Japan, explained by Chie Nakane (1967)—the crisis-management responsibilities went unassigned in most of Japan's big companies.

As a result, Japan's corporate system, known worldwide for its economic prominence, stability, and exacting precision, has come down from its peak in the 1980s to face increasing threats of corporate crises.

CHARACTERISTIC 2: CONCEALMENT AS A RESPONSE TO AN INCIDENT

Another characteristic that demonstrates the vulnerability of Japanese businesses to crisis occurrences is the tendency to conceal a crisis incident and to avoid disclosing details to the public or regulatory agencies. Such a response serves to complicate and aggravate the crisis situation. For example, Mitsubishi Motor Company, here referred to as "MMC,"[1] intentionally concealed information about a manufacturing flaw in one of its automobiles. MMC neglected to recall the vehicles (that is, to notify consumers of free repairs or returns), even though the recall system in Japan was established in 1969 to protect the general public. MMC should also have notified the Japanese Ministry of Land, Infrastructure and Transport (JMOLIT) immediately upon discovering the flaw, which is required when there appear to be manufacturing flaws that could cause dangerous accidents. Compliance with safety regulations should be the company's top priority, but MMC concealed the facts from the government and also from the public.

MMC's problem first occurred in the process of designing the hub, a critical component in connecting the wheels to the axle and frame of the automobile. The structural flaw, which caused the deterioration of metal parts, was possibly overlooked due to the fact that MMC neglected to test the design on actual cars. MMC has changed the design of the hub for large-sized cars six times since 1983, with the hub types labeled A through F in sequence. It was the D-type hub, manufactured since 1993 and used for large-sized trailers, that caused a fatal accident in the city of Yokohama, near the Tokyo metropolitan area. In January 2002, the left wheel came off a moving trailer and struck a woman walking with her children, instantly killing the woman and injuring both children.

According to records, the design of the hub was changed from the C-type to the D-type hub when the company was rushing to get the car model on the market in order to compete with other car manufacturers. MMC, threatened with the potential loss of competitive advantage and a declining market share, decided on the cheaper hub design, even though the D-type hub had a high probability of failure at that time. Rather than taking responsibility for the faulty engineering, MMC instead blamed the car owners for insufficiently fastening the bolts. It was not until later that the company admitted to any wrongdoing.

MMC continued to conceal information, submitting falsified test reports to the investigative authorities, claiming that the D-type hub had sufficient strength and durability. At the same time, an internal MMC memo showed that the reports were not based on any actual experiments. MMC claimed that the internal memo was merely the conclusion of inexperienced technical workers and was not authorized by the company.

Another example of the tendency to conceal information involved Tokyo Electric Power Co. (TEPCO) in late 2002. TEPCO—the largest power company in Japan, serving more than 27 million customers with numerous power plants—was ordered to shut down all of its nuclear power plants for safety checks after it was revealed that the company had falsified nuclear safety documents to hide information about cracks in nuclear power plant structures. A subcontract employee eventually reported the falsified repair records to the authorities, and after an investigation, TEPCO was found to be guilty of wrongdoing.

CHARACTERISTIC 3: THE INFLUENCE OF CORPORATE TRADITIONS AND MANAGEMENT CULTURE

Organizational structure and decisions are often the result of corporate traditions and management culture, rather than thoughtful consideration and analysis. Traditions and internal pressures impact the perspective of management decision-makers and can increase the company's tendency toward crisis situations, as in the following example.

MMC, one of the Mitsubishi group's leading companies, was once a subsidiary of Mitsubishi Heavy Industries (MHI), one of the core companies of the Mitsubishi group. Traditionally, the CEO of MHI has been chosen from among some executive managers, and whoever was not chosen for MHI was expected to become the CEO of the subsidiary, MMC. This, in effect, branded the MMC CEO and the company as "secondary" and cultivated an environment of "catching up" instead of manufacturing high-quality vehicles. Reducing total cost was the first priority for the company, and safety management was regarded as an obstacle to that priority. MMC tried to evade costs associated with safety design as much as possible. Top technicians who focused on safety features were outsourced. In order to maintain their influence in the company, technician managers concentrated their efforts on cost reduction rather than on the safety procedures. As mentioned, MMC denied that the D-type hub had structural problems and instead blamed the accidents on the trailer drivers, which perpetuated the problematic management culture.

Because of an alliance with Daimler Chrysler, the CEO of MMC has more recently come from Germany and introduced European and American management practices, including safety as a priority. The corporate culture of MMC has been gradually changed. Evidence of this is that in early 2004, MMC set up an "MMC hot line," which employees can call to report illegal activities within the company. The hot line goes directly to a third-party lawyer who is under obligation to keep all reports confidential. The lawyer's photograph, address, phone number, and e-mail address were published in the MMC employee magazine. MMC had tried to encourage this type of internal watchdog practice earlier in 2000, shortly after the D-type hub recall cover-up, when an "employee consulting room" was developed. The move was mostly ineffective at that time, however, owing to the fact that there were no provisions for confidentiality and no means to protect the employee "whistleblower" from retaliation within the company.

Recently, the Japanese government has contributed to the changing climate in Japanese business culture. Congress has passed a new law to protect employees who report negative internal information (whistleblowers). The law is controversial, and not enough to completely protect the whistleblowers, but it is still in the development stage. The actions by the government are intended to establish greater corporate compliance and to advance the social movement to protect public interest.

In light of the new Japanese law, the role and effectiveness of JMOLIT will also need to be reviewed. When the JMOLIT's official governmental inspection of MMC was done as scheduled by the regulations, the agency did not notice the structural flaws in the D-type hub. This may have been because of the vertical type of bureaucracy in both private and public organizations in Japan, with strong superior-subordinate relationships adding to the tendency to narrow the scope of responsibility in order to avoid blame within territories. Another contributing problem is that JMOLIT does not have any compulsory investigation rights, and they have few technical experts for the inspection of vehicles. Therefore, JMOLIT may bear some of the blame in the D-type hub crisis, because it was ineffective in holding MMC accountable for their safety responsibilities.

CHARACTERISTICS 4, 5, AND 6: INSENSITIVITY, SLOW RESPONSIVENESS, AND LACK OF LEARNING FROM MISTAKES

While tradition and culture played a role in the problems at MMC, three different management behaviors made things worse: insensitivity to complex work environments, slow response time, and lack of learning from prior experiences. Understanding work environments, especially in foreign countries, is a critical factor in a company's success. Also, swift action on the part of management can avert a crisis, where a slow response time can make a critical difference in public perception of a situation. And not learning from mistakes can prove to be disastrous.

In the case of the U.S. subsidiary of MMC, several personnel issues grew to be major problems in the 1990s. All management decisions at U.S. MMC had traditionally been made exclusively by the expatriate Japanese managers. This practice, combined with poor cross-cultural public relations skills, risk management, and personnel supervision, created an environment where a sexual-harassment charge in 1994 became a major problem. U.S. MMC's response internally and in the media was slow and ineffective, and the result was that by 1996 the "Mitsubishi" public image was badly damaged, with sales falling roughly 7%. In the sexual-harassment suit brought against U.S. MMC in 1996, the company paid the 300 female employees 34 million U.S. dollars in 1998, the highest payment for a sexual-harassment charge up to that time.

In 1999, U.S. MMC was sued again, this time by seven plaintiffs on behalf of the company's 250 African-American and Hispanic-American employees for discrimination in the workplace and in promotion practices. The suit suggested that U.S. MMC's discriminatory workplace be corrected immediately. The suit cost U.S. MMC 3.2 million U.S. dollars in 2001, a cost that could have been avoided with management practices that were more sensitive, more responsive, and better at learning from the previous litigation experience. It was apparent that the management of U.S. MMC practiced the same management characteristics as the head MMC office in Japan, and was not sensitive enough to the complicated work environment in the United States.

Returning to the defective D-type hub case in MMC Japan, the Japanese police investigated the head office of MMC in January and March of 2004. The company admitted that the hub had a design flaw that required recall notifications. The investigators found that MMC cut corners in safety management that would have incurred high costs if done properly. MMC executives believed they could save money if no accidents occurred. While the objective of cost savings is typical for corporate management, it is unusual that safety-management costs would be regarded as a wasteful investment.

In June 2004, Daimler Chrysler wanted to withdraw from the alliance with MMC. Meanwhile, MMC has suffered from a heavy sales slump, with total sales figures for 2004 expected to fall approximately 50% compared to 2003. These figures are indicative of an organization in the midst of a real corporate crisis.

MMC's tendency to conceal information could be attributed to the corporate culture of Mitsubishi Heavy Industries, which had long been engaged in manufacturing military equipment such as tanks and jet fighters. Confidentiality is often required and considered an admirable trait in the military arena. In the eyes of the organization's management, there is little distinction between keeping confidential secrets and hiding the facts from outsiders. Therefore, whether or not they were revealed, hiding the recall information did not seem to MMC's management to be a poor decision for the company. The former CEO, Kawazoe, apologized about concealing the first recall information in 2002, but MMC continued to hide recall information systematically.

It has been reported that over the years, MMC has concealed information about 159 defective parts, causing 24 accidents resulting in injury or death, 63 property-loss accidents, and 101 vehicle fires.

Definition of a Crisis

It is helpful to consider a definition of "crisis" and an analysis of its components. There is no established definition in the field of crisis management; but to define a crisis, two conditions are generally required, according to Pauchant and Mitroff (1992). The two conditions are displayed in the grid in Figure 9.1.

First, the primary condition considers the area involved in the situation. It is divided by whether the whole organization or system was involved, or only a section or subsystem. The second condition considers the level of impact to the organization; that is, whether physical damage alone is involved or the impact reaches further to the symbolic, or social, level.

According to this definition, a crisis occurs when the phenomenon involves the whole organization, or system, and when its impact goes beyond material damage to having a symbolic effect by disturbing the corporate culture and the social assumptions of the group and its identity.

An example of the symbolic—or corporate identity—crisis can be seen in the case of widespread food poisoning from Snow Brand Milk Products Co., Ltd. in 2000. This situation became a crisis owing to almost all of the

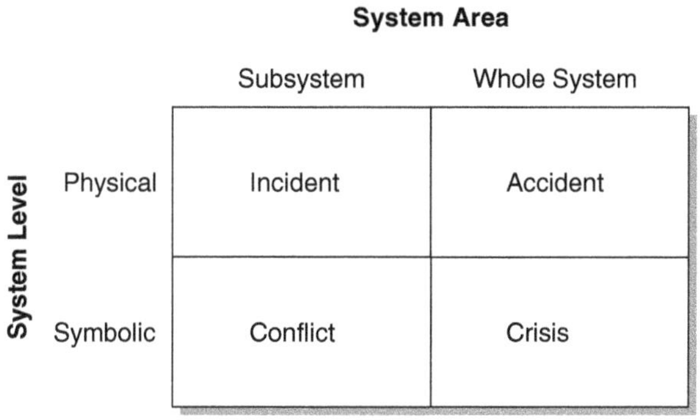

The Eight Characteristics of Japanese Crisis-Prone Organizations

System Area

	Subsystem	Whole System
Physical	Incident	Accident
Symbolic	Conflict	Crisis

(System Level)

Figure 9.1 Defining a Crisis

SOURCE: Thierry C. Pauchant and Ian I. Mitroff, *Transforming the Crisis-Prone Organization*, Jossey-Bass Publishers, 1992. Used with permission of John Wiley & Sons, Inc.

characteristics covered in this chapter, but the way it unfolded in the media gives an insightful view of the unraveling of the company's internal social and symbolic identity.

It all began when more than 15,000 people living in western Japan became ill from food poisoning, eventually traced to milk products made by Snow Brand's factory in Osaka. At first, management tried to downplay the severity of the situation, then tried to cover up incriminating investigation facts and also proved to be reluctant to cooperate with recall procedures. The Snow Brand management appeared to be self-serving and arrogant, instead of being concerned about the welfare of the public.

This was apparent during a press conference when the company president, Tetsuro Ishikawa, along with other executives explained the cleanliness and sanitary guidelines of the factory. Suddenly, a factory manager stepped forward and admitted that, in fact, the workers would "skip washing the valves." The response from the audience—made up of the media as well as the food-poisoning victims—was immediate and critical. The president's face turned red, and he said, "What are you saying? Is that true?" The public-relations manager, who was as surprised as everyone else by the bold remark, tried to take charge of the scene and said, "He is just commenting on the possibility." But the factory manager held firm, saying, "It is a fact," as if to reveal that such a practice was within the normal cost-cutting routine—and yet he could no longer go along with it, or tolerate the management's arrogance.

At that moment, the corporate culture of Snow Brand turned to chaos, and the situation moved from merely a physical level to the symbolic level. To make matters worse, the press conference was broadcast on television, and the result was that the public became completely skeptical of the company's quality control and its trustworthiness.

President Ishikawa attempted to restore order within the corporate culture by visiting the sales shops and the customer-service departments, to apologize and to encourage the workers during the difficult public response. On at least one occasion, he was met with critical responses from workers that would have been unthinkable before the crisis. Snow Brand found itself in a true corporate crisis, one that impacted the material operations as well as the symbolic internal identity of the company.

By the time a crisis occurs, it may be the "tip of the iceberg" that is visible, but under the surface there are many occurrences of incidents, conflicts, and accidents making up 90% of the total phenomenon. Thinking in this way, the crisis can also be defined as the prolongation of a trivial matter. In the beginning, the phenomenon is usually a simple or trivial matter, or just friction within the organization.

In some cases, the phenomenon continues to develop and can grow sequentially into a crisis. For example, in the MMC case, when the former CEO apologized in 2002 about concealing the first recall information, the company was not yet in real crisis; they were probably still in the incident or conflict phase. These occurrences can "snowball" into greater problems, following the sequence: Incident → Conflict → Accident → Crisis.

Cost Implications of Crisis

When a crisis occurs, a typical organization takes preventative measures or develops corrective plans through a careful and detailed investigation of the crisis, and renews the internal corporate system of checks and balances. But in the examples presented, why did crises occur repeatedly within the same organization? A graphical presentation of the costs generated in a crisis provides an aid to the analysis. The upward slant of the cost curves shows the seriousness of the situation, because unlike traditional cost curves, costs involved in a crisis situation only increase.

With MMC, for example, it is assumed that management considered the different cost impacts before making decisions. Cost curve A in Figure 9.2 shows the cost impact if MMC does not conceal the information and complies with Japanese law requiring a recall. Cost curve B shows the assumed cost impact when the information is concealed and no recall action is taken. Choice B is clearly more appealing to the management of MMC as they consider their objective keeping costs down, an important proposition to the corporation. Implementing a recall is very expensive, and in the case of MMC it can cost over billions of yen. Of course, cost curve B assumes ex ante that concealing the recall information will succeed. Also, generally speaking, the more serious the situation becomes, the farther apart cost curve A and cost curve B will become. This is because of the cost the corporation will have to pay in order to recover the trust of consumers.

In Figure 9.3, the cost curve C, which the organization faces ex post, assumes that concealing the recall information fails, perhaps owing to

The Eight Characteristics of Japanese Crisis-Prone Organizations

Figure 9.2 Cost Curves of a Crisis

some inside whistleblowers. Then, in this case, too, the more serious the situation becomes, the farther apart the cost curve C and the cost curve B will be. An organization that finds itself in a crisis typically faces these cost structures. In other words, the organization that has not chosen compliance (cost curve A) faces two choices: cost curve C, where the effort at concealing damaging information fails and costs increase in efforts to recover the lost credibility; and cost curve B, where a company succeeds in concealing information.

Another way to look at this is that management considers cost curve D, ex ante, that synthesizes the ex post expected value of cost curve B and cost curve C. This can be displayed as

Formula 1: D = E (B) + E (C), where E is the expected value of B or C.

The comparison will be between the ex ante cost curve A and the ex ante synthesized cost curve D as defined by Formula 1. (Cost curve D' is addressed later.)

The primary hypothesis here is that an organization moves into a crisis when the management makes decisions based solely on the economically rational cost considerations of comparing cost curves A and D.

In fact, the main factor to consider in these decisions is the position of cost curve D, which is a result of the positions of cost curves B and C, and the probability of the occurrence of the phenomena. As the probability increases, cost curve D moves toward D', which has a much greater overall

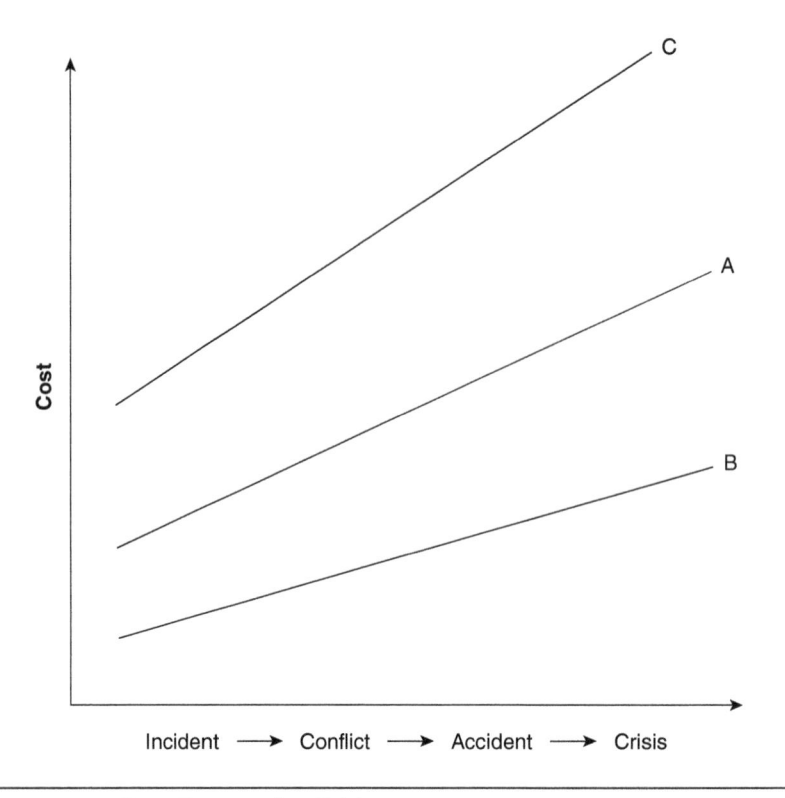

Figure 9.3 Cost Curves of a Crisis

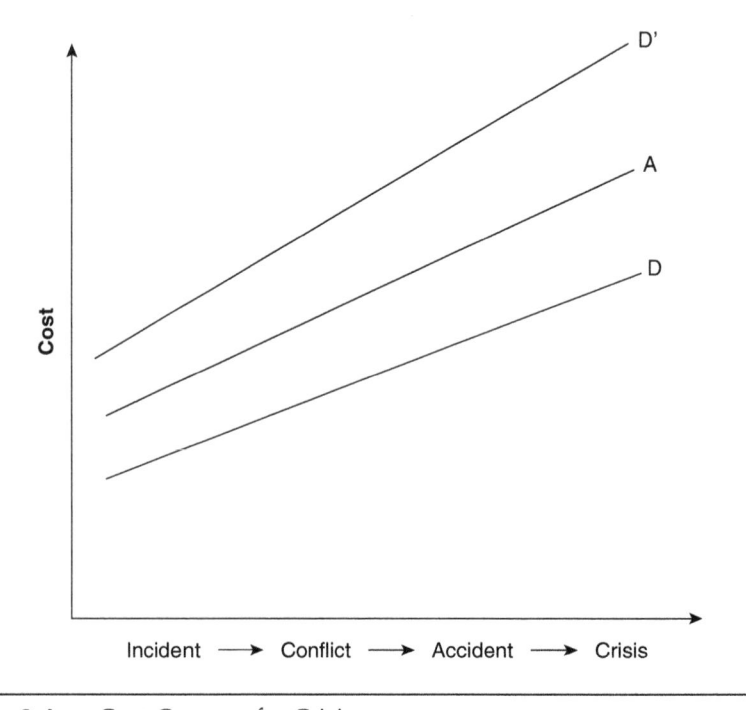

Figure 9.4 Cost Curves of a Crisis

cost to the organization. If management considers the threat of the higher cost curve, they will make crises-averting decisions for the organization.

Comparisons to U.S. Examples

It can be said that businesses in the United States have comparatively fewer disgraceful crisis situations than those in Japan. The United States seems to have greater societal pressure against such business behavior and therefore more severe sanctions as a result. When a crisis occurs, the position of cost curve C ex post is relatively higher than in Japan.

Two very good examples of this can be taken from the United States in the late 1970s. The first involved Procter & Gamble, Inc. (P&G), the manufacturer of a brand of tampon called OB. P&G developed a new fiber for the OB tampon that increased absorption, a quality which could increase market share for the product. Shortly after its introduction, there were several cases of illness and even death that came to be attributed to a condition named Toxic Shock Syndrome, or TSS. TSS was at first not thoroughly understood, but was suspected to be related to the long-term use of the OB tampon.

Because of the difficulty in proving the causality between TSS and the OB tampon, P&G could have ignored the situation and avoided any responsibility, as might be typical for an organization. Instead, P&G immediately withdrew the product from the market. It was not until nearly 5 years later that the cause of TSS was proven to be from toxic bacteria that could grow readily in the fiber developed for the OB tampon. But P&G's swift action, perceived by the public as a safety precaution, averted further problems, and even increased P&G's reputation as a trustworthy company. In fact, a redeveloped OB tampon is still on the market today.

A contrasting example is the case of the A. H. Robbins Company, a U.S. pharmaceutical manufacturer and developer of the Dalkon Shield contraceptive device. In the early 1970s, the Dalkon Shield was put on the market with claims of being a safe form of birth control. However, a flaw in the product design reduced its contraceptive efficacy and also caused thousands of injuries from pelvic inflammatory disease. These reports were ignored by the management at A. H. Robbins, and for 3 years production was continued along with an aggressive marketing campaign. In 1974, the company finally pulled the Dalkon Shield from the market but still refused to recall the product; meanwhile, it continued to defend the product's safety and reliability, and even deflected blame by claiming that pregnancies and injuries resulted from improper use, not from faulty design. It was later discovered that in advance of releasing the product on the market, the company had received cautionary medical reports and had chosen to ignore them.

Litigation was forthcoming, with more than 12,000 suits filed in U.S. courts. A. H. Robbins, however, continued to deny any flaws in the contraceptive device, and increased spending on legal personnel and litigation costs. In the end, A. H. Robbins paid claims of more than 500 million in

U.S. dollars, and in 1985, the company declared bankruptcy as a direct result of the costs involved with the defective Dalkon Shield.

P&G chose to take the cost curve A in compliance with the related regulations, and as a result, the company is a globally prosperous business. On the other hand, A. H. Robbins erroneously believed that the ex ante cost curve was at position D, when, in fact, it was at position D', and the company suffered a tremendous setback.

The difference between cost curve D and cost curve D' can be attributed to social factors that influence organizations to choose compliance and honest disclosure to consumers. The threat of economic damage caused by negative public sentiment and litigation can have an effective impact on management decisions. This social pressure seems to be greater in the United States than in Japan, which may be part of the reason Japanese companies are more prone to crisis situations.

Recently the Japanese government came up with a policy to protect employees against repercussions from reporting wrongdoing within organizations, and also introduced a public-interest communicator protection system.

In Japan, most of the corporate crises—such as the recall concealment case at MMC, the nuclear safety cover-up at Tokyo Electric Power Co., and the tainted milk scandal at Snow Brand Milk Products—were derived from cost-cutting activities. In other words, management decisions in all of these cases were focused on cost curve D. Now, owing to the response of the public and the government, it is socially required to put higher sanctions on cost-cutting activities that endanger consumers.

CHARACTERISTIC 7:
THE IMPACT OF AGENCY COSTS

Another characteristic of crisis-prone organizations in Japan has to do with agency costs. Agency costs are those that are made by the agents, or employees, of a company. There are various kinds of agency costs defined by many scholars, but the focus here is on x-inefficiency costs.[2] The definition of the x-inefficiency cost is the cost of reduced effort on the part of employees, especially in lower-level positions. There seems to be a tendency for them to reduce their work efforts and to fall into inertia, whether consciously or unconsciously. There is an important relationship between x-inefficiency costs and the occurrence of crisis situations. For example, with scheduled maintenance checks on aircraft equipment, if a worker does not work at full effort and cuts corners, the cost to the individual worker is reduced, but the possibility of a mechanical breakdown causing an aircraft accident increases.

The cumulative x-inefficiency cost can play an important role in organizations, but the tendency for an individual to reduce work effort declines as employees receive promotions and have more discretionary tasks.

While a higher level of employment means a lower likelihood of x-inefficiency costs, there is an increased agency cost of another kind at higher employment levels, called influence cost.

Influence cost relates to the inefficient distribution of management resources, caused by employees' self-interest and an organization's internal politics.[3] That is, when an employee becomes a senior manager in an organization, there is a tendency to use resources to preserve status and maintain power instead of to benefit the organization as a whole.

Influence costs can impact safety management. If, for example, a middle or senior manager is nearing the mandatory retirement age, and a situation arises in which an important but unpleasant decision must be made (such as the reporting of a design flaw or production mistake), there is a tendency for the employee to avoid such a report in order to maintain good employment status until retirement. Influence costs from within the organization can impact the effectiveness of the company's crisis management.

These agency costs tend to accumulate within the organization as it expands, especially in larger and more profitable organizations. But because agency costs are not directly identifiable, they are difficult to analyze. However, in some cases, the analysis of agency costs can be the key to understanding the underlying causes of a corporate crisis.

In the official report of the Tokyo Electric Power nuclear power plant case, an individual employee stated that he could not help but follow the way things were being done, although he felt that it was not right. The factory manager of Snow Brand Milk Products may have felt the same way. It was not worth it to expend the effort to do things differently. This is evidence of the x-inefficiency cost within the organization. The report also said that the employees felt a strong responsibility to process the electricity for scheduled uses rather than report the accident to the government,

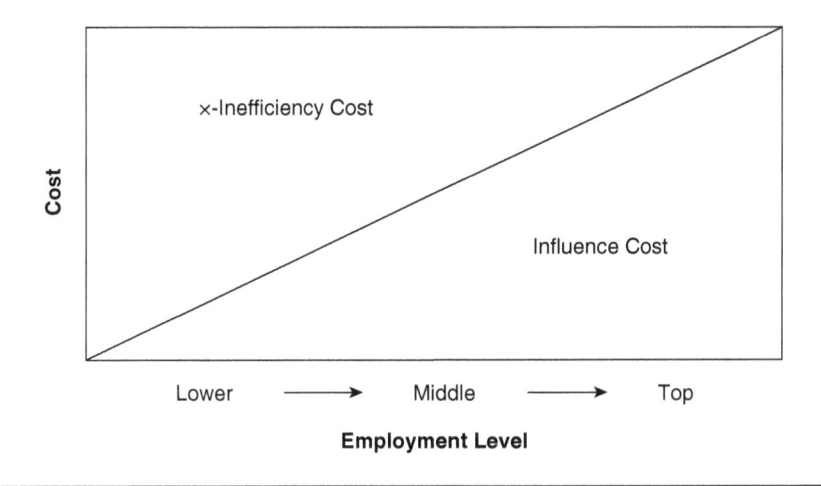

Figure 9.5   Agency Cost

which would result in inspections and the shutting down of the power plant. If there is a safety problem, the trouble should be reported to the local and central government authorities, and then reported to the top management of the Tokyo Electric Power. It was inevitable that there was the psychology to want to avoid reporting a problem for self-preservation reasons. This is evidence of the existence of the influence cost.

CHARACTERISTIC 8: POOR QUALITY-CONTROL DECISIONS

The last characteristic to be examined here is that of poor quality-control decisions within Japanese organizations. The six sigma technique, developed by U.S. Motorola, Inc. in the 1980s to improve the production process, was also implemented by manufacturers in Japan. Six sigma became famous after General Electric published the implementation of "the quality 2000 plan" on the basis of operation management techniques that had been developed by Motorola in 1996. It could also be said that six sigma originated from Motorola's research of Japanese quality-control management, but with a new focus to work with the top-down technique used in many U.S. companies. Six sigma addresses solutions to wasteful cost problems and the cost of poor quality (also known as "COPQ"), which reduces overall quality.

To begin with, there are two perspectives of concept of "quality" that need to be examined. The first is where the average quality level should be set for the product. The second is where the standard deviation of the product quality should be set for production. Both of these quality issues are related to costs, including the cost to discover defective products, the cost to sort out the defective products, the cost to repair the defective products, the cost to dispose of defective products, the cost to manufacture the defective products, the cost to collect the defective products that have been distributed to the market, the opportunity cost of sales lost, and the cost to recover the trust of the consumers.

But organizations tend to overlook the increased production cost by focusing on the higher average quality level, or by compressing the standard deviation of the product quality.

Costs for quality include the cost for the prevention of production errors and the cost for quality evaluation, both of which are discretionary costs of the company. Figure 9.6 shows that there is a trade-off between quality cost and failure cost, and the total cost curve is always U-shaped with a minimum point. This is important for the discussion of the traditional quality theory. 100% quality can be chosen as the goal of the quality level, but in most cases, the minimum total cost at the optimal quality level (shown by the dashed line in Figure 9.6) is chosen as the target.

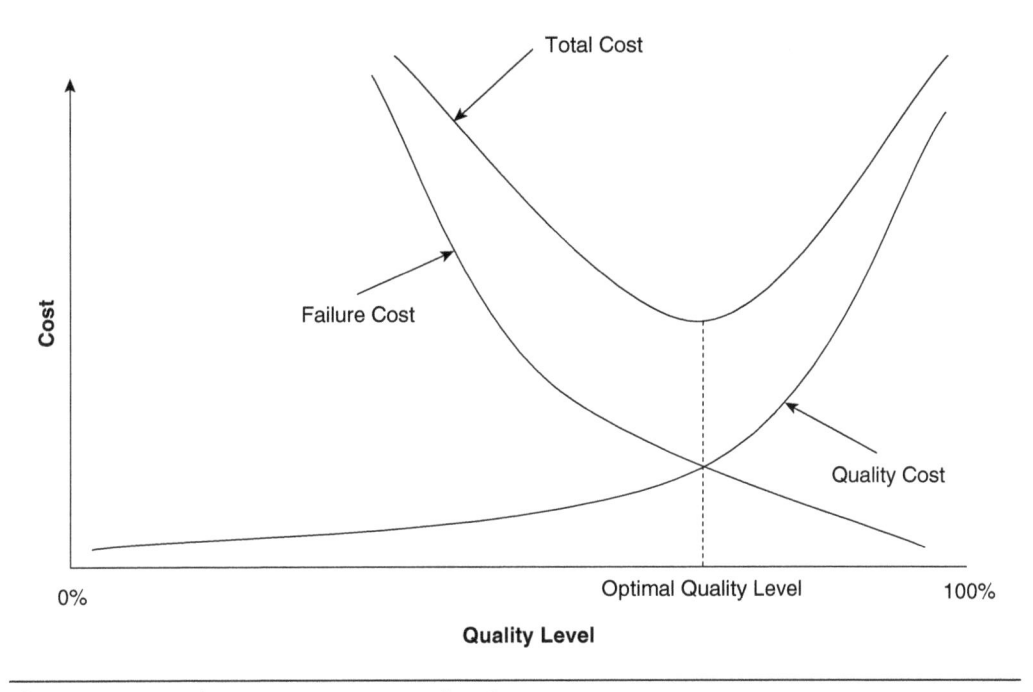

The Eight Characteristics of Japanese Crisis-Prone Organizations

Figure 9.6 Failure Cost Versus Quality Cost

On the other hand, the development of some ground-breaking new products, such as technology hardware and software, generate large profit margins, and it can be easier to upgrade product quality. The relationship between the total cost curve and the product specification range will be A in Figure 9.7. At that point, the quality improvement is always compatible with the profit increase.

But in the case of commodity products such as milk, the relationship between the total cost curve and the product specification range will tend to be range C in Figure 9.7. At that point, there is little room for quality improvement without either additional investment or disruptive innovation and reengineering of current processing.

If the total cost curve and the product specification range is located in A, the company will try to achieve A', which represents the highest quality level within range A. This position seems to occur frequently in innovative industries because new processes are open to cost improvements.

If the total cost curve and the product specification range is located in range B, the company will try to achieve B', which represents the company's most suitable economic operation point. This position seems to be normal and healthy because total cost can be minimized within regular operations.

If the total cost curve and the product specification range is located in range C, the company will try to achieve C', which represents the lowest

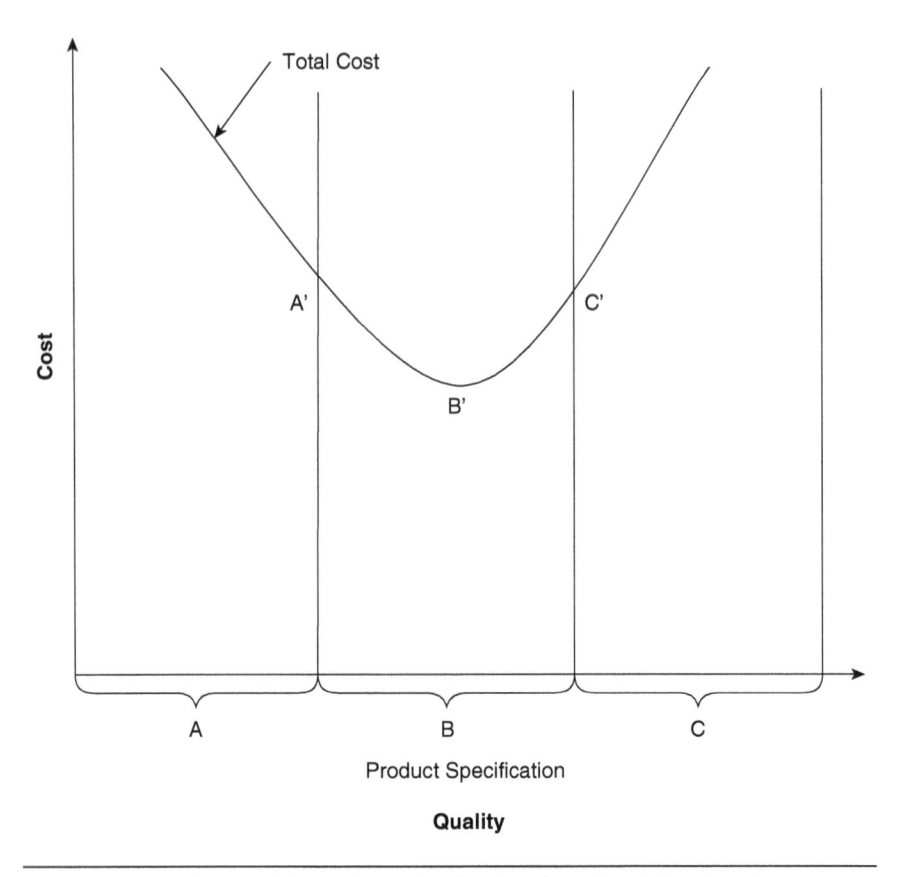

Figure 9.7 The Total Cost Curve in the Product Specification Ranges

quality within the C range of product specification. This position seems to occur frequently in commodity industries because there is little opportunity for cost improvement. The fact that commodity producers focus on the lowest possible quality level, however, can create an environment open to serious corporate crises.

As with Snow Brand Milk Products and the tainted milk due to improper product line sanitation, the crisis was caused by focusing on lower quality levels and giving priority to cost-cutting activities. This strategy, targeting quality levels at the lowest point to meet—but never exceed—authorized specifications, seems to have been adopted by the leading companies in oligopolistic industries.

Another example, Asahi Glass Co., Ltd., one of the biggest glass and chemical product manufacturers in Japan, produced a batch of sodium bicarbonate (baking soda) at the Kashima factory in 2004 that was contaminated with an alien substance. The substance was the scale of fluoric resin that was used for manufacturing machine parts. Asahi Glass received notification of the contamination from a pharmaceutical company that had the most rigid specifications for purchasing sodium bicarbonate. Asahi Glass decided to collect approximately 1,900 tons that had already been shipped to pharmaceutical and food-additive companies. While collecting the contaminated product was a wise decision, the original error was due to cost-cutting from focusing on the lower-quality strategy.

Under the Japanese management environment today, safety management is not always a primarily concern, especially for leading companies, since it can be regarded as a wasteful investment. If situations arise that expose a lack of safety management, those companies could encounter a real corporate crisis.

While quality control is an issue for consideration in crisis management, it is also a topic for consumer protection advocates. In fact, the International Organization for Standardization (ISO) created ISO 9000, a set of voluntary technical standards that companies can implement in production or services in order to earn the ISO certification. The ISO 9000 requires that an organization set technical standards by developing quality-control policies and following through with quality guidelines. The standards are expected to consider the consumer's point of view and should result in a constant high level of quality within the organization. Therefore, if an organization wants ISO 9000 certification, it must have systematic quality-control measures and internal policies that are compliant with the ISO standards. Since the late 1980s, most of the larger manufacturers in Japan have earned the ISO 9000 certification. It is surprising, then, that every company mentioned above had acquired the ISO 9000 certification before the time of its crisis. This shows that even when important systematic quality-control measures are in place and policies are made known to employees, they are only manually based certifications; poor management decisions can be made, and x-inefficiency and other agency costs can still be incurred. It is, in fact, the actual circumstances of the ISO 9000 implementation that are important.

Japan also has public policies regarding quality control and consumer protection. The product liability (PL) law was passed in Japan in 1995, and can hold companies responsible for damages incurred in any liability occurrences. This law serves as a reminder to Japanese crisis-prone organizations about the importance of high quality and quality improvement.

Conclusion

While it is helpful to evaluate these eight characteristics in the context of Japan's business culture, they could apply to organizations worldwide. While there are aspects of the Japanese culture that might contribute to the occurrence of crises in Japanese organizations, it is important to acknowledge that not only do similar phenomena occur elsewhere, but preventions can be accomplished in any economic culture. All cultures can learn from the examples here.

Notes

1. Mitsubishi Motor Company later transferred its large-sized vehicle operations to The Mitsubishi Fuso Track and Bus, Inc. in 2003; but for purposes of this article, "MMC" refers to the organization as it existed at the time of the incident.

2. H. Leibenstein explained that the members of an organization did not always show the maximum effort and defined the ×-inefficiency costs as those arising from the difference between the members' maximum effort and their actual effort.

3. Milgrom and Roberts defined the influence cost as the cost that relates to the inefficient distribution of the management resources that are caused by internal organizational politics.

Bibliography

Andriole, S. J. (1984). *Corporate crisis management.* Princeton, NJ: Petrocelli Books.

Christensen, C. M. (1997). *The innovator's dilemma.* Boston: Harvard Business School Press.

Dougherty, D. (1992). *Crisis communications.* New York: Walker and Company.

Leibenstein, H. (1978). *General X-efficiency and economic development.* London: Oxford University Press.

Milgrom, P., & Roberts, J. (1992). *Economics, organization & management.* Englewood Cliffs, NJ: Prentice Hall.

Nakane, C. (1967). *The human relationship in the vertical society.* Tokyo: Koudansha.

Pauchant, T. C., & Mitroff, I. I. (1992). *Transforming the crisis-prone organization.* San Francisco: Jossey-Bass.

Pearson, C. M., Harrington L. K., & Mitroff, I. I. (1996). *Managing corporate crises.* London: Oxford University Press.

Voices From the Terraces

10

From "Mock Bureaucracy" to "Learning From Crisis" Within the UK's Soccer Industry

Dominic Elliott and Denis Smith

On a warm Saturday in 1989, 96 people who went to watch a game of soccer lost their lives in a crowd-crushing accident at Sheffield's Hillsborough Soccer Stadium. It was the 45th such incident, involving fatalities or multiple injuries, to occur within a British soccer stadium during a 40-year period (see Elliott & Smith, 1993, 1997, 2006). While the issue of risk associated with "football" in the United Kingdom (UK) has had something of a checkered history, notably around crowd violence, there was a general assumption that it was relatively safe as a spectator sport. This "crisis" highlighted the apparent vulnerability of crowds within soccer stadiums and pointed to the limitations of those who were responsible for the management of such events. The fact that there had been eight previous official investigations into the causes of systemically similar disasters suggested that there may well have been a set of deep-seated problems within the management of this industry. What is apparent from a review of these various (and varied) accidents is that there seemed either to be a fundamental problem associated with the ways in which the sport was run in the UK, or that there were considerable design flaws in the physical fabric of those stadiums that were used to host the sport. It was also clear that many of the accidents displayed common elements (Elliott & Smith, 1993) and that these might also have been problems that were more generic within the industry sector. Add to this the fact that the football industry involves collaboration between a number of organizations, each with different cultures and operating processes and procedures, and brings together many thousands of people into a confined space at designated points in time, and it is clear that there is a complex mosaic of elements that could interact together to create a potential for harm.

Our aim in this chapter is to explore the nature of these accidents and also to explore the barriers to organizational learning within the UK's soccer industry. Of importance here are the fundamental questions: Why did history seem to repeat itself so often? And what were the barriers that obviously existed to making this industry safer, especially given the number of formal inquiries into the earlier accidents, and how could these be overcome? We argue that by seeking to highlight and understand the nature of these barriers, organizations can attempt to strengthen their defenses and, potentially, prevent incidents from escalating into accidents. Our discussions around these issues are informed by a perspective that focuses on organizational learning from crisis, which is utilized to better understand why such "pathways of vulnerability" (Smith, 2000b) persist despite their identification.

Given the millions of global spectators attending soccer matches each year, it is not seen as a particularly hazardous activity. Comparing the risks of attending a sports stadium with other forms of activity with more obvious hazards makes the scale and frequency of fatalities within the UK seem, at the very least, peculiar. A culture of complacency within the industry may have emerged, leading to the creation of many of the preconditions of the subsequent crises. In addition, those problems that were perceived as requiring action were often attributed to hooliganism—an issue so embedded within the sport in the UK that it was termed the "English disease." As a result much of the attention of policy-makers and "managers" has been focused on the strategies for dealing with hooliganism and this may have created many of the conditions that allowed subsequent incidents to escalate into crises (see Elliott & Smith, 2006). In order to examine these issues in more detail it is first necessary to set out the theoretical background.

Theoretical Background

In terms of its theoretical roots, this chapter draws upon the developing organizational learning literature and Gouldner's (1954) work on "patterns of industrial bureaucracy" (a study that has been too widely neglected within the literature). By bringing these theoretical perspectives together, it is hoped to show how policy responses over time have contributed to the creation of barriers to learning and the "incubation" (Turner, 1976, 1978) of crisis potential. For Turner (1976, 1978), direct experience of a catastrophic event provided the motivation for cultural readjustment, or in other words, the translation of new beliefs about the world into new operating norms. The fact that an accident had occurred should provide managers with an indication that the dominant views around controls were somewhat flawed. However, it is clear from a number of industrial sectors that there are often several reasons why such cultural readjustment is not necessary. Managers seem to find it difficult to accept that their organizations are as vulnerable as those that have experienced a crisis—after all, they believe that they work in well-managed organizations!

There are close parallels between Turner's notion of cultural readjustment and a number of the subsequent definitions of organizational learning. These invariably share the view that learning may be equated with the translation of knowledge into different patterns of behavior (see, for example, Argyris, 1991, 1994; Garvin, 1993; Levitt & March, 1988; Nonaka, 1991; Senge, 1990; Toft & Reynolds, 1997), and this behavioral change process is clearly linked to Turner's notion of cultural readjustment. Although knowledge acquisition is a consistent element within many definitions of learning, it does form only one part of the learning process. There are a number of distinct phases in organizational learning from crisis, including knowledge acquisition, dissemination, and transfer, and its absorption into new operating practices. (See, for example, Garvin, 1993; Levitt & March, 1988; Nonaka, 1991; Senge, 1990; Toft & Reynolds, 1997). In addition, knowledge can also be categorized in a number of ways.

Nonaka (1991), for example, distinguishes between tacit and explicit forms of knowledge. Tacit knowledge is personal and difficult to formalize, while explicit knowledge is formal and "easily" communicated. Nonaka (1991) uses the example of a craftsman to highlight the nature of tacit knowledge. Knowledge and skill develop during a long apprenticeship served working alongside a master craftsman. Such knowledge cannot be made explicit easily; that is, it cannot be readily transferred to others in the way that the logic of a computer program might be demonstrated. Senge (1990) made a similar distinction when he argued that the term "learning" had lost its central meaning, stating that it had become synonymous with absorbing facts. Learning, argued Senge, should also involve "a fundamental shift or movement of mind" that flows into changed behavior. The manner in which knowledge is coded prior to dissemination is also an important element of the process. In some cases, the expression of information in technical language can prove to be a major barrier to the dissemination of the underlying "knowledge" to nonexpert groups (see, for example, Smith, 1990b).

In the case of the soccer industry the primary means of knowledge acquisition around crises was undertaken via the public inquiry process. Clearly, such a process brings with it several major problems around dissemination, the codified nature of the "information," and the sense of the problem being "located elsewhere" (and therefore not relevant to other organizations). In addition, there are problems surrounding the investigative aspects of the inquiry process itself, and the outcomes of any investigation, not least among them the public inquiry, will be determined by a range of factors. First, the skill set and disposition of the inquirers will play a key role. For example, McClean and Johnes (2000) suggested that a particular academic was appointed assessor to the Court of Inquiry, following the sinking of the *Titanic*, because his views favored the Board of Trade. The utilization of power and influence (both directly and through the use of technical expertise) is also a major factor in determining the "neutrality" of the inquiry process (see Collingridge & Reeve, 1985; Smith, 1990b; Smith & Sipika, 1993). While setting the scope and scale of an investigation will determine clear boundaries and may have a major impact upon findings, there is always room for powerful groups to lobby government agencies to restrict the terms of reference for any inquiry, especially where the boundaries of the issues are somewhat blurred (see, for example, Elliott & McGuinness, 2002; Elliott & Smith, 1993; Smith, 1990b; Toft & Reynolds, 1997). Hutter (1992), for example, reported that there was some controversy regarding the scope of the inquiries regarding a series of railway accidents. Although the immediate circumstances of the accidents were investigated, other key issues—including the wider organizational, political, social, and economic contexts of the railway industry—were ignored, as was government policy toward the railway industry (Hutter, 1992, p. 188). Indeed, Woolfson (1999) argued for an extension of Cullen's terms of reference for the public inquiry following the Paddington train crash:

> Let us hope that the impact of cost-cutting pressures accompanying privatization on the effectiveness of the regulatory regime is subject to proper scrutiny. If so, then the results of the Paddington inquiry may have wider, beneficial results for safety. (p. 23)

Within the UK, the system of "public inquiry" has been criticized for its tendency to apportion blame (see, for example, Peay, 1996), an observation reinforced in other studies of crisis (see, for example, Elliott & Smith, 1997; McClean & Johnes, 2000; Smith, 1990a; Smith & Sipika, 1993). If we add to this critique the difficulties in problem recognition, structuring, and information handling, it is clear that the process of knowledge acquisition may be fundamentally flawed (see Perrow, 1999; Turner, 1976).

The role of decoy phenomena may also play a role in shaping the processes of learning around crises. Within the UK soccer industry there was, historically, a demonstrable focus upon hooliganism—despite evidence that its significance was dramatically exaggerated (see, for example, Elliott et al., 1997). The inquiry into the Bradford Fire provides an illustration of this, as Justice Popplewell (1986) felt able to conclude his report into the causes of the fire (in which 56 people were burned to death): "I do not pretend that my Report can be all embracing or provide a simple solution to a complex problem. There is no panacea. There is no one solution to violence" (p. 61).

These concluding remarks are all the more peculiar as there was never any suggestion that hooliganism played any part in the disaster. The Bradford Fire occurred close to other major loss-of-life events where the behavior of fans had been called into question, and this may in some way provide insight into the comments by Lord Justice Popplewell. It did seem that Government and its nominees had already decided what was to be done to address the problems in "football"—a view reinforced by the observation that new legislation was introduced prior to Popplewell's report being completed (Elliott & McGuinness, 2002; Elliott & Smith, 1993).

With regard to the issue of knowledge transfer and dissemination, Elliott and McGuinness (2002) have demonstrated that the patterns of regulation that are introduced following a public inquiry will play a key role in shaping the process. The view has often been expressed that the only way to change behavior is to introduce legislation that highlights the need to change. While there are a number of arguments that can be made against such a view, it is clear that by failing to address the "behaviors" through the tightening of rules it leaves organizations with sufficient latitude to avoid changing their own behaviors by claiming that "if government wanted behaviors to change, they would have legislated for it!" There is also the question of the degree of the receptiveness of any organization within an institutional field to "institutionalize" newly acquired knowledge into new forms of practice (see, for example, Elliott & Smith, 2006).

Finally, with regard to the processes by which organizations absorb newly acquired knowledge and translate it into new operating practices, Elliott and Smith (in press), in a more comprehensive study of crisis and organizational learning, have identified a range of barriers to organizational learning from crisis (see Table 10.1). These barriers to learning include the rigidity of core beliefs, values, and assumptions; ineffective communication; peripheral inquiry and decoy phenomena; cognitive narrowing; maladaptation and threat reduction; and a focus upon single-loop learning and a lack of corporate social responsibility (see Smith & Elliott, in press; Smith, 2001). For the purposes of our discussion here, we would like to highlight one aspect of this complex process that has not had the attention it deserves, namely Gouldner's notion of a "mock bureaucracy." The next part of this chapter is concerned with utilizing Gouldner's (1954) concepts as a lens through which to examine the UK soccer industry.

In his initial research, Gouldner (1954) examined different patterns of safety practices within a gypsum mine. Gouldner was especially concerned with internal compliance with organizational rules. For example, despite the presence of "cues" such as posters and inspections, most employees in Gouldner's study failed, initially, to comply with the "no smoking" rules.

Table 10.1 Barriers to Organizational Learning From Crisis

Barrier to Learning	Source		Soccer Industry Case
Rigidity of core beliefs, values, and assumptions	Argyris & Schön, 1974, 1978; Kets de Vries & Miller, 1984; Miller, 1990; Pauchant & Mitroff, 1988, 1992; Turner, 1976, 1978	Denial is powerful barrier to learning through the creation of deeply held values and assumptions that create problems of sensemaking when things appear to be "not as expected."	Focus upon crowd control over safety with belief that hooliganism is the prime concern (Elliott & Smith, 2006) "Rosy memories" of well behaved crowds (Elliott & Smith, 1997) It couldn't happen here mentality (Taylor, 1989; Elliott, 1998)
Ineffective communication and information difficulties	Argyris, 1999; Barton, 1993; Smart & Vertinsky, 1977; Smith, 1990b, Toft & Reynolds, 1992; Turner, 1976, 1978	Communications may become distorted through making issues "undiscussable," through cultural and self-censorship means as articulated by Argyris (1999) or by conducting any discourse in the technical language of experts (Smith, 1990b). Information difficulties may include, for example, "noise," overload, "groupthink," and "bounded rationality."	Reluctance of football clubs to participate in representative forms of regulation and in earlier inquiries (Elliott & Smith, 1993, 2006; Shortt, 1924) Clubs ignore official warnings prior to both the Ibrox and Bradford disasters (Inglis, 1987; Popplewell, 1985, 1986; Wheatley, 1972)
Centrality of expertise, and the disregard of outsiders	Senge, 1990; Smith, 1990b, 1995; Turner, 1976, 1978	Early development of core beliefs and values, will lead to the use of evidence (often scientific) to support the core paradigm. Those outside of the organization do not have the power, or	Use of technical advisers on public inquiries (Elliott & McGuinness, 2002) Exclusion of spectators from decision making bodies (Elliott & Smith, 2006)

Barrier to Learning	Source		Soccer Industry Case
		resources, to challenge that dominant view and science is often used as a barrier to entry into the discourse.	
Peripheral inquiry and decoy phenomenon	Schön, 1983; Turner, 1976, 1978	Organizations, and individuals, may prioritize actions to deal with well defined problems to the detriment of those that are ill structured.	Response to disasters focused upon technical issues to detriment of human and organizational failures (Canter, 1989; Elliott & Smith, 1993, 1997)
Cognitive narrowing and fixation (reductionist)	Senge, 1990; Starbuck & Milliken, 1988; Weick, 1988, 1993, 1995	Reductionist approaches tend to focus upon "manageable chunks" of a problem.	The piecemeal development of the Hillsborough stadium created a death trap. Until the disaster occurred no one considered viewing the construction holistically (Elliott & Smith, 1993)
Maladaptation, threat minimization, and environmental shifts	Smith, 1995; Toft & Reynolds, 1992; Turner, 1976, 1978	An emergent property of rigid core beliefs and ineffective communication is the reduction of risk through threat minimization (in which temporal and spatial factors are used to deny the existence of worst case scenarios) or the concerns are dismissed because of the person who raised the concerns.	Low perceived odds of disaster (Elliott & Smith, 2006)

(Continued)

Table 10.1 (Continued)

Barrier to Learning	Source		Soccer Industry Case
Lack of corporate responsibility	Smith, 1999b; Smith & Tombs, 1995	The social responsibility argument is a powerful one in that it is used to surface the constraints around rigid core beliefs. General problems around ethical behavior are important in shaping the climate in which risk taking is contextualized.	Deliberate avoidance of regulation (Elliott & Smith, 1997; Popplewell, 1985, 1986)
Focus on single-loop learning	Argyris & Schön, 1978; Ashby, 1940; Schön, 1983; Toft & Reynolds, 1992	The reluctance to challenge the manner in which organizations learn (and frame that learning) is a key barrier to dealing with the incubation of crisis potential within organizations.	The persistence of the soccer industry's concerns with hooliganism reflected in ongoing government investment in hooligan-focused research and heavy-handed policing of soccer events in 2005–2006

This open noncompliance with the established rules was described as "mock bureaucracy" by Gouldner, who argued that these develop when rules are held to possess little value and breaking them brings no harm or punishment to the rule-breaker. Thus, the rules can be seen to possess little or no legitimacy. The issues of rules and rule compliance were also matters that Turner (1976, 1978) highlighted in his own early research to indicate how organizations might incubate the potential for crisis. Gouldner also identified an indulgency pattern (in which no rules existed) and a punishment-centered pattern (which emerges when only one group, management or employees, views rules as legitimate). In this latter case, either party would seek to force compliance from the other through the use of punitive measures. Gouldner argued that each of these patterns could play a major role in generating problems for the organization. In Gouldner's case study, management's enforcement of a no-smoking policy underground became more stringent as a response to rising insurance premiums. Disciplinary measures imposed by the management sought to secure employee adherence to the policy. A final pattern was described as "representative" in which safety rules were both enforced and adhered to on the basis of a consensus that everyone benefited. For employees, legitimacy was linked to real concerns about personal injury and, potentially, inadequate compensation. For managers, accidents interrupted the efficient flow of production and could increase insurance premiums.

Gouldner's (1954) work suggested that the means by which regulations are introduced and enforced will determine, in large part, the responses of managers and workers. Although Gouldner was concerned with one organization, he recognized the institutional context through his identification of the interplay with other stakeholders, such as the mine's insurers. In a study of the Westray mining disaster, Hynes and Prasad (1997), drawing from Gouldner, questioned the focus of public inquiries upon tightening safety regulations without fully understanding the institutional and social context in which organizational decisions are taken. They argued that "formal rules are clearly subordinate to workplace norms and ideologies" (p. 619) and that changing these is no easy task. These issues are important within the context of our present discussion, and the chapter will now move on to consider a number of crises within the UK's football industry from the perspective of Gouldner's work.

Elements of a Crisis Within Soccer

A number of observers have commented on the similarity between many of the crises within soccer in the UK. For example, Scraton (1999) observed that a description of the Bolton Stadium disaster of 1946 could easily be confused with a portrayal of the Hillsborough disaster of 1989, so closely did the latter mirror the former. In both cases too many spectators were permitted to access a tightly constricted area. In both cases police and officials failed to recognize the significance of a build-up of people within these areas. In both cases, police and officials were reluctant to open exit gates and permit escape because they believed that their primary role was to maintain law and order. The police, in both events, were convinced that the problem was one of crowd (mis)behavior. In both cases the police and officials reacted slowly, as they seemed unable to comprehend the severity of the emerging situation. Given the common ground that seems to exist between the two events, then one would be forgiven for expecting that the inquiries into such accidents would generate lessons that would allow organizations to strengthen the defenses in place to prevent the recurrence of such accidents. Indeed, this was without doubt the principal aim of those carrying out the inquiries. The Moelwyn-Hughes report (1946) made recommendations that were aimed at ensuring that there could be no repeat of such a disaster. Perhaps the key to understanding why such an important aim failed to materialize can be found in the manner in which the various recommendations were interpreted and implemented.

In this case, a voluntary licensing scheme was introduced to improve the safety of grounds—a system of self-regulation that was largely ignored and rarely enforced by those who managed grounds and enforced "regulation." Indeed, such was the weakness of the regulatory framework that it might best be described as a "mock bureaucracy" (Elliott & Smith, 1997, 2006; Gouldner, 1954), a situation in which the veneer of regulation and control could be seen to overlie a vulnerable framework of culture, complacency, and complicity that ensured the repetition of a similar accident pathology. The extent of the problem can be encapsulated in Scraton's (1999) observation: "Outside Bolton, one of the most significant lessons in football's history was laid to rest alongside those who died" (p. 19).

Unfortunately, the aftermath of the Bolton accident was to be replicated in other accidents. Following a series of fatal accidents, Lord Justice Taylor's (1989) opening statement at the Hillsborough Inquiry stated, "After eight previous reports... it seemed astounding that 95 people could die from overcrowding before the very eyes of those controlling the event."

Taylor (1989) seemed to believe that the knowledge necessary to prevent the Hillsborough disaster had been published in an inquiry report some 43 years previously. The recurrence of so many incidents within the industry, including the virtual replication of the Bolton disaster and the persistence of a mock bureaucracy, challenge the assumption implicit within Turner's (1976, 1978) work that cultural readjustment would occur. The many incidents identified by Elliott and Smith (1997) indicated that there was an ongoing "mindset of vulnerability" (Wicks, 2001) within the industry. This is illustrated by reference to the history of soccer disasters in the UK, which have been the scene of at least 45 incidents involving multiple casualties or fatalities since 1945 (see Table 10.1).

The scale and occurrence of these incidents suggest a particular problem for the safe management of crowds in UK soccer stadiums. Until recently the issue of managing crowds, as opposed to managing hooligans, has received low priority. In support of this argument, Inglis (1987) commented,

> A century ago clubs did virtually nothing to protect spectators. Thousands were packed onto badly constructed slopes with hardly a wooden barrier in sight. About the best that can be said of the early grounds is that with only ropes around the pitches there was little to stop a build up of pressure sending hundreds pouring onto the pitch. (p. 28)

A brief history of the UK soccer industry indicates that many crisis incidents have taken place and that there have been many public inquiries that have aimed at learning lessons from those accidents. For example, the Shortt (1924) report, commissioned in response to more than a thousand injured spectators during the 1923 Wembley Cup Final, concluded,

Where then, a measure of self government has been developed, it would seem a pity that, without real need, it should be destroyed for the sake of concentrating in the present system of national and local government the immediate administration of regulations affecting sports grounds... We are assured that these governing bodies are only too anxious to secure that their sport is carried on under conditions which will promote public safety, and we feel at this stage that it is safe to leave the matter to them. (p. 27)

The final sentence is remarkable given the failure of the governing bodies to cooperate with Shortt's committee. Some 20 years later, the Moelwyn-Hughes report (1946), concerning the Bolton stadium disaster, concluded, in contrast to Shortt,

The preceding safety measures cannot be secured without legislation.... Compliance with the recommendations of this report will cost money. They will involve grounds in a loss of gate money on popular days. Human beings will not station themselves scientifically on a terraced enclosure; among the crowd there will be thin patches and gaps to grieve the sight of club directors and secretaries. The insurance for greater safety for the public demands a premium. (pp. 11–12)

However, their recommendations were not always listened to. Moelwyn-Hughes, for example, concluded with the ominous warning,

The helpful representative of the Football Association... feared that the disaster at Bolton might easily be repeated at 20 or 30 other grounds and would welcome such measures as I have suggested for securing a safety capacity. (p. 12)

Despite Moelwyn-Hughes's recommendation for legislation, a voluntary licensing system for grounds with a capacity of 10,000 or more was introduced. Thus, the lessons learned between the 1923 and 1946 accidents were lost as the dominant strategy employed by the regulators, despite rhetoric to the contrary, was one of self-regulation.

Mock Bureaucracy and the Management of Risk

The manner in which organizations and regulatory authorities respond to catastrophic events has been the subject of discussion within the literature and remains a major policy problem (Smith, 2002; Smith & Tombs, 1995). In order to develop a discussion around this process, it is possible to use Gouldner's (1954) label of a "mock bureaucracy" to describe an extremely lax process of enforcement and a failure to comply with the rules that are set in place. There are some specific issues that relate to the process of soccer regulation. First is the lack of data regarding near-misses and the smaller number of incidents involving multiple injuries and deaths. Government interest in soccer was primarily concerned with its finances and the growing media interest in soccer hooliganism. Such a "distraction" from the main issue of ground safety was a major factor in shifting the focus of concern. For example, Chester's (1968) report examined the organization and finances of the soccer industry. Its main observation concerning crowds was to note an increase in spectator disorder; this is an early example of "hooliganism" deflecting attention from issues of crowd safety. In fact, the problem of spectator disorder was an issue deemed sufficiently serious to require its own investigation, undertaken by Harrington (1968), who reported:

> The absence of national legislation outlining minimum standards of safety and amenity at football grounds means that some club managements do not feel obliged to put their grounds into a state considered by the police to be necessary for crowd control.... Clubs often seem keener to spend money on the purchase of players than to undertake any major spending on ground improvement which would increase safety and make hooligan control easier.... Letters from members of the public suggest that already some are staying away because of their dislike of poor facilities ... so that the neglect of ground improvement may ultimately be self defeating. (pp. 33–34)

Harrington's (1968) observations indicated the continued existence of laxity in which guidelines were frequently ignored and club executives demonstrated relaxed attitudes toward safety.

The following year, Lang (1969) also recommended a voluntary licensing system overseen through the sport's governing bodies, ignoring Moelwyn-Hughes's (1946) earlier call for legislation. The Lang report (1969) may be seen as a further endorsement of the well-established mock bureaucracy, and there was a general tendency toward minimum regulation (a process that was to reemerge in the 1980s with the onset of a forceful policy of deregulation). Clearly, there is invariably a difficult policy line to follow in encouraging organizations to conform to best practice and to work within a highly regulated (and some might argue, stifling) environment. However, as has been common throughout the history of risk-related policy, it was to take another disaster to lead to legislation.

In 1971, 66 people died on the Ibrox Stadium's stairway 13, the site of three major incidents involving death and multiple injuries in the preceding 10 years. One explanation of the disaster was provided by Canter (1989):

When spectators who had started to leave early from a new year local derby match turned back at the sound of cheering from the stands. In the crush which resulted between those leaving and those returning, 66 people died and 140 were injured. Steel barriers were bent in the crush, which suggests that a force of at least 4,450 newtons was exerted at that point. (p. 89)

The subsequent inquiry (Wheatley, 1972) found the Ranger's management complacent in its attitude toward previous problems and official warnings. Despite the number of deaths, there was limited coverage of the disaster in the national (British) press, reflecting a low degree of public interest and indicating that, like the Bolton disaster (which was also investigated via the public inquiry process), the Ibrox tragedy did not have a major symbolic resonance. The Wheatley report led to the passing of the 1975 Safety at Sports Ground Act, although this was implemented in a halfhearted way that encouraged the continuation of a lax regulatory regime (Elliott et al., 1997). The Ibrox stadium disaster highlighted the inadequacies of the voluntary licensing scheme. That four serious incidents could happen upon the same stairway within a 10-year period indicated that a problem had been clearly identified but that no effective learning had taken place. This was not to be the only catastrophic event for which the lack of learning was to prove a major factor.

Lord Justice Taylor noted (1989) in the wake of the Hillsborough disaster, "Despite all the accumulated wisdom of so many previous reports and guidelines [that Hillsborough was allowed to happen] must indicate that the lessons of past disasters and the recommendations following them had not been taken sufficiently to heart" (p. 4).

In 1985, 56 people died when part of the Bradford Stadium was destroyed by fire. Correspondence between Bradford AFC and the Health and Safety Executive (HSE) and the local authority indicated that the potential fire hazard had been identified for some time. For example, Popplewell (1985) reported the following warning:

1. Main Grandstand
    (a) The unusual construction of this stand makes an appraisal of structural adequacy desirable.
    (b) The timber construction is a fire hazard, and in particular, there is a build up of combustible materials in the voids beneath the seats. A carelessly discarded cigarette could give rise to a fire risk. (p. 20)

Once the fire broke out, on the day of the disaster, the efforts made to respond to the demands of the event were impeded for several reasons.

First, fire extinguishers had been removed due to fears of them being misused by hooligans. Second, the exits had been locked to prevent spectators getting in without paying. Both of these factors might have made a difference to the number of fatalities that were incurred, but they did point to a wider set of issues relating to the culture of football clubs. This was reinforced less than 3 weeks later when a further disaster at the Heysel Stadium, Belgium, resulted in 33 deaths. Despite the contribution of inadequate incident management and the poor structure of the ground, hooligan behavior played a key role as a direct cause of the deaths (Elliott & Smith, 1993).

The consequences of these crises were considerable. Twenty-seven grounds were closed immediately because they failed to comply with regulations, an indicator of the laxity of the preceding period, and there was considerable media questioning about the nature of the problem within football. The publication of the inquiry documents saw recommendations being made that echoed those of Wheatley, although public funds were provided for the introduction of CCTV to help monitor hooligan behavior. Other legislation included the Public Order Act (1984) and the Football Spectator's Act (1989) highlighting the continuing focus upon hooligan behavior (Elliott et al., 1997).

Four years after the Bradford Fire, another 96 people died at the Hillsborough Stadium in Sheffield. Early reaction to the disaster gave Taylor's (1989, 1990) subsequent recommendations the status of criminal law. The speedy implementation of changes in planning, responsibilities, and structures required considerable energy from soccer clubs, local government, and the police (see Elliott & Smith, 1993, 2006). This chronological account highlights the persistent failure of organizational learning in the face of a series of crisis events. We now turn to reflect upon why organizational learning was persistently deficient within the industry.

Organizational Learning and the Crisis of Legitimation

There have been several observations that postcrisis learning generates problems owing to the need for organizations to resecure their legitimacy in the wake of major catastrophes. The postevent "crisis of legitimation" (Smith, 1990a, 1995; Smith & Sipika, 1993) has the potential to generate a second-order crisis for an organization and, to an extent, those who regulate the industry in which they operate. However, despite the significance of this phase, there would appear to be several major barriers to learning within this phase of a crisis (Smith & Elliott, in press) and there are also problems associated with interorganizational learning, as many managers may believe that the problems that generated the crisis would not apply to their organizations. It has been argued elsewhere that there is little evidence of any cultural readjustment taking place in this period within the football industry (Elliott et al., 1997) and this issue needs to be explored in more detail.

One key issue of importance surrounds the remarkable degree of similarity in terms of the response of regulators to the various stadiums disasters. In the initial postcrisis phase, legislative controls were developed to deal with the demands of a particular incident, reflecting the tendency for learning to be constrained to incident-specific lessons (Toft & Reynolds, 1992); there was also a focus upon technical solutions (Canter et al., 1989; Elliott & Smith, 1993; Turner, 1976, 1978) leading to the development of a piecemeal framework of control. John De Quidt, chief executive of the FLA, reported, "All football legislation might be described as tombstone legislation, driven by emotion, hurried, things overlooked, the end result is that we finished with legislation that is flawed" (private communication, 1997).

More fundamental problems associated with managing crowds within "complex space" were not addressed in any holistic way. For example, the Moelwyn-Hughes report (1946) recommended that the maximum capacities for grounds be determined and enforced. "The Guide to Safety at Sports Grounds" (or Green Guide) was published as a response to the Ibrox disaster as an attempt to provide guidelines to clubs on ground safety, paying particular attention to the problems of crowd egress from grounds that had triggered the tragedy. The Popplewell report (1985) sought to control the sale and consumption of alcohol in and around soccer grounds. In the wake of the Bradford fire, specific recommendations concerning the maintenance and construction of grounds were put forward. In 1969, the *Fire Prevention Association Journal* had published recommendations following a series of "near misses" in which fires had broken out in soccer stadiums. These recommendations were not acted upon until Popplewell's inquiry some 17 years later, an example used by Toft and Reynolds (1992) as "the failure of hindsight." That is, the knowledge had been collected and disseminated through "appropriate" channels, but it was not acted upon. Finally, the Taylor report (1989) made specific recommendations about the control of crowds and the use of wire cages to prevent pitch invasions.

This fragmented approach brings particular problems as Canter et al. (1989) argued,

> As a consequence there is never any possibility of examining the system of legislation as a whole, of seeing the directions in which it is accumulating or of developing radical solutions that will deal with fundamental problems. A further problem is that rules and principles get built into the legislation in the early years and provided it cannot be demonstrated that somebody has been injured because of these rules, there is a powerful inertia in the system of controls operating against changing the rules. (p. 92)

Canter et al.'s argument is that once the problem of crowd safety and control is seen as a technical question (for example, determined by barrier strengths, the width of passageways) the mindset becomes one that seeks only technical solutions. In essence, a technical paradigm is created, one that then becomes impossible to shift. This culture of technocracy is important in luring organizations into a false sense of security.

Even as late as 2006, the FLA continues to warn of creeping complacency on the part of clubs and identified that over an 18-month period, some 13 clubs (out of 94) had received prohibition notices because they had failed to respond to identified problems with stewarding. Also noted in the FLA annual report (2005) were examples of clubs that for one reason or another were temporarily exempted from regulation, and reverted to significantly bad practices in the absence of enforcement.

ORGANIZATIONAL LEARNING AND THE UK SOCCER INDUSTRY

Drawing on our earlier discussion, it may be seen that the dissemination of knowledge, within the organizational learning from crisis process, has taken many forms. Within the soccer industry the many official reports were one key means. Another means concerned patterns of regulation. Elliott and Smith (2006), echoing Gouldner (1954), argued that patterns of regulation play an important role in the knowledge-dissemination process. Their findings suggested that more participative styles of regulation encourage greater cultural readjustment. Alternatively, a punitive approach to regulation may achieve rigid compliance, but no more than this (Elliott, 1998; Elliott & Smith, 2006). This has particular implications for learning from crisis as it emphasizes the importance of the broader institutional context in which cultural readjustment may occur (see, for example, Elliott & Smith, 2006; Wicks, 2001). Learning from crisis results from the interaction of the norms, values, and objectives of the stakeholders within an industry. This has an important practical implication for policy-makers and legislators regarding the role of the public inquiry.

Organizational Interpretation: Barriers to Learning From Crisis

Smith (2001) has suggested a number of barriers to learning, as summarized in Table 10.1. Although it is not argued that there is any form of hierarchy for these barriers, a case can be made that many of the barriers listed are consequences of rigid core beliefs and ineffective communications.

The key role of core beliefs in predisposing organizations toward or away from crisis has been developed in many earlier studies (see, for example, Pauchant & Mitroff, 1988, 1992). Pauchant and Mitroff's four-layer "onion" model of crisis management, drawing on Schein (1985), distinguishes between the plans and strategies formulated by organizations and the individual and collective beliefs and assumptions that drive them. Although they depict an unusually symmetrical onion, they emphasize the messy nature of the reality that they seek to model. Each of the layers, they argued, influences the others (echoing Chandler's strategy or structure first). Communication, effective or otherwise, is one vehicle by which this interplay between the different layers is achieved. Unsurprisingly, the barriers outlined in Table 10.1 are also closely connected.

Drawing from Turner (1978), rigidities in beliefs lead to misunderstandings because of erroneous assumptions and the distractions offered by decoy phenomena. For example, in the case of the UK soccer industry, the ongoing focus upon hooliganism and crowd control ensured that limited time, resources, and mental energy were invested in crowd safety. Thus hooliganism distracted managerial attention away from the more fundamental problems of ground safety and design. Although stewards increasingly received training in safety, prior to 1995 they were largely used to control crowds (Elliott & Smith, 1997), reflecting the deeply held view that hooliganism remained the principal problem.

Ineffective communications and difficulties in information handling may arise from a number of causes. A first issue is that the availability of information will help or hinder the identification of vulnerabilities. Within the soccer industry, prior to 1989, vulnerabilities were seen as technical. The limited data collected regarding the potential failures were technical in nature, ensuring that there was no opportunity for identifying the social dimension of any vulnerability (Elliott, 1998). A second key issue is that even where there is considerable communication between organizations and their stakeholders, the language of the discourse may be too technical for nonexperts. This may result in the exclusion of some stakeholders, especially those with fewer resources, from relevant discussions (see, for example, Smith, 1990a, 1990b). Indeed, "legitimized" expertise may be used to prevent some outside groups from entering into debates on risk and hazard (Smith, 1990b). A further complication thwarting good communications is the diversity of stakeholder objectives. Following the Hillsborough Disasters, official police policy was to withdraw from their previously leading role in managing match-day operations. Elliott (1998) reports that a key to this strategy was a desire for the police service to avoid the possibility of being blamed for future incidents. The desire for blame avoidance permeated all discussion between the police, local authority regulators, and soccer clubs.

Another major group of barriers centers on the tendency to give only scant attention to the lessons of accidents from other organizations or near-miss events. Elliott (1998) reported a lack of awareness about the scale of the poor crowd-safety problem within the soccer industry. This lack of attention could be a result of decoys distracting managers from core issues (Turner, 1976, 1978), or the process of threat minimization and maladaptation (Senge, 1990; Smith, 1995; Toft & Reynolds, 1992). The distraction offered by hooliganism to lure attention away from the problem of crowd safety has been raised already. Close parallels with the *Titanic* may be drawn here. The core belief that the ship was unsinkable created a context in which investing less in safety appeared to make sense. The process of threat minimization may be seen in the following typical response from executives within the soccer industry:

> I suppose that when you assess the odds then it won't happen, you know the number of disasters when you consider the number of football matches, its one of the safest past times isn't it, it really is low, low odds. (Elliott, 1998, p. 275)

These pressures continue, as is evident from the following extract of the FLA's annual report (2005), which identified a reduction in injuries within soccer stadiums for the preceding year:

> Statistics can only record the injuries that have occurred, not those that have been prevented. We are concerned that some clubs and/or local authorities (at times reflecting the views of supporters) have challenged particular safety measures on the grounds that nobody has been seriously injured. We must all remain vigilant. (p. 6)

An additional barrier that emerges out of these processes is the process of event fixation and cognitive narrowing (Starbuck & Milliken, 1988; Weick, 1988, 1993, 1995). The assumption that catastrophic events are unique and constrained in both space and time can also lead to constraints on the learning process. Dismissing an event as a function of a particular organization's technology, operating systems, or culture results in a lack of interorganizational learning. For example, superficially the disasters at Bradford and Hillsborough were markedly different. Elliott and Smith (1993), however, have argued that when viewed at a systemic level the two disasters share many characteristics and that the underlying causality emerges from a "mindset of vulnerability" (Wicks, 2001). Despite these similarities, soccer club executives fixated upon the particular detail of each incident before reaching the conclusion that such events could not happen to them (Elliott & Smith, 1997). This "it couldn't happen here" syndrome prevents managers from picking up cues from events that happen elsewhere (Elliott & Smith, 1993, 1997).

Finally, there are two other barriers toward learning that are of emerging importance. The first is a lack of corporate responsibility on the part of the organization. There is a tendency to conform to, but not exceed, the current regulatory requirements, which inevitably constrains the lessons that can be drawn from events. Such an approach is manifest within a large proportion of soccer clubs within the UK. One respondent reflected on the value of increased regulation following the Hillsborough Disaster: "That they make you follow it to the letter... now whether the Club would do that I don't know" (Elliott, 1998, p. 224).

Other respondents referred to regulations as the bible or the gospel, reporting that they often prevented regulators from being flexible and using common sense because they were fearful of being criticized. Another view was expressed "that they nit-pick, to justify their existence, its jobs for the boys" (Elliott, 1998, p. 225).

The second barrier, of emerging importance, concerns the tendency to scapegoat; this will also constrain this learning (see Smith, 1999b; Smith & Tombs, 1995; Tombs & Smith, 1995) and may be reflected in an organization's tendency to focus on single-loop rather than double-loop learning (Ashby, 1940; Schön, 1983). While some learning does take place here, it tends to occur within the dominant organizational paradigm. The problem is that this paradigm may well have given rise to the conditions for the failure in the first place. An inability to challenge that paradigm through effective double-loop learning seems destined to ensure that organizations fail to learn effective lessons from crisis events.

Conclusions

Despite experiencing a series of major disasters, each investigated via a public inquiry, the UK soccer industry has shown only limited evidence of cultural readjustment. This chapter has sought to explore three of the stages through which learning has progressed within the industry. It has been argued that learning may be inhibited because of flaws in the ways in which knowledge is acquired. The skill set and mindset of the investigators and the political context in which such inquiries are made have been identified as key factors. The chapter has focused upon the role of regulations as a key means of disseminating knowledge. We have alluded to the different patterns of regulation that may help or hinder the effective communication of findings and recommendations. Gouldner (1954) depicts a number of ideal types that may provide practical insights that lead to the development of more effective regulatory regimes. Gouldner's work, as well as that of Hynes and Prasad (1997), Wicks (2001), and Elliott and Smith (2006), all indicate the importance of an industry-level approach to learning.

Finally, we have identified a number of barriers to learning present within the UK soccer industry. It is evident from this somewhat depressing analysis that there is still much to be done in better understanding the processes of organizational learning from crisis and feeding this back into practice. Given the terrible events of the opening years of this century, the issue of learning from crises has taken on a new dynamic, and it is important that our academic and practical understanding of these is improved considerably. A failure to do so will condemn our own and subsequent generations to making the same mistakes.

Bibliography

Argyris, C. (1976). Single-loop and double-loop models in research on decision-making. *Administrative Science Quarterly, 21,* 363–377.

Argyris, C. (1977). Double-loop learning in organizations. *Harvard Business Review, 55*(5), 115–134.

Argyris, C. (1999). *On organizational learning* (2nd ed.). Oxford, UK: Blackwell Business.

Argyris, C., & Schön, D. A. (1978). *Organizational learning: A theory of action perspective.* Reading, MA: Addison-Wesley.

Ashby, W. R. (1940). *An introduction to cybernetics.* London: Chapman and Hall.

Baier, A. (1986). Trust and antitrust. *Ethics, 96*(2), 231–60.

Barton, L. (1993). *Crisis in organizations: Managing and communicating in the heat of chaos.* Cincinnati, OH: South-Western.

Beck, U. (1992). *Risk society: Towards a new modernity.* London: Sage.

Berger, P. L., & Luckman, T. (1967). *The social construction of reality.* New York: Doubleday Anchor.

Bignall, V., & Fortune, J. (1984). *Understanding systems failures.* Manchester, UK: Manchester University Press.

Billings, R., Milburn, T., & Schaalman, M. (1980). A model of crisis perception. *Administrative Science Quarterly, 25,* 300–16.

Blois, K. J. (1999). Trust in business relationships: An evaluation of status. *Journal of Management Studies, 36*(2), 197–215.

Bood, R. P. (1998). Charting organizational learning: A comparison of multiple mapping techniques. In C. Eden & J.-C. Spender (Eds.), *Managerial and organizational cognition. Theory, methods and research* (pp. 210–230). London: Sage.

Brown, A., & Jones, M. (2000). Honourable members and dishonourable deeds: Sensemaking, impression management and legitimation in the arms to Iraq affair. *Human Relations, 53*(5), 655–689.

Burgelman, R. (1994). Fading memories: A process theory of strategic business exit in dynamic environments. *Administrative Science Quarterly, 39,* 24–56.

Calman, K., & Smith, D. (2001). Works in theory but not in practice? Some notes on the precautionary principle. *Public Administration, 79*(1), 185–204.

Cangolisi, V., & Dill, W. R. (1965). Organizational learning: Observations toward a theory. *Administrative Science Quarterly, 10*(2), 175–203.

Canter, D., Comber, M., & Uzzell, D. (1989). *Football in its place: An environmental psychology of football grounds.* London: Routledge.

Chester, D. N. (1968). *Report of the Committee on Football.* London: Department of Education and Science, HMSO.

Collingridge, D., & Reeve, C. (1985). *Science speaks to power.* London: Francis Pinter.

Crainer, S. (1993). *Zeebrugge: Learning from disaster.* London: Herald Charitable Trust.

Crossan, M. M., & Guatto, T. (1996). Organizational learning research profile. *Journal of Organizational Change Management, 9*(1), 107–112.

Crossan, M. M., White, R. E., Lane, H. W., & Klus, L. (1996). The improvising organization: Where planning meets opportunity. *Organizational Dynamics 24*(4), 20–35.

Cyert, R., & March, J. G. (1963). *A behavioral theory of the firm.* Englewood Cliffs, NJ: Prentice Hall.

Donaldson, M. (1992). *Human minds—An exploration.* Harmondsworth: Penguin Books.

Easterby-Smith, M., & Araujo, L. (1999). Organizational learning: Current debates and opportunities. In M. Easterby-Smith, J. Burgoyne, & L. Araujo (Eds.), *Organizational learning and the learning organization.* London: Sage.

Easterby-Smith, M., Crossan, M., & Nicolini, D. (2000). Organizational learning: Debates past, present and future. *Journal of Management Studies, 37*(6), 783–796.

Eberwein, W. D. (1978). Crisis research—the state of the art: A Western view. In D. De Frei, *International crises and crisis management* (pp. 126–143). Conference Proceedings, University of Zurich.

Elliott, D. (1998). *Organizational learning from crisis: The UK football industry since 1945.* Unpublished doctoral dissertation, University of Durham, UK.

Elliott, D., Frosdick, S., & Smith, D. (1997). The failure of legislation by crisis. In S. Frosdick & L. Walley (Eds.), *Sport and safety management* (pp. 85–107). Oxford, UK: Butterworth-Heinemann.

Elliott, D., & McGuinness, M. (2002). Public inquiries, panacea or placebo? *Journal of Contingencies and Crisis Management, 10*(1), 14–25.

Elliott, D., & Smith, D. (1993). Football stadia disasters in the United Kingdom: Learning from tragedy. *Industrial and Environmental Crisis Quarterly, 7*(3), 205–229.

Elliott, D., & Smith, D. (1997). Waiting for the next one. In S. Frosdick & L. Walley (Eds.), *Sport and safety management* (pp. 85–107). Oxford, UK: Butterworth-Heinemann.

Elliott, D., & Smith, D. (2006). Patterns of regulatory behavior in the UK football industry. *Journal of Management Studies, 43*(2), 291–318.

Elliott, D., & Smith, D. (in press). *Learning from crisis.*

Fiol, C. M., & Lyles, M. A. (1985). Organizational learning. *Academy of Management Review, 19*(4), 803–813.

Football Licensing Authority. (2005). *Annual report and accounts.* London: HMSO. Retrieved February 7, 2006, from http://www.flaweb.org.uk/docs/thefla/anrep05.php

Fortune, J., & Peters, G. (1995). *Learning from failure: The systems approach.* Chichester, UK: Wiley & Sons.

Furedi, F. (1997). *Culture of fear: Risk-taking and the morality of low expectation.* London: Cassel.

Garvin, D. A. (1993). Building a learning organization. *Harvard Business Review, 71*(4), 78–91.

Giddens, A. (1990). *The consequences of modernity.* Stanford, CA: Stanford University Press.

Gioia, D., & Chittipeddi, K. (1991). Sensemaking and sensegiving in strategic change initiation. *Strategic Management Journal, 12,* 433–448.

Gouldner, A. (1954). *Patterns in industrial bureaucracy.* New York: Routledge & Kegan Paul.

Grint, K. (1997). *Fuzzy management. Contemporary ideas and practices at work.* Oxford, UK: Oxford University Press.

Harrington, J. (1968). *Soccer hooliganism.* Bristol, UK: John Wright.

Hermann, C. F. (1963). Some consequences of crisis which limit the viability of organizations. *Administrative Science Quarterly, 8,* 61–82.

Hofstede, E. (1990). Measuring organizational cultures: A qualitative and quantitative study across twenty cases. *Administrative Science Quarterly, 35,* 286–316.

Hosmer, L. T. (1995). Trust: The connecting link between organizational theory and philosophical ethics. *Academy of Management Review, 20*(2), 379–403.

Huber, G. (1991). Organizational learning: The contributing processes and the literature. *Organizational Science, 2*(1), 88–115.

Hutter, B. M. (1992). Public accident inquiries: The case of the Railway Inspectorate. *Public Administration, 70*(3), 177–192.

Hynes, T., & Prasad, P. (1997). Mock bureaucracy in mining disasters. *Journal of Management Studies, 34,* 601–623.

Inglis, S. (1987). *The football grounds of Great Britain.* London: Collins-Willow.

Janis, I., & Mann, L. (1977). *Decision making.* New York: Free Press.

Kets de Vries, M. F. R., & Miller, D. (1984). *The neurotic organization: Diagnosing and changing counterproductive styles of management.* San Francisco: Jossey-Bass.

Kim, D. M. (1993). The link between individual and organizational learning. *Sloan Management Review, 35,* 37–50.

Kramer, R. M., & Tyler, T. R. (Eds.). (1996). *Trust in organizations.* Thousand Oaks, CA: Sage.

Lang, J. (1969). *Report of the Working Party on crowd behaviour at football matches.* London: HMSO.

Levitt, B., & March, J. G. (1988). Organizational learning. *Annual Review of Sociology, 14,* 319–340.

Marquardt, M., & Reynolds, A. (1994). *The global learning organization: Gaining competitive advantage through continuous learning.* Burr Ridge, IL: Irwin.

McLean, I., & Johnes, M. (2000). *Aberfan: Government and disasters.* Cardiff, UK: Drake.

Miller, D. (1990). *The Icarus paradox: How exceptional companies bring about their own downfall.* New York: HarperCollins.

Mishra, A. K. (1996). Organizational responses to crisis: The centrality of trust. In R. M. Kramer & T. R. Tyler (Eds.), *Trust in organizations.* Thousand Oaks, CA: Sage.

Mitroff, I., Pauchant, T., Finney, M., & Pearson, C. (1989). Do (some) organizations cause their own crises? Culture profiles of crisis prone versus crisis prepared organizations. *Industrial Crisis Quarterly, 3,* 269–283.

Mitroff, I., Pauchant, T., & Shrivastava, P. (1988). The structure of man-made organizational crisis. *Technological Forecasting and Social Change, 33,* 83–107.

Moelwyn-Hughes, R. (1946). *Inquiry into the disaster at the Bolton Wanderers' football ground on the 9th March 1946.* Cm 6848. London: HMSO.

Nathan, M., & Kovoor-Misra, S. (2002). No pain, yet gain: Vicarious organizational learning from crises in an interorganizational field. *The Journal of Applied Behavioral Science, 38*(2), 245–266.

Nonaka, I. (1991). The knowledge creating company. *Harvard Business Review, 69,* 96–104.

Nonaka, I. (1994). A dynamic theory of organizational knowledge creation. *Organization Science, 5*(1), 14–37.

Osborn, A. (2002, December 6). EC plans cuts of up to 80% in white fish quotas. *The Guardian,* p. 7.

Pauchant, T. C., & Douville, R. (1993). Recent research in crisis management: A study of 24 authors' publications from 1986 to 1991. *Industrial and Environmental Crisis Quarterly, 7*(1), 43–66.

Pauchant, T. C., & Mitroff, I. (1988). Crisis prone versus crisis avoiding organizations: Is your company's culture its own worst enemy in creating crisis? *Industrial Crisis Quarterly, 2,* 53–63.

Pauchant, T. C., & Mitroff, I. (1992). *Transforming the crisis-prone organization. Preventing individual organizational and environmental tragedies.* San Francisco: Jossey-Bass.

Pearson, C. M., & Clair, J. A. (1998). Reframing crisis management. *Academy of Management Review, 23*(1), 59–76.

Peay, J. (1996). *Inquiries after homicide.* London: Duckworth.

Pedlar, M., Burgoyne, J., & Boydell, T. (1991). *The learning company: A strategy for sustainable development.* Maidenhead, UK: McGraw-Hill.

Perrow, C. (1999). *Normal accidents: Living with high risk technologies* (with a new Afterword). Princeton, NJ: Princeton University Press.

Popplewell, O. (1985). *Committee of inquiry into crowd safety and control at sports grounds: Interim report.* Cm 9585. London: HMSO.

Popplewell, O. (1986). *Committee of inquiry into crowd safety and control at sports grounds: Final report.* Cm 9710. London: HMSO.

Prange, C. (1999). Organizational learning—desperately seeking theory. In M. Easterby-Smith, J. Burgoyne, & L. Araujo (Eds.), *Organizational learning and the learning organization.* London: Sage.

Reason, J. T. (1987). Cognitive aids in process environments: Prostheses or tools. *International Journal of Man-Machine Studies, 27,* 463–70.

Reason, J. T. (1990). *Human error.* Oxford, UK: Oxford University Press.

Reason, J. T. (1995). Understanding adverse events: Human factors. *Quality in Health Care, 4,* 80–89.

Reger, R. K., Mullane, J. V., Gustafson, L. T., & DeMarie, S. M. (1994). Creating earthquakes to change organizational mindsets. *Academy of Management Executive, 8*(4), 31–43.

Reilly, A. (1993). *Vicarious organizational learning: The example of crisis management.* Paper presented at the 13th Annual Strategic Management Society, Chicago.

Schein, E. H. (1985). *Organizational culture and leadership.* San Francisco: Jossey-Bass.

Schön, D. A. (1983). Organizational learning. In G. Morgan (Ed.), *Beyond method: Strategies for social research.* Beverly Hills, CA: Sage.

Scraton, P. (1999). Policing with contempt: The degrading of truth and denial of justice in the aftermath of the Hillsborough disaster. *Journal of Law & Society, 26*(3), 273–297.

Senge, P. M. (1990). *The fifth discipline: The art and practice of the learning organization.* New York: Doubleday.

Shrivastava, P. (1983). A typology of organizational learning systems. *Journal of Management Studies, 21*(1), 7–28.

Shortt, Rt. Hon. E. (1924). *Report of the departmental committee on crowds*. Cm 2088. London: HMSO.

Sipika, C., & Smith, D. (1993). From disaster to crisis: The failed turnaround of Pan American Airlines. *Journal of Contingencies and Crisis Management, 1*(3), 138–151.

Smart, C., & Vertinsky, I. (1977). Designs for crisis decision units. *Administrative Science Quarterly, 22,* 640–657.

Smith, D. (1990a). Beyond contingency planning—toward a model of crisis management. *Industrial Crisis Quarterly, 4*(4), 263–275.

Smith, D. (1990b). Corporate power and the politics of uncertainty: Conflicts surrounding major hazard plants at Canvey Island. *Industrial Crisis Quarterly, 4*(1), 1–26.

Smith, D. (1993). The public sector in crisis? The case of the UK Prison Service. In J. Wilson & P. Hinton (Eds.), *The public services and the 1990s: Issues in public service, finance and management* (pp. 142–170). London: Tudor Press.

Smith, D. (1995). The dark side of excellence: Managing strategic failures. In J. Thompson (Ed.), *Handbook of strategic management* (pp. 161–191). London: Butterworth-Heinemann.

Smith, D. (1999a). A dance of interactive parts: Making sense of disaster. *Mimeo.* Centre for Risk and Crisis Management, University of Durham, UK.

Smith, D. (1999b). Crisis as a catalyst for change? Changing corporate approaches to responsibility. In U. Rosenthal, L. Comfort, & A. Boin (Eds.), *From crises to contingencies: A global perspective.* Springfield, IL: Charles C Thomas.

Smith, D. (2000a). Crisis management teams: Issues in the management of operational crises. *Risk Management: An International Journal, 2*(3), 61–78.

Smith, D. (2000b). On a wing and a prayer? Exploring the human components of technological failure. *Systems Research and Behavioral Science, 17,* 543–559.

Smith, D. (2001). Crisis as a catalyst for change: Issues in the management of uncertainty and organizational vulnerability. In BBA (Ed.), *E-risk: Business as usual* (pp. 81–88). London: British Bankers Association/Deloitte and Touche.

Smith, D. (2002). Not by error, but by design—Harold Shipman and the regulatory crisis for health care. *Public Policy and Administration, 17*(4), 55–74.

Smith, D. (2004a). In the eyes of the beholder? Making sense of the system(s) of disaster(s). In E. L. Quarantelli & R. Perry (Eds.), *What is a disaster?* Philadelphia, PA: Xlbris.

Smith, D. (2004b). *Mind the gap! Exploring emergence and escalation in the creation of vulnerability in organizations.* Liverpool, UK: Centre for Risk and Crisis Management, University of Liverpool.

Smith, D. (in press). For whom the bell tolls: Imagining accidents and the development of crisis simulation in organizations. *Simulation and Gaming.*

Smith, D., & Elliott, D. (in press). Moving beyond denial. *Management Learning.*

Smith, D., & Sipika, C. (1993). Back from the brink—Post-crisis management. *Long Range Planning, 26*(1), 28–38.

Smith, D., & Tombs, S. (1995). Self regulation as a control strategy for major hazards. *Journal of Management Studies, 32*(5), 619–636.

Sparrow, P. R. (1999). Strategic management in a world turned upside down: The role of cognition, intuition and emotional intelligence. In P. Flood, S. Carroll, L. Gorman, & T. Dromgoole (Eds.), *Managing strategic implementation.* London: Blackwell.

Stacey, R. D. (1991). *The chaos frontier: Creative strategic control for business.* Oxford, UK: Butterworth-Heinemann.
Stacey, R. D. (1993). *Strategic management and organizational dynamics.* London: Pitman.
Starbuck, W. H., & Milliken, F. J. (1988). Executives' perceptual filters: What they notice and how they make sense. In D. C. Hambrick (Ed.), *The executive effect: Concepts and methods for studying top managers.* Greenwich, CT: JAI.
Taylor, Rt. Hon. Lord Justice. (1989). *The Hillsborough Stadium disaster: Interim report.* Cm 765. London: HMSO.
Taylor, Rt. Hon. Lord Justice. (1990). *The Hillsborough Stadium disaster: Final report.* Cm 962. London: HMSO.
Taylor, S. E. (1989). *Positive illusions.* New York: Basic Books.
Toft, B., & Reynolds, S. (1992). *Learning from disasters.* London: Butterworth.
Toft, B., & Reynolds, S. (1997). *Learning from disasters* (2nd ed.). Leicester, UK: Perpetuity Press.
Tombs, S., & Smith, D. (1995). Corporate social responsibility and crisis management: The democratic organization and crisis prevention. *Journal of Contingencies and Crisis Management, 3*(3), 135–147.
Turner, B. A. (1976). The organizational and interorganizational development of disasters. *Administrative Science Quarterly, 21,* 378–397.
Turner, B. A. (1978). *Manmade disasters.* London: Wykeham Press.
Turner, B. A., & Toft, B. (1988). Organizational learning from disasters. In H. B. F. Gow & R. W. Kay (Eds.), *Emergency planning for industrial hazards.* London: Elsevier Applied Science.
Wicks, D. (2001). Institutionalized mindsets of invulnerability: Differentiated institutional fields and the antecedents of organizational crisis. *Organizational Studies, 22*(4), 659–692.
Weick, K. E. (1988). Enacted sensemaking in crisis situations. *Journal of Management Studies, 25,* 305–317.
Weick, K. E. (1993). The collapse of sensemaking in organizations: The Mann Gulch disaster. *Administrative Science Quarterly, 38,* 628–652.
Weick, K. (1993). The vulnerable system: An analysis of the Tenerife Air disaster. In K. Roberts (Ed.), *New challenges to understanding organizations.* New York: Macmillan.
Weick, K. E. (1995). *Sensemaking in organizations.* Thousand Oaks, CA: Sage.
Weinberg, A. M. (1972). Science and trans-science. *Minerva, 10,* 209–222.
Wheatley, Rt. Hon. Lord (1972). *Report of the inquiry into crowd safety at sports grounds.* Cm 4952. London: HMSO.
Williams, A., Dobson, P., & Walters, M. (1989). *Changing culture* (2nd ed.). London: Institute of Personnel Management.
Woolfson, C. (1999, October 8). Rights and retribution. *The Guardian,* p. 19.

Part IV

New Crises, New Solutions

A "Total" Responsibility Management Approach to Crisis Management and Signal Detection in Organizations

Judith A. Clair and Sandra Waddock

In this chapter, we propose a "total" responsibility management approach to crisis management, which embraces a systemic, integrated, and consistent approach like that taken in the quality, environmental management, and responsibility management movements. We suggest that such an approach involves inspiration, integration, and innovation through assessment, improvement, and learning systems. In the first part of the chapter we explore implications of a total responsibly management approach for crisis management in general. And then, in the second part of the chapter we describe how such an approach would be applied to a specific crisis-management challenge: the detection of early warning signals of crisis.

Crisis seems to characterize the world that managers face these days. From threats of terrorism that could conceivably destroy entire companies to the discovery of internal wrongdoings that can send a company plummeting into bankruptcy, threats abound. Clearly, companies cannot be prepared for every contingency that might present itself; however, this chapter will argue that by adopting approaches from both the quality and responsibility management movements, companies can better prepare themselves to face the particular threats that are most likely within their domains. While some scholars have long urged a systems approach to crisis management (e.g., Mitroff and colleagues), most companies fail to adopt such an approach. Rather, most companies adopt an "after-event" approach where actions have a relatively narrow purview. What may be stopping these companies from adopting this type of systems approach is the belief that crises are rare events, and substantial time and resources should not be devoted to unlikely occurrences.

While a systems approach to crisis management is rare in companies, such an approach to managing company systems to achieve high quality and to meet company responsibilities is actually quite common. If a company could adapt already existing systemic approaches to include its crisis-management activities, then it might be more likely to address the crises proactively rather than after the fact.

In this chapter, we explore this idea in two primary ways. First, we discuss how companies would be better served with a more proactive and even stakeholder-interactive "total" responsibility management approach (TRM; Waddock & Bodwell, 2002) to managing a company's relationships with stakeholders. A TRM approach, which is inspired by the total quality movement and includes a crisis-management component, can help companies deal holistically with potential crises, establish interactive working relationships with key stakeholders, think about the breadth of responsibilities they need to manage, think through a responsibility vision and consider how to integrate it into the organization before a crisis hits, and potentially avoid the reputational damage that occurs in the aftermath of a crisis.

Second, we apply the TRM approach to explore one of the least-understood and least-researched parts of crisis management: signal detection. In so doing, we attempt to demonstrate how the TRM approach would inspire a systemic approach to early crisis detection, one that is focused on revealing and acting on early warning signals.

Organizational Crisis

Organizational crises are not everyday events; however, they are common enough that company leaders need to be well aware of their possibility—and prepare their companies to cope effectively with them. Pearson and Clair (1998) summarized the literature on crisis management and offered the following definition:

> An organizational crisis is a low-probability, high-impact event that threatens the viability of the organization and is characterized by ambiguity of cause, effect, and means of resolution, as well as by a belief that decisions must be made swiftly. (Pearson & Clair, 1998, p. 60)

Such relatively unusual but increasingly notable events include computer tampering or a new virus that shuts the company down (e.g., Google's facing a new version of the "MyDoom" virus on the very day it announced its initial public offering), terrorist attacks such as the one on New York City's World Trade Center in 2001, and a major product recall—such as Firestone's recall of more than six million faulty tires—that threatens a company's future. Clearly, leadership in the company needs to be aware of the possibility that such disasters may occur and ensure that systems are in place for dealing with the unexpected and the unpredictable.

Crisis-management systems typically follow a pattern that begins with executive perceptions about risk, including awareness of the need for preparations to be put in place (Pearson & Clair, 1998). This awareness is moderated by the environmental context within which a specific company operates, including the extent of industry regulation and institutionalized practices across the industry and within the company (Pearson & Clair, 1998). For example, the type of crisis that Coca-Cola might face, and has faced, with respect to the quality of water used in its products in Great Britain is quite different from the type of crisis that Putnam Investments faced with its market timing scandal in 2003, which caused customers to withdraw millions in investment and created ripple effects across the entire mutual-fund industry.

Executives need to be aware of the life cycle of crises. Becoming aware of the possibility that a crisis may occur—or signal detection—is only the first of five phases in a developing crisis (Pearson, Clair, Kavoor-Misra, & Mitroff, 1997). Once awareness occurs, the company needs to begin preparing to deal with the potential crisis. Steps include adopting a "crisis-management mindset," creating a team to deal with the crisis, ensuring that the company's values with respect to the issue and strategies for coping are widely known, and even engaging in simulations of the crisis so that responders will have direct experience in dealing with that type of crisis (Pearson et al., 1997).

When a crisis has actually occurred and the crisis-management plan has been implemented, the company now needs to deal with the third phase—damage containment. Steps at this phase can involve turnaround initiatives aimed at reducing the impact of the crisis (Pearson et al., 1997). Putnam, for example, tried to reassure its clients during this phase by agreeing to repay its investors and by implementing governance reforms, including oversight by a third party (Wallace, 2003).

After the crisis has peaked, companies enter into a recovery phase. For example, as the marketing timing scandal in 2003 spread across the mutual fund industry, numerous pension plans began offering a wider array of choices to investors, while simultaneously those funds caught in the scandal began cleaning up their acts and putting safety measures and lower fees in place (Harris, 2004). The final phase of the crisis involves learning from it and improving the internal systems of the company so that the same thing does not happen again (Pearson et al., 1997).

Responsibility Management: Systemic Approaches to Crisis Management

If the steps of managing a crisis are known, as they are, and if the elements of a good crisis management system are clear, then why do so many presumably avoidable crises seem to be occurring? Too often, the problem lies in the fact that crisis management is an "after-the-event" set of actions, reactive rather than proactive, with commitment to action embedded too low in the organization to make a difference when a real crisis occurs (Mitroff, 2001) as opposed to being approached as a possibility to keep constantly in mind as part of a holistic responsibility management approach. Rather than focusing on coping with the aftermath of a crisis, as most crisis-management systems do, Mitroff (2001) suggests a proactive approach that focuses primarily on prevention through a systemic and integrated approach linked to other systems in the enterprise. Such an approach involves truth-telling, dealing with the emotions involved, ensuring that the crisis is thoroughly studied by an independent investigator, and putting in place appropriate scanning mechanisms to ensure that new potential crises are averted.

More is necessary. We want to argue here that crisis management needs to be considered an integral element of the core responsibilities that any company has for its impacts on stakeholders and the natural environment (cf. Waddock, 2002) and, in particular, an important element that assures the survival of the firm and helps manage its external reputation. Crises themselves may not necessarily be avoidable, but as Mitroff (2001) argues, with sufficient vision and foresight, crises can be managed as systematically and as well as any other managerial issue. We take this lesson from the experiences that companies have had in managing other relatively intractable issues and producing consistently powerful results; for example, quality (Evan & Lindsay, 2001), environment (Hart & Milstein, 2003; Thomas & Harris, 2004), and, most recently, stakeholder and environmental responsibilities (Waddock, & Bodwell, 2002, in press).

We argue that by taking a systemic, integrated, and consistent approach to crisis management, much as companies have done with quality, environmental management, and (more recently) responsibility management, companies can place themselves in a better position to ensure their long-term survival. We further argue that because a crisis is potentially life-threatening for an organization, creating a systemic crisis-management system can be conceived to come under the logic of the company's overall approach to managing its responsibilities (Waddock & Bodwell, 2002). The elements of responsibility management, which are drawn from approaches to quality management, are the very elements that can help a company avoid a crisis in the first place or, should one occur despite having the system in place, cope with it effectively once it happens. In other words, crisis management needs to be integrated directly into the overall responsibility management system that a company evolves to deal with its stakeholder and environmental impacts.

Responsibility and Crisis Management

Responsibility management involves taking seriously all of a company's relationships with stakeholders and impacts on the natural environment. It means putting into place systemic approaches for working interactively with stakeholders in an engaged way so that there are fewer surprises. Similarly, advance preparation for crises needs to be considered an important element of managing responsibility because of the negative impacts on stakeholders that inevitably follow from a crisis; whether it is the financial impact on shareholders and pension-fund holders of a scandal that results in bankruptcy, as the Enron scandal did, the loss of customer (investor) trust associated with Putnam's market timing scandal, or the ecological and human costs of an *Exxon Valdez* oil spill, it is clear that companies experiencing the types of crises that are generated by their lack of fully managing all of their responsibilities effectively have not served their stakeholders—or their shareholders—well. And when crises are caused by unavoidable external events, such as an environmental disaster like a hurricane or a terrorist attack on the company's facilities, having an effective responsibility management approach in place, one that encompasses how the company will deal with crises, can help mitigate negative impacts.

Waddock and Bodwell (2002) have outlined the core elements of approaches to (total) responsibility management that have emerged as companies recognized the integral nature of their stakeholder and environmental responsibilities—and the fact that they are increasingly being held accountable for those impacts by their many constituencies. Responsibility management means integrating awareness of the responsibility for stakeholder and ecological impacts into the company's vision, strategy, and management systems. A holistic approach like those of quality management, but applied to a broader set of stakeholders (Waddock & Bodwell, in press), responsibility management takes a systemic view of a firm's impacts and adjusts cross-organizational processes accordingly. It is not a big step to recognize that effective crisis management is an important part of this holistic approach. Below we will identify the specific ways in which crisis management is related to responsibility management.

Responsibility management approaches start with *inspiration*. Inspiration or vision-setting is the process through which the company articulates a values-driven vision to which top management is committed. The vision involves an aspiration about how a company will affect the world, hopefully positively (Senge, 1990). In this respect, responsibility management is very similar to crisis management in the traditional sense, which requires that companies articulate their values (Pearson & Clair, 1998). This vision provides inspiration because it creates meaning for stakeholders engaged in a range of processes, partnerships, and other relationships with the business.

Built on generally agreed-upon foundational standards and values that provide a *floor* of expectations about company practices and performance, vision guides strategy development and implementation. Foundation values, of course, combine with the company's own values and goals to provide guidance and direction for the overall enterprise consistent with the company's strategies, goals, and objectives (Waddock, 2004). Constructive values (Waddock & Bodwell, 2002) are important to both responsibility management and crisis management because the way that a company handles a crisis, as was aptly demonstrated in Johnson & Johnson's Tylenol crisis in the early 1980s, directly relates to how strongly felt and lived the company's values are.

In a crisis, it is critical that the company's values already be widely known and deeply felt, because there is little time to think things through and the company's managers and leaders are likely to respond based on what they already know well—how we do things here. Responsibility management approaches ensure that the values are already widely disseminated, since every employee has to take responsibility for their implementation. It is very likely that the best responses to crisis will be derived from the kinds of values that have inspired the company's stakeholders to be loyal in the first place, as J&J found when executives realized that the famous J&J credo dictated "customers first"—and those values became the basis of the company's effective actions to cope with the crisis. In contrast, lack of attention to important constructive core values seems to have been partially at the root of problems faced by Japan's Snow Brand Milk Products Company when, in 2000, the company was faced with more than 15,000 people suffering from food poisoning after consuming Snow Brand milk-related products (Baker, 2004). In that situation, a typical nightmare scenario for a food company, the company's low hygiene standards resulted in *Staphylococcus aureus* bacteria infecting a valve used in the processing of low-fat milk because the valve was not regularly cleaned—and inspections claimed that the standards were in fact appalling (Baker, 2004). Unlike J&J, which put stakeholders first, Snow Brand "by all accounts, ... initially sought to downplay the incident, and gave the impression of being more concerned for its reputation and standing than it was for the victims of the outbreak" (Baker, 2004, p. 1).

An important aspect of responsibility management's inspiration processes involves stakeholder engagement (Svendsen, 1998). By engaging with their stakeholders, companies can more readily be apprised of any pending or extant concerns of which they should be aware, as well as how their actions are being viewed both internally and externally. There are obvious important reputational aspects to stakeholder engagement processes from which the company can benefit, as well as important feedback loops to be established so that issues associated with the company's responsibilities do not create surprises. Consider, however, the impact of poor stakeholder engagement in Snow Brand's situation. According to Baker (2004), the company tried to convince local government officials not to publicly issue a recall order so that it would appear that the recall was voluntary. The recalcitrance backfired, as local officials not only issued the public recall but also publicized the company's request not to make it public (Baker, 2004).

The link to crisis avoidance is clear. Consider, for example, how Enron's ultimate collapse might have been avoided had financial analysts concerned about the company's practices and sudden rise been engaged with the company more closely; they could have fed back their concerns to the company or made them public sooner. Or consider how Snow Brand Milk might have avoided damage to its reputation had it been both more proactive in dealing with the food-poisoning situation and simultaneously in closer communication with local city officials before the incident spiraled out of the company's control. Stakeholder engagement, of course, cannot avoid all crises for companies, but it can be the basis of important scanning processes that allow companies to become aware of (and, more importantly, deal with) potential future issues—before they actually become issues.

Should a crisis actually happen, especially one beyond the company's control, the responsibility vision can help employees and other stakeholders better understand the actions that are being undertaken, because they will be aligned with the company's already well-articulated vision. Key stakeholders will be familiar with the company's procedures and vision, and fewer questions are likely to be asked because the basis upon which decisions are being made and communicated will be available to interested parties.

The next major component of responsibility management approaches is *integration* of the company's vision and values into the company's management systems and human-resource practices. Responsibility management approaches *integrate* the company's inspirational vision into its strategies, employee relationships and working standards, functional/divisional operating practices, and management systems that support strategies. Integration is the core of responsibility management, because it is based on what the firm does on a daily basis, the activities and outputs that determine what the firm does to achieve its responsibility vision. Integration includes human-resource policies and practices, training to health and safety guidelines, marketing and promotion, and other daily processes and functions that impact whether a firm achieves its responsibility goals—and avoids crises.

Crisis management involves much the same type of thinking. It is helpful to consider the benefits that could accrue if all of a company's management systems and employee policies were designed with an eye toward how effective they would be in times of crisis. In this respect, planning for crisis management, as with responsibility management, is simply another step in a company's path toward managing itself as effectively as possible under whatever circumstances develop. Rather than thinking of crisis management as something beyond daily responsibilities, the responsibility management approach simply recognizes that many of the same systems in place for typical operations will be those called upon during a crisis—and they need to be designed to work well under the entire spectrum of conditions they might face. Having the responsibility and crisis-prepared dimensions of management systems well thought out in advance is particularly important during the actual crisis, when all the system's and employees' resources are likely to be stretched thin.

Snow Brand's attempt to make a comeback is illustrative of these processes. Although the company was still underperforming several years after the food-poisoning incident, it had taken multiple steps aimed at improving its responsibility management, including hiring a new president who admitted the mistakes and tried to move the company forward. Steps were also taken to improve quality assurance, including a new corporate philosophy (i.e., inspiration or vision, with associated values), emphasis on customer-focused management, better corporate governance, and risk-management training for managers (Baker, 2004, p. 2). This case not only demonstrates the importance of having an effective responsibility and crisis management approach in place before a crisis hits, but also highlights the difficulty of recovering from a crisis as well as changing organizational culture, particularly since the company once again found itself having difficulties in 2002, when it deliberately mislabeled beef so it could falsely claim government subsidies in the "mad cow" scare (Baker, 2004).

Responsibility management approaches also foster *innovation through assessment, improvement, and learning systems* in management systems by carefully designing responsibility objectives for each of the company's core stakeholders, starting with the company's employees. As Pearson et al. (1997) suggest, the aftermath of a crisis involves post hoc analysis that creates learning—so that crises do not repeat themselves and so that, where needed, new procedures, policies, and practices can be put in place in the event of a new crisis, although as the Snow Brand case illustrates, changing a company's internal practices significantly is far from easy. Innovations and improvements in various operating practices that affect different stakeholders, boost performance, and improve results are a consistent feature of responsibility management approaches—and will also be of great benefit during and after a crisis.

Transparency and accountability, typically in the form of reporting out how the company is performing along social and environmental lines, has become increasingly important to external stakeholders concerned about corporate responsibility. Similarly, transparent communication is a key to effectively handling a crisis (Mitroff, 2001; Pearson & Clair, 1998). Consider the contrast between J&J's open communication with the press and the general public about the Tylenol situation and the stonewalling by Firestone around its defective tires.

A Total Responsibility Approach to Signal Detection in Organizations

So far, we have discussed the relationship between total responsibility management systems and crisis management in broad terms. Now, we provide a specific focus on the case of signal detection in organizations. This focus gives us an opportunity to demonstrate how a total responsibility approach that embraces the systemic and integrative nature of crisis management is implemented as an organization attempts to undertake signal detection—in other words, the detection of a crisis' warning signals prior to the onset of significant damage and harm.

While many factors conspire in the development of an organizational crisis, one of the most insidious catalysts is the inability of organizations to detect warning signals present prior to the onset of damage (Pauchant & Mitroff, 1992). In fact, research demonstrates that almost without exception, a trail of early warning signals is left during the earliest stage of a crisis (Bowonder & Linstone, 1987; Pearson & Mitroff, 1993). Warning signals can be recognizable for a substantial period of time before the full-blown eruption of the crisis. For example, in one study, warning signals were detectable for up to 10 years (Hambrick & D'Aveni, 1988).

A total responsibility management approach suggests that that approaches to signal detection need to be systemic in nature (Pauchant & Mitroff, 1992). Based on this assumption, diagnostic systems and structures for signal detection need to be integrated throughout all levels and areas of an organization. Signal detection methods need to be qualitative and quantitative. All systems of the organization need to be an integral part of an overall diagnostic system; methods for signal detection need to involve strategic, technical, structural, diagnostic, communication, psychological, and cultural aspects of an organization (Pearson & Mitroff, 1994). In addition, signal detection should not be contained within the organization. Rather, a total responsibility management approach suggests that organizations need to bring stakeholders into the process. Prior research supports this contention, as signals can first be detected by external stakeholders rather than by internal systems for detection.

We suggest that the design of a formal system for signal detection should involve five categories of activities: (1) getting top management support and assigning accountability for design; (2) conducting a cultural audit and undertaking psychological preparations; (3) identifying organizational vulnerabilities and symptoms; (4) developing methods for scanning, evaluation, and diagnosis; and (5) enhancing communication systems. An organization that engages in each of these five categories of activities will be better prepared to detect the warning signals of a crisis.

Top Management Support and Accountability for Design

Top management commitment to, and visible support for, early detection is absolutely vital. Leadership involvement at the highest levels seems to be crucial to the success of crisis-management programs (Pearson & Mitroff, 1994); time, resources, and willingness by organizational members to support efforts at signal detection are likely to be limited without top management involvement and support. An explicit policy statement regarding crisis prevention and expectations for dealing with potential warning signals of a crisis provides organizational members at all levels with needed direction and guidance in their decision-making when they are faced with an abnormality.

While one employee, ideally a top manager, needs to be given oversight responsibility for all signal-detection programs, different groups of employees need to be made accountable for the design of formal signal-detection methods and procedures for *each* type of crisis. These "intelligence groups" (Smart & Vertinsky, 1977) are responsible for identifying rare events with threat potential and designing methods to detect them.

Criteria used to select individuals for leadership positions and for participation on task forces will need to be established. Such criteria can be based on what top managers believe are important prerequisites for involvement in a comprehensive detection program. Some criteria might be individuals' functional expertise and knowledge, demonstrated integrity and ethics, and commitment to the deterrence and detection of certain crises.

Culture Audit and Psychological Preparation

An organization should undertake an analysis of its culture to see whether norms, values, and behaviors seem to deter attention to potential warning signals. Certain cultural characteristics may lead organizational members to ignore, misinterpret, or hide knowledge of a potential warning signal.

For example, a propensity to punish organizational whistleblowers may make organizational members less likely to report perceived abnormalities.

Outside consultants may need to be brought into an organization to gain an accurate assessment of its culture and assist with change efforts. Though there is some question about whether culture change is even possible, research suggests that leaders may be able to enact organizational change through their stated beliefs and actions (Schein, 1985). One way top managers facilitate a supportive cultural environment is actively demonstrating that signal detection is important for the organization's future functioning. For example, whistleblowers or external stakeholders who convey critical information about a potential warning signal could be provided with a safe, anonymous method for reporting an abnormality.

Inevitably, employees will experience strong negative cognitions and emotions such as fear, confusion, and anxiety when faced with the possibility of a crisis. Methods to counteract these responses need to be implemented. Simulations or psychodramas (Pauchant & Mitroff, 1992; Smart & Vertinsky, 1977) may give employees exposure to the emotions and cognitions that are likely to arise in the event of a crisis. If appropriate responses to a serious threat and methods to reduce stress are modeled, employees may be more psychologically prepared for a crisis that could arise. To reduce feelings of ambiguity and confusion, employees could participate in training programs that increase problem solving and recognition skills. Such training may increase employees' confidence and ability when they are actually faced with a possible warning signal. In summary, interest in the psychological and physical safety of employees and other stakeholders who could be involved in a crisis needs to be demonstrated (Regester, 1987); attention to these human concerns may increase the likelihood that employees and others are able to respond to an abnormality.

Identification of Vulnerabilities and Symptoms

As mentioned, signal detection needs to be specific to a particular crisis. Since an organization cannot possibly prepare for all types of crises, organizational members need to identify several crises to which a company is most vulnerable (Pauchant & Mitroff, 1992). One way to identify vulnerabilities is through a historical analysis. If an organization has had a history of certain types of problems or crises, then it may be vulnerable to experiencing such situations in the future.

A second way to identify vulnerabilities is to conduct an external analysis of an organization's environment. Problems or crises experienced by similar companies, or within the industry or a related industry, may also be worthy of attention. For example, food manufacturers and distributors are likely to find that faulty or dangerous products and product-tampering incidents are crises to which the food industry is particularly vulnerable. Trends in the external environment may also suggest organizational vulnerabilities. Finally, research suggests that considering worst-case scenarios and conducting risk audits can also be useful methods for clarifying organizational vulnerabilities (Waugh & Hy, 1990).

Once one or more vulnerabilities are identified, organizational members need to catalogue symptoms that indicate that a certain type of crisis is developing.

METHODS FOR EVALUATION AND DIAGNOSIS

Ideally, an organization will develop specific systems to scan, monitor, and screen potential warning signals of a certain crisis. Such systems will ideally be designed so that individuals or technical systems monitor all vulnerable areas of an organization. The systems need to embrace quantitative as well as qualitative methods for data collection and analysis so that all types of warnings are identified.

Periodic tests of such systems by a review committee can help ensure their effectiveness. This committee could critically analyze current systems by conducting vulnerability analyses that surface weak points in an organization's current structures and technologies, and inadequacies in detection capabilities. Such a review committee needs to be independent from other detection-reporting relationships because, as Vaughan (1996) reports in her study of the explosion of the space shuttle *Challenger,* interdependencies between regulating bodies and those being regulated can lead to the repression of warning signals.

It is important to establish clear thresholds for action once potential warning signals surface through an organization's detection systems. Such triggering mechanisms provide employees with a standard, accepted decision rule to report and act upon warning information. In addition, training sessions need to be designed and implemented to increase employees' and managers' awareness about the severity and importance of detecting potential warning signals and to train employees in how to manage the organization's signal detection systems. The benefits of such training sessions include decreasing employee and managerial apathy about detecting warning signals and generating a better overall understanding of how to systematically detect and respond to potential warning signals.

Mechanisms for Communication

An integrative structure for communication with external and internal stakeholders will also help increase awareness of, and commitment to, the detection of potential warning signals. Structures should focus on integrating diverse information and disseminating critical data to key individuals. Specifically, the free flow of internal and external communication can help ensure that people who need information have access to it and that individuals who have contributed information receive feedback.

Several tactics may further facilitate appropriate speed and direction of communication. A "safe" location to report information (e.g., anonymous "800" numbers) may make employees less hesitant to report potential warnings. The distribution of issue-status reports and analyses can increase key decision-makers' awareness and understanding of potential warning signals.

Maintenance of open and close communication with the top management team may also ensure that those with discretionary power are aware of key issues. Finally, Smart and Vertinsky (1977) suggest that "extraordinary channels" to cut through hierarchy (Smart & Vertinsky, 1977) may also be necessary.

One company that appears to be taking responsibility management—as part of reputational crisis prevention—seriously is Nike, although it might not call its approach TRM or crisis management. In 1997, faced with a serious reputational crisis because of activism against Nike's relationships with supplier factories that had been discovered to have significant labor abuses, Nike began to focus on working conditions in its supply-chain factories. In the ensuing years, Nike implemented many changes in how it managed its supply chain, including the implementation of factory monitoring and improving working conditions, by first establishing a code of conduct and then seeing to it that factories adhered to that code. Early signals, however, were missed, and Nike made several missteps, as CEO Phil Knight admits in Nike's most recent triple-bottom-line report (Knight, 2004). In the interests of transparency and to meet stakeholder demands, Nike also published in 2004 the entire list of its suppliers, and began working toward common industry standards around supply-chain issues. This type of proactive and interactive stance places the company at the forefront of trying not only to detect signals before they become problematic, but also to take significant internal actions to forestall problems.

Conclusion

Preparing for a crisis obviously requires planning and foresight, but it also demands, as we have argued, close attention to early signals that can easily be ignored. These signals can frequently be found by heeding input from, and paying attention to, the interests, demands, and needs of stakeholders—and this attention can result from the implementation of a responsibility management system that takes a wide range of stakeholders into consideration. Stakeholders and the issues they raise or have concerns about can play an important role in signal detection that can help avert or at least mitigate the impacts of crises. Even when crisis cannot be avoided, the solid relationships established by managing stakeholder-related responsibilities well may help the company deal with a crisis more effectively and efficiently.

Responsibility management can arguably help companies avoid or mitigate some of the worst internally generated and industry-specific crises, especially those associated with irresponsible internal actions. If the entire system is set up to foster integrity, then early signals will be more likely to be noted rather than ignored. Further, responsibility management can help managers prepare for unusual and unforeseen events, because they become more aware or mindful of the full scope of their responsibilities and impacts and know where to place their attention and what needs to be managed. Conversely, listening to the concerns of stakeholders provides early entry into potential crises related to human factors or concerns about a company's practices that might otherwise explode into not only a reputational nightmare but events of significant cost to stakeholders and the company itself. While no manager is omniscient, taking a holistic approach to responsibilities as outlined above can represent an important corporate asset that helps forestall and mitigate foreseeable risks.

Bibliography

Baker, M. (2004). *Companies in crisis—What not to do when it all goes wrong: Snow Brand Milk Products Co.* Retrieved April 20, 2006, from http://www.mallenbaker.net/csr/CSRfiles/crisis04.html

Bowonder, B., & Linstone, H. (1987). Notes on the Bhopal accident: Risk analysis and multiple perspectives. *Technological Forecasting and Social Change, 32,* 183–202.

Evans, J. R., & Lindsay, W. M. (2001). *The management and control of quality* (5th ed.). New York: West.

Harris, R. (2004). Malfeasance insurance: How plan sponsors are coping with the mutual fund scandal. *CFO Magazine.* Retrieved July 29, 2004, from http://www.cfo.com/article/1,5309,12858||M|886,00.html

Hart, S. L., & Milstein, M. B. (2003). Creating sustainable value. *Academy of Management Executive, 17*(2), 56–69.

Knight, P. H. (2004). *Nike: FY 04 Corporate Responsibility Report.* Retrieved April 20, 2006, from http://www.nike.com/nikebiz/nikebiz.jhtml

Mitroff, I. (2001). Crisis leadership. *Executive Excellence, 18*(8), 19.

Pauchant, T. C., & Mitroff, I. (1992). *Transforming the crisis-prone organization. Preventing individual organizational and environmental tragedies.* San Francisco: Jossey-Bass.

Pearson, C. M., & Clair, J. A. (1998). Reframing crisis management. *Academy of Management Review, 23*(1), 59–76.

Pearson, C. M., Clair, J. A., Kovoor-Misra, S., & Mitroff, I. (1997). Managing the unthinkable. *Organizational Dynamics, 26*(2), 51–64.

Schein, E. H. (1985). *Organizational culture and leadership.* San Francisco: Jossey-Bass.

Senge, P. (1990). *The fifth discipline.* New York: Free Press.

Smart, C., & Vertinsky, I. (1977). Designs for crisis decision units. *Administrative Science Quarterly, 22,* 640–657.

Svendsen, A. (1998). *The stakeholder strategy: Profiting from collaborative business relationships.* San Francisco: Berrett-Koehler.

Thomas, J., & Harris, J. (2004). Clear advantage: Building shareholder value, environment: Value to the investor. *Global Environmental Management Initiative (GEMI), 2004.* Retrieved April 15, 2004, from http://www.gemi.org/GEMI%20Clear%20Advantage.pdf

Vaughan, D. (1996). *The* Challenger *launch decision: Risky technology, culture, and deviance at NASA.* Chicago: University of Chicago Press.

Waddock, S. (2004). Creating corporate accountability: Foundational principles to make corporate citizenship real. *Journal of Business Ethics, 50,* 313–327.

Waddock, S., & Bodwell, C. (2002). From TQM to RESPONSIBILITY MANAGEMENT: Emerging responsibility management approaches. *Journal of Corporate Citizenship, 7,* 113–126.

Waddock, S., & Bodwell, C. (in press). Managing responsibility: What can be learned from the quality movement? *California Management Review.*

Wallace, K. (2003). Fund Times: Putnam's SEC settlement unsettles some. *Morningstar.* Retrieved July 29, 2004, from http://news.morningstar.com/archive/archive.asp

Waugh, W. L., Jr., & Hy, R. J. (Eds.). (1990). *Handbook of emergency management: Programs and policies dealing with major hazards and disasters.* New York: Greenwood.

Crisis Management Simulations 12

Flaws and Remedies

Bertrand Robert and Christopher Lajtha

Crisis-management training focuses principally on simulations and exercises. The nature of these exercises is the subject of much recent review and redesign in response to an evolution in the crisis landscape. Empirical evidence confirms that the frequency, complexity, and degree of unexpectedness of crises have increased materially over the last 2 decades.

It is necessary to move to the next paradigm—from the repetition of mechanical and relatively meaningless exercises to genuinely reflecting on, and learning about, the real nature of crisis situations.

The Argillos consultants have more than 20 years of experience in providing advice, research, and training in crisis preparation and management.

Use and Limitations of Conventional Training Exercises

Traditional crisis-management exercises are useful for taking stock of a number of issues. They enable certain critical components of a crisis-management response to be tested under conditions resembling those of a real crisis. Such components might include the suitability of the crisis command center(s); the efficiency of the alert and mobilization procedures; the robustness of materials used at the crisis location; the efficiency of the various communication systems; and the communication and coordination between the various crisis-management participants. Training exercises can also bring to light a number of structural and procedural weaknesses in the crisis response, and can stimulate ideas for improvement that would not otherwise have been considered. In most cases, exercises serve to convince the crisis-management teams that there is always room for improvement in their response preparation and implementation efforts. These represent reasonably unequivocal, positive aspects to the conventional training process.

However, there are limitations and weaknesses inherent in such exercises that are frequently either not understood or ignored altogether. When questioned afterward, participants in traditional crisis-management training exercises often express disillusionment and even discomfort with the experience, and express skepticism with respect to the real value of lessons learned from the exercise—if any. Furthermore, whether or not appreciated by the participants or the training organizers, the tendency to focus on a half-day or one-day "annual exercise" reveals an incomplete understanding of the crisis-management process and the kind of response capability that can and should be developed.

A crisis situation is likely to involve many members of an organization, even if only peripherally. Clearly the members of the crisis management team(s) (CMTs) and their backups or substitutes will be directly implicated in parallel with the senior management team. However, many other members of the organization will be implicated to a greater or lesser extent because of additional, covering workloads, temporarily reassigned tasks and responsibilities, the absence of their colleagues assigned to the CMT(s), and questions from family members and friends outside of the workplace. It is important that they share an awareness that there is a credible crisis-response capability in the organization—one that is not undermined by inadequate or inappropriate training.

There are three principal drawbacks to the traditional approach to crisis management training—the periodic "day out" to participate in a crisis simulation and training exercise, described below.

1. Such exercises provoke adverse psychological reactions—feelings of dissatisfaction, doubt, and distrust—on the part of the participants.

Dissatisfaction results from the frequently justified perception that a crisis simulation exercise represents a period of stress and discomfort with little upside potential for the participant. The only certainty is that a day will be lost from a hectic work schedule and time will have to be found to make up for it. There may well be a feeling that since a similar exercise was performed last year, there is little point in repeating the disruption again so soon. In many cases, there may also be a feeling that such an exercise serves only to highlight personal management weakness and that the exercise represents a moment of exaggerated personal risk in the workplace environment.

Doubts may be felt or expressed with respect to the design and execution of the training exercises themselves. Typically, there are difficulties in making scenarios unfold realistically because of the behavior of the crisis-management team and because of the artificially distorted time frames and scales that are necessitated by other competing operational agendas. Doubts may also exist with respect to the efficacy of the logistical support, much of which cannot be tested during a periodic, one-off exercise.

More critically, there may well be feelings of distrust with the training process or the motivation of the managers designing and running the training exercise. If key participants are conspicuously absent ("*too busy on more important operational issues*") or choose to get involved in the organization of the training but not participate themselves, then the whole process is undermined. If the key senior managers do not participate in the training process, for whatever reason, then the crisis management training exercise may well be reasonably considered as a potentially career-limiting minefield—and treated with distrust in addition to dissatisfaction and doubt.

2. There may be doubts about the learning value attaching to such exercises.

Traditional exercises tend to follow a predictable annual cycle and are frequently linked to fire and emergency evacuation drills. How wise is such a predictable and repetitive routine? How smart is it to link a fire evacuation drill (other than perhaps that relating to the evacuation of skyscrapers) to the potential complexities of a real-life crisis? How would a sports team be judged that is scheduled to compete against a talented opponent ("the crisis") in an important competition, yet trains only once during the pre-season—and with neither its team captain's participation nor the participation of the team substitutes? And in real life, the game does not concern the winning of trophies but the preservation of the quality of many lives—any of the multiple stakeholders in the organization.

Many people do not seek to be exposed to stressful situations, nor do they necessarily react well under them. Ill-designed, incomplete, or inadequately explained stressful training exercises can trigger a long-term rejection of the process and mental blockage with respect to any lessons that may have been learned. Infrequent exposure to constrained training exercises is not likely to reinforce the learning process or overcome distaste for the process. Nor are such exercises particularly suited to testing and revealing the kinds of psychological profiles that are needed in a crisis-management team.

What happens after most exercises? After another, similar exercise twelve months later? In the interim, who owns the crisis-management process? How many of the observed weakness or system errors are corrected? How many of the suggestions for improvements are followed up? What level of resources is allocated to making such enhancements?

One of the key learning and progress factors in crisis-management training lies with the use of professional observers who are charged with reviewing and critically commenting on the exercise as it unfolds. Such external observers are not always used because of the perceived sensitivity of the subject matter. Further, there are issues relating to field experience, personal biases, their reporting lines, and their role in between crisis-management exercises that need to be addressed.

A final, important issue with respect to the learning value of traditional exercises is the extent to which they address real weak points or sensitive issues. There are taboo subjects that can have significant destructive value, yet are rarely raised from within the organization. As a consequence, they are rarely made the subject of crisis-management scenarios. (The use of trusted, external observers and advisors can be particularly useful with respect to the posing of otherwise career-limiting questions.)

3. Traditional crisis-management exercises are based on flawed assumptions about the nature of crises and the practical implications for effective response.

The most glaring flaw in traditional approaches to crisis management and training lies with the notion that the key to crisis management lies with developing a detailed plan or set of procedures. There is a qualitative difference between peril and hazard-specific emergency response planning and the development of a crisis response capability. Crises are, by definition, sufficiently surprising and unpredictable to preclude the notion of conventional written plans and procedures.

Another example of flawed thinking lies with the notion that the nature of crises has not changed over the last two decades and that traditional crisis-management exercises are as relevant and effective today as they have been in the past—despite their limited and highly structured focus on conventional problem situations.

The concentration of training into single "D-Day" exercises can lead to the false impression that crisis-management skills are uniquely devoted to sudden and immediate responses. Such a skewed focus ignores the many facets of crisis-management preparation that can be developed outside of a "hot" situation. Examples of initiatives that should be taken in constant preparation for a truly material and unexpected event or situation include an effective system for "weak signal" detection and media surveillance training of the members of the crisis-management team in their specific crisis command center roles; the continuous updating of the key contact network's analysis of, and lessons learned from, crisis situations and their management in other organizations; and the development of "off-the-wall" scenarios against which to test response capabilities.

In summary, traditional crisis-management exercises achieve very little with respect to the development of an improved crisis response capability. Too often, they are considered as tiresome annual rituals rather than as opportunities to step aside from day-to-day tasks and participate in an unusual, yet critically important, management process.

A new approach is needed, with new crisis response techniques.

New Crisis Management Training Practices

Argillos has developed many different crisis-management training initiatives, 20 of which are described here. They are grouped and allocated to seven fundamental crisis-management objectives that are applicable to just about any organization. These innovative training initiatives have been developed as a result of nearly 20 years of practical intervention in real-life crisis situations. Many are based on simple common sense. Others have been inspired by practices observed in teams that have to confront extreme situations (notably training for extreme sports or Special Forces training).

The exercises described in the following pages neither pretend to address every possible aspect of crisis-management preparation nor seek to provide a series of obligatory steps to follow. Instead, they represent a consolidation of real-life experiences and techniques that have proved their worth in a wide variety of crisis situations.

Crisis-management preparation and training needs to be customized to each organization and aligned with its particular exposure profile, its business objectives, its time frames, and the maturity of its crisis-management capability. It is possible to create hybrid training programs that combine various exercises or parts of various exercises. Another way of looking at the development of an effective crisis-management capability is to respond with the same exceptional qualities that characterize the crisis itself: creativity, guile, speed, surprise, symbolic value, and so on.

1. Making the transition to crisis mode successfully

The need to react quickly and effectively at the critical early stages of a crisis, combined with the potential for all kinds of unexpected hiccups to arise during such a period of high stress, means that the Crisis Alert and Crisis Management Team (CMT) Mobilization phases need to be crafted, practiced, and recrafted.

MOBILIZATION DRILL

The first step consists of simulating the mobilization of the CMT and the activation of the Crisis Command Center (CCC). What are the first reactions and actions to be taken during the first hour(s)? What are the mandatory steps that must be taken—and in what order of priority? Does everyone know what he or she has to do (especially the CMT)? Is everyone familiar with the layout and functionality of the CCC? Until the responses to these basic questions become second nature, there is no point in moving further into the crisis-management process.

CMT 101

The roles played by the CMT members in the CCC *do not correspond to traditional job functions* and therefore need to be understood and learned. For example, how many CMTs contain an Information Manager, a Scenarist, a Stress Manager, or an external Observer? How many of these roles appear in a conventional corporate job-title or job-description database? Both the primary CMT members and their role substitutes need to understand their particular nonstandard roles and responsibilities in the CCC, and rehearsal of the interaction with other CMT members is essential during crisis simulation exercises.

2. Master the basic elements of crisis management

Instead of repeating error-filled exercises that demonstrate a lack of understanding of the basics of crisis management, why not design the exercises to reinforce such understanding?

EXERCISE INVERSION

Transform some of the characteristics of traditional exercises into positive features: Let the participants choose the crisis scenarios rather than imposing them. Idea ownership will alleviate much of the initial angst and suspicion over motives. Take plenty of time to prepare the exercise participants *before* the scenarios and exercises are played out. Explain the crisis-management process and introduce some of the techniques and skills that constitute an effective response capability. Explain that the D-Day exercise is not important in itself but is simply a pretext for developing skills and reinforcing lessons learned. Underscore the fact that the primary objective is team building and team learning rather than worrying about weaknesses in the exercise execution.

FRAGMENTED EXERCISE

Focus on the *positive aspects* of the exercise. Instead of approaching the exercise as a sporting contest with points to be won (or, more usually, lost), break the exercise into segments and work on the training method: The various phases of the crisis can be played and replayed so that positive lessons can be reinforced.

REPEAT EXERCISE

Replay the same exercise with the same participants after the lessons learned have been assimilated. This reinforces the lessons learned and helps to motivate the participants by providing evidence of learning.

3. Build a sense of teamwork and team spirit

Knowing the rules of football does not mean that one will necessarily win the match. Even the best of procedures will serve little purpose if the crisis-management team does not function well as a unit.

MINIATURE MODELING

Using a real or imaginary model of the CCC, work through the CMT procedures and move the CMT members around in the CCC model as they perform their tasks. The use of a kind of "doll's house" model in this way allows a better understanding of each of the CMT member roles and the ways in which they should work together.

ROLE CHANGE

The CMT members exchange roles for an exercise so that they can better understand the constraints and difficulties of the roles that other team members must play—and thus develop an enhanced mutual respect and collective efficiency. This is especially useful for the guardian of the logbook.

SAQS

An extensive, self-assessment questionnaire (SAQ) that is built around 150 questions grouped into 11 categories enables the CMT to address all aspects of crisis management. It provides common reference points, facilitates the sharing of prior experiences, and tackles the pertinent questions.

4. Reinforce the links between the various participants

There is a predictable group of internal and external participants necessary for the successful management of a crisis. It is therefore prudent to develop strong working relationships with them during periods of calm.

KEY PARTICIPANTS' EXERCISE

Work with the CMT members and key participants to iron out any communication or operational constraints. The objective is to identify and address issues of nonalignment of interests between the participants so as to permit smooth relationships during the next crisis.

EXTENDED, CROSS-CULTURAL EXERCISE

Run simulation exercises with, and invite critical input from, organization managers from other parts of the world. These managers may prove to be valuable supporters of the crisis-management team during "hot" situations.

5. Preparation and support for decision-making

Decision-making lies at the heart of crisis management. This is a particularly difficult skill to master and merits special attention.

MAZE

The decision-making process is mapped out using real cases or hybrid extracts from real cases. The important decisions are examined in detail and alternatives are debated. The exercise consists of uncovering the traps that surround the taking of decisions. Familiarity with questioning is developed. Above all, the exercise reveals the components of confidence capital and the key values that help determine how to choose between multiple options. For example, this kind of exercise can be used to develop different decision trees with respect to product recall problems, an epidemic response, or an imminent coastal pollution disaster.

COPILOT

No single person owns all the attributes of the ideal decision-maker (pilot) in a crisis situation. His or her inevitable areas of weakness need to be filled by the qualities of a specially created crisis-management team. This exercise explores the eight key CMT roles that have been designed to support the decision-maker (pilot).

REWRITING HISTORY

To facilitate the creation of common points of reference, certain exercises can be built using important historical events and key decision-making moments (crises). The advantage of this kind of exercise lies with the change of focus: reference to issues of general cultural interest rather than operational efficiency. References to teams that have confronted extreme (often life-threatening) conditions—successfully and unsuccessfully—provide excellent simulation models (e.g., the *Titanic* disaster).

TAKE THE CONTRARIAN VIEW

It is useful to look at crisis situations from all angles and perspectives—including the roles and objectives of the most difficult stakeholders—to appreciate the real nature of a crisis. A significant degree of mental agility and flexibility is required to make the exercise fruitful.

6. Develop an enhanced capability to react to the truly unexpected

Crises are occurring for the increasingly unpredictable and surprising reasons. It is therefore well worth analyzing the nature of surprise in order to develop of robust reactive capability.

Instead of reusing crisis scenarios and crisis-management exercises that have been used in the past (which really do not address the truly unpredictable event or series of events), much more value is created by simulating truly surprising, even shocking, scenarios and analyzing the CMT reactions.

"ALPHABET OF SURPRISE"

Surprise is never total—it has roots. An "alphabet of surprise" has been created that highlights each of the 26 elements of surprise. The exercise consists of learning the alphabet and using it either to construct relevant scenarios or explore the elements of surprise in crises that have already played out. This approach has been deployed in analyses of terrorist threats and conditions of extreme temperatures (e.g., heat waves).

FLASH/RAPID EXERCISE

The exercise consists of making a CMT respond to an unconventional situation with a much-reduced reaction time. Use of e-mail enables the same problem to be posed to each member of the CMT, integrating the contributions of a previous CMT to each iteration of the problem, all within the same day. For example, such exercises have been used to test responses to blackmail threats made against postal services and shipping companies.

MIRROR EXERCISE

The exercise consists of breaking up a real crisis into its chronological elements. The CMT meets each day, for 2 hours, to examine and discuss how the other organization reacted to the unfolding situation and to raise questions about the choices available at each stage. Ideally, after the exercise, it would be rewarding to contact the organization that lived through the real crisis and exchange ideas and lessons learned. For example, a metropolitan crisis-management team can usefully benefit from real-life examples experienced by their counterparts in other cities (e.g., severe flooding; power outages; road and bridge collapses; underground railway closures; health alerts; major events).

FIVE SENSES (DON'T OVERLOOK OR UNDERESTIMATE THE SIXTH SENSE!)

The ability to respond effectively to surprise depends largely on the intuition and spontaneity of the decision-makers. There are a number of exercises that can used to test and improve the reactivity to surprise—notably from theatrical schools and from the world of martial arts.

THE ODYSSEY

Stories of exploration and navigation offer numerous analogies for crisis-management exercises and numerous examples of surprises. The exercise consists of spending time (2–3 days) offshore in small sailing boats with professional captains experiencing and analyzing the nature of surprise.

7. Communicate acquired knowledge within the organization
The ultimate goal of the training exercises is enhanced robustness of, and continuity prospects for, the organization. This assumes a certain degree of autonomy built on the capitalization of the training process through the communication of the lessons learned to other managers in the organization.

DYNAMIC FEEDBACK

Organize an immediate postmortem following a crisis and use the CMT participants as internal experts with respect to the development of lessons learned for future CMT members.

DAMOCLES

Damocles is a crisis-management training software tool that is build around the model of an aircraft cockpit and flight. The tool can be adapted to the particular structure and culture of an organization and operates on two levels—as a pedagogic tool in periods of calm and as a reference guide in the CCC during "hot" situations.

MEDIA TENNIS

Media Tennis is a software tool that stimulates the learning of the essential elements of crisis communication—using game of tennis as a reference. This tool provides an amusing way of learning important techniques, in a structured manner, very quickly.

These new forms of training form a central part of a new thinking about the nature of surprise and the development of effective crisis-management skills. They should be supplemented by further research to develop a better understanding of the components of confidence, the art of anticipation, the nature of fear, and the elements of surprise.

Author Index

Abrassart, C., 58
Ackermann, F., 169
Acquier, A., 58
Adams, J., 13, 15
Aggeri, E., 58
Aguilera, D. C., 109
Allard-Poesi, F., 169
Alvesson, M., 147
Angelmar, R., 165
Argyris, C., 236, 276 (tab), 278 (tab)
Arnold, T., 47, 72
Arrow, K., 77
Ashby, W. R., 277 (tab), 289
Audet, M., 167
Augoustinos, M., 165
Austin, J. L., 38, 64
Axelrod, R., 167

Baccus, M. D., 150
Baecker, D., 9
Baker, M., 304, 305, 306
Bantel, K. A., 234
Barnard, C., 10, 63, 229
Barnes, J., 55
Barry, D., 5, 133
Barthes, Y., 79n17
Barton, L., 95, 125, 276 (tab)
Baumol, W. J., 72
Beamish, T. D., 126, 127
Beardon, C., 27
Beavin, J. H., 78n8
Beck, U., 5, 6, 8, 11, 13, 17, 18, 21n1,
   21n6, 221
Benton, T., 8
Berger, P., 148
Berle, A., 72
Berleur, J., 27
Bernstein, P. L., 5
Bettenhausen, K. L., 90
Bettleheim, B., 214

Bieri, F., 17
Bigley, G., 109, 112
Billings, R. S., 226
Blair, J. D., 97
Blommaert, J., 176, 180
Bodwell, C., 300, 302, 303
Bogen, D., 142–146
Boje, D., 125
Boli, J., 17
Boltanski, L., 80n27
Bonß, W., 5
Bonss, W., 8
Borland, J., 86, 88
Bourgeois, E., 177
Bowonder, B., 227, 307
Boyer, W. W., 130
Bradbury, H., 121
Brockner, J., 238
Brody, H., 133
Brown, A. D., 125, 134, 135, 154, 156,
   222, 236, 237
Brown, D., 52
Brunsson, N., 21n8
Bryant, J., 169
Buckley, M. R., 237, 240
Burlaud, A., 27, 80n27

Callahan, A. L., 238
Callon, M., 79n17
Canter, D., 277 (tab), 282–283, 285–286
Caron, D. D., 79n17
Chandler, A. D., 73
Charny, B., 93
Chester, D. N., 282
Cicourel, A. V., 137
Clair, J., 90, 109, 224, 225, 226, 227,
   230, 233, 244, 245, 300, 301, 302,
   304, 306
Clarke, L., 9, 11, 15
Cohen, A. R., 236

Collingridge, D., 274
Comber, M., 285–286
Cook, F. L., 130
Cossette, P., 167
Cottraux, J., 165
Coulon, A., 136
Crocker, J., 164, 165
Cropper, S., 169
Cruver, B., 206
Cyert, R., 234

D'Aveni, R. A., 90, 307
De Quidt, J., 285
de Saint Georges, I., 176, 177, 186
Delli Carpini, M. X., 130
Desai, V., 120, 121
Deschamps, I., 227, 230
Dewey, J., 16, 21n9
Donaldson, T., 20
Douglas, M., 21n3, 25, 35, 36–42, 44, 45, 49, 61, 69, 141
Doyle, A., 5
Dror, Y., 224
Dunn, W. N., 240
Dutton, J. E., 109, 111, 163, 165, 166, 236

Edelman, G. M., 162
Eden, C., 167, 169
Elliott, D., 271, 272, 274, 275, 276 (tab), 277 (tab), 278 (tab), 280, 283, 284, 285, 286, 287, 288, 289
Elliott, M. A., 17
Ellis, R., 21n3
Elmes, M., 133
Ericson, R. V., 5
Evans, J. R., 302
Evers, A., 5
Ewald, F., 5, 6, 71, 80n31

Ferris, G. R., 237, 240
Filliettaz, L., 176
Fink, S. J., 163, 164
Fink, S. L., 90, 95
Fletcher, K. E., 169
Føllesdal, A., 17
Football Licensing Authority, 286, 288
Forgues, B., 162, 163, 165, 224, 229, 230
Foti, R. J., 165
Freeman, R. E., 20, 97
Freud, S., 32, 78n3
Friedman, M., 17
Frosdick, S., 274, 283, 285
Frost, P., 110

Funtowicz, S. O., 11
Fusaro, P. C., 206

Gabriel, Y., 204, 213, 214
Garfinkel, H., 124–125, 136, 137
Garvin, D. A., 273
Gatot, L., 162, 163, 164, 168, 169, 176, 231
Gephart, R. P., 123, 124, 125, 129, 131, 132, 134, 137–138, 139, 140, 141, 147, 148, 149, 150, 154, 156
Giddens, A., 8
Gioia, D. A., 165
Global Exchange, 18
Goestschin, P., 163
Golding, D., 15
Gouldner, A., 272, 275–276, 279, 280, 281–282, 286, 289
Grandy, C., 51
Grant, D., 176
Greve, A., 238
Grolin, J., 18
Grosz, E., 186

Habermas, J., 79n17, 80n27, 125, 147, 148, 149, 245
Halpern, J., 234
Hambrick, D. C., 90, 233, 307
Handel, W. H., 124, 136
Harrington, J., 282
Harris, J., 302
Harris, M., 218
Harris, R., 301
Hart, S. L., 302
Harvey, M. G., 237, 240
Heap, J., 136
Hedberg, B. T., 238
Hermann, C. F., 163, 165, 226
Holsti, O. R., 163, 165
Holzer, B., 13, 17, 18, 21n7
Huff, A. S., 169
Hutchins, E., 108
Hutter, B. M., 274
Hy, R. J., 310
Hynes, T., 279, 289

Iedema, R., 176
Inglis, S., 276 (tab), 280

Jackson, D. D., 78n8
Jackson, S., 109
Jackson, S. E., 236
Jacobs, L. R., 130
Jacques, E., 236

Author Index

Jacques, J. M., 161, 162, 163, 164, 166, 167, 168, 169, 176, 177, 180, 186, 187, 188, 231
Janis, I. L., 237
Janoff-Bulman, R., 244
Jeanson, B., 167
Jensen, M., 233
Johnes, M., 274

Kahneman, D., 164
Keenoy, T., 176
Kelly, G., 167
Kelsen, H., 79n12
Kemp, R., 129, 131, 147, 149, 150
Kets de Vries, M. F. R., 236, 276 (tab)
Kletz, T., 163
Klienfield, S., 238
Knight, F. H., 21n2, 43–44, 45, 54, 55, 72, 79n10
Knight, P. H., 311
Kojeve, A., 79n12
Kovoor-Misra, S., 90, 95, 100, 162, 163, 227, 301, 302, 306
Krimsky, S., 15
Krohn, W., 12, 14

Lagadec, P., 35, 164, 223, 224, 226, 244
Lalonde, M., 227, 230
Lang, J., 282
Laroche, H., 164
Lascoumes, P., 79n17
Lash, S., 8
Latour, B., 79n17
Lau, C., 5, 8, 13
Laufer et al., 81n35
Laufer, R., 27, 46, 62, 74, 79n16, 79n20, 80n27, 162
Laughlin, H. P., 237
Laurent, N., 161, 166, 176, 187, 188
Lawrence, T., 141
Lawton, R., 231
Leben, C., 79n17
Leibenstein, H., 270n2
Leiter, K., 124, 125, 136–137
Lemos, R., 93
Levitt, B., 273
Lichtenstein, B. B. B., 121
Lindsay, W. M., 302
Linstone, H., 227, 307
Lomborg, B., 54, 56
Lord, R. G., 165
Louis, M., 111
Luckmann, T., 148

Luhmann, N., 9, 21n4
Lynch, M., 141, 142–146

Madsen, P., 120
Madsen, P. M., 121
Manz, C. C., 165
March, J. G., 11, 166, 234, 241, 273
Mason, P., 233
Masuch, M., 165
McClelland, D. C., 80n28
McCloskey, D. N., 127, 134
McDermott, I., 230
McGuinness, M., 196, 274, 275, 276 (tab)
McKechnie, P. I., 237–238
McLean, I., 274
Means, G., 72
Metais, E., 163
Micheletti, M., 17, 18
Miglani, A., 109, 125, 126, 162, 225
Milburn, T. W., 224–225
Milgrom, P., 270n3
Miliken, F., 222, 235
Millburn, T. W., 226
Miller, D., 109, 125, 126, 162, 225, 242, 276 (tab)
Miller, R., 206
Milliken, F., 111
Milliken, F. J., 277 (tab), 288
Milstein, M. B., 302
Mintzberg, H., 10, 20
Mitroff, I., 85, 90, 95, 98, 109, 125, 126, 128, 129, 162, 163, 164, 221, 224, 225, 226, 227, 228, 229, 230, 235, 238, 244, 258, 259 (fig), 276 (tab), 287, 301, 302, 306, 307, 309
Moelwyn-Hughes, R., 279, 281, 282, 285
Moldoveanu, M., 18
Morgan, G., 110
Morin, E., 228
Morris, P., 244
Morrison, A. B., 53
Musil, S., 93

Nader, R., 28
Nakane, C., 254
Narapereddy, V., 169
Nathan, M. L., 100
Nioche, J. P., 164
Nix, T. W., 97
Nizet, J., 177
Nonaka, I., 273
Novicevic, M. M., 237, 240

Nowotny, H., 5
Nystrom, P. C., 85, 163, 165, 166, 234

O'Connor, J., 230
Offe, C., 147
O'Riordan, T., 131
Oswick, C., 176

Paine, L. S., 18
Paradeise, C., 27, 46, 79n16
Parker, D., 231
Pauchant, T. C., 90, 95, 162, 221, 224, 225, 226, 227, 228, 229, 230, 235, 238, 244, 258, 259 (fig), 276 (tab), 287, 307, 309
Pearson, C. M., 85, 90, 95, 98, 109, 128, 129, 224, 225, 226, 227, 230, 233, 244, 245, 300, 301, 302, 304, 306, 307, 308
Peay, J., 274
Perelman, C., 80n36
Perrow, C., 9, 12, 30, 109, 110, 156, 163, 229, 274
Pezet, E., 58
Phelps, N. L., 226
Piret, A., 177
Pitter, R., 125, 147, 148
Pondy, L., 110
Popplewell, O., 274–275, 276 (tab), 278 (tab), 283–284, 285
Porfiriev, B., 224
Posner, R., 78n1, 79n14
Post, J. E., 18
Prasad, P., 279, 289
Preble, J. F., 162
Preston, L. E., 20
Puffer, S. M., 237–238
Purdue, M., 131

Quarantelli, E. L., 109, 224, 227

Ramaprasad, A., 165
Ravetz, J. R., 11
Rayner, S., 21n3
Reason, J., 231, 232, 242
Reeve, C., 274
Reilly, A. H., 225, 226
Reivich, K., 202
Reynolds, S., 273, 274, 276 (tab), 277 (tab), 278 (tab), 285, 288
Ridington, R., 133
Riessman, C. K., 125, 132, 133
Roberts, J., 270n3

Roberts, K., 108, 109, 112, 121
Roberts, K. H., 120, 187
Rosenthal, U., 221–222, 223, 224, 226, 227
Roth, R., 112
Roux-Dufort, C., 162, 163, 164, 187, 224, 226, 231, 244, 247
Rumelhart, D. E., 165

Salter, L., 123, 129, 130, 154
Sandoval, G., 94
Savage, G. T., 97
Schaalman, M. L., 226
Schein, E. H., 287, 309
Schmeltzer, J., 89
Schneider, C., 165
Schön, D. A., 276 (tab), 277 (tab), 278 (tab), 289
Schuler, R. S., 224–225
Schwartz, H. S., 227, 235
Schwarz, M., 21n3
Schwenk, C., 238
Schwenk, C. R., 164
Scollon, R., 186
Scollon, S., 186
Scraton, P., 279, 280
Senge, P., 304
Senge, P. M., 273, 276 (tab), 277 (tab), 288
Sethi, S. P., 18
Shamir, J., 222, 237, 238
Shamir, M., 222, 237, 238
Shatte, A., 202
Short, J. F., Jr., 9, 15
Shortt, Rt. Hon. E., 276 (tab), 280–281
Shrivastava, P., 90, 109, 125, 126, 162, 163, 165, 222, 225, 226, 227, 228, 229, 231, 232
Sikkink, K., 18
Simon, H. A., 11, 29–30, 164, 234
Sipika, C., 274, 284
Slaco, D., 123, 129, 130, 154
Slatter, S. P., 165, 166
Smart, C. F., 226, 308, 309, 311
Smith, D., 230, 232, 233, 271, 272, 273, 274, 275, 276 (tab), 277 (tab), 278 (tab), 280, 281, 283, 284, 285, 286–287, 287, 288, 289
Sørensen, M. P., 17
Sproull, L. S., 166, 241
Starbuck, W., 111, 222, 234, 235, 238
Starbuck, W. H., 85, 163, 165, 166, 277 (tab), 288
Starkey, K., 222, 236
Staw, B. M., 237–238

Author Index

Steier, L., 141
Stolle, D., 17, 18
Stubbart, C. I., 163, 164, 165, 166
Sutcliffe, K. M., 41, 222, 229, 234, 242, 247
Sutton, R., 111
Sutton, R. I., 238
Svendsen, A., 305

Tamuz, M., 166, 241
Taylor, Rt. Hon. Lord Justice, 280, 283, 284
Taylor, S. E., 164, 165, 276 (tab), 284.285
Thevenot, L., 80n27
Thiétart, R. A., 229, 230
Thomas, J., 302
Thompson, M., 21n3
Toft, B., 273, 274, 276 (tab), 277 (tab), 278 (tab), 285, 288
Tombs, S., 278 (tab), 281, 289
Tononi, G., 162
Toulmin, S., 76–77
Tsoukas, H., 18
Turner, B. A., 90, 126, 131, 154, 165, 166, 226, 227, 228, 229, 232, 273, 274, 276 (tab), 277 (tab), 278, 280, 285, 287, 288
Tversky, A., 164

Ulrich, P., 20
Uzzell, D., 285–286

Varela, F. J., 165
Vaughan, D., 222, 235, 240, 242, 243, 310
Verschueren, J., 176, 180
Vertinsky, I., 163, 164, 165, 166, 226, 276 (tab), 308, 309, 311
Vidaillet, B., 165, 167, 244
Vogel, D., 18

Waaub, J. P., 227, 230
Waddock, S., 300, 302, 303, 304
Wahlström, B., 163

Walker, I., 165
Wallace, K., 301
Wallemacq, A., 161, 162, 167, 168, 176, 177, 186, 187
Watman, K. H., 224–225
Watson, T. J., 236
Watts, P., 19
Watzlawick, P., 78n8
Wätzold, F., 18
Waugh, W. L., Jr., 310
Weber, M., 64, 80n25
Weick, K., 31, 41, 49, 108, 110, 111, 112, 123–124, 163, 165, 166, 168, 187, 188, 222, 225, 226, 228, 229, 230, 231, 234–235, 237, 240, 242, 244, 245, 247, 277 (tab), 288
Weil, E., 55
Weiner, B., 237, 242
Weiss, J. W., 20
Welch, J., 245
Weyer, J., 12, 14
Wheatley, Rt. Hon. Lord, 276 (tab), 283
Whetton, D. A., 238
Whitehead, C. J., 97
Wicks, D., 280, 286, 288, 289
Wiersema, M. F., 234
Wildavsky, A., 141
Wildavsky, A., 8, 21n3
Willetts, P., 19
Williamson, O., 80n27
Wilmot, H., 147
Wodak, R., 176
Wong, D., 120
Woolfson, C., 274
Worf, B., 168
Wrightson, M. T., 169
Wybo, J. L., 164, 186, 232

Zajac, E. J., 233
Zammuto, R. F., 95

Subject Index

Abramoff lobbying scandal, 53
Accountability
   decision-making and, 19
   external stakeholders and, 307
   sensemaking and, 130–131, 136
   social, 5, 6
Action, definition of, 73
AFNOR (French Association for Normalization), 55
Agency cost impact, 264–266, 265 (fig)
A. H. Robbins Company, 263–264
AIDS, 60
Akamai, denial-of-service attack on, 92, 98
Alberta Energy Resources Conservation Board, 139–140
Alexa, and customer privacy, 95
Allitt Inquiry report, 134–135
Amazon.com, and customer privacy, 95
Anthrax, 29, 224
Anthropology, symbolic, 141
Anticipatory crisis management model, 164
Antisweatshop campaign, 18, 311
Antitrust law, 47, 50–51, 70–71, 72–73, 80n30
Argillos consultants, 315, 319
Argument of the cauldron, 32, 78n3
Aristocracy principle, 80n29
Aristotle, 54, 55, 77
Arthur Andersen bankruptcy, 29, 30, 52, 80n33, 200
Artificial procreation, ethics of, 55
Asahi Glass Co., Ltd., 268–269
Asbestos, 28, 54, 223
Atomic radiation, 7
Atomistic firm, 69–70
Attributional egotism, 237
Attribution theory, 237
Automobile recall/safety, 28
   See also Mitsubishi Motor Company

Avian flu, 60
AZF industrial accident, 223

Bankruptcy, 72
   Arthur Andersen, 29, 30, 52, 80n33, 200
   Enron, 29, 30, 52, 80n33, 200, 206, 303, 305
   REFCO, 52
Basel 2 regulation, 58
Baumol, William J., 80n32
Belgium, Heysel Stadium disaster in, 284
Bernanke, Ben, 53
Betrayal
   defining, 206–207
   See also Betrayal, psychological effects of
Betrayal, psychological effects of, 205–211
   betrayal by boss, 207–208 (fig)
   cold-blooded betrayer, 210 (fig)
   splitting/demonizing, 210 (fig)
   view of self vs. betrayer, 208–211, 209 (tab)
Bhopal, India, disaster, 11–12, 28, 56–57
Big City Police Department (BCPD) study
   data sample, 114–115
   early model adoption practice, 116–117
   having the bubble practice, 119–120
   model migration/resetting practice, 117–119
   research setting for, 112–114
   sensemaking practices, 115–120
Bolton Stadium disaster, 279, 280, 281, 283
Border-spanning economic decision-making, 19
Bovine spongioform encephalopathy (BSE), 14, 34, 60
Bradford Stadium fire, 274–275, 283–284, 285, 288
Brain cancer risk/cell phone rumor, 34

333

Brent Spar affair, 18, 19–20
BSE (bovine spongioform encephalopathy), 14, 34, 60, 223
Buffalo Grill crisis, France, 246
Butterfly effect, 33

Calculus of risk, 5–6
　in modern organization, 10–11
　social function of, 6
Caribou Coffee, 89
CD Universe, hacker theft of credit card information, 93
Central-limit theorem, 71
Certainty
　as basis for settling disputes, 36–37
　as institution, 36
　of scientific knowledge, 75
　See also Uncertainty
CERT (Computer Emergency Response Team), 97
Challenger accident (NASA), 11, 235, 240, 243, 310
Chaos theory, 33–34
Charisma, 79n24–80n24
Charismatic authority, 65, 66, 77
Chat group, online, 96–97
Ch-Ch-syndrome, 11
Chemical pollution, 7
Chernobyl disaster, 11, 13, 28
Chrysler, 72
Class action, 51, 73
　asbestos use, 28
　health hazard, 78n6
　tobacco company, 28
Classical free-market theory, 69–70
Classical microeconomic theory, 65
Classical model of economic theory, 39, 67
Climatic catastrophe, 58, 223, 242, 245, 323
Cloning, 28, 54
Closed system, 75
　finality of power and, 40
　in positivism, 46
　vs. open system, 29–30
CNIL (Commission Nationale Informatique et Liberté), 53
Coca-Cola, 301
Communication system, role in major risk management, 56–61
　at global level, 59–61
　at intermediate level, 58–59
　at local level, 56–58

Communicative speech acts, 149
Complex organization vs. complex system, 29–30
Computer Emergency Response Team (CERT), 97
Comte, Auguste, 59, 75, 76, 81n35
Consensus conference, 48–49, 56
Constative speech acts, 149, 150
Consumer relationship management (CRM), in online environment, 99
Contraceptives, 263–264
Conversational analysis, 141–146, 151, 153 (tab), 155
　production of conventional history in, 143–144
　production of plausible deniability in, 145–146
　witness interrogation in, 144–145
Creutzfeldt-Jakob disease (CJD), 14, 246
Crisis
　characteristics of, 162–163
　damage containment phase, 301
　defining, 125, 162, 223, 225, 258, 259 (fig)
　direct/indirect consequences of, 163
　event approach to, 225–226, 228
　industrial, features of, 125–126
　learning phase of, 301–302
　meaningfulness dimension of, 127
　motivational, 148
　planning stage of, 301
　process approach to, 226–228
　process vs. self-contained event view of, 221–222, 224–228
　recovery phase of, 301
　rhetorical dimension of, 127
　sequence of events in, 126, 224–225, 301–302
　signal detection phase, 301
　triggering event, 225, 226, 228, 232
　See also Major risk
Crisis Command Center (CCC), 319–320, 324
Crisis leadership vs. crisis management, 126
Crisis management
　"after-event" approach to, 300, 302
　anticipatory model, 164
　defining, 109, 127–128
　limitations of traditional requiring new perspective, 223–224
　need for systemic approach to, 302–303
　"onion" model of, 287

Subject Index

phases of, 128, 301–302
renewing, 223
sensemaking/information provision role in, 128–129
steps in, 301
systems approach to, 300
trauma approach to, 233
vs. crisis leadership, 126
See also Crisis management, cognitive approach to; ; Crisis management, paradox in; Crisis-management training, new practices; Crisis-management training, traditional; Legitimacy, and crisis management; Online environment crisis management strategies; "Total" responsibility management
Crisis management, cognitive approach to
architecture-of-thought-level discussion, 183–185
cognitive elaboration process, 165
cognitive mapping, 167
cognitive reduction process, 165
cognitivist paradigm, 165–166
groupthink phenomenon, 166
organizational-crisis-level discussion, 185–188
schema theory and, 165
semantic mapping, 167–168
structuralist paradigm, 166
See also Crisis management, empirical evidence for cognitive approach
Crisis management, empirical evidence for cognitive approach, 168–183
aggravating factors, cognitive mapping of, 169–175
aggravating factors, macro level, 186–187
aggravating factors, micro level, 186, 187–188
aggravating factors, steps in identifying, 170, 172
aggravating factors list, 171 (fig)
causal vs. semantic concept of language, 184–185 (fig)
cognitive map example, 170 (fig)
data sources, 168, 176–177
"Management of the Crisis Center" strategic action example, 172–175
semantic mapping using Evoq, 176–183
validity, 160
Crisis management, paradox in, 29–32

complex organization vs. system, 29–30
in area of responsibility, 31–32
physical paradox emergence, 30
technology/crisis management examples, 30–31
Crisis Management Team (CMT), 316, 319–320, 321, 322, 323, 324
Crisis-management training, new practices, 319–324
"alphabet of surprise" exercise, 323
basic elements of crisis management, 320
build sense of teamwork/team spirit, 321
CMT 101 exercise, 320
communicate acquired knowledge in organization, 325–326
copilot exercise, 322
Crisis Command Center and, 319–320, 324
Crisis Management Team and, 316, 319–320, 321, 322, 323, 324
Damocles training software exercise, 324
decision-making preparation/support, 322–323
develop capability to react to truly unexpected, 323–324
dynamic feedback exercise, 324
exercise inversion, 320
extended cross-cultural exercise, 321–322
five/six senses exercise, 324
flash/rapid exercise, 323
fragmented exercise, 320
key participant exercise, 321
maze exercise, 322
Media Tennis software exercise, 325
miniature modeling, 321
mirror exercise, 323–324
mobilization drill, 319
Odyssey exercise, 324
reinforce links among participants, 321–322
repeat exercise, 320
rewriting history exercise, 322
role change exercise, 321
self-assessment questionnaire (SAQ), 321
take contrarian view, 322–323
transition to crisis mode, 319–320
See also Crisis-management training, traditional

Crisis-management training, traditional, 315–318
  adverse psychological reactions to, 316–317
  doubts about learning values attached to, 317–318
  flawed assumptions of, 315–318
  See also Crisis-management training, new practices
Cultural rationalities study, 141
Culture of uncertainty, 3, 5, 11–12, 21n3
  vs. safety culture, 15–16
Curador (hacker), 86
Cyndinics (science of danger), 232

Daimler Chrysler, 256
Dalkon Shield contraceptive device, 263–264
Danger vs. risk, 9
Decoy phenomena, 274–275, 287
Deforestation, 28
Denmark, consensus conference in, 49, 56
Deterministic scientific knowledge, 74, 75
Dioxin catastrophe, 28, 54, 223
Disney, 94
Drug Czar, 48
D-type hub. See Mitsubishi Motor Company
Dunne-za people, 133

EBay, 88
Economic crisis, 147–148
Educational institutions, and copyright, 94
Egghead.com, hacker theft of customer information, 93
Electromagnetic field density, 54
Emergency response organization, sensemaking in. See Big City Police Department (BCPD) study
England
  information privacy in, 53
  nuclear waste fuel reprocessing plant in, 149–150
  See also Soccer industry, in United Kingdom; United Kingdom
Enron bankruptcy, 29, 30, 52, 80n33, 200, 206, 223, 303, 305
Environmental Assessment Institute (Denmark), 56
Erika oil tanker wreck, 223, 245
Etcetera principle, in ethnomethodology, 137
Ethical hacking, 98

Ethics, and modern medical technology, 55
Ethnomethodology, 136–141, 151, 152 (tab), 155
  analysis of sensemaking practices study, 137–139
  cultural rationalities study, 141
  descriptive vocabulary in, 137
  etcetera principle in, 137
  focus of, 136–137
  indexicality in, 136
  normal form use in, 137
  quantitative sensemaking study, 139–140
  reciprocity of perspective in, 137
  reflexivity in, 136
Ethos, 77
eToys, 89, 93
European Union (EU)
  precaution principle in, 56
  transnational decision making bodies in, 14
  See also *individual country*
Evoq. See Semantic mapping using Evoq
External analysis, 309–310
External observer/advisor, 317–318
External stakeholders, 91 (tab), 96, 171 (fig), 233, 307, 309
Exxon Valdez oil spill, 11–12, 303

Fairy tale, as coping mechanism, 214–215
Fayol's principles of administration, 31
Federal Emergency Management Agency (FEMA; U.S.), 58, 245
Federal Reserve Board, 53
Financial empire collapse
  Enron, 29, 30, 52, 80n33, 200, 206, 223, 303, 305
  Parmalat, 223
Firestone, tire recall by, 301, 307
First Modernity, 11
Food and Drug Administration (FDA), 55
Food poisoning, in Japan, 258–260, 264, 265, 268, 304, 305
Football Spectator's Act (1989; UK), 284
France
  consensus conference in, 49
  crisis of administrative law (from 1945/1960 to present), 68
  criterion of Public Power (from 1800 to 1880/1900), 68
  heat wave in, 223, 242
  information privacy in, 53

Subject Index 337

lobbying in, 53
normalization processes in, 55
oil tanker wreck in Brittany, 245
precaution principle as constitutional principle in, 56
primacy of Public Service (from 1880/1900 to 1945/1960), 68
restaurant crisis, 246
symbolic definition of public sector in, 68–69
Free-market, 65, 69, 70, 80n30
French Association for Normalization (AFNOR), 55
French Ministry of Environment, 80n27
French Revolution, 65, 66–67
Freud, Sigmund, 32, 78n3, 203, 213, 214

Galilean science, 67
Garrison state, 39, 68
Gas disaster, 133, 139–140
Genetically modified (GM) organisms, 7, 12, 15, 13, 28, 54
Genetic engineering, 8, 28
  as techno-science, 77
  legal regulation of, 47
Global crisis vs. local crisis, 65–66
Globalization
  effect on emergence of risk society, 7–8
  politicization of risk and, 14
Google, 301
Grandiosity, 238
Grantham and Kesteven Hospital, United Kingdom, 134–135
Greater Manchester Police Department (GMPD)
  bomb threat/reaction to, 107–108, 109
  lack of recognition of anomaly at, 108, 111
Greenhouse effect, 28
Greenpeace, protest against Shell, 18, 21n7
Greenspan, Alan, 53
Groupthink, 166
Gypsum mine safety practices, 275, 278–279

Habermasian critical theory, 125, 147–154, 153 (tab), 155
  communicative speech acts in, 149
  constative speech acts in, 149, 150
  crisis cycle in, 147–149
  regulative speech acts in, 149, 150
  representative speech acts in, 149
  speech acts/ideal speech situation in, 149–151

Having the bubble, 119–120
Health Canada, 79n11
Health crisis
  anthrax, 29, 224
  asbestos, 28, 54, 223
  contaminated blood, 223
  dioxin, 28, 54, 223
  hydrogen sulfide gas flow, 139–140
  mad cow disease, 14, 34, 60, 223
  ozone layer, 28
Health hazard legal class action, 78n6
Heat wave, in France, 242
Herald of Free Enterprise (HFE) ferry catastrophe, 241, 243
Heysel Stadium disaster, 284
Hidden risk, of risk models, 3
Hierarchical rationality, 141
High reliability organization (HRO), 31, 35, 229, 231, 247
Hillsborough Stadium disaster, 279, 280, 283, 288, 289
Historical analysis, 309
HOT (Human, Organizational, Technological) components, 232
Hunt, Bob, 200–202
Hurricane Katrina, 58, 245
Hydrogen sulfide gas flow, 139–140

Ibrox Stadium stairway 13 disaster, 282–283
ICO (Information Commissioner's Office), 53
Ideal-type theory, 80n26
Impossible, management of, 45–47
  communication processes level, 46–47
  retrospective anticipation and, 45
  rule of law level, 45–46
  science level, 46
Industrial accident, major
  AZF, 223
  Bhopal, India, disaster, 11–12, 28, 56–57
  Chernobyl nuclear disaster, 11, 13, 28
  Erika oil tanker wreck, 223, 245
  Exxon Valdez oil spill, 11–12, 303
  gas disaster, 133, 139–140
  mining, 28, 35, 275, 278–279
  nuclear power plant crisis in Japan, 255, 264, 265–266
  Prestige oil spill, 223
  Sandoz factory fire, 57, 58–59
  Three Mile Island, 11–12, 28
  See also Industrial crisis

Industrial crisis
    features of, 125–126
    legitimation and, 148
    See also Industrial accident, major
Industrial vs. religiously motivated risk, 4–5
Information Commissioner's Office (ICO), 53
Information processing
    as techno-science, 77
    privacy issues, 28, 51, 53
    Year 2000 "bug," 28, 60
Inside trading, 46
Insurance contract, 5, 6
Insurance industry
    challenge to modern, 77
    natural disaster as financial catastrophe in, 27–28
    product liability and, 77
Intel, 99
International Organization for Standardization (ISO), 269
Invisible Hand, 69–70, 73
Iran-Contra congressional hearings, 142–146
Ishikawa, Tetsuro, 259, 260

Japan
    cost implications of crisis in, 260–263, 261 (fig)–262 (fig)
    crisis in, compared with crisis in U.S., 263–267
    food poisoning in, 258–260, 264, 265, 268
    nuclear power plant crisis in, 255, 264, 265–266
    product liability law in, 269
    sodium bicarbonate contamination, 268–269
    symbolic/corporate identity crisis in, 258–260
    See also Japan, characteristics of crisis-prone organization in; Mitsubishi Motor Company
Japan, characteristics of crisis-prone organization in, 253–270
    agency costs, 264–266, 265 (fig)
    concealment as response to incident, 254–255
    corporate tradition/management culture influence, 255–257
    insensitivity, 257
    lack of learning from mistakes, 258
    poor quality control decisions, 266–269, 267 (fig), 268 (fig)
    restructuring, 253–254
    slow responsiveness, 257–258
Japanese Ministry of Land, Infrastructure and Transport (JMOLIT), 254–255, 256–257
Johnson & Johnson (J&J) Tylenol crisis, 304, 307

Kant, Emmanuel, 74, 76, 79n21
Klein, Melanie, 213–214
Knight, Frank, 45
Knight, Phil, 311
Knowledge
    nondeterministic, 40
    nonpositivistic, 44–45
    scientific, 39–40, 74, 75

Labor abuse, by Nike, 18, 311
Legal-rational authority, 65, 66–67, 77
Legal-rational system of legitimacy, 37, 38, 50, 67
Legal system, defining, 79n11
Legal system, role in major risk management, 50–53
    at level of laws/norms, 50–52
    communication processes, 53
    third party intervention, 52–53
Legitimacy, and crisis management
    action at global/local level, 50
    agreement vs. knowledge as problem, 37–38
    authority role in, 38
    belief changes effect on, 36–42
    certainty in, 36–37
    legitimization at global/local level, 41
    major risk and (See Major risk)
    open enquiry role in, 38–39
    uncertainties in, 26
    See also Legitimacy, and crisis management; Legitimacy, crisis of social system of; Legitimacy systems; Legitimacy systems, history of
Legitimacy, crisis of social system of, 39–43
    first period (from 1800 to 1880/1900), 39
    second period (from 1880/1900 to 1945/1960), 39–40
    third period (since 1880/1900 to 1945/1960), 40
Legitimacy gap, in transnational corporation, 17–20
Legitimacy systems, 61–77

Subject Index

conflict resolution in modern
societies and, 62–64
See also Legitimacy systems, history of
Legitimacy systems, history of
charismatic authority, 65, 66, 77
epistemological paradigms/symbolic
structures, 73–77
legal-rational authority, 65, 66–67, 77
legal-rational system, 66–68
limits between nature/culture, 74
nature/culture confusion, 75
origins of power, 74
radicalization of complexity/science of
artificial, 76–77
symbolic definition of public sector in
France, 68–69
symbolic definition of public sector in
U.S., 69–73
traditional authority, 65, 77
Weber's types of legitimate
authority, 64–77
Lobbying, 48, 53
Local crisis vs. global crisis, 65–66
Logos, 77
Loosely coupled system, 31
Love Bug virus, 87

Mad cow disease. *See* Bovine spongioform
encephalopathy
MafiaBoy (hacker), 85–86, 87
Major risk, 27–36
accounting/financial scandal, 29
causal chain of, 33–34
characteristics of, 40–43
definition of, 73, 76
definition of management of, 41
definitions, objections to, 34–35, 41–42
formal definition of, 32–36
frame of anticipation in, 34
industrial catastrophe and, 28
insurance industry and, 27–28
life cycle of, 60–61
management of, 42–49
product liability, 28
size of, 33
terrorism, 29
See also Major risk, characteristics of
management of; Major risk,
scope/methods of management of
Major risk, characteristics of
management of, 43–49
institutions, 45–47
symbolic methods, 47–49
uncertainty, 43–45

Major risk, scope/methods of
management of, 49–61
communication system, 56–61
legal system, 50–53
scientific system, 54–56
"Management of the Crisis Center"
strategic action example, 172–175
CPC/PCO coordination problems, 173
CPC/PCO function ambiguity, 172–173
general coordinator role ambiguity, 174
insufficient exchange between
disciplines, 173
lack of coordination in medical
discipline, 175
lack of priorities, 174
lack of standardized vocabulary, 175
postcrisis management problems, 175
Managerial ignorance. *See*
Organizational imperfections,
managerial ignorance of
Managerial theory of firm, 72
Mann Gulch disaster, 234–235
Market rationality, 141
Market theory, 69
Maxus (hacker), 88
Merck, 46, 79n11
Mercury Interactive, 92, 95
Methyl isocyanate (MIC) gas. *See*
Bhopal, India, disaster
Microsoft
antitrust law and, 51, 72
denial-of-service attacks and, 94, 98
Mill, John Stuart, 81n35
Mining, 28, 35
gypsum mine safety practices,
275, 278–279
Westray mining disaster, 279
Mitsubishi Heavy Industries (MHI),
256, 258
Mitsubishi Motor Company (MMC)
concealment as response to crisis at,
254–255, 258, 264
cost implications of crisis at, 260–263,
261 (fig)–262 (fig)
insensitivity at, 257
lack of learning from mistakes at, 258
sexual harassment charges against, 257
slow responsiveness to crisis at,
257–258
tradition/culture influence on, 256–257
workplace discrimination at, 257
Mobile phones, brain cancer risk
rumor and, 34
Modernization, reflexive, 8–9, 10, 12

Modernity, as self-endangering, 11
Modern society, as risk society, 4–6
Moelwyn-Hughes report, 279–280, 281, 282, 285
Montesquieu, 80n29
Motivational crisis, 148
Motorola, Inc., six sigma technique of, 266
Mutual-fund scandal, 301
MyDoom virus, 301

Nader, Ralph, 18, 28
Napster, 90, 94
Narrative analysis, 132–133, 151, 152 (tab), 154–155
NASA. See *Challenger*
National Energy Board of Canada, 141
Natural disaster, as financial catastrophe, 27–28
Natural gas leak, 138–139
Natural laws of market equilibrium, 65
Nestlé infant-formula marketing, in Third World, 18
Newtonian science, 39, 67, 74
New York Stock Exchange, avoiding registering in, 52
Nike, antisweatshop campaign against, 18, 311
9/11, 197, 200, 201–202, 205, 207, 211, 214, 224, 301
Nonpositivistic knowledge, 44–45
Normalization, 237
Normative phenomenology of common sense, 63, 64
North, Oliver, 145, 146
Northern Pipeline Agency, 133
Noumenon vs. phenomenon, 79n21
Nuclear energy, as techno-science, 77
Nuclear power, concealment as response to incident, 255
Nuclear power accident
 at Chernobyl, 11, 13, 28
 at Three Mile Island, 11–12, 28
 in Japan, 255, 264, 265–266
Nuclear radiation, 54
Nuclear waste fuel reprocessing plant (Windscale, England), proposed, 149–150

OB tampon, 263
Official Secrets Act (England), 150
Oil spill
 Erika, 223, 245
 Exxon Valdez, 11–12, 303
 Prestige, 223
Oligopolistic industry, 268
Ombudspersons, increase in number of, 48
"Onion" model of crisis management, 287
Online environment
 architecture of Internet as threat, 87
 brick-and-mortar online organization, 86
 centralized operations as threat, 87
 copyright/privacy issues as crisis, 94–95
 denial-of-services attack as crisis, 90, 92–93, 98, 99
 easy accessibility as threat, 86–87
 forms of online crises, 90–95, 91 (tab)
 future research directions, 100–101
 hackers as threat, 85–86, 88, 89, 97, 98
 high visibility as threat, 88
 high volumes of customer data as threat, 88
 24/7 operation as threat, 88
 pure play online organization, 86
 quick dissemination of information/rumors as threat, 88–89
 threats in, 86–90
 virtual blackmail/sabotage by hackers as crisis, 93
 virtual boycott of product/services as crisis, 93–94
 viruses, 87
 Web site failure as crisis, 91–92
 See also Online environment crisis management strategies
Online environment crisis management strategies, 95–100, 96 (tab)
 address nontechnical aspects, 98–99
 consumer relationship management, 99
 develop crisis portfolio, 97–98
 identify key stakeholders, 97
 institute secondary data centers, 98
 monitor technology/chat groups, 96–97
 share crisis learning across online organizations, 99–100
Open system
 methods of power and, 40
 science of artificial and, 76
 vs. closed system, 29–30
Ordinary risk, 33
Organization
 anticipatory resistance to decisions in, 10

Subject Index

highly reliable, 31, 35, 229, 231, 247
in risk society, 9–12
See also Organizational crisis development model; Organizational imperfections; Organizational imperfections, managerial ignorance of; Organizational learning
Organizational crisis, defining, 300
Organizational crisis development model, 239–246
  phase 1, anomalies/unnoticing, 239–241
  phase 2, vulnerabilities/normalizing, 241–243, 244
  phase 3, disruptions/denying, 243–245
  phase 4, crisis/escalation, 245–246
  phase 5, research/practice implications, 246–248
  summary of, 240 (fig)
Organizational imperfections, 228–233
  anomaly as lowest level of, 231
  crisis as ultimate degree of, 233
  defining, 228–229
  degrees of imperfections, 231–233
  development of crisis-prone environment, 230–231
  disruption as catalyst for crisis, 232–233
  vulnerabilities, 232
  See also Organizational crisis development model; Organizational imperfections, managerial ignorance of
Organizational imperfections, managerial ignorance of, 222, 233–239
  cultural perspective on, 235
  denial and, 237–238, 244
  escalating commitment and, 238–239
  psychoanalytical perspective on, 235
  psychodynamic perspective on, 236–239
  psychological perspective on, 234–235
  rationalization, 237
  sociopolitical perspective on, 235
Organizational learning
  barriers to, 275, 276 (tab)–277 (tab), 286–289
  crisis of legitimation and, 284–286
  cultural readjustment and, 273
  decoy phenomena in, 274–275, 287
  explicit knowledge and, 273
  industrial bureaucracy patterns and, 272
  knowledge acquisition and, 273–274
  knowledge transfer/dissemination and, 275
  mock bureaucracy and, 275, 278–279
  tacit knowledge and, 273
Organized irresponsibility, 13
Ozone layer, 28

Paddington train crash, 274
Paradoxes of risk/uncertainty, 29–32
Pareto optimum, 69
Parmalat, collapse of, 223
Pathos, 77
Performative statement, 64
Perrier water, 57
Phantom risk, 12
Pharmaceuticals
  Tylenol, 304, 307
  Vioxx, 46, 79n11
Pipeline accident, 138–139, 150–151
Pluralistic ignorance, 237
Political crisis, 148
Politicization, of risk conflicts, 12–17
Popplewell report, 285
Positivism, 40, 46
  founder of, 59
  quasi-positivism, 44–45, 49–50, 60
Positivistic epistemology, 75
Power, definitional authority and, 13
Pragmatic ignorance, 240–241
Precaution principle, 54, 55, 56
Prestige oil spill, 223
Privacy issues, 28, 51, 53, 94–95
Probabilistic risk, 21n2
Procter & Gamble (P&G), 89, 263, 264
Product liability. *See* Product recall
Product liability (PL) law in Japan, 269
Product recall, 28
  automobile tires, 301, 307
  contraceptive device, 263–264
  tampon, 263
  See also Mitsubishi Motor Company; Snow Brand Milk Products Co., Ltd.
Product tampering
  Tylenol crisis, 304, 307
  See also Rural Books, major crisis at
Profit maximization, 80n28
Progress notion, and finality of power, 40
Property rights, 54, 69
Prudence (practical wisdom), 54–55

Psychological effects of crisis
  assumption collapse/invalidation, 217–219 (fig), 218 (fig)
  betrayal, 205–211, 208 (fig), 209 (tab), 210 (fig)
  defense mechanisms, 203 (tab)–204
  demonization process, 209–211, 215 (fig)
  denial vs. trauma, 204–205
  guilt feelings, 205
  lessons learned, 197, 212
  major crisis at Rural Books and, 198–199
  recovering from crisis, 211
  self-reflection and, 211–212
  Splitting/Compartmentalization, 210 (tab), 213–219
Public inquiry
  accountability and, 130–131
  before/after crisis, 127, 131
  difference from courtroom proceedings, 130
  emergence of, 129
  features of, 139
  final inquiry report, 154
  goal of inquiry board, 148–149
  in United Kingdom, 274
  nature of, 129–132, 154
  political/legal characteristics of, 130–132
  postcrisis, 127, 131
  predevelopment hearings, 127, 131
  See also Public inquiry sensemaking research approach
Public inquiry sensemaking research approach, 132–151
  conversational analysis, 141–146, 151, 153 (tab), 155
  ethnomethodology, 136–141, 151, 152 (tab), 155
  Habermasian critical theory, 147–154, 153 (tab), 155
  implications for practitioners, 156–158
  legitimacy issues, 150, 155
  narrative analysis, 132–133, 151, 152 (tab), 154–155
  rhetorical analysis, 134–135, 151, 152 (tab), 155
  summary of, 151–154, 152 (tab)–153 (tab)
Public Order Act (1984; UK), 284
Public relations, and customer privacy, 94–95
Public sector, symbolic definition of
  in France, 68–69
  in United States, 69–73
Pure risk, 32, 71, 77
Putnam Investments, 301, 303

Quantitative sensemaking study, 139–140
Quasi-positivism, 44–45, 49–50, 60
Quicken (software), 97

Rating agency, 59
Rationalization vs. normalization, 243
Reality show, 214–215
Recall, automobile, 28
  See also Mitsubishi Motor Company
REFCO bankruptcy, 52
Referendum, on nuclear energy in Sweden, 56
Reflexive modernization, 8–9, 10, 12
Reflexive risk society, 7–8
Regulative speech acts, 149, 150
Regulatory standards
  regional variations of, 18–19
  transnational diversity of, 14
Religiously motivated vs. industrial risk, 4–5
Representative speech acts, 149
Residual risk, 8, 15
Residual risk society, 6–7
Responsibility management. *See* "Total" responsibility management
Retrospective anticipation, 45
Revolution, role in legitimacy system evolution, 65
Rexao technique, 185–186
Rhetorical analysis, 134–135, 151, 152 (tab), 155
Risk
  acceptability of, 14–15
  as unlimited in time/space, 13
  calculus of risk and, 5–6
  contradictions of globalization and, 13–14
  culture of uncertainty and, 5
  defining, 5, 9
  elements of, 13–17
  irreversible consequences of, 13
  known unawareness as, 14
  "new," 13
  ordinary, 33
  phantom, 12, 14
  probabilistic, 21n2
  public perception of, 12–13

Subject Index

pure, 32, 71, 77
residual, 8, 15
speculative, 26, 31, 71, 77
subjective nature of, 33
unreliability of knowledge as, 14
virtual, 12, 14
vs. danger, 9
Risk audit, 309
Risk factor production
    ignoring/enforcing risk production, 7
    inaccessibility of human senses, 7
    metanorms of risk definition, 7
Risk society, 221
    reflexive, 7–8
    residual, 6–7
Risk zero, 221
Royal Dutch/Shell, protest against, 18, 19–20, 21n7
Rural Books, major crisis at
    background to, 198–199
    betrayal and, 205
    crisis vs. risk management at, 200–202
    defense mechanisms used in, 204
    Denial used in, 204
    Disavowal used in, 204
    Idealization used in, 204
    normal vs. abnormal business demands and, 202–203
    precrisis psychological training need, 203
    reasons for inability to meet challenges, 199–200

Safety at Sports Ground Act (1975), 283
Safety culture vs. culture of uncertainty, 15–16
Safety logic, top-down, 150–151, 155
Safety norms, 54
Sandoz factory fire, 57, 58–59
Sarbanes-Oxley Act of 2002, 52–53
Satisficing, 29–30
Say, Jean-Baptiste, 67, 74
Science
    artificial, 76
    nondeterministic, 76
Science/technology development, effect on terrorism, 29
Scientific knowledge, 39–40, 75
    deterministic, 74, 75
Scientific management, 70–71
Scientific system, role in major risk mangagement, 54–56
    at communication processes level, 56
    independent third party and, 55
    at laws/norms level, 54–55
Second Modernity, 11, 12
Sectarian rationality, 141
Securities and Exchange Commission (SEC), 72
Self-aggrandizement, 238, 243
Self-conscious risk society, 11
Semantic mapping using Evoq, 176–183
    coding process, 177
    interface of Text/Dictionary Modules, example, 178 (fig)
    interview transcripts, 180–183, 181 (fig)–182 (fig)
    interview transcripts, crisis center/on the ground distinction in, 183, 184 (fig)
    screenshots of animated 2-/3-D maps, 178 (fig)–179 (fig)
    webs of meaning and, 176
Sensemaking
    accountability and, 130–131, 136
    See also Sensemaking, crisis
Sensemaking, crisis
    ambiguity effect on, 124
    cognitive psychology conception of, 124
    defining, 109–110, 123–124
    defining crisis in, 127
    difficulty of, 110–112
    ethnomethodology conception of, 124–125
    future research needs, 120–121, 155–156
    in emergency response organization (*See* Big City Police Department [BCPD] study)
    narrative methods and, 125
    public inquiry and (*See* Public inquiry)
    uncertainty effect on, 124
Shared symbol system, 63
Sherman Antitrust Act, 51
Simon, Herbert, 29–30, 40, 76
Simulations, 76
    See also Crisis-management training, new practices; Crisis-management training, traditional
Six sigma technique, 266
Sizewell B Inquiry, 131
Smith, Adam, 67, 74
Smithian economic theory, 39
Snow Brand Milk Products Co., Ltd., 258–260, 264, 265, 268, 304, 305, 306

Soccer industry, in United Kingdom
  barriers to organizational learning from crisis, 276 (tab)–277 (tab)
  Bolton Stadium disaster, 279, 280, 281, 283
  Bradford Stadium fire, 274–275, 283–284, 285, 288
  core belief effects in, 287, 288
  corporate responsibility lack in, 289
  crisis elements in, 279–281
  decoy phenomena and, 274–275, 287
  event fixation/cognitive narrowing in, 288
  FLA and, 285, 286
  Hillsborough Stadium disaster, 279, 280, 283, 288, 289
  hooliganism/crowd control focus of, 272, 274–275, 276 (tab), 278 (tab), 280, 282, 284, 287, 288
  Ibrox Stadium stairway 13 disaster, 282–283
  ineffective communication in, 287
  knowledge acquisition and, 273–274
  lack of national safety legislation in, 281, 282
  mock bureaucracy and management of risk in, 281–284
  national safety legislation and, 283, 284
  organizational learning and, 284–286
  organizational learning/legitimization in, 284–286
  other accident/near-miss event effect on, 288
  scapegoating in, 289
  single-/double-loop learning focus in, 289
  voluntary licensing scheme, 280, 281, 282, 283
  vulnerability mindset in, 280, 288
  weak regulatory framework in, 280–281
Social movement, and legitimacy, 18
Social optimum, 65, 69
Social realities, constructivism on, 183–184
Social system of legitimacy, 38
Sodium bicarbonate contamination, 268–269
Speculative risk, 26, 31, 71, 77
Stem cell research, 54
Sweden, nuclear energy referendum in, 56
Symbolic anthropology study, 141
Symbolic/corporate identity crisis, in Japan, 258–260
Symbolic methods, role in major risk mangagement, 47–49
  laws and norms, 47
  social communication/social negotiation, 48–49
  third-party intervention, 47
System
  loosely coupled, 31
  tightly coupled, 30–31
Systemic analysis of crisis, 227
System of legitimacy of actor, 37
Systems analysis, 40, 230
  nonpositivistic knowledge and, 44–45
Systems theory, 29–30

Taylorism, 81n35
Taylor report, 285
Technological moralization, 6
Technological risk/crisis management literature, paradox in, 30–31
Techno-sciences, 46, 77
  See also Genetic engineering; Information processing; Nuclear energy
Terrorism
  anthrax, 29, 224
  9/11, 197, 200, 201–202, 205, 207, 211, 214, 224, 301
  psychological effects of, 205, 214
  science/technology effect on, 29
Third party intervention, 48, 52–53, 59, 256, 301
Three Mile Island, 11–12, 28
Tightly coupled system, 30–31
Tobacco company, class action against, 28
Tokyo Electric Power Co. (TEPCO), 255, 264, 265–266
"Total" responsibility management (TRM)
  assessment/improvement/learning systems and, 306–307
  communication mechanisms in, 310–311
  cultural audit/psychological preparation in, 308–309
  defining, 303
  evaluation/diagnosis methods in, 310
  inspiration/vision-setting in, 304
  relationship with crisis management, 303–307
  signal detection activities for, 308–311
  signal detection and, 307–311
  stakeholder engagement in, 305

Subject Index

top management support/design
  accountability in, 308
value dissemination and, 304
vision/values integration in, 304–305
vulnerability/symptom identification
  in, 309–310
Toxic Shock Syndrome (TSS), 263
Toysmart.com, 94
Toysrus.com, 99
Toywar, 89
Traditional authority, 65, 77
Trailing concepts, 169
Train crash, Paddington, 274
Transparency, 52, 59, 307
Triggering event, crisis, 225, 226, 228, 232
Tsumani, 2004, 28, 60
Turnbull, Robert, 198–199, 200
Tylenol crisis, 304, 307
Typology of organizational systems, for
  crisis risk, 163

Uncertainty, role in major risk
  mangagement, 43–45
  management of impossible, 45
  management of improbable, 43–45
  management of probable, 43
Uncertainty trap, 3
Union Carbide, 56–57
United Kingdom
  murder of children in hospital in,
    134–135
  public inquiry in, 274
  See also Soccer industry, in United
    Kingdom
United Nations, on catastrophic risk, 60
United States
  antitrust laws (from 1880/1900 to
    1945/1960), 70–71

normalization processes in, 55
reign of Invisible Hand (from 1800 to
  1880/1900), 69–70
reign of very large firm (from
  1945/1960 to present), 71–73
symbolic definition of public sector in,
  69–73
Upper-echelon theory, 233–234
U.S. Post Office, and anthrax scare, 29

Vioxx, 46, 79n11
Virtual risk, 12
Visible Hand, 73

Wal-Mart, online boycott of, 93–94
Water-based nuclear reactor, 131
Weber, Max
  ideal-type theory, 80n26
  on legal-rational legitimate
    authority, 37
  on legitimacy systems, 61
  on state and legitimate violence,
    37, 64, 72
Welfare state, 39
Wembly Cup Final disaster, 280–281
Western Union, hacker theft of credit card
  information, 93
Westray mining disaster, 279
Whistleblower, 256, 261, 309
Work-related accident, social acceptability
  of, 71–72
World Trade Organization, 72
World Wide Web, and
  uncertainty, 59–60

Yahoo!, 85, 92
Yahoo! Finance, 97
Year 2000 bug, 28, 60

About the Editors

Christine M. Pearson, Thunderbird, The School of Global Management, Glendale, Arizona, U.S., is Professor of Management—Global Business at Thunderbird. Prior to joining Thunderbird, Pearson was a professor at the Kenan-Flagler Business School (University of North Carolina) and the Ivey Business School (University of Western Ontario), and she was the Associate Director and Senior Research Scientist of the Center for Crisis Management (University of Southern California). Additionally, she has held visiting professor appointments in Hong Kong, France, and Brazil. Pearson studies two related workplace phenomena: organizational crisis management and dysfunctional behavior in organizations (i.e., as incivility/aggression/violence). Her research has been featured in over 400 international/national/regional media outlets through television, radio, and print press. She has consulted about crisis management with organizations such as Pepsi-Co., Dow, Clorox, Mobil, Transamerica, Kraft, LAPD, Red Cross, BellSouth, and Nortel. In this role, she has helped organizations plan for, avert, and contain crises such as workplace homicide, product tampering, executive kidnapping, product recalls, consumer fraud, and aircraft accidents. Her research has appeared in *Harvard Business Review, Academy of Management Review, Organizational Dynamics, Academy of Management Executive, Organization Science,* and *Human Relations.* She is currently writing her fifth book, *It Pays to Be Civil: Workplace Incivility, Its Causes, Consequences and Cures.*

Christophe Roux-Dufort, E.M. Lyon, France, is a Professor of Strategic Management at Lyon School of Management, where he teaches and coordinates seminars on crisis management for students and executives. In 1994 Roux-Dufort was one the first professors to introduce a crisis management seminar in the regular curriculum of a French business school. At E.M. Lyon, Roux-Dufort teaches crisis management in the executive M.B.A., the International M.B.A., the international masters program in management and in various executive programs. Christophe Roux-Dufort has also written nearly 30 scientific and professional articles and 4 books on crisis management. He also works as a consultant on crisis management for French multinational companies in France and in the United States: Michelin, Danone, Tupperware, Renault, Chanel, Airbus, among others. His comments on corporate crises are regularly published in national newspapers. He is regularly featured in national radio broadcast. Christophe Roux-Dufort received his M.B.A. degree (1990) from the University Laval (Quebec, Canada) and his Ph.D. degree (1997) from University Paris Dauphine, France. His research interests lie in risk and crisis management, organizational learning, and the management of change. Christophe Roux-Dufort is regularly holding visiting appointments in INSEAD (France), Thammasat University (Thailand), ICHEC (Belgium) and Aarhus School of business (Denmark) where he teaches Crisis Management.

Judith A. Clair, Boston College, Chestnut Hill, Massachusetts, U.S., received a B.A. in psychology from the University of California at Los Angeles and a Ph.D. in business management from the University of Southern California. She joined the Department of Organization Studies at Boston College in 1993 and served as the Department Chairperson for 4 years. She has consulted for organizations in the areas of crisis management, natural environmental management, fraud detection, and performance enhancement. Her current research interests include how individuals manage identities at work and how individuals and organizations experience, make sense of, and take action on critical organizational events such as organizational crises and downsizings. Her publications have appeared in journals such as *Academy of Management Review, Human Relations, Organizational Dynamics, Academy of Management Executive, Academy of Management Learning and Education, Advances in Qualitative Organizational Research,* and *Industrial and Environmental Crisis Quarterly.* Dr. Clair teaches courses in organizational behavior, leadership, and management of multicultural diversity. She teaches at the undergraduate, M.B.A., Ph.D., and executive levels. She is a faculty partner with Leadership for Change, an executive education program in the Carroll School of Management.

About the Contributors

Ulrich Beck, Ludwig-Maximilians-Universität, Munich, Germany, is professor for Sociology at the University of Munich and the British Journal of Sociology Visiting Centennial Professor at the London School of Economics and Sciences. Ulrich Beck is co-editor of *Soziale Welt* and editor of *Zweite Moderne* at Suhrkamp (Frankfurt a.M.). His interests focus on risk society, globalization, individualization, reflexive modernization, and cosmopolitanism. He is founding director of a research center at the University of Munich (in cooperation with four other universities in the area)—Reflexive Modernization—financed since 1999 by the DFG (German Research Society).

Vinit Desai, University of California, Berkeley, is a doctoral candidate and researcher in Organizational Behavior and Industrial Relations at the Walter A. Haas School of Business, University of California at Berkeley. His research interests include organizational learning, decision-making, crisis management, and the study of organizations in which error can have catastrophic consequences. He examines organizations that operate with hazardous technologies yet experience extremely low error rates, and his work spans various industries including space exploration, healthcare, telecommunications, naval aviation, and natural gas. He has worked in the private and public sectors and has a B.A. in business administration from the University of Texas at Austin.

Dominic Elliott, University of Liverpool, England (Paul Roy Professor of Business Continuity and Strategic Management), is currently head of the Management Division at the University of Liverpool Management School. He has published many articles and books in the fields of strategic and crisis management and business continuity. Reflecting the practical focus of his work he has worked with senior executives from a range of organizations including IBM, Philips, Government of Lesotho, Football Association, Merrill Lynch, BNP-Paribas, Royal Mail, Transco, and the Department of Trade and Industry. Dominic has been editor of *Risk Management: An International Journal* since 2000. He is particularly interested in how organizations learn from crisis and the barriers that prevent it. He is currently engaged in a study of how the learning organization is being used as a mechanism for reducing workplace sectarianism in Northern Ireland. He retains an ongoing interest in soccer crises.

Laurent Gatot, Université Notre-Dame de la Paix, Namur, Belgium (M.A. in Economy and Ph.D. in Management Science from the FUNDP), is the head of the AML team of an international bank and assistant professor at the University of Namur (FUNDP), where he teach Risk and Crises Studies. As a member of the Research Center for Crises and Conflict Management (ReCCCoM) he conducted a 4-year longitudinal study of the Crisis Center of the Province of Namur. He has been a Belgian expert for three OECD missions (environmental audit of Spain, Finland, and Belgium).

Robert P. Gephart, Jr., University of Alberta, Edmonton, Canada, is professor of Strategic Management and Organization at the University of Alberta. He received his Ph.D. in Commerce and Business Administration from the University of British Columbia. His current research addresses stakeholder sensemaking concerning the risks of energy development as well as sensemaking about new media and broadband technologies. He is the author of *Ethnostatistics* (Sage, 1988) and co-editor, with D. Boje and T. Thatchenkery, of *Postmodern Management and Organization Theory* (Sage, 1996).

Toshihiko Hagiwara, Nagoya Economics University, Japan, is associate professor of Strategy and Management at Nagoya Economics University. Hagiwara received his Ph.D. from the Aoyama Gakuin University, MBA from the University of Washington, and B.A. from the University of Tokyo. He has published two books (Toyo Keizai), including a popular management textbook. His current research focuses on crisis management of Japanese corporations especially in the large commodity industries. Hagiwara is a member of the Academy of Management and the Strategic Management Society. He consults with numerous companies and organizations, including the Japanese government.

Boris Holzer, Ludwig-Maximilians-Universität Munich, Germany (Ph.D., London School of Economics and Political Science, 2001), is lecturer in the Department of Sociology, Ludwig-Maximilians-University Munich, and associated with the research center Reflexive Modernization. His current research focuses on development and modernization, political sociology and social networks. Recent publications include "Rethinking Subpolitics: Beyond the 'Iron Cage' of Modern Politics?" in *Theory, Culture & Society*, (2003) (with Mads P. Sørensen), "From Risks to Second-order Dangers in Financial Markets: Unintended Consequences of Risk Management Systems," in *New Political Economy* (2005) (with Yuval Millo), and *Netzwerke* (in press).

Jean-Marie Jacques, Université Notre-Dame de la Paix, Namur, Belgium (Ph.D. in Biology and in Organization Science), is professor of Organisation

Sciences and Qualitative Research Methodology at the University of Namur (FUNDP) and at the University of Louvain (UCL), where he is head of Research Center for Crises and Conflict Management (ReCCCoM). He is also invited professor at the Ecole de Mines de Paris/Ecole Nationale de Chimie de Paris and at ENSAM/ESTP. He conducts research on individual and collective cognition in crises situation, cognitive mapping, and epistemology. He developed a semantic mapping software application (Evoq) with Prof. Anne Wallemacq. In 2001 he was elected executive secretary of IGBP at the Belgian Academy of Science. Jacques is a founding member of the Mediterranean Disaster Information Network (EU Medin). His research appears in international books and scientific journals in French and in English.

Sarah Kovoor-Misra, University of Colorado, Denver, is an associate professor of Management in the Business School, University of Colorado, Denver. She has published a number of peer-reviewed articles on crisis preparedness, crisis management, and crisis learning. She has also consulted with a range of organizations in the public and private sectors enabling them to be better prepared for crises. Her other research interests focus on organizational change and organizational identity. She received her Ph.D. from the University of Southern California where she also worked as a research scientist in the Center for Crisis Management.

Christopher Lajtha, Argillos, was corporate risk and insurance manager of Schlumberger until the end of 2004, having been appointed to the position in 1992. He previously worked in various risk management roles for Schlumberger subsidiary operations, based in Europe and North America since 1981. Prior to joining Schlumberger, Lajtha worked for Sedgwick Forbes (U.K.) Ltd. (now part of Marsh & McLennan group of companies) as a Lloyd's broker and with B.T.R. Industries as the acting insurance manager—both posts based in London. Lajtha graduated from Manchester University. He is a fellow of the Chartered Insurance Institute and an associate in Risk Management. In 2001, he completed a new higher education initiative—a European fellowship in Applied Risk Management. Lajtha is a frequent speaker at national and regional risk management conferences and an active member of several risk management forums.

Romain Laufer, HEC Paris, France, is professor of services marketing at the HEC School of Management and chair of ACCOR, Air France, and SNCF. His research is devoted to the notions of legitimacy and system of legitimacy. These notions allow establishing links between the fields of philosophy, social sciences, and management. This approach permits developing an understanding of the reason why nowadays the notion of major risk tends to characterize the context of all managerial decisions. He is the author/co-author of *Marketing Democracy, Public Opinion and Media Formation in*

Democratic Societies (1990); *Les Nouvelles Fondation des Sciences de Gestion, Elément d'Epistémologie de la Recherche en Gestion* (2001); *L'Entreprise Face aux Risques Majeurs: À propos de L'incertitude des Normes Sociales* (1993).

Peter Madsen, University of California, Berkeley, is an assistant professor in the Marriott School at Brigham Young University. His doctoral degree is from the University of California, Berkeley's Walter A. Haas School of Business. Madsen's research interests focus on organizational reliability and on the interrelationship between organizational and environmental change. His current research deals with high reliability organizations and institutional and technological change. Specifically, he is examining the relationship between organizational reliability (and its converse, organizational catastrophe) and the legitimacy of organizations, organizational forms, and technological systems. He has studied these issues in the aerospace, healthcare, and insurance industries.

Manavendra Misra, Ph.D., cofounder of StorePerform Technologies, Inc., Denver, Colorado, was previously the senior director of strategy at KBtoys.com, where he also led the Business Intelligence team in building a data warehouse, decision support system, and Intranet DSS portal. He also led the development of KBToys.com's customer interaction analytics suite that served as its centralized CRM solution. Earlier, he was a professor of computer science at the Colorado School of Mines where he performed research in Intelligent Systems and High Performance Computing. His specific interests were in data analytics, and mining large data sets. He has a B.S. (Electrical Engineering) from the Indian Institute of Technology–Kanpur and a Ph.D. (Computer Engineering) from the University of Southern California.

Ian I. Mitroff, University of Southern California, Los Angeles, is the Harold Quinton Distinguished Professor of Business Policy at the Marshall School of Business, University of Southern California, and professor of Journalism at The Annenberg School of Communications at USC. He was the founder of the USC Center for Crisis Management, which he directed for 10 years. He is widely recognized as a founder of the discipline of crisis management. As a teacher, writer, and consultant, Dr. Mitroff specializes in crisis prevention, strategic planning, and the design of ethical work environments. He is the author of more than 300 articles and 26 books on a wide range of topics, including crisis management, corporate culture, business policy, current events, organizational change, and spirituality in the workplace. His most recent books include *A Spiritual Audit of Corporate America* and *Managing Crises Before They Happen*.

Bertrand Robert, founder and president of Argillos, focuses on leading edge crisis management practices, notably in the areas of crisis anticipation and leadership during crisis situations. Robert supports both commercial and public service organizations in understanding the nature of crisis situations and developing appropriate crisis response capabilities. He has more than 20 years of practical, "hands on" experience, with as much as 30% of this time spent supporting crisis management teams in "hot situations." Robert has developed new techniques and training approaches with respect to the management of surprise; the preservation of trust; pressured decision-making; and enhanced anticipation performance. He is an experienced teacher, public speaker, and creator of atypical workshops and training exercises—employing many eclectic references to, for example, the theater, ancient music, sailing, aikido, and mountain climbing. Robert was educated at Hypokhagne, Institut d'Etudes Politiques de Paris, ESSEC.

Karlene H. Roberts, University of California, Berkeley, is a professor at the Walter A. Haas School of Business at the University of California, Berkeley. Roberts earned her bachelor's degree in Psychology from Stanford University and her Ph.D. in Industrial Psychology from the University of California at Berkeley. She also holds an honorary Ph.D. from Paul Cezanne University, Aix en Provence. Roberts currently investigates the design and management of organizations and systems of organizations in which error can result in catastrophic consequences. She has studied both organizations that failed and those that succeed in this category. Some of the industries Roberts has worked in are the military, commercial marine transportation, healthcare, railroads, petroleum production, commercial aviation, banking, and community emergency services. Roberts is a fellow in the American Psychological Association, the Academy of Management, and the American Psychological Society.

Denis Smith, University of Liverpool, England, is the professor of Management at the University of Glasgow. Prior to moving to Glasgow, he held chairs in Management at the Universities of Liverpool, Sheffield, Durham, and Liverpool John Moores. He was also the founding director of the University of Liverpool Management School and had been the director of the business school at Liverpool John Moores University. He has also held visiting chairs at the University of Kobe (Japan) and the University of Innsbruck (Austria) and was a visiting associate professor at San Diego State University (U.S.). Aside from his academic appointments, he has been a non-executive director of Mersey Regional Ambulance Service, St Helens Rugby League Club, and Aintree University Hospital NHS Trust and a director of CSC Consulting and HARM Consulting. Smith's main research interests are in risk assessment within socio-technical systems, adverse events in healthcare, complexity, and crisis management. He is the joint editor of two journals: *Clinician in Management* and *Risk Management: An International Journal*.

Sandra Waddock, Boston College, Chestnut Hill, Massachusetts, is professor of Management at Boston College's Carroll School of Management and senior research fellow at BC's Center for Corporate Citizenship. She has published extensively on corporate responsibility, corporate citizenship, and inter-sector collaboration in journals such as *The Academy of Management Journal, Academy of Management Executive, Strategic Management Journal, The Journal of Corporate Citizenship, Human Relations,* and *Business & Society.* Author of *Leading Corporate Citizens* and co-editor of *Unfolding Stakeholder Thinking* and *Learning to Talk,* she is a founding faculty of the Leadership for Change Program, edited the *Journal of Corporate Citizenship* from 2003 to 2004, and received the 2004 Sumner Marcus Award for Distinguished Service and the 2005 Faculty Pioneer Award for External Impact.

Anne Wallemacq, Université Notre-Dame de la Paix, Namur, Belgium (Ph.D. in Sociology), is professor of Organisation Sciences, Human Resources, and Sociology at the University of Namur (FUNDP). She is a member of the Research Center for Crises and Conflict Management (ReCCCoM) and invited professor at the University of Louvain (UCL). She conducts research on organisational discourse and cognitive mapping. Wallemacq developed a semantic mapping software tool (Evoq) together with Prof. Jean-Marie Jacques. She was a member of the Fond voor Wetenchap Onderzoek and is a member of the scientific board of the International Network Organisational Discourse. She publishes in international books and journals in French and in English.

Milton Keynes UK
Ingram Content Group UK Ltd.
UKHW030607130324
439198UK00001B/20